DISPOSED OF
BY LIBRARY
HOUSE OF LORDS

D1429530

ADVENTURES OF THE LAW

A VIEW OF THE FOUR COURTS.

This etching by Brocas (hand-coloured in water colour) entitled 'A View of the Four Courts' shows this celebrated Dublin building itself in the picture in the background, but focuses on the heads of the four separate courts at some point between 1807 and 1822 when all of them held office together. L to R are featured Standish O'Grady, 1st Viscount Guillamore (1766–1840), CB Exch; John Toler, 1st earl of Norbury (1745–1831), CJCP; Thomas Manners-Sutton, 1st Baron Manners (1755–1842), LC; and William Downes, 1st Baron Downes (1752–1826), CJKB. Downes lived for many years in a house that still stands on the Belfield campus of University College, Dublin. Reproduced courtesy of National Library of Ireland.

Adventures of the Law

Proceedings of the Sixteenth British Legal History Conference, Dublin, 2003

PAUL BRAND, KEVIN COSTELLO
& W.N. OSBOROUGH
EDITORS

FOUR COURTS PRESS
in association with
THE IRISH LEGAL HISTORY SOCIETY

Typeset in 10.5pt on 12.5pt EhrhardtMt by
Carrigboy Typesetting Services, County Cork for
FOUR COURTS PRESS LTD
7 Malpas Street, Dublin 8, Ireland
e-mail: info@four-courts-press.ie
and in North America for
four courts press
c/o ISBS, 920 N.E. 58th Avenue, Suite 300, Portland, OR 97213.

© the several authors and the publishers 2005

A catalogue record for this title is available
from the British Library.

ISBN 1–85182–936–9

All rights reserved.
Without limiting the rights under copyright
reserved alone, no part of this publication may be
reproduced, stored in or introduced into a retrieval system,
or transmitted, in any form or by any means (electronic, mechanical,
photocopying, recording or otherwise), without the prior
written permission of both the copyright owner and
publisher of this book.

Printed by MPG Books, Bodmin, Cornwall.

Contents

Contributors

DR PAUL BRAND All Souls College, Oxford

KEVIN COSTELLO Faculty of Law, University College, Dublin

PROFESSOR NORMA DAWSON School of Law, Queen's University, Belfast

DR JULIE EVANS Department of Criminology, University of Melbourne

PROFESSOR ROGER D. GROOT School of Law, Washington and Lee University

DR JOSHUA GETZLER St Hugh's College, Oxford

RICHARD W. IRELAND Department of Law, University of Wales, Aberystwyth

EMERITUS PROFESSOR DAFYDD JENKINS Department of Law, University of Wales, Aberystwyth

DR COLUM KENNY School of Communications, Dublin City University

PROFESSOR DANIEL M. KLERMAN Law School, University of Southern California

DR THOMAS KRAUSE Law Library, Christian-Albrechts-Universität, Kiel

DR MIKE MACNAIR St Hugh's College, Oxford

PROFESSOR PAUL G. MAHONEY School of Law, University of Virginia

EMERITUS PROFESSOR W.N. OSBOROUGH Faculty of Law, University College, Dublin

PROFESSOR RUSSELL K. OSGOOD Grinnell College, Iowa

DR FREDERIK PEDERSEN School of History and History of Art, University of Aberdeen

W.D.H. SELLAR School of Law, University of Edinburgh

PROFESSOR PETER SPILLER School of Law, University of Waikato

PROFESSOR DR C.H. VAN RHEE Department of Metajuridica, Law School, Maastricht University

DR RICHARD WHITING School of History, University of Leeds

PROFESSOR DAVID V. WILLIAMS Faculty of Law, University of Auckland

Ceterum ex aliis negotiis quae ingenio exercentur,
in primis magno usui est memoria rerum gestarum.
Cuius de virtute quia multi dixere, praetereundum puto,
simul ne per insolentiam quis existumet memet
studium meum laudando extollere.

The British Legal History Conference

The first British Legal History Conference was held in 1972 in Aberystwyth on the initiative of Professor Dafydd Jenkins. Since then there have been meetings at London / Cambridge (1974 and 1975), Edinburgh (1977), Birmingham (1979), Bristol (1981), Norwich (1983), Canterbury (1985), Cardiff (1987), Glasgow (1989), Oxford (1991), Exeter (1993), Durham (1995), Cambridge (1997), Edinburgh (1999), and Aberystwyth (2001). The Conference has become established as a leading forum for the discussion of all aspects of the history of law in Britain, and indeed further afield.

Proceedings of the Conference have been published as follows:

Legal History Studies 1972, ed. D. Jenkins (University of Wales Press, Cardiff, 1975).

Legal Records and the Historian, ed. J.H. Baker (Royal Historical Society, London, 1978).

Law-Making and Law-Makers in British History, ed. A. Harding (Royal Historical Society, London, 1980).

Law, Litigants and the Legal Profession, ed. E.W. Ives and A.H. Manchester (Royal Historical Society, London, 1983).

Law and Social Change in British History, ed. J.A. Guy and H.G. Beale (Royal Historical Society, London, 1984).

Customs, Courts and Counsel, ed. A. Kiralfy, M. Slatter and R. Virgoe, in *Journal of Legal History*, 5 (1984), and as a separate volume (Frank Cass, London, 1985).

The Political Context of Law, ed. Richard Eales and David Sullivan (The Hambledon Press, London, 1987).

Legal Record and Historical Reality, ed. Thomas G. Watkin (The Hambledon Press, London and Ronceverte, West Virginia, 1989).

Legal History in the Making, ed. W.M. Gordon and T.D. Fergus (The Hambledon Press, London and Rio Grande, Ohio, 1991).

The Life of the Law, ed. Peter Birks (The Hambledon Press, London and Rio Grande, Ohio, 1993).

Law Reporting in Britain, ed. Chantal Stebbings (The Hambledon Press, London and Rio Grande, Ohio, 1995).

Community and Courts in Britain, 1150–1900, ed. Christopher W. Brooks and Michael Lobban (The Hambledon Press, London and Rio Grande, Ohio, 1997).

Learning the Law: Teaching and the Transmission of English Law, 1150–1900, ed. Jonathan A. Bush and Alain Wijffels (The Hambledon Press, London and Rio Grande, Ohio, 1999).

The Dearest Birthright of the People of England: The Jury in the History of the Common Law, ed. John W. Cairns and Grant McLeod (Hart Publishing, Oxford and Portland, Oregon, 2002).

Legal Cultures, Legal Doctrine, ed. Richard W. Ireland, in *Cambrian Law Review*, 33 (2002).

Irish Legal History Society Publications

ALSO AVAILABLE

* Volumes 1–7 are published by Irish Academic Press.

Preface

The theme selected for the first British Legal History Conference in the biennial series to be held outside Britain itself, and brought into service again as the title of the present volume, was suggested by the choice of metaphor that an Irish author adopted when writing in the *Law Quarterly Review* in 1920. There, in volume 36, the reader will encounter W.J. Johnston's pioneering essay, 'The first adventure of the common law', an exercise undertaken by the then county court judge for Monaghan and Fermanagh to describe the transplantation of the common law of England into Irish soil, a process that begins in the final decades of the twelfth century, and which continues. A former editor of the *New Irish Jurist* and of the *Irish Law Times and Solicitors' Journal*, Johnston had previously written practitioners' manuals on such disparate topics as local government, old age pensions, labourers' legislation and land purchase. Plainly therefore, what was his second appearance in the hallowed pages of the *LQR*[1] with another offering in the area of medieval legal history will have constituted for him something of a challenge – a personal adventure of sorts. The storming of the bastion in question in this repeat performance will, of course, have been assisted to no small degree by the availability to Johnston of recently printed relevant source material – the production between 1875 and 1886 of the five volumes of the *Calendar of documents relating to Ireland* (1171–1251), between 1905 and 1914 of the first two volumes in the series of *Calendars of the justiciary rolls, or proceedings in the courts of the justiciar of Ireland* (1295–1302) and between 1907 and 1914 of the first three volumes in the *Early Irish statutes* series (John–12 Edward IV). In 1920, too, it scarcely needs to be added, Ireland, its history and its problems, were frequently in the news. Concerned to prove that the initiatives of 1918 and 1920 constituted no mere flash in the pan, Johnston followed up with a third piece for the *LQR* four years later – 'The English legislature and Irish courts': *LQR*, 40 (1924), 91.[2]

Students of medieval Irish history may be a tad embarrassed by the picture Johnston draws in his second piece in the *LQR*, by way of illustrating the arrival of the common law in the emerald isle, of showing Henry II and his equipage riding north from Waterford in the autumn of 1171 to the accompaniment of 'jingling spur' and 'clanging armour'. But the calibre of Johnston's credentials is surely established in his 1924 offering where he furnishes the reader with a glimpse of the exact state of the statute-roll

---

1 Johnston's 'The parliament of the Pale' had been published two years earlier: *LQR*, 34 (1918), 291.
2 Johnston's 'Ireland in the medieval law courts' had been published elsewhere in the interval: *Studies*, 12 (1923), 553.

The Honourable Mr Justice William J. Johnston
Reproduced courtesy of Mr Micheal Johnston

containing the statutes of Sir Edward Poynings's Irish parliament of 1494–95 and which he had actually examined before its destruction, along with that of so many other Irish public and legal records, in the explosion and fire at the Dublin Four Courts in 1922.

On the partition of Ireland, Johnston, though a native of Magherafelt, Co. Londonderry, elected to continue his professional career in the South. From 1921 he acted as county court judge for Monaghan and Louth (partition had occasioned the swapping of Louth for Fermanagh), until, in 1924, he was elevated to the High Court bench in the Irish Free State. In 1939 he was promoted to the Supreme Court. Johnston died in November 1940.[3]

Though no one perhaps could have anticipated this, least of all Johnston himself, questions of great moment in Irish legal history were destined to pursue him on the bench. The manner of their resolution at the time wrote a not unimportant chapter in modern Irish history and law. In the Erne several fishery case, *Moore* v. *A.-G.*, Johnston was in the end to be overruled by the Supreme Court, the Judicial Committee of the Privy Council later declining to intervene[4]; but in the comparable Moy several fishery case, on

3 *Irish Law Times and Solicitors' Journal*, 74 (1940), 320.
4 [1929] IR 191, [1934] IR 44, [1935] IR 472. See, too, *R. (Moore)* v. *O'Hanrahan* [1927] IR 406.

the two separate occasions the matter was litigated, no appeals were lodged and Johnston's views here were fated to prevail.[5] Both cases turned on intricate questions of brehon law and the precise impact that Magna Carta might be thought to have had in medieval Ireland.[6]

A conundrum of a very different kind faced Johnston when elevated temporarily to join Chief Justice Kennedy and Mr Justice Murnaghan on the Supreme Court to hear the appeal in the Erasmus Smith Schools case: was the educational charity established by Erasmus Smith in seventeenth-century Ireland exclusively designed to advance Protestantism or could it rather be interpreted as non-denominational? In 1931, in the High Court, Mr Justice Meredith supported the narrower interpretation.[7] An appeal to the Supreme Court followed, but no decision had been handed down when, late in 1936, Kennedy died. The following January, the two remaining members of the court who had heard the appeal – Murnaghan and Johnston – revealed that they did not agree as to the result. The prospect beckoned of the parties in dispute having to commence litigation all over again. In the end, the government of Eamon de Valera proposed a compromise which gave the critics of the administration of the charity something of what they had demanded, and this compromise, somewhat unusually, was given effect to by a private Act of the Oireachtas.[8] Though the judgements prepared by Murnaghan and Johnston were then suppressed, I happen to have been fortunate to see part of the 40-page judgement prepared by Johnston. It is a very small part – just page 1 and page 40 – but these fragments reveal an intellect very much aware of what was at stake and blessed with a capacity to write about it in attractive and fluent prose.

The invitation that went out for papers to be delivered at the 2003 conference, having identified 'Adventures of the Law' as the theme, attempted to provide a little more guidance. The theme, it was suggested, might attract the presentation of papers on the penetration of a legal system, such as that of the common law, into new lands ('adventures' in a geographical sense), or, equally, papers on doctrinal inventiveness in the law ('adventures' in an intellectual sense), such inventiveness, of course, including novel ways of thinking about, or interpreting, the law. The hope is here expressed that the eighteen papers selected for inclusion in the present volume are worthy of incorporation under one or other of these very broad headings.

The Sixteenth British Legal History Conference (designated a British and Irish Legal History Conference) was held on the Belfield campus of University College Dublin from 2 to 5 July 2003, under the joint auspices of

5 *Little* v. *Moylett* [1929] IR 439, *Little* v. *Cooper* [1937] IR 1.

6 Bryan Murphy, 'The lawyer as historian: Magna Carta and public rights of fishery', *Irish Jurist*, 3 (1968), 137; Thomas Mohr, 'Salmon of knowledge', *Peritia*, 16 (2002), 360.

7 *Governors of Erasmus Smith Schools* v. *A.G.* (1932) 66 ILTR 57.

8 Erasmus Smith Schools Act, 1938, No. 1 (private) of 1938.

the College's Faculty of Law and of the Irish Legal History Society. (Information concerning the latter Society will be found elsewhere in the present volume.) The conference was financially sponsored not only by University College Dublin, but also by both branches of the legal profession in the Republic of Ireland and in Northern Ireland, by Cambridge University Press and other publishers, and by Fáilte Ireland. The Irish attorney-general, Mr Rory Brady SC, also gave generous support. Thanks are also owed to Mr Jonathan Armstrong, the Librarian at King's Inns, and to Round Hall Press.

My co-editors, Paul Brand and Kevin Costello, join me in extending our thanks to all the authors represented in this collection (from eleven different jurisdictions, as it happens) and, indeed, to all the participants in the conference itself, including the chairpersons who presided at the several sessions in the two different venues. A word of thanks is also due to Caroline Dowling in the College's Conference and Events Office, to the administrative staff in the College's Law Faculty (especially Karen Smith, Bianca Cranny, Liesanne Dean and Fiona Murphy), and to several office-holders in the Irish Legal History Society, including, in particular, Mr Justice Hart, now of the Northern Ireland High Court.

Our main debt of gratitude in respect of the present volume is owed, of course, to our score of contributors. We should like to thank them all for making their papers available and for their patience and forbearance as this volume progressed through its various preliminary stages.

W.N. Osborough

Abbreviations

N.B. For a separate list for Wales, see p. 19.

Add. MS	Additional manuscript (British Library)
All ER	All England Reports
APS	*Acts of the parliaments of Scotland*
BL	British Library
Bodl.	Bodleian Library, Oxford
Cal. anc. rec. Dublin	*Calendar of ancient records of Dublin*
Cal. S.P. dom.	*Calendar of state papers, domestic series*
Cart. St Mary's Dublin	*Cartularies of St Mary's Abbey, Dublin and annals of Ireland, 1162–1395*
ChD	Chancery Division
CLR	Commonwealth Law Reports (Australia)
DLR	Dominion Law Reports (Canada)
DNB	*Dictionary of national biography*
DOST	*Dictionary of the older Scottish tongue*
Eng. Rep.	English Reports
F	Federal reports (USA)
FSR	Fleet Street Reports
HC	House of Commons
HC Deb.	Debates of the House of Commons
ILTR	Irish Law Times Reports
IPR	Intellectual Property Reports
IR	Irish Reports
ITR	Industrial Tribunal Reports
JSSISI	*Journal of the Statistical and Social Inquiry Society of Ireland*
LQR	*Law Quarterly Review*
McGill U. Lib.	McGill University Library
NAI	National Archives of Ireland
NAS	National Archives of Scotland
OED	*Oxford English dictionary*
OR	Ontario Reports
Pollock and Maitland	F. Pollock and F.W. Maitland, *The history of English law before the time of Edward I*, 2nd ed., 2 vols. (Cambridge, 1898, repr. 1968)
PRO	Public Record Office, London
Reg. Tristernagh	*Register of the priory of the Blessed Virgin Mary at Tristernagh*
RIA	Royal Irish Academy

RPC	Reports of Patent Cases
SC	Session Cases (Scotland)
SND	*Scottish national dictionary*
Stat. realm	*The statutes of the realm* [of England and Great Britain]
TNA	The National Archives, London
US	United States Supreme Court Reports
WLR	Weekly Law Reports
WR	Weekly Reports

Isolt's trial and ordeal: a legal–historical analysis

ROGER D. GROOT*

IN ITS SEVERAL VARIATIONS, the love affair of Tristan and Isolt is one of the great medieval stories. In general and in short, Tristan is dispatched by King Mark to bring Isolt, an Irish princess, to become King Mark's queen. On the return voyage, Tristan and Isolt unwittingly share a potion which causes each to love the other. They become physical lovers. Although Isolt marries King Mark, Tristan and Isolt continue their affair. King Mark, having become suspicious, plans to catch them trysting under a tree. He hides himself in the tree; Tristan and Isolt do meet under it, but each has observed King Mark's shadow. Isolt speaks of gossip and rumour, asserts her fidelity and sends Tristan away. King Mark, mollified, allows Tristan back within the court, where the affair is renewed. An evil dwarf then spreads flour on the floor between Tristan's bed and Isolt's to obtain proof of transit between them. Tristan, leaving some evidence, does go to Isolt's bed and returns to his own. King Mark seeks retribution through some form of trial.

Thomas of Britain was a twelfth-century redactor of this story. His contribution centres on his insertion of Isolt's acquittal by ordeal after she had sworn an equivocal oath. Thomas understood that to have these events sensibly occur, he needed a trial that would permit Isolt's denial; to have such a trial he needed to alter the legally significant facts in the flour-on-the-floor episode. His skill in describing and fitting the new portions into his source measures his legal expertise as well as literary talents. I propose to examine the sequence from the flour-on-the-floor through Isolt's vindication by ordeal to reveal that Thomas had a close familiarity with law generally and with the procedure in trials before the *magna curia* and an awareness of royal consideration of legal change.

I believe that Thomas's comprehension of legal events which inform the discovery-trial-ordeal sequence places the date of his *Tristram and Ysolt* closely around 1166. I also believe he could have attained that sophisticated comprehension only through close association with the court of Henry II.

---

* Research for this paper was assisted by the Frances Lewis Law Center, Washington and Lee University. I am grateful to many colleagues for their helpful suggestions.

I do not attempt to identify Thomas,[1] but suggest that he must be found in the circle around Henry II rather than in that around Eleanor of Acquitaine.

THE ESTOIRE

There is general agreement that a written Tristan story, the *estoire*, existed in France about 1150[2] and that it divided. One branch contains Thomas of Britain's *Tristram and Ysolt*, Brother Robert's *Saga of Tristram and Isond* and Gottfried of Strassburg's *Tristan*. Robert and Gottfried, scions of Thomas, have permitted the lost portions of Thomas to be reconstructed.[3] The other branch contains Eilhart of Oberge's *Tristrant* and Beroul's *Romance of Tristan*.[4] This branch is thought to be closer to the *estoire* than is the Thomas branch.[5]

Eilhart, Beroul and Thomas all contain the tryst under the tree. In each, King Mark, convinced that Isolt is faithful, permits Tristan to sleep in the royal bedchamber.[6] In each, Tristan's return is followed by the flour-on-the-floor episode. Here Eilhart and Beroul differ from Thomas. In Eilhart, as

---

1 He has been identified as Thomas of Kent, the author of *Roman du toute chevalerie:* D. Legge, *Anglo-norman in the cloisters* (Edinburgh, 1950), pp. 38–43. Legge is followed by Lejeune: Rita Lejeune, 'Rôle littéraire d'Alienor d'Aquitaine et de sa famille', *Cultura Neolatina*, 14 (1954), 24. But see Bartina Wind, 'Faut-il identifier Thomas, auteur de *Tristan*, avec Thomas de Kent?' in *Saggi e ricerche in memoria di Ettore Li Gotti*, Centro di Studi Filologici e Linguistici Siciliani (Palermo, 1962), pp. 479–90.

2 J. Bedier, *Le roman de Tristan par Thomas: poème du XIIe siècle* (Paris, 1905), ii, 313–14; G. Schoepperle, *Tristan and Isolt: a study in the sources of the romance* (2d ed. New York, 1963), i, 183. The scholarship is collected in R. Picozzi, *A history of Tristan scholarship*, Canadian Studies in German Language and Literature no. 5 (Berne and Frankfurt, 1971); Roger Loomis's addenda to Schoepperle, 'Survey of Tristan scholarship after 1911' and 'A bibliography of Tristan scholarship after 1911' in Schoepperle, *Tristan and Isolt*, ii, 565–92; J. Bruce, *The evolution of the Arthurian romance from the beginnings down to the year 1300* (Baltimore, 1923), I, chap. v. It is conventional to date the *estoire* to about 1150 and to see it as the basis for Eilhart, Beroul and Thomas: P. Schach, *The saga of Tristram and Isond* (Lincoln, Neb., and London, 1973), p. xiv; A. Hatto, *Gottfried von Strassburg: Tristan* (New York, 1960), p. 8.

3 I will use the reconstruction of Thomas by Loomis: R. Loomis, *The romance of Tristram and Ysolt by Thomas of Britain* (1931; reprint, New York, 1982). Bedier's reconstruction of Thomas, from the tryst under the tree through Isolt's vindication, is virtually identical: Bedier, *Le roman de Tristan*, i, 202–11.

4 Bedier, *Le roman de Tristan*, ii,192. Beroul is in two parts: the poem and the continuation. My references to Beroul are to the poem rather than the continuation unless otherwise specified.

5 Schoepperle, *Tristan and Isolt*, i, 66–111. See also the authorities cited by J. Thomas, *Eilhart von Oberge's Tristrant* (Lincoln, Neb., and London, 1978), p. 42, n.1; and see Hatto, *Gottfried von Strassburg: Tristan*, p. 8; Schach, *Saga of Tristram and Isond*, p. xiv.

6 Thomas, *Eilhart ... Tristrant*, pp. 85–91; A. Fedrick, *The romance of Tristan by Beroul* (New York, 1970), pp. 47–59; Loomis, *Tristram and Ysolt*, pp. 154–58.

King Mark leaves the bedchamber, the dwarf spreads flour on the floor and hides under Isolt's bed. Tristan leaps from his bed to Isolt's. A wound opens so that he bleeds in her bed. The dwarf sounds the alarm. Tristan's returning leap falls short and leaves a footprint in the flour. King Mark then captures them and calls a council for purposes of condemning them. Tristan escapes and rescues Isolt.[7]

In Beroul, the dwarf leaves the room after spreading the flour, but somehow watches the lovers. Tristan's leap to Isolt's bed opens a wound so that he bleeds in it. When the dwarf sounds the alarm, Tristan leaps back, but bleeds on the floor during the return leap. After the capture, King Mark proposes to condemn the pair without trial. Again Tristan escapes and rescues Isolt.[8]

I believe that the *estoire* contained an episode in which Tristan was the only source of blood, the dwarf witnessed the adultery[9] and sounded the alarm, and Tristan left some evidence of transit in the flour. I also conclude that the *estoire* had the lovers, upon discovery and capture, condemned or about to be condemned when Tristan escaped and rescued Isolt; there was no plenary trial nor an equivocal oath nor an ordeal.[10]

In Thomas, the dwarf spreads the flour and disappears.[11] Tristan leaps from his bed to Isolt's. *Both* have been bled on the preceding day. It is his bloodletting lesion which opens. Isolt has a similar lesion. No alarm is sounded. After he wakes, Tristan leaps back without leaving any mark in the flour. King Mark sees blood in both beds; Isolt asserts that the blood in her bed is her own.[12] King Mark summons a council at which Isolt is accused of adultery and is adjudged the ordeal of hot iron. She arranges her encounter with Tristan, disguised as a pilgrim; the encounter permits her equivocal oath and her equivocal oath permits her success at the ordeal.

As I will explain, Thomas's changes in this episode were necessary for his insertion of the oath and ordeal.

7 Thomas, *Eilhart ... Tristrant*, pp. 92–97.

8 Fedrick, *Tristan ... Beroul*, pp. 60–75.

9 Nichols has suggested that the dwarf, in Beroul, only saw Tristan and Isolt talking: Stephen Nichols, 'Ethical criticism and medieval literature: Le roman de Tristan' in W. Mathew (ed.), *Medieval secular literature: four essays* (Berkeley and Los Angeles, 1965), p. 74. Tristan, however, was so 'intent on his pleasure' that he did not notice his bleeding wound: Fedrick, *Tristan ... Beroul*, p. 63.

10 The Beroul *continuation* contains a different equivocal oath sequence.

11 The dwarf is crucial. Bedier thought Beroul and Thomas concorded because in each the dwarf leaves the room, and that Eilhart was divergent: Bedier, *Le roman de Tristan*, ii, 249. I believe Eilhart and Beroul concord because the dwarf in each is an eyewitness and that Thomas diverges. Schoepperle, *Tristan and Isolt*, i, 92. Bedier asserts that in Eilhart, Beroul and Thomas, King Mark is accompanied by the dwarf when he reenters the bedchamber. Bedier, *Le roman de Tristan*, ii, 249. In fact, the dwarf has already dropped out of Thomas's story: Loomis, *Tristram and Ysolt*, p. 159; Bedier, *Le roman de Tristan*, i, 204.

12 Loomis, *Tristram and Ysolt*, pp. 158–59.

THE EQUIVOCAL OATH MOTIF

There are many ancient oriental stories containing an equivocal oath.[13] The stories involve sexual misconduct suspected by the husband/father of the female protagonist. She proposes to prove her innocence by an oath (and sometimes by an ordeal). She arranges for her lover to disguise himself and make contact with her. She then swears that she has had contact with no man but the lover under his assumed identity, or with no man but him and her husband. The deity invoked to judge this oath, relying on the absolute truth of the oath, signals its veracity and so the innocence of the miscreant.[14]

Thomas's *Tristram and Ysolt* employs this exact narrative pattern. Isolt instructs Tristan to disguise himself as a pilgrim and meet her at the ordeal ground. She then asks the 'pilgrim' to carry her ashore. At the shore, on her instructions, Tristan falls with and upon her. Isolt then swears that she has lain with no man but King Mark and the pilgrim. In the following ordeal she is unburned, the veracity of her oath is verified and she is acquitted of the charged adultery.[15]

MANIFEST GUILT OR SUSPICION

A medieval English criminal trial proceeded through accusation, pre-proof, denial, medial judgment, proof and final judgment. To maintain the prosecution, the accuser needed evidentiary support (pre-proof) for his accusation. In an accusation of wounding, for example, display of the wounds was sufficient pre-proof.[16] The accuser needed also to offer his mode of proof. An able-bodied male offered to prove 'by his body', i.e., by combat. The accused then needed to deny the accusation, for lack of denial constituted acknowledgement and hence guilt. The accused then offered his mode of proof, usually combat or ordeal. The presiding judge then made a medial judgment. This judgment assigned the proof.[17] Failure of the accused at his proof – defeat in combat or unsuccessful ordeal – elicited a final judgment of conviction. Victory in combat or a successful ordeal produced an acquittal.

These processes could be truncated. Confession (or failure to deny) is one example. Another is manifest guilt. When a malefactor captured by the hue and cry was brought to his trial, the accusation was supported by presentation

---

13 The term 'equivocal oath' comes from R. Hexter, *Equivocal oaths and ordeals in medieval literature* (Cambridge, Mass., 1975), pp. 2–3.

14 Id., pp. 10–13; Shoepperle, *Tristan and Isolt*, i, 223–26.

15 Loomis, *Tristram and Ysolt*, pp. 163–68.

16 *Select pleas of the crown, AD 1200–1225*, ed. F. Maitland, Selden Society vol. 1 (London, 1888), plea 41 (1202).

17 F. Pollock and F. Maitland, *History of English law* (2d ed. Cambridge, 1968), ii, 598–609.

of evidence surrounding his flight and capture. This supporting evidence – the pre-proof – could be so overwhelming that he was not permitted to deny and the presiding judge proceeded directly to a final, condemnatory judgment.[18]

The Tristan *estoire* of Eilhart/Beroul is a case of manifest guilt. The dwarf observed the adultery and sounded the alarm; the responding lords observed substantial evidence corroborating the dwarf's perception; they captured Tristan and Isolt. The trial that should follow needs only contain accusation, pre-proof and final judgment. However the accusation is made, the dwarf and the lords will present supporting evidence and a final, condemning judgment is inevitable.[19] Of course, in the *estoire* the escape and rescue thwart prosecution.

Once Thomas decided that his story should include an equivocal oath and ordeal, he needed to amend the flour-on-the-floor episode so that the evidence found in it would permit, but not pretermit, a full trial. He deleted the dwarf as witness and the evidence of transit between the beds; he added Isolt's lesion as a possible source of the blood in her bed. These changes significantly reduce the impact of the evidence.[20]

It is clear that Thomas understood the legal import of his alterations. When King Mark entered the bedchamber, he 'wist [that] naught was proved save of the blood ... and that was not certain accusation nor trusty tokening,'[21] that is, that there was not manifest proof of guilt. Because the evidence only raises suspicion, denial will be permitted and a full trial will be necessary. That trial will adjudge proof by one of the purgative tests.

The eventual test is the hot-iron ordeal; that ordeal tests Isolt's oath; Isolt's oath is equivocal. I suggest that Thomas had decided to insert an equivocal oath and ordeal. He understood that to do so, he would first need to alter the flour-on-the-floor episode to render the evidence less certain. Otherwise, the following oath and ordeal would not have been sensible to his auditors.

---

18 E.g., *Curia regis rolls*, vi, p. 351 (1212) ['the whole township came to the hue and took him in the very act. So let him be hanged.']

19 Failure to distinguish between the response (probably) permitted a husband who found his wife *in flagrante delicto* and the legal treatment of a person captured in manifest guilt has caused much confusion. Newstead, for example, says that the lovers were 'not actually discovered *in flagrante delicto*': Helaine Newstead, 'The equivocal oath in the Tristan legend' in *Mélanges offert à Rita Lejeune* (1969), ii, 1077–78. That assertion answers a question that need not be asked. The lovers were discovered in manifest guilt, but should still have had a trial. At that trial they surely would have been condemned without resort to a purgative proof. Nichols recognized the distinction, but understated the evidence: Nichols, 'Ethical criticism', pp. 71–76.

20 The evidence is reduced so much that Bedier questions whether it was sufficient pre-proof to elicit proof by ordeal: Bedier, *Le roman de Tristan*, ii, 251.

21 Loomis, *Tristram and Ysolt*, p. 159. Compare King Mark's comment at the same point in Beroul: 'This is only too clear proof. You are guilty': Fedrick, *Tristan ... Beroul*, p. 64.

Thomas's treatment of legal issues is not incongruous. In his treatment of the offence, penalty and trial, Thomas's description tracks closely twelfth-century English law and process.

CRIME AND PENALTY

Isolt's offence was adultery – generally a matter for the ecclesiastical courts.[22] In the particular case, however, the adultery is a form of treason. Establishing that it was treason in mid-twelfth century England is made difficult by the lack of contemporary legal materials.[23] What legal materials there are tend to focus only on the male partner rather than on the royal female.

Roman law included adultery with an imperial princess as treason.[24] At another temporal extreme, defiling the queen was, by statute, made treason in England in the fourteenth century.[25] The primary legal materials do not close this gap. *Glanvill*, a text of the late twelfth century, does not mention reginal adultery within treason.[26] Neither does *Bracton*, a text of the earlier thirteenth century.[27] The late thirteenth century gives us three texts. *Fleta* is silent on reginal adultery as treason.[28] *The Mirror* specifically states that adultery *with* the queen is treason.[29] *The Mirror* is supported by *Britton*, which states that adultery with the wife of one's lord is a form of treason, and extrapolates to the royal situation.[30] *Britton* pushes adultery as treason only back to the late thirteenth century and then only as to the male partner.

There are, however, stories pre-dating the mid-twelfth century involving adultery *by*, rather than *with*, a queen and so are analogues to Isolt's situation. Queens Teutberga, Richardis, Cunigunda, Gunhilda and Emma are all possibilities.

---

22 M. Bigelow, *History of procedure in England* (1880; rep., New York, 1983), p. 50; Pollock and Maitland, *History of English law*, i, 130; ii, 543.

23 Two separate concepts of treason, Roman (offences against the *imperium*) and Germanic (breaches of faith), were simultaneously operating: Floyd Lear, *Treason and related offenses in Roman and Germanic law*, Rice Institute Pamphlet, vol. 42, no. 2 (Houston, 1955); J. Bellamy, *The law of treason in England in the later middle ages* (1970; rep., Holmes Beach, Fla., 1986), pp. 1–7; S. Cuttler, *The law of treason and treason trials in late medieval France* (Cambridge, 1981), p. 8.

24 Lear, *Treason and related offenses*, p. 27. Lear hypothesizes that adultery was also a form of treason in early Germanic law. Id., p. 52.

25 25 Edw. III, stat. 5, ch. 2.

26 *The treatise on the laws and customs of the realm of England commonly called Glanvill*, ed. G. Hall (1965; rep., Holmes Beach, Fla., 1983), pp. 171–73.

27 *Bracton on the laws and customs of England*, ed. S. Thorne, 4 vols. (Cambridge, Mass., 1968–77).

28 *Fleta*, vol. II, ed. H. Richardson and G. Sayles, Selden Society vol. 72 (London, 1955).

29 *The mirror of justices*, ed. W. Whittaker, Selden Society vol. 7 (London, 1895), p. 15.

30 *Britton*, ed. F. Nichols (1865; rep., Holmes Beach, Fla., 1983), i, pp. 41, 108.

Teutberga was accused of incest, but was successful, through a proxy, at an ordeal of boiling water. Richardis offered to prove her innocence by hot iron after being accused of adultery. Cunigunda, accused of adultery, successfully walked the hot ploughshares. Gunhilda, accused of the same, was proven innocent through a trial by combat in which she was represented by a young retainer.[31]

These accounts may not be historically accurate,[32] but they were widely disseminated. Christopherson has traced the merger of the Richardis-Cunigunda stories and the confusion of Cunigunda with Gunhilda.[33] He posits a continental Gunhilda song, based in the merged Richardis-Cunigunda stories, which came to England and was the model for William of Malmesbury's chronicle entry about Gunhilda's accusation and trial.[34] If he is right, the Gunhilda story had an established authenticity in England by the 1120s.[35]

Queen Emma was the mother of Edward the Confessor. Her story has her accused of adultery with a bishop after Edward became king and has her prove her innocence by walking the hot ploughshares. Emma's story would have made a better model for Isolt than would Gunhilda's, for Emma's case would have provided an English precedent and her trial was by ordeal rather than combat. Unfortunately, a written Emma legend cannot be traced anterior to the late twelfth century.[36] Elements in the Emma story, however, correspond very closely to those about Richardis and Cunigunda.[37] It is quite possible that an Emma story preexisted its earliest extant recordation, and that it was known to Thomas.

31 Teutberga was married to Lothair II of Burgandy; she may have performed her ordeal (*c.* 860) in person or by proxy. Her case produced early ecclesiastical debate about the efficacy of ordeals: H. Lea, *Superstition and force* (4th ed. Philadelphia, 1892), pp. 281–82; S. Grelewski, *La réaction contre les ordalies en France depuis le IXe siècle jusqu'au decret de Gratian* (Rennes, 1924), pp. 58–62. Richardis was married to Charles the Fat; she was accused of adultery with a bishop in 887: Lea, *Superstition and force*, p. 293; P. Christopherson, *The ballad of Sir Aldinger* (Oxford, 1952), p. 98. Cunigunda (d. 1033) was married to Emperor Henry II: Lea, *Superstition and force*, p. 293; Christopherson, *Sir Aldinger*, pp. 97–98. Gunhilda (d. 1038), half-sister of Edward the Confessor, was married to Emperor Henry III: *William of Malmesbury's chronicle of the kings of England*, trans. and ed. J. Giles (London, 1876), pp. 207–08.
32 Christopherson, *Sir Aldinger*, pp. 94–95.
33 Id., pp. 95–100.
34 Id., p. 31.
35 Giles dates that portion of William of Malmesbury which contains the Gunhilda story to the 1120s: *William of Malmesbury's chronicle*, p. viii : n. * 1.
36 Giles attributes the Emma ordeal story to Richard of Devizes: *William of Malmesbury's chronicle*, p. 215 n.* Richard wrote at the end of the twelfth century: John Appleby, 'Richard of Devizes and the annals of Winchester' in *Bulletin of the Institute of Historical Research*, 36 (1963), 71.
37 In the story Emma, like Richardis, was accused of adultery with a bishop. She, like Cunigunda, performed the hot iron ordeal in the form of ploughshares, and also like Cunigunda, called upon Susanna to deliver her: Christopherson, *Sir Aldinger*, p. 100.

The important point remains that these stories were believed sufficiently authentic to be included in the chronicles. That level of authenticity should have permitted Thomas to believe that they were historically accurate and so serve as precedents for the proposition that an adulterous queen was to be tried in a secular court and subjected to a purgative proof.[38]

Because Isolt eventually succeeded at her ordeal, the question of punishment is not officially addressed. But at the point of her denial and acceptance of the ordeal, Isolt recognized that a finding of guilt would result in her being burned or torn apart by horses.[39] The thirteenth-century English treatises prescribe burning for female traitors[40] and female felons were burnt as early as 1198.[41] This evidence implies that burning would have been the appropriate penalty for female traitors earlier in the twelfth century. The other penalty – tearing apart by horses – is less certain. The reference might be to that mode of execution *per se* or to quartering. There is some evidence in older Germanic law that traitors were torn asunder by horses, but I have found no English example.[42] Quartering was practised in England, especially in treason cases, but might be a later development.[43]

TRIAL

Adultery as treason lies in the secular jurisdiction. But Isolt is not remanded to a regular secular court. Rather, King Mark 'sent for all his councilors ... bishops and barons and all the wisest men that were in England'.[44] What King Mark has done is call a great council, a *magna curia*, to try Tristan and Isolt. There are several reasons why this procedure is appropriate.

First, there is substantial evidence that cases of treason against the king were tried in the great council.[45] Second, Isolt is noble in her own right and

---

38 'This charge and this form of proof belonged together': R. Bartlett, *Trial by fire and water* (Oxford, 1986), p. 19.

39 Loomis, *Tristram and Ysolt*, p. 162.

40 *Britton*, i, 41; *Fleta*, pp. 58–59.

41 *Rotuli curiae regis*, ed. F. Palgrave (London, 1835), ii, 204. See also J. Reinhard, 'Burning at the stake in medieval law and literature' in *Speculum*, 16 (1941), 186–209.

42 F. Riedel, *Crime and punishment in the Old French romances* (New York, 1966), p. 80. Lear, *Treason and related offenses*, however, does not mention it. See also Kathryn Huganir, 'Equine quartering in The Owl and the Nightingale' in *Publications of the Modern Language Association of America*, 52 (1937), 935–45. Huganir seems to believe that equine quartering (tearing asunder) was practised in twelfth-century England.

43 Bellamy, *Treason in England*, p. 21. The earliest recorded example appears to be 1238: Pollock and Maitland, *History of English law*, ii, 501 n.1.

44 Loomis, *Tristram and Ysolt*, p. 159.

45 Bellamy remarks that in England treason was tried in the regular secular courts: Bellamy, *Treason in England*, p. 12. I have found no examples until the reigns of John and Henry III:

is also the queen. A male in her position was without doubt entitled to the benefit of the maxim *minor majorem judicare non possit* and so would be entitled to judgment by his peers[46] – by the great council. But, Isolt is a female. I have not found direct authority for trial of a peeress by the peers. The only apparent options are trial in the regular courts or direct adjudication by the king. The former would be jarringly incongruous as the social structure of the day. The latter would have excluded the peers from judging treason, a matter of great political importance. I conclude that Isolt was entitled to trial by peers.[47] The need to try an important person by peers, as is recorded from the conquest through the twelfth century, caused the convocation of a great council – all of the bishops and barons,[48] precisely the persons summoned by King Mark.

An ancient bishop speaks to the council and notes that no one will make a direct accusation against Tristan because no accuser would dare offer proof against him.[49] The reference is to accusation by appeal and trial by combat. Combat was appropriate when one able-bodied male appealed (accused) another of treason. Thomas had a contemporary example. Henry of Essex, who fled a battle during one of Henry II's Welsh campaigns, was appealed of treason by Robert de Montfort in 1163; Robert defeated Henry in the ensuing trial by combat.[50] If one of the lay peers had accused Tristan, proof would have been by combat. The accusing peer would have fallen to Tristan, the greatest knight.

The bishop then turns to Isolt's case. He notes that the king cannot 'manifestly show [her] guilt', but because of suspicion she must be summoned to

Curia regis rolls, vii, pp. 168–73 (1214); id., xii, plea 1055 (1225). During the twelfth century, treason clearly was tried in the great council: *English lawsuits from William I to Richard I*, *vol. II*, ed. R. van Caenegem, Selden Society vol. 107 (London 1991), pleas 407B (1163), 421A (1164).

46 B. Keeney, *Judgment by peers* (Cambridge, Mass., 1949), pp. 39–43.

47 Much later, in 1441, the duchess of Gloucester, accused of sorcery and treason, was tried before a royal commission, humiliated and banished. A statute passed the next year, established that great ladies indicted for treason or felony were to be tried by the 'Judges and Peers of the Realm' : stat. 20 Hen. VI, c. 9. The statute recites that the matter had been in doubt, but it looks quite like an abrogation of the novelty applied to the duchess of Gloucester. See also Keeney, *Judgment by peers*, p. 103.

48 See especially the following cases: William, bishop of Durham (1088) in G. Adams, *Council and courts in Anglo-norman England* (New York, 1965), pp. 48–65; William of Eu (1096): 'The King [William II] and all of his councillors' in *English lawsuits*, vol. I, plea 143B; Robert de Montfort (1107): 'King Henry [I] called together his magnates' in ibid., plea 176; Henry of Essex (1163): 'Henry [the accused] withstood the said Robert [the accuser] in the assembly': *The chronicle of Jocelin of Brakelond*, trans. and ed. H. Butler (London, 1949), p. 70; Thomas Becket (1164) in F. Barlow, *Thomas Becket* (Berkeley and Los Angeles, 1986), p. 109; Girard de Camvill (1193): 'King Richard [I] celebrated the fourth and last day of his council': Bigelow, *Placita Anglo-normannica*, p. 283.

49 Loomis, *Tristram and Ysolt*, p. 160.

50 *Jocelin of Brakelond*, pp. 70–71.

answer, and she was summoned.[51] This was the usual procedure in council cases. One or two peers were designated by the council to summon the accused peer.[52]

When Isolt responds to the summons the bishop states the case against her. He notes again the absence of manifest guilt but that suspicion exists.[53] He then makes the accusation: 'I appeal thee of these crimes, and I require of thee a straight ordeal that thou mayest free thee and deliver the King of this annoyance.'[54] In trials before the great council, when the king was an interested party, the accusation was made on his behalf by one of the peers. When the Bishop of Durham was summoned before William II's great council in 1088, Hugh de Beaumont spoke for the king and appealed the bishop[55] and in 1163 Robert de Montfort appealed Henry of Essex of treason against Henry II. Clearly King Mark is as much an interested party in Isolt's case as was William II or Henry II in those cases. The stating of the formal accusation by the ancient bishop on behalf of King Mark thus corresponds to actual practice.

Once the accusation had been made, Isolt could challenge the accusation on technical grounds,[56] admit or deny. Isolt chose denial – 'I am guiltless of this slander.'[57] It is important to distinguish this denial from the later oath. The records do not indicate that the denial immediately responsive to the accusation was sworn,[58] but it was necessary, in ordinary procedure, for the

51 Loomis, *Tristram and Ysolt*, p. 160.
52 Adams, *Council and courts*, pp. 50–51.
53 '[The King] hath not seen openly ... but only this slander ... and that with no sure tokening of your deeds': Loomis, *Tristam and Ysolt*, p. 161.
54 Ibid., p. 161.
55 Adams, *Council and courts*, pp. 56–58. In general, an appellor was required to allege that the deed complained of occurred within his sight and hearing; the ancient bishop could not and did not make this allegation. But neither did Hugh de Beaumont when he made his accusation against the bishop of Durham. Apparently the pleading rule was relaxed in cases, at least treason cases, before the great council. Glanvill permits an appeal of treason by one who 'saw ... or knew with certainty' that the treason had taken place: *The treatise ... called Glanvill*, p. 172 (emphasis added). What is important is that Thomas has again gotten the procedure right.
56 One appealed of treason could, for example, plead that his accuser was a confessed criminal: See *Curia regis rolls*, xii, plea 1055 (1225). The technical pleas of William, bishop of Durham, are described in detail in Adams, *Council and courts*, pp. 54–60; those made by Thomas Becket are well known.
57 Loomis, *Tristram and Ysolt*, p. 162.
58 Ernest York, 'Isolt's ordeal: English legal customs in the medieval Tristan legend' in *Studies in Philology*, 68 (1971), 4–5, goes wrong when he identifies Isolt's equivocal oath as her denial. The denial and the oath tested by ordeal were acts distinct in place and time. The denial followed immediately upon the accusation, and 'there is no trace of any foreoath, nor of an oath of any kind from the parties': Adams, *Council and courts*, p. 57 n.31. Glanvill says purgative proof is adjudged after 'the accused denies everything in court in the proper manner': *The treatise ... called Glanvill*, p. 172. Records of twelfth- and thirteenth-century trials invariably note that the accused '*defendit totum de verbo in verbum*' ('denies everything

denial to meet the accusation word for word. In trials by council, however, the process seems to have been less formal.[59] It can fairly be said that the bishop's accusation was properly met by Isolt's claim that she was guiltless.

Once accusation had been met with denial it became necessary for the court to pronounce its medial judgment. That judgment implicitly decided that the accusation and denial were sufficient and that the issue had been properly joined; it explicitly announced what form of proof would be required. In Isolt's case the bishop had sought proof by ordeal and as part of her denial Isolt had accepted proof by 'the hot iron or other ordeal'.[60] It only remained for the medial judgment to be announced – King Mark ordained proof by ordeal in one month.[61] That the king himself announced the medial judgment is unusual. The general practice was that one of the peers announced the judgment of the council.[62] King Mark's personal announcement of the judgment may be a reflection of Henry II's propensity to act in the same way.[63]

Isolt's offer of proof, phrased in the alternative, is appropriate in every way. First, the form is appropriate. In 1157, a cleric offered to prove in similar language: by the ordeal of the glowing iron plate or by whatever justice might dictate.[64] Second, the choice is appropriate. Recall the bishop's early recognition that no man would dare face Tristan in a trial by combat and that the bishop has made an appeal against Isolt. The usual proof in a case begun by appeal was combat, but since Isolt was female she could not fight. Isolt's case, however, is not a common criminal case. Perhaps she would have been permitted a champion.[65] If she were permitted one, it would have been Tristan. That would not do for Thomas because the primary literary task he had undertaken was to insert the equivocal oath/ordeal into the story.

word for word'). This denial was unsworn: *Placita corone*, ed. J. Kaye (London, 1966), pp. 2, 5, 8, 10, 12, 13, 15. With these denials, compare the oath sworn in preparation for, and at the place of, the combat. Id., p. 7.

59 See generally Adams, *Council and courts*, pp. 52–64. The late thirteenth-century treatises, discussing appeals of treason, specifically permit general denials: *Britton*, i, 101–02; *Fleta*, p. 57.

60 Loomis, *Tristram and Ysolt*, p. 162.

61 Ibid.

62 When the proceeding was against a peer, rather than between peers, '[t]he monarchs ordinarily avoided pronouncing judgment personally ...': Keeney, *Judgment by peers*, p. 39; Adams, *Council and courts*, p. 63.

63 Id., p. 57, n. 32.

64 *Placita Anglo-normannica*, p. 196. This is not a criminal case, but the fact of choice is historically accurate. See *English lawsuits*, vol. II, plea 520A (1156) (accuser, in council, offered ordeal of hot iron or other proof); *Select pleas*, plea 68 (1203) (accused elected ordeal of hot iron).

65 There is some evidence that champions were permitted in English criminal cases. When the Conqueror introduced judicial combat into England, he permitted an infirm Englishman to find a substitute: The Ten Articles of William I, ch. 6, § 1, in *The laws of the kings of England from Edmund to Henry I*, ed. A. Robertson (1925; rep., New York, 1974), p. 241. Relatives or retainers were sometimes proffered in the early thirteenth century, but I have

Thomas therefore made his accuser an ancient bishop. Now there are two additional reasons why combat is inappropriate. First, the accuser is a cleric who could not make proof by combat.[66] Second, he is ancient; persons past fighting age did not make proof by combat.[67] The choice of the ancient bishop as accuser when there were clearly other choices must have been purposeful. I suggest that the choice was made to exclude any question of Tristan becoming Isolt's champion and so to exclude any question of proof by combat.[68]

Once that has been done, the ordeal of hot iron is inevitable. In England, free men and all women made proof by hot iron.[69] Isolt is both female and high-born and so would naturally make proof by hot iron.

THE OATH AND ORDEAL

Isolt's medial judgment set the ordeal at Caerleon in one month. Isolt sent word to Tristan that he should disguise himself and meet her there. He did so disguised as a pilgrim; she called upon him to carry her ashore; while he was carrying her she instructed him to fall upon her at the shore. After he had done so, Isolt immediately and publicly laments that she can no longer swear that she has lain with no man but King Mark.[70]

At the ordeal site the iron has been heated and blessed by three bishops. Holy relics are presented for Isolt to swear upon. She places her hand on them and swears her equivocal oath – that she had lain with no man but King Mark and the pilgrim.[71] This procedure precisely follows the pattern of real ordeals. The elements of the ordeal were blessed and adjured. The oath to be tested by the ordeal was sworn upon sacred relics.[72]

found no example of one actually fighting a combat: e.g., *Pleas before the king or his justices, 1198–1202*, vol. II, ed. D. Stenton, Selden Society vol. 68 (London, 1952), pleas 284, 619 (1201); *Curia regis rolls*, ii, p. 50 (1201).

66 G. Neilson, *Trial by combat* (Glasgow, 1890), p. 46, notes that in 1176 Henry II conceded to the pope that no cleric would be forced to fight a duel and extrapolates that before that date clerics did fight duels. I doubt that was so. Bishop Remigius, accused of treason during the reign of William I, proved his innocence by a proxy who performed the ordeal of hot iron: Bigelow, *Placita Anglo-normannica*, p. 30. When William II suspected Bishop Hildebert of Le Mans of treason, the ordeal of hot iron was adjudged (but never performed): Grelewski, *La réaction contre les ordalies*, p. 75.

67 *The treatise ... called Glanvill*, p. 173. Glanvill's reference is to an aged accused, but it is quite clear the aged accusers were also exempt.

68 The choice of bishop as accuser may also be an artifact of general ecclesiastical authority over adultery.

69 Id.; every extant instance of a female adjudged an ordeal in England is an instance of the hot iron: e.g., *Pleas before the king ... , 1198–1202*, vol. II, ed. Stenton, plea 359 (1201) ('let the males purge themselves by [cold] water ... and Maud by the judgment of [hot] iron').

70 Loomis, *Tristram and Ysolt*, pp. 163–64.

71 Id., p. 167.

72 P. Hyams, 'Trial by ordeal: The key to proof in the early common law,' in M. Arnold et al.

Isolt then carried the iron and 'God in his fair mercy granted her clean purgation'.[73] The legal side of the statement is cryptic. Thomas is clear that the iron was borne. His description, however, indicates that Isolt was not burned at all and that her success was immediately perceived. The actual practice was to bind the burned hand and open the bandages after three days for inspection of the healing process.[74] The immediate perception of innocence, however, is a dramatic device common in the oriental equivocal oath/ordeal stories and in the legends of the accused queens. Only here does Thomas finally diverge from actual practice to dramatic effect.

THE EQUIVOCAL OATH AND ORDEAL REVISITED

The most dramatic aspect of the ordeal episode is not, however, the immediate perception of innocence. Rather it is that Thomas has chosen to combine the christianized ordeal with the equivocal oath motif.

An ordeal story that does not expose its auditor to the underlying truth or falsity of the charge tested by the ordeal can never have narrative purpose. A story which tells that a person was suspected of a crime, was adjudged an ordeal, made an oath of denial, and either passed or failed the test can only describe a legal process. To attain narrative impact both the underlying truth and the ordeal outcome must be known.[75] When both are known a comparison of them – a judging of the judgment – by the auditor can elicit some response: outrage at injustice; satisfaction with justice; glee at a cruel judge thwarted.

The equivocal oath stories originated in the non-Christian east. Repetition of those stories in the Christian west, without changing their context, can easily be accepted; to the extent the invoked deity was perceived as ineffective the stories might even have been didactic. But in western Europe the ordeals had been fully assimilated into Christianity. They were commonly used as proof in both ecclesiastical and secular courts. They were dependent upon

---

(eds.), *On the laws and customs of England: essays in honor of Samuel C. Thorne* (Chapel Hill, 1981), p. 92.

73 Loomis, *Tristram and Ysolt*, p. 168.

74 Lea, *Superstition and force*, p. 288.

75 This idea was suggested to me by Bloch's reference to 'the reader's privileged perspective': R. Bloch, *Medieval French literature and law* (Berkeley and Los Angeles, 1977), p. 41, and by the title, although not the content, of his chapter IV, 'The text as inquest'. The text, known to the auditor, describes the historical events as a full evidentiary inquest would do. An ordeal cannot do this. The text, then, serves the reader as an inquest. A perceptive auditor concerned with crime and judging must have made the connection and so understood that an inquest would be superior to the ordeal as a method of determining past reality. This, of course, is precisely what Henry II did understand and partially implemented in the Assize of Clarendon (1166) through communal accusation.

Christian ritual.[76] These proofs, frequently called *judicia dei*, were truly thought
to be judgments of God.[77]

The equivocal oath motif, when it has been christianized and includes an
ordeal as proof, is remarkable. To tell the auditor the underlying facts and the
ordeal outcome necessarily puts him in the position of judging the judgment.
To put him in that position *vis-à-vis* a story containing a christianized ordeal
is to call upon him to judge the judgment of God. Thomas seems to call
upon his auditors to do precisely that.

This is the crux of Thomas's redaction. He has brought the non-Christian
equivocal oath motif into a Christian context. It is clear that Thomas made
considerable effort to make the oath and ordeal fit into his source. It is clear that
he was at pains to structure his trial episode to make proof by ordeal inevitable.
Yet in doing so, he knew that if Isolt failed the ordeal, he would need to describe
her condemnation. At that point, he could have permitted her to suffer the
penalty and his story would end; or, he could have followed his source, the
estoire, more closely and permitted Isolt, after condemnation, to be rescued by
Tristan. Rather, Thomas brought himself, through much careful thought and
work, to reach Isolt acquitted upon an equivocal oath and apparently expended
that effort to bring his auditor to questioning a judgment of God.

THE TWELFTH-CENTURY ORDEAL

As early as the ninth century some popes had decreed against specific ordeals
in specific instances. Early in the twelfth century Ivo of Chartres had
collected these decrees, as well as those condoning ordeals. Gratian, about
1140, was ambivalent, as were other canonists until the 1180s. In general,
they were concerned about the souls of those who officiated at ordeals. It is a
sin to tempt God and the canonists tended to view an ordeal, at least when
other proof was available, as tempting God.[78] To the extent the ordeals were
under theological attack by 1150, the attack did not precisely doubt the ordeal
as a judgment of God;[79] rather, it questioned the propriety of demanding

---

76 So fundamental were the religious rituals to the ordeals that when the church, in 1215,
    forbad priests to perform rites and blessings in conjunction with them, they were 'abolished'
    in England almost immediately.

77 Bartlett, *Trial by fire and water*, pp. 159–66.

78 The prohibition is stated thrice: Deut. 6.16; Matt. 4.7; Luke 4.12. The development of
    canonist thought is detailed in John Baldwin, 'The intellectual preparation for the canon of
    1215 against ordeals' in *Speculum*, 36 (1961), 617–21 and Bartlett, *Trial by fire and water*,
    pp. 81–88.

79 When Ivo of Chartres, a critic of ordeals, confronted a case in which an accused had
    succeeded at a hot-iron ordeal, but the public clamoured for another trial, he opined that
    the proband's innocence had been proven, and that the divine judgment should not be
    challenged by human investigation: Grelewski, *La réaction contre les ordalies*, pp. 80–81.

that judgment. It was only later, when Peter the Chanter began his vigorous attack in the 1180s, that accuracy was questioned.[80]

The conventional dating for Thomas's story is 1155–1170.[81] If Thomas were closely attuned to canonist thought, and there is no evidence that he was, he most likely would have thought that ordeals were sinful if other proof was available. But recall that Thomas very carefully reconstructed the flour-on-the-floor episode so that other proof was not available. The ordeal in Thomas, in terms of contemporary canonist thought, was appropriately adjudged. But the canonists did not question the accuracy of ordeals. Thomas does so. He was either willing to judge a judgment of God or he did not entirely believe that an ordeal was such a judgment.

THOMAS'S MILIEU

Thomas has been connected to the court(s) of Henry II and Eleanor of Aquitaine.[82] I believe it is more likely that Thomas was associated with Henry II than with Eleanor.

Thomas's legal sophistication places him amidst detailed knowledge about the conduct of trials, particularly treason trials, by the great council. His use of the christianized equivocal oath/ordeal implies an audience that would not be scandalized by a doubtful *judicium dei*, and probably implies that he expected receptivity.[83] Both conditions should have been present in the circle surrounding Henry II during the mid-1160s.

During that period several notable legal events transpired: on the judicial side the treason trial of Henry of Essex (1163) and the aborted council trial of Thomas Becket (1164); on the legislative side the Assize of Clarendon (1166) and its predecessor enactments, the Edict of Falaise (1159) and the Constitutions of Clarendon (1164). The trials provided an interested observer

---

80 J. Baldwin, *Masters, princes and merchants, the social views of Peter the Chanter & his circle* (Princeton, 1970), i, 327–28.

81 Bedier, *Le roman de Tristan*, ii, 46, 55. Schoepperle collects several authorities. She accepts 1155 as the *terminus a quo*, but is uncertain about the *terminus ad quem*: Schoepperle, *Tristan and Isolt*, i, 178. Wind suggested 1180–1190 in her first edition, but moved back to 1150–1160 in her second: Wind, *Les fragments du roman de Tristan* (1st ed. 1950), p. 16; (2nd ed. 1960), p. 17.

82 E.g., Rita Lejeune, 'Rôle littéraire d'Alienor d'Aquitaine et de sa famille' in *Cultura Neolatina*, 14 (1954), 35.

83 About 1115, this statement appears: 'By whatever mode of expression a person [making proof] may swear, God accepts it in the way in which he to whom the oath is made understands it.' *Leges Henrici primi*, ed. and trans. L. Downer (Oxford, 1972), c. 5, 29a. Obviously, neither Thomas nor his audience believed this. The persons present understood Isolt's oath to be a denial of adultery; if God had understood it that way as well it would not have been equivocal. Without equivocation, the whole motif fails.

the procedural detail replicated in Isolt's case; the Assize of Clarendon informed an acute observer that the outcome of an ordeal could be questioned.

The Essex trial was certainly a major judicial event. The antagonists were important individually and by heredity. Essex was the king's standard bearer. Montfort made a spectacular accusation against him – that he had cried the king's death and thrown down the king's standard while engaged. In essence, the charge was treason through cowardice by a powerful member of the military aristocracy.[84] Combat was adjudged as proof and it was fought on an island before a multitude. Its climax was astonishing. Essex was defeated and thought dead, but revived while being prepared for burial; he became a monk.[85] The participants, the charge and the outcome all make this the kind of event that is pondered, dissected and discussed.

Becket's trial the following year was unspectacular in its conclusion – Becket fled before judgment. But the events preceding it were momentous. The squabble between King Henry and Becket had become a feud. As the positions hardened and the stakes increased, there must have been careful consideration of each royal move. As each move was made, there must have been lively discussion among those within the court. We know, for example, that as the decision to force Becket to trial was being taken, Bishop Odo's council trial for treason in 1082 was recalled.[86]

As these events of 1163–64 unfolded, an observer in Henry's court would have heard discussions about the details of trial by council. Who makes the accusation? What does he say? What must the accused then say? What judgment can there be? Who pronounces it? These topics must have been worked out by the king and his counsellors while they were simultaneously discussed within the larger circle around the king.

The Assize of Clarendon issued in 1166, but it was preceded by the Edict of Falaise and the Constitutions of Clarendon. Many have noted that Henry's innovations were worked through adaptation.[87] By the 1150s, however, archdeacons had acquired prosecutorial power that displaced private or communal accusations. Henry faced complaints about abusive exercise of this power in England in 1158 and in France in 1159. By his Edict of Falaise, Henry (re)instituted communal accusation in French church courts. But this edict also required communal accusation, or at least communal verification of accusations, in French secular courts.[88] Here is innovation derived from adaptation.

---

84 '... cowardice and desertion on the field of battle (*herisliz*) are treason of the basest sort': Lear, *Treason and related offenses*, p. 57.

85 *Jocelin of Brakelond*, pp. 68–71.

86 Adams, *Council and courts*, p. 63, n.43.

87 E.g., J. Goebel, *Felony and misdemeanor* (Philadelphia, 1976), p. 334; Warren, *Henry II*, p. 317.

88 Raoul Van Caenegem, 'Public prosecution of crime in twelfth-century England,' in C. Brooke et al. (eds.), *Church and government in the middle ages ... essays presented to C.R. Cheney* (Cambridge, 1976), pp. 69–70, 72.

In England, during January 1164, Henry promulgated the Constitutions of Clarendon. Partly, the constitutions were directed toward Becket's claim to ecclesiastical jurisdiction over criminous clerks[89] and were closely tied to the movement toward Becket's trial. The constitutions also dealt with the problem of abusive archdiaconal prosecution.[90] Henry displaced the archdeacons' prosecutorial power by reestablishing communal accusation in English church courts. The innovation here is that the sheriff, upon the bishop's request, was to produce twelve lawful men to serve as accusers.[91] This secular aid in ecclesiastical cases is new.

These developments cannot have been solely the work of the king himself. Since each involved the ecclesiastical courts, there must have been consultation with some representatives of the church; there must also have been careful consideration of how to meld the old with the new. In the case of the constitutions, the breach between king and archbishop should have heightened the care with which these questions were approached. As with the council trials, those issues occupying the king's immediate circle should have overflowed into more general discussions around the court.

The Assize of Clarendon (1166) dealt solely with secular criminal justice. Before the assize, criminal prosecutions began by a private accusation or through a local prosecuting official; the system was haphazard and subject to abuse.[92] In the assize, Henry extrapolated communal accusation from the edict and the constitutions into English secular courts. Twelve lawful men were to name those 'accused or publicly known' as felons. Those accused were to make proof by the traditional ordeal. Those who failed were to be mutilated. But here is the fillip: those who successfully performed their ordeals could nonetheless be exiled.[93]

There is only one way in which the exile clause can have come into the assize. Someone asked what was to be done with those who should have been convicted by their ordeals, but were cleared. The answer is the exile clause. An accused of bad repute and heavily suspected was to be exiled. That accused, implicated by the jury, would be either mutilated or exiled. The ordeal determined *which* rather than *whether*. Necessarily those God had signified as innocent by verifying their oaths of denial were still treated as guilty by man. The Assize of Clarendon called upon royal officials to do precisely what Thomas called upon his auditors to do – to question a judgment of God.

---

89 Criminous clerks were treated in c. iii of the constitutions: W. Stubbs, *Select charters illustrative of English constitutional history* (Oxford, 1881), p. 138.
90 Van Caenegem, 'Public prosecution,' p. 69.
91 The constitutions of Clarendon, c. vi, in Stubbs, *Select charters*, pp. 138–39.
92 Van Caenegem, 'Public prosecution', p. 71.
93 The Assize of Clarendon, cc. 1, 2, 14, in Stubbs, *Select charters*, pp. 143–45.

I am not arguing that the royal circle wanted or expected to change society's view of ordeals. The opposite is probably true. Retention of ordeal-proof was the conservative feature of the assize. The conventional religious trappings were maintained. The royal treasury in fact paid priests to bless new ordeal pits made necessary by the assize.[94] This implies that Henry and his advisors thought ordeal-proof was acceptable to society and they thought the success of their new criminal process depended upon its retention. Within the royal circle, however, the consultations preceding the assize had necessarily touched the possibility of ordeals that acquitted guilty persons. That possibility was thought sufficiently strong that the exile clause was drafted into the assize.[95]

CONCLUSION

Thomas proved his legal sophistication when he altered the flour-on-the-floor episode to make his equivocal oath story sensible. His description of the council trial follows closely what actual records we have of such trials. I believe this knowledge of council trials places Thomas generally within the royal circle. Because the council trials of Essex and Becket would have produced within the royal circle concern and knowledge about council trials, Thomas may have been within the orbit of Henry II in the mid-1160s. Moreover, Thomas's use of the equivocal oath and 'false' ordeal at least corresponds to Henry II's concern about 'false' acquittals by ordeal when the Assize of Clarendon was issued in 1166.

I believe, then, that Thomas was somehow connected to the court of Henry II. He may well have come there through an association with Eleanor, but if so, he must have moved, by about 1160, from her orbit into that of Henry. There, whether as an interested but uninvolved accessory or a more active participant, Thomas would have been exposed to the legal sophistication necessary for his description of process. Simultaneously, he would have been exposed to enough frank debate about ordeals as infallible judgments of God that he would have felt secure in adapting the equivocal oath into his *Tristram and Ysolt*.

94 J. Holt, 'The assizes of Henry II: the texts,' in D. Bullough and R. Storey (eds.), *A study of medieval records, essays in honor of Kathleen Major* (Oxford, 1971), p. 104.

95 It is possible to believe that God would never issue a false judgment of conviction, but that He might, in His mercy, issue a 'false' acquittal. The exile clause deals only with the latter. To me, that clause necessarily implied doubt, within the royal circle, about the validity of successfully performed ordeals. I do not extrapolate from this either royal cynicism or a general disbelief in ordeals. See Bartlett, *Trial by fire and water*, pp. 67–69. The merciful acquittal may have been in Thomas's mind when he wrote of Isolt's ordeal, 'God in his fair mercy granted her clean purgation': Loomis, *Tristram and Ysolt*, p. 168.

Borrowings in the Welsh lawbooks

DAFYDD JENKINS

IT MAY SEEM TACTLESS to begin a paper published in Ireland with the assertion 'that the Welsh mediaeval jurists were far better lawyers than their Irish colleagues', even though those words are a quotation from the father-figure of Celtic legal history, the late Professor Daniel Binchy. But Binchy said also that 'the native Welsh polity had been profoundly affected by the struggle with the Anglo-Saxons', so that 'institutions, and even a number of technical terms, were taken over from the Anglo-Saxon system'. Moreover, he rebuked us – for these borrowings had 'been almost entirely ignored by Welsh scholars, perhaps owing to a mistaken impression that such borrowings are a sign of weakness on the part of the recipients. Nothing could be farther from the truth. All great legal systems have progressed by judicious borrowings from more advanced systems' – and, I would add, perhaps from less advanced systems.[1]

ABBREVIATIONS

A   Manuscript Peniarth 29, NLW.
B   Manuscript Cotton Titus D.ii, BL.
Bleg *Cyfreithiau Hywel Dda yn ôl Llyfr Blegywryd*, ed. Stephen J. Williams and J. Enoch Powell (Cardiff, 1942; second edition 1961).
C   Manuscript Cotton Caligula A.iii, BL.
Col Manuscript Peniarth 30, NLW; references with § are to numbered sentences in *Llyfr Colan*, ed. D. Jenkins (Cardiff, 1963).
D   Manuscript Peniarth 32, NLW.
E   Manuscript Additional 14931, BL.
L   Manuscript Cotton Titus D.ix, BL.
LatA Latin Redaction A, in LTWL 109–158, from manuscript Peniarth 28, National Library of Wales, Aberystwyth.
LatB Latin Redaction B, in LTWL 193–259, from manuscript Cotton Vespasian E.xi, BL.
LatD (D1) Latin Redaction D, in LTWL 316–397, from manuscript Rawlinson C821, Bodleian Library, Oxford.
LatE Latin Redaction E, in LTWL 434–509, from manuscripts Corpus Christi College, Cambridge, 454 (E1) and Merton College, Oxford, CCCXXIII (E2).
Llyfr Iorwerth Llyfr Iorwerth, transcribed and ed. Aled Rhys Wiliam (Cardiff, 1960). References (of the type §1/1) are to numbered paragraphs and unnumbered sentences within paragraphs.
LTMW *The Law of Hywel Dda: law texts from medieval Wales*, tr. and ed. D. Jenkins (Llandysul, 1986; second edition 1990).
LTWL *Latin texts of the Welsh laws*, ed. Hywel David Emanuel (Cardiff, 1967).
Mk The Bodorgan manuscript of Welsh Law.
NLW National Library of Wales, Aberystwyth.
O   Manuscript Peniarth 36a, NLW.
Rec. Caern. Registrum vulgariter nuncupatum "The Record of Caernarvon", [ed. Henry Ellis] (Commissioners of the Public Records of the Kingdom, 1838).
Tim Manuscript Llanstephan 116, NLW. References by page and line to facsimile edition by Timothy Lewis (London and Aberystwyth, 1912).
U   Manuscript Peniarth 37, NLW.
V   Manuscript Harley 4353, BL.
W   Manuscript Cotton Cleopatra A.xiv, BL.
WM *The White Book Mabinogion*, ed. J. Gwenogvryn Evans (Pwllheli, 1907; text reprinted with new Introduction by R. M. Jones as *Llyfr Gwyn Rhydderch*, Cardiff, 1973).
WML *Welsh medieval law*, ed. A. W. Wade-Evans (Oxford, 1909, reprinted, Aalen, 1979).
X   Manuscript Cotton Cleopatra B.v, BL.
Y   Manuscript NLW 20143, NLW.
Z   Manuscript Peniarth 259b, NLW.

---

1   We cannot claim that *Cyfraith Hywel* was a more advanced system than twentieth-century English law, but it could have suggested *cyfraith cyhydedd*, 'the law of equality' (LTMW 95.6, 104.23, translating Ior §§80/3, 85/4) as a solution of the problem set by Devlin L.J. (as

Though the Welsh legal material has had a good deal of attention in the
years since Binchy wrote, the study of legal history has not gone very far in
Wales as yet – in the sense that there has been comparatively little work on the
practical aspect or on the thought which especially interests the lawyer-historian
of law. This is neither surprising nor discreditable, for (as Maitland said so long
ago) 'the materials provided by the Ancient Laws and Institutes of Wales should
only be used with the greatest caution'.[2] Like any other historical material they
must not be innocently taken at their face value, but these materials of ours do
indicate that some Welsh lawyers at some period knew some Anglo-Saxon, some
French, and some Latin; and some of them at some period understood some of
the law of England and of the law of Rome, though they had some difficulty in
finding Latin equivalents for Welsh terms of art.[3] When the classical scholar M.
Gwyn Jenkins began a study of the Latin of Redaction A which he did not live
to finish, he saw traces of translation from the Welsh in the Latin, and these
traces will have much of our attention.

Again, in a paper given in 1974 and published in 1980, Professor Rees Davies
gave a warning against rash interpretation of statements in the lawbooks:

> A passage from the law-texts themselves may serve to illustrate the
> point: more than one text dwells on the rights of an estranged husband,
> overcome with memories of former marital bliss, to reclaim his former
> wife if he caught her with one foot in and one foot out of her intended
> second husband's bed. Interesting as is the argument as an example of
> the sophisticated legal casuistry of native Welsh lawyers, it has about it
> that air of unreality which hardly fosters confidence in the validity of
> the law-texts as a guide to the central issues of social custom.[4]

The passage does indeed suggest to me the response of an advocate who has
argued for the husband's right in less extreme circumstances, and is

---

he then was) in his dissenting judgement in *Ingram* v. *Little* [1961] 1 Q.B. 31, at p.73, 'For
the doing of justice, the relevant question in this sort of case is not whether the contract was
void or voidable, but which of two innocent parties shall suffer for the fraud of a third. The
plain answer is that the loss should be divided between them in such proportion as is just in
all the circumstances. If it be pure misfortune, the loss should be borne equally.' For
Binchy's words see *Proceedings of the International Congress of Celtic Studies held in Dublin,
6–10 July, 1959* (Dublin, 1962), pp. 119–20.

2   'The laws of Wales – the kindred and the blood feud' in *The collected papers of Frederic
William Maitland*, ed. H.A.L. Fisher (Cambridge, 1911; reprinted Abingdon, 1983), i,
202–29 at p. 204. The paper was first published in *Law Magazine and Review*, August 1881.

3   The person responsible for the cross-heading 'De leyrewittis' in manuscript LatD1 (LTWL
346.1) seems to have been showing off, for the word is not used in the text, and it occurs only
rarely in the record material from Wales: see the Index to *Rec. Caern.*

4   R.R. Davies, 'The status of women and the practice of marriage in late-medieval Wales' in D.
Jenkins and M.E. Owen (eds.), *The Welsh law of women* (Cardiff, 1980), pp. 93–114 at 93–94.

answering the judge's question where he will draw the line; but the casuistry is not in fact exclusive to Wales, but has parallels from France and in canon law.[5] We should not expect to find record evidence for application of the rule, for such matters are not minuted: in Professor Davies's words, with a different emphasis, 'We will never square our conventional historical evidence completely with the legal and textual studies of the law-texts, for they are based on different *genres* of material and often relate to different periods. That, however, is no reason for being unwilling to learn from both sources.'[6]

Before saying anything more specific, we must look at our sources. A detailed account of these is given in Professor Charles-Edwards's *The Welsh laws*;[7] here we note first that (in contrast to England), Wales has neither Year Books nor Court Rolls, but has some forty lawbooks which were the working tools of teachers or practitioners of Welsh law in the period before 1536 when Welsh law was still to some extent a living system. For those men, and for students today when speaking Welsh, that law was *Cyfraith Hywel*, 'the law of Howel', and it is accepted that this Hywel was the Hywel ap Cadell who died as king of all Wales except the extreme south-east in 949 or 950. This has led too many 'innocent' scholars to cite passages from the lawbooks as evidence for tenth-century legal, economic, or social conditions in Wales; but since the earliest surviving lawbooks were written in the thirteenth century, no Welsh lawbook can safely be taken as giving a faithful account of tenth-century conditions. Nor can it be assumed that a manuscript gives a faithful account of conditions in the period in which it was written, since it is quite clear that obsolete law was often copied, whether *ex abundante cautela* or from indolence. Then again, it should not be thought that Hywel created a body of law 'from scratch': there was surely some law before his day, and of this he made some use. That this was realised by those who produced the manuscripts is very prettily demonstrated by a short passage which was quoted in the first printed notice of Welsh medieval law. This was a bilingual Protestant pamphlet which cited passages from a Welsh lawbook as evidence that 'priestes had lawfully maried wyues' in Hywel's time.[8] The Welsh passage[9] is best translated 'Here is a book of law which Hywel the Good made in the White House on Taf, though there are also other things in it of good laws which wise ones made both before that and after that'. The pamphlet's English

---

5 Mr Dafydd Walters pointed this out in the course of a seminar; practical difficulties of access to records have prevented him from giving me references to sources.

6 loc.cit.

7 T.M. Charles-Edwards, *The Welsh laws* (Writers of Wales, Cardiff, 1989).

8 *Ban wedy i dynny* (London, 1550), [A i *recto*]; reprinted in *Yny lhyvyr hwnn a Ban o gyfreith Howel*, ed. John H. Davies (Bangor and London, 1902).

9 Lyma lyuyr kyfreith a wnaeth Hywel da yn y ty gwyn ar daf / kyn bot heuit petheu erill yndaw o gyfreithieu da a wnayth doethion / a chyn no hynny a gwedy hynny.

version of this passage, 'Thys is the boke of the law which Hoel da made at
Tuy gwyn ar daf' does not mention the other wise ones; and the triad which is
cited in support of the claim shows that in fact there was at least an element of
irregularity in the marriage of priests.[10] For us, its reference to the wise ones
is evidence for recognition that the lawbooks are composite collections, and
it can be said with some confidence that the rule about the priest's son is an
innovation which reflects the activity of Norman reforming clergy.

The lawbooks which we have can be divided into two contrasting groups
in several ways. There are late antiquarian copies of existing medieval manuscripts, to be contrasted with their medieval archetypes, which had practical
use-value.[11] There are lawbooks in Welsh to be contrasted with lawbooks in
Latin. There are lawbooks which purport to present a comprehensive account
of Welsh law, and lawbooks which are miscellanies with little pattern. There
are practitioners' lawbooks and library lawbooks, which contrast sharply in
appearance, but do not necessarily differ in content.[12] But one feature seems
to be common to all these manuscripts, and it is a feature which modern
lawyers can explain from their own experience as teachers or practitioners.
Without exception, so far as my experience goes, the lawbooks contain larger
or smaller blocks of material which does not fit quite tidily into the general
pattern of the book. The attention of Welsh scholars was first drawn to these
'floating sections' by the late J. Enoch Powell in 1937 in a paper based on a
comparison of five manuscripts.[13]

10 Christine James, '*Ban wedy i dynny*: medieval Welsh law and early Protestant propaganda',
     in *Cambrian Medieval Celtic Studies*, xxvii (1994), 61–86, at pp. 69–71.
11 Antiquarian or semi-antiquarian copies can be used for the study of the text of lost
     manuscripts from the period of living Welsh law. The lost Llanforda manuscript (the *Ll* of
     Ancient Laws) has been partly reconstructed from eighteenth-century selections: *Bulletin of
     the Board of Celtic Studies*, xiv (1951), 89–104. Peniarth manuscript 259b in the National
     Library of Wales at Aberystwyth is a fairly complete sixteenth-century copy of a lost
     manuscript probably written early in the fifteenth century: Daniel Huws, 'Yr Hen Risiart
     Langfford' in *Beirdd a Thywysogion*, ed. Brynley F. Roberts and Morfydd E. Owen (Cardiff
     and Aberystwyth, 1996), pp. 308–09.
12 Some manuscripts are very small: these could have been carried to court by practitioners in
     pockets or the sleeves of gowns, and the many lost pages of these small volumes may well
     have fallen out under handling. The larger manuscripts are usually more calligraphic and
     better preserved, and it is natural to think that these were written for the libraries of
     Church or State, where access to Welsh law would be needed – and needed in Latin by
     Norman lords and abbots. The finest of the library manuscripts is of medium size: this is
     the Latin Peniarth 29 in the National Library of Wales, which was probably the lawbook
     from which Archbishop Peckham got the idea that Hywel made his law by the authority of
     the devil: Daniel Huws, 'Leges Howelda at Canterbury' in *National Library of Wales
     Journal*, xix (1976), 340–44, reprinted in Daniel Huws, *Medieval Welsh manuscripts* (Cardiff
     and Aberystwyth, 2000), pp. 169–76.
13 J. Enoch Powell, 'Floating sections in the laws of Howel' in *Bulletin of the Board of Celtic
     Studies*, ix (1937), 27–34. Powell's system for showing the order of passages in the

If now we think about our own practice, we may remember starting out as teachers to prepare a course on some subject, or deciding as practitioners that an orderly statement of some aspect of the law would help us when we came to prepare for presenting a client's case persuasively to a court. We then made a draft in a more-or-less-carefully considered pattern, so as to present the subject really effectively. The first time round, the draft may have been used as planned; but it may well have been amended at some points, and if the draft was used a second time, there will certainly have been amendment. The need for amendment arises most obviously in response to new legislation or a new judicial decision, but may come from realisation that the existing draft is inadequate. Faced with this need to amend, we take immediate care to record the new point, and slot it in on our typescript *somewhere*, without necessarily worrying much about whether that somewhere is the best place for it: perhaps *somewhere* is only the first big-enough blank space on a page of the typescript. Untidiness in medieval texts can be explained in much the same way: we can be sure that in one particular manuscript a miscellany comes at the end of a quire which was not filled by the material for which it had been reserved.[14] Again, there are many legal statements which are appropriate to more contexts than one: a rule about the contracts of women can appear (perhaps indeed ought to appear) in the contract context and the woman context; and this will explain the fact that the same passage sometimes appears more than once in the same manuscript.

It has long been recognised that the 'comprehensive' texts are of more than one kind. This fact was first made public in the Record Commission's *Ancient laws*, published in 1841;[15] there three forms of comprehensive text were interpreted as intended for different parts of Wales and named 'Venedotian Code', 'Dimetian Code', and 'Gwentian Code'. In that paper of 1881 Maitland had said that 'it is very apparent that a large part of these masses of rules is neither law made by any "sovereign one or many" (to use Austin's phrase), nor yet "judge-made" law, nor yet again a mere record of

manuscripts seems peculiar, and at a few points makes it impossible to tell what the order in a particular manuscript is. Morfydd Owen has examined the relation of all sixteen manuscripts of the Redaction in *Cyfreithiau Hywel Dda yn ôl Llawysgrif Coleg yr Iesu LVII*, ed. Melville Richards (revised edition, Cardiff, 1990), pp. xiv-xx.

14 Daniel Huws has shown that manuscript *W* of the Cyfnerth Redaction 'comprised three free-standing parts, quires 1–3, 4–8, and 9–10': T.M. Charles-Edwards et al. (eds.), *Lawyers and laymen* (Cardiff, 1986), p. 132. 'The text [of the Laws of Court] ends on the penultimate leaf of quire 3' [ibid.], but two, or perhaps three, floating sections which have nothing to do with the Laws of Court follow, on the penultimate leaf and the last leaf of that quire.

15 *Ancient laws and institutes of Wales* [ed. Aneurin Owen], (Commissioners on the Public Records of the Kingdom, 1841). There were two editions, an octavo in two volumes and a folio in one volume; references are most often to the two-volume edition, but thoughtful editors use book-chapter-section references, which are very nearly the same for the two editions.

popular customs. It is lawyer-made law, glossators' law, text-writers' law.'[16]
Two generations later, in 1951, the late Professor T. Jones Pierce gave effective
expression to the view which has since been accepted as a valid starting-point
for the more detailed study which is slowly going on: 'from the point of view
of content the books of *Cyfnerth*, *Blegywryd* and *Iorwerth* stand in related
chronological sequence – and in the order named'.[17] The names 'Cyfnerth
Redaction', 'Blegywryd Redaction', and 'Iorwerth Redaction' have by now
displaced 'Gwentian Code', 'Dimetian Code', and 'Venedotian Code' respectively, and it is clear that the chronological sequence is a sequence of increasing
sophistication. We must also take in the Latin texts, which seem to start from
a translation of a text related to the surviving Cyfnerth manuscripts; its
Latinity was improved in the other Latin redactions, which drew on each
other and on Welsh-language material. The Blegywryd Redaction is now
known to be a re-translation from an intermediate Latin text which is not
extant, though Latin Redaction D is derived from it.[18] That the nucleus of
the Cyfnerth Redaction goes back to Hywel's time is suggested by the
presence in the later manuscripts of some older Welsh forms which have
been eliminated from the Blegywryd Redaction: thus in the specification of
the compensation for insult (*sarhaed*) payable to a king, the silver rod which
is part of this is to be *kyr refet ae aran vys*,[19] whereas the Blegywryd Redaction
makes it [*k*]*yn vrasset a'e hirvys*.[20] After the rapid Norman Conquest of
England, any linguistic contact at official level will have been between Welsh
and French; hence the persistence in later manuscripts of words taken from
Anglo-Saxon will mean that those words had been 'naturalised' in Welsh, and
were open to develop like words of more native origin: there will have been no
borrowing from English *via* French, nor from French *via* English. Here there
is a clearly recognisable contrast with the vocabulary of English law, whose
technical terms are French: only where England had an institution unknown
to Normandy (such as soke and sake) were English-language terms used.

16 *Collected Papers* (as n. 2), i, 202.
17 J. Beverley Smith (ed.), *Medieval Welsh society* (Cardiff, 1972), p. 295. The passage comes
    from a lecture delivered in 1951 and published in 1952.
18 The strongest evidence for translation is in mistranslations: see Hywel D. Emanuel, 'The
    Book of Blegywryd and Ms. Rawlinson 821' in *Celtic law papers*, ed. D. Jenkins (Brussels,
    1973), pp. 163–70; this translates a paper in Welsh, *Bulletin of the Board of Celtic Studies*, xix
    (1960), 23–28. References to the redactions will use the abbreviations listed on p. 19, above;
    the sigla IorA and IorB are needed because for one 'chapter' of the Iorwerth Redaction
    there are two forms, which are printed on the upper and lower parts of the pages of *Ancient
    laws*. IorA follows manuscript *A* and, for the lacunae in *A*, manuscript *E*, and gives variants
    from other manuscripts; IorB follows the one manuscript of its class, *B*, which is the main
    source of the edition *Llyfr Iorwerth*.
19 WML 3.2.
20 Bleg 3.20.

Though familiarity with *Ancient laws* has made it natural for us to speak of Books I, II, and III of the comprehensive texts, this usage has no support from the manuscripts: the designation *book* (Welsh *llyfr*) is there used for the Justices' Test Book (*Llyfr Prawf Ynaid*), the Book of Case-law (*Llyfr Damweiniau*), and the Book of Procedure (*Llyfr Cynghawsedd*)[21], for the books of named jurists, and for the Book of the White House, but the main divisions of the texts are not called 'books'. According to one of the expanded accounts of the work of Hywel, when he had got the laws and usages of Wales 'the nearest possible to truth and justice', 'he commanded them to be written in three parts: the first the law of his daily court; the second the law of the country; the third the usage of each one of them'.[22] The first two parts stand out clearly enough in the three redactions; there is very little sign of the third part in the Cyfnerth and Blegywryd Redactions, and though the Iorwerth Redaction has a clearly-marked third part, this is not concerned with usage, but is an expanded Justices' Test Book.

'Book I' in all three redactions contains the Laws of Court. This part of the law has been very fully examined in *The Welsh king and his court*,[23] and without going into detail it can be said that the Laws of Court, far more than any other provisions of the lawbooks, reveal a strengthening of the state (which in that age was the king). Hywel's close relations with the court of Athelstan are clearly reflected in the language of the Laws of Court, and the desire for precision as a spur to borrowing can be seen at different levels here. At the level of the court's daily sport, the lawbooks show the Welsh language adapting an Anglo-Saxon word to meet a need which appeared (as it would seem) when contact with the English court introduced the Welsh to the sport of hunting with birds. The Anglo-Saxon *heafoc* is represented in modern English by *hawk*, and that word is today used in the wide sense of 'hunting bird', as well as in the narrower sense in which hawks are contrasted with falcons; but in the lawbooks *hebog* has been specialised for 'falcon'.[24] At the level of the court's evening junketing, which would be intertwined with political significance, the Anglo-Saxon *distain* seems to displace Welsh *swyddwr*. At various points in *The Welsh king and his court*[25] the names *swyddog*,

---

21 This translation seems more satisfactory than the 'Book of Pleadings' which has been used more often: see Morfydd E. Owen in *Y Traddodiad Rhyddiaith yn yr Oesau Canol*, ed. Geraint Bowen (Llandysul, 1974), p. 237.

22 *The Laws of Hywel Dda* (*The Book of Blegywryd*), translated by Melville Richards (Liverpool, 1954), p. 23.

23 ed. T.M. Charles-Edwards, Morfydd E. Owen, and Paul Russell (Cardiff, 2000).

24 D. Jenkins, '*gwalch: Welsh*' in *Cambridge Medieval Celtic Studies*, xix (1990), 55–67.

25 See especially Chapters 12 and 24, and the passages indexed under *swydd* and extensions of that word. The Latin texts seem to me to make unnecessarily heavy weather of the translation of *swydd*, and to be at fault in the passage 'ebedyw optimatis qui habet hereditatem, id est swyd'; the unusual translation may however be a reaction to what seems

swyddwr, and *distain* have been discussed in more detail than can be allowed here, without resulting in any very clear conclusion. However, it can be said that the lawbooks seem to use *swyddog* (for which *officer* is the usual translation) as the wider-sense designation for all members of the court, while the singular *swyddwr* (for which *official* is conveniently different from *officer*) and the plural *swyddwyr* have the narrower sense of those members who dealt with food and drink. One *swyddwr* would stand out as superior to his fellows, and it would be awkward that his designation did not stand out like his function – until the alien word *distain* was adopted for him, and for him alone. There is no doubt that *distain* is a Welsh form of the Anglo-Saxon *discthegn*, 'dish-servant', whose pronunciation involved the quite un-Welsh medial combination *shth*. There could be dishthanes in the plural, but a Welsh visitor to Athelstan's court might meet the leading dishthane and learn his title, without realising that his undistinguished assistants were also dishthanes. Hence the alien word, re-shaped to a Welsh form, could conveniently be used as the distinctive designation for the one officer who is usually called *steward* in English. With the centuries this officer's function changed (as, of course, the function of the royal Stewarts or Stuarts of Scotland changed): it had already begun to change in the England of Hywel's day, and in thirteenth-century Wales Goronwy ab Ednyfed, who is *distein y'r tywyssawc* in *Brut y Tywysogion*,[26] is *senescallus noster* in the Latin of a charter of Prince Llywelyn ap Gruffudd.[27] For most of the year, Goronwy's food-serving duties would have been performed by deputy, but it is likely enough that (like comparable officers in England in much later times) Goronwy would himself serve the prince with food on special occasions.

Similar reasons may explain the adoption of *edling*, and the later development of its meaning. It comes from the Anglo-Saxon *ætheling*, and for its meaning we look at the Iorwerth Redaction's version of the Laws of Court:

> The heir-apparent, to wit the edling, who is entitled to reign after the King, is entitled to be the most honoured in the court, except the King and Queen. It is right for him to be a son or a nephew of the King. ...
> These are the King's members: his sons and his nephews and his male first-cousins. Some say that each of these is an edling; others say that no-one is an edling save him to whom the King gives hope and prospect.[28]

The word translated *heir-apparent* is *gvrthdrych*. In modern Welsh this has become *gwrthrych*, and is the ordinary word for some senses of the noun

---

to be a fact of thirteenth-century Wales, that certain offices were 'running in the family'. See also n. 48.

26 Thomas Jones (ed.), *Brut y Tywysogyon, Peniarth ms. 20* (Cardiff, 1941), 218b.16.

27 J. Goronwy Edwards (ed.), *Littere Wallie* (Cardiff, 1940), p. 28.

28 LTMW 6.20–23, 7.1–4, translating Ior §4/1,2,7–9.

'object'; that meaning is ultimately derived from the concept of something looked at. The lawbooks' word, which was more usually *gwrthrychiad*, 'an older word with Irish parallels ... seems to imply a looking forward by the heir or a looking up to him'.[29] The identification of member with edling surely goes too far, for there could certainly be 'members' of royal blood (brothers and uncles of the king, to say nothing of his female relatives) who were not edlings though some of them would have been edlings to earlier kings. We remember that it has been persuasively argued that the many conflicts over kingship in Ireland and Wales are explained by the rules which meant that a particular man would realise that if he did not secure the kingship for himself, he and his descendants would cease to be eligible when the reigning king's successor was appointed. He would, that is, no longer be a *gwrthrychiad*, but he would still be a member of the royal blood.

So it looks as though the Welsh adopted *ætheling* and made it Welsh as *edling*, in the first place to identify those royal members who were eligible for kingship; and at that stage there would be many edlings in a Welsh kingdom. The Laws of Court as we have them, however, tell us a good deal about *the* edling, and show that there has been a change in the concept. The change was undoubtedly a change for the better, but it was made in Wales independently of England, for *ætheling* did not come to mean 'designated heir' in England.[30] We have no positive evidence for the date of its adoption in Wales, and there is some temptation to connect it with Llywelyn ab Iorwerth's designation of his younger son Dafydd (by his wife Joan, the legitimated daughter of King John of England), in preference to Gruffudd, who was older and was acknowledged by his father though his mother, Tangwystl Goch, was not canonically married to that father.

At a less political level, borrowing in the interest of precision is particularly evident in the lawbooks' words for horses, which seem to show a continued course of finding names which will identify more exactly a particular kind of horse. The basic word which gives *equus* in Latin and *ech* in Irish does not appear in a simple form in Welsh, though the basic word must have been known. The 'general' word which has survived to the present day is *ceffyl*, represented in Vulgar Latin by *caballus*; the forms which this word has taken in Latin, in the Romance languages, and in the Celtic languages have much exercised the linguistic specialists, but 'no generally accepted theory has been advanced'.[31] In Welsh medieval verse and prose stories romantic words

---

29 LTMW 222. See also T.M. Charles-Edwards, 'The heir-apparent in Irish and Welsh law' in *Celtica*, ix (1971), 180–90.

30 David N. Dumville, 'The ætheling: a study in Anglo-Saxon constitutional history' in *Anglo-Saxon England*, viii (1979), 1–33.

31 Patricia Kelly, 'The earliest words for "horse" in the Celtic languages' in Sioned Davies and Nerys Ann Jones (eds.), *The horse in Celtic culture: medieval Welsh perspectives* (Cardiff, 1997), p. 50.

appear, but for the lawbooks *march*, whose origin has not been traced, is the most usual word. This has survived into Modern Welsh: in southern dialects, it is the normal word for 'stallion'; for other dialects *march* is poetic and Biblical, while the entire horse has a name, *stalwyn*, also found in the lawbooks and borrowed from some form of *stallion*. The English word is based on *stall*, so that the original stallion was a stalled horse – and that concept leads us to another line of development in Welsh. Latin had nouns *admissarius* and *admissus* (representing *equus admissus ad equam*), meaning 'stallion'; by the normal process of adaptation *admissus* gave in Welsh *emys*, which in turn (because *emys* sounded like a plural) gave *amws*. *Amws* does occur in Welsh in the sense of 'stallion', but in the lawbooks it has the narrower sense of a horse adapted to the needs of battle. The Western medieval mind thought castration would make a horse too timid for battle, so we can assume that the *amws* was still a stallion; but what the lawbooks are concerned with is ensuring that it is kept in fighting condition by adequate feeding. It could not be allowed to graze freely except for a few weeks in spring; at all other times it must be kept in the stall which the name 'stallion' implied.[32] In the Latin redactions *amws* is usually represented by *dextrarius*, and can be translated 'destrier'; but *dextrarius* occurs for 'stallion' at LatA 156.21 and LatD 362.6. More often forms representing Welsh *stalwyn* occur in the Latin redactions; and at LatB 235.30 and LatD 360.34 (in unrelated passages), the stallion is *emissarius*.

The name *amws* was found by narrowing an earlier borrowing; other names use varying techniques. For a working horse, the lawbooks have the compound *gweinyddfarch*, 'serving horse', where both elements are native. In *swmerfarch*, corresponding to the Latin redactions' *equs*[33] *summarius*, 'sumpter-horse', a mixed compound noun has been produced, and it is most likely that the borrowing is from French, for 'other languages show the same kind of French influence, because the Normans were largely responsible for developments in the culture of the horse in Western Europe'.[34] The Iorwerth Redaction's 'Rvnsy neu sumeruarch, chue ugeynt yu y werth'[35] might

---

32 A Welsh brocard wholly forbids open grazing: 'A destrier grazing in the open and a greyhound without its collar lose their status', LTMW 173.8–9, translating WML 67.20–21 = Bleg 53.19–20. In the Latin redactions this appears only at LatD 380.8, in Welsh; and other passages in the Welsh-language redactions are more detailed and more generous: e.g. 'A destrier does not lose its value or its status in spite of grazing out during three seasons, which are these: from the middle of April to the middle of May, and the whole of October', LTMW 172.3–8, translating Ior §121/4.

33 The Latin manuscripts in general prefer *equs* to *equus*: does this tell us something about medieval Welsh speech? The *q*-sound found in French does not occur in Welsh: in any word picked up, a *q*-sound is naturalised as a *k*-.

34 Patricia Kelly, *The horse in Celtic culture*, p. 64. For a wide-ranging study of the development of horses in Western Europe and its background, see R.H.C. Davis, *The medieval warhorse* (London, 1989), especially pp. 55–60 for the Normans.

35 Ior §121/6.

perhaps mean that the two names were being offered as alternative names for the same animal; it is more likely that they are names for different animals of the same value. The Cyfnerth Redaction does not mention the *swmerfarch*, and the Blegywryd and Latin redactions give different values: 120*d*. for the *rwnssi* and 80*d*. for the *swmeruarch*.[36] The medieval horseman is likely to have distinguished clearly enough between the load-carrying sumpter-horse and the rowney which would be ridden by an esquire. For the *palffrai* we look to the French form, which lies behind the English *palfrey* too, and note that the common German word for 'horse', *Pferd*, is derived from the same *paraverdus* which gave us *palffrai* for the horse which could amble, moving the two legs on one side together.[37] We can assume that it was this ambling which made a horse a *palffrai*, though the lawbooks do not say so. This is surprising, for they so often specify the *teithi*, the features which justify treating something (whether it be an animal or a human being or an offence) as a member of a named class. So for the mare 'Her properties are, to draw a car uphill and downhill, and to carry a cross-load, and to bear foals.'[38] The verb *rhygyngu*, which is accepted as meaning 'amble' does not occur in the lawbooks; it is also used in a looser sense, '*mince, stalk, strut*' in Isaiah iii.16: see *Geiriadur Prifysgol Cymru* 3138b. At WM 168.18–20 the romance of Peredur describes a knight coming out on a 'palfrei gloy6du ffroenuoll ymdeithic. A rygig wastadualch escutlym ditramg6yd gantha6', but none of the extant English translations uses *ambling*. The two sentences can be run together and translated 'a shining-black wide-nostrilled fast-moving palfrey with a proudly-even sharply-swift unobstructed amble'.

If there has been borrowing to define the trained grown horse, its first months are firmly native. There seems to be only the one word *caseg* for 'mare', in medieval as in modern Welsh; and though the elementary counterpart of *equus* has been lost, it has not been lost without trace, for a pregnant mare is *cyfeb*, 'with-horse', and the lawbooks give the value of a mare's *cyfebrwydd*, 'with-horseness'. When delivered the product is *ebol* or *eboles* according to sex.

Horses provided for military service are the subject of rules which give significant information about the grammar of Welsh as well as about

36 Bleg 91.11–12, LatA 154.31–2, LatB 234.7–8, LatD 360.10–11. LatA has *Precium runci*, LatB the more regular *Runcinus*, LatD *runcius*, editorially emended to *runcinus*. This seems to imply that LatD was following LatA rather than LatB, and that LatA was latinising from the Welsh, which in turn will have come 'by ear' from the French; the Welsh form always has the –*s*–, which suggests borrowing from French *rouncy* rather than English *rowney*.

37 Davis, *The medieval warhorse*, p.137, s.vv. *Palefridus, Paraveredus*. Werner König, *dtv-Atlas zur deutschen Sprache* (Munich, 1978), pp. 210–11, shows that *Pferd* has superseded *Ross* (cognate with English *horse*) in most of Germany, while *Ross* survives in Austria and southern parts of Germany.

38 LTMW 175.2–4, translating Ior §125/3/1,2.

Table 1. Texts of a rule on supplies for hosting

WML 57.21	Latin Redaction A 137.9	Latin Redaction B 205.1	Latin Redaction D 377.24	Bleg 47.15	Ior §93/3.4
Y gan y tayogeu	Rex debet*	Rex a villanis suis	Equos summarios	Y gan y tayogeu	meybyon eyllyon … a deleant
y *dyly** y brenhin	a villanis	debet habere equos	in expeditione sua	y keiff y brenin	rody pynueyrch e'r brenhyn
pynueirch	summarios	summarios, id est penueirch,	rex a villanis suis habere debet,	pynueirch	
yn y luyd;	in expedicione sua,	in expeditione sua,		yn y luyd,	en e luedeu,
ac	et	et	et	ac	[§43/5] E brenhyn
o pop taya6ctref y keiff	de qualibet villa rusticana	de qualibet villa	de qualibet villa rusticana	o pob tayawctref y keiff	a dele o pob byleyntref
g6r a march a b6ell	hominem cum securi et cum equo,	hominem cum securi et cum equo,	hominem cum securi et cum equo	gwr a march a bwell	den a march a bueall
ar treul y brenhin	qui castra regis edificent:	qui castra regis edificent;	ad castra regis edificanda;	y wneuthur y gestyll,	y wneythur lluest e'r brenhyn,
y wneuthur lluesteu ida6.	sed interim erunt	sed ipsi		ac	ac
	ad expensam regis.	ad expensam regis erunt.	ad regis tamen sint expensa.	ar treul y brenhin y bydant.	vynteu a deleant bot ar e cost ef.

* ms. keiff.   * LTMW inserts [habere] here

subordinate status in medieval Wales. In Table 1 forms of these rules from the three Welsh-language redactions, and from three Latin redactions, are compared. The extant Cyfnerth versions are close to the Blegywryd version, but for a reason which will appear, the Cyfnerth version has been emended in italics.

All the versions can be fairly enough rendered in English by 'The king is entitled to have from the villeins packhorses in his hostings, and from each villein townland a man with an axe and a horse, to make the king's camps, at the king's expense'; but the various forms call for comment. First then comes the 'Rex debet ... summarios' of LatA. Emanuel has added *habere* after *debet*, and LatB and LatD agree in making what I think any Latinist would regard as a necessary correction (and a modern Welsh-speaker would also perceive as natural). But *debet* without *habere* is best understood as over-literal translation of a Welsh idiom, which appears in the emended Cyfnerth form and can be translated 'The king is entitled to packhorses from the villeins'. Like English *ought*, which has won a special meaning for an oblique tense of the verb *to owe*, modern Welsh *dylai* has won a similar meaning for an oblique tense of a verb, most of whose tenses have disappeared from modern Welsh. The form *dyly* is the third person singular of the present indicative, and has a double possibility: it may mean 'is entitled to' or 'is bound to', and has a related action-noun *dylyed*. This has given in modern Welsh the forms *dlêd* and *dyled*, with the one meaning 'debt', but in medieval Welsh that noun could be used equally for what one was entitled to have and for what one was bound to give, whether in money, in kind, or in some act.[39] A similar word was found by Gluckman in the juristic language of the Barotse: 'in Barotse both right and duty are covered usually by a single word, derived from a verbal form which we can translate as "ought".'[40] LatA then seems to be treating the Latin *debet* as though it could, like the Welsh *dyly*, mean 'is entitled to'. Part of the entitlement is to *pynfeirch*, which are *summarii* in the Latin, though LatB may have added the Welsh word so as to make it clear that the *summarii* of this rule were not necessarily of the value set down in the lists. Those lists do not mention the *pynfarch*, whose primary meaning was 'packhorse', so that the rule can be interpreted as fulfilled by any horse which could carry a *pwn* (a load, from Latin *pondus*[41]).

---

39 LTMW p.xli. Irish has the cognate noun *dliged*: see *Crith Gablach*, ed. D.A. Binchy (Dublin, 1941), pp. 50, 84.

40 Max Gluckman, *The ideas in Barotse jurisprudence* (New Haven, Conn., and London, 1965; reprint with minor amendments and new preface, Manchester, 1972), p. 21.

41 *Geiriadur Prifysgol Cymru, a dictionary of the Welsh language* (Cardiff, 1950–2002), pp. 2941–2. In the lawbooks *pynfarch* appears also in the eight 'packhorses' of the king, which bring him income unpredictably (like the 'incidents' of English land tenure); see D. Jenkins, 'A second look at Welsh land law' in *Transactions of the Honourable Society of Cymmrodorion*, viii (new series, 2002), 69. In modern Welsh *pynfarch* is alive in the sense 'leat', which is also

What the king *debet*, then, was horses (of any kind) which could carry loads; but who were the givers for whom these were an obligation? In English they can safely be called *villeins*, but we have in Welsh several words which may not be synonymous, as we might tend to assume. The understanding of subordinate status in any society is bedevilled by attempts to create a package of features, all of which are applicable in all cases. In practice, the features of any particular status in any particular place will depend on local conditions and on the way the status came into effect; but lawyers want tidy statements, and patrons and would-be patrons want to be able to invoke the whole package by proving one fact from the package, in order to claim some other advantage offered by the package. Thus in the English case of 1308, *Paris v. Page*[42] the defendants sought (but failed) to justify their treating one brother as a villein by showing that another brother was an admitted villein. In that case, the status of the villein brother might be evidence that the plaintiff brother *had been* a villein, but proof that he had become a citizen of London overrode the original status so that the villein package could not be applied.

For an introduction to the pattern of medieval Welsh society we can turn to a sentence in the Laws of Court at LatB 207.30–31: 'Tres solum sunt homines: scilicet, rex, optimas, villanus; et eorum membra.' LatD 318.22 has much the same wording, and Bleg (5.12–13) has perhaps chosen his terms for the sake of the alliteration: 'Tri ryw dyn yssyd: brenhin, a breyr, a bilaen, ac eu haelodeu.' Welsh and Latin can both be translated 'There are three kinds of man ['human being']: a king, a breyr, and a villein, and their members.' There were of course other human beings in Wales, but aliens and slaves were not counted as part of the community, and the lawbooks have to make special provisions for associating them with the community: we shall look at these a little later. Meanwhile we notice that the classes are named from their heads, but we have already seen the importance of the king's 'members', and the members of any group headed by a breyr are quite as important. For the breyr is the head of a group made up of his descendants, and has become breyr by succeeding to his family inheritance on the death of the last of his direct male ancestors. It would indeed be more illuminating to call the class that of the *bonheddig*, since the breyr's members have that name until they succeed to the inheritance, and we are specifically told that if a breyr's land is given up in settlement of a claim for *galanas* (the Welsh parallel to English *wergeld*), his son (who will find that there is no land to inherit) 'will not be an alien, but an innate bonheddig. An innate bonheddig is a person whose

found in place-names in the twelfth century: *The text of the Book of Llan Dâv*, ed. J. Gwenogvryn Evans with the co-operation of John Rhys (Oxford, 1893; reprinted Aberystwyth, 1979), pp. 42,134.

42 *Year Books 1 &2 Ed.* 2 (1307–09), ed. F.W. Maitland, Selden Society xvii (1903), pp. 11–13.

complete stock is in Wales, both from mother and from father.'[43] The Blegywryd Redaction brings this out clearly and simply when it values the life of an innate bonheddig and his sarhaed at half those of a breyr without office. We have seen that the breyr becomes *optimas* in Latin, and I am not qualified to quarrel with that translation; but it is certainly unfortunate that *gwerth bonhedic canhwynawl* has become *Precium nobilis qui dicitur canhwynawl* at LatD 339.40, since this has led so many scholars to refer in English to 'nobles'. In modern Welsh *gŵr bonheddig* means 'gentleman', and 'gentry' is the best name for the medieval class.

For the third of the classes of Welsh society there are several names: *taeog* seems to be the oldest, and always seems to imply non-free status, but we need to do some deeper thinking about the matter. We can start with the *meybyon eyllyon* of Ior, and from the proposition that unfree status cannot arise while unoccupied land is accessible to able-bodied men. In support of that proposition I quote the experience (of which Karl Marx made use) of 'a Mr. Peel, who, in the early days of Australian colonization ... took with him to the Swan River Settlement, Western Australia, 3,000 people of the working class and £50,000 worth of capital. Instead of being able to "exploit" the proletarians, he found himself left "without a servant to make his bed or to fetch him water from the river" ... for there was an abundance of unused land, as open to them as to him.'[44] A clientship relation is not inconsistent with superfluity of land (if only because livestock may be needed for effective use of the land), and though in most of the extant references the *aillt* is semi-free, the *aillt* is primarily a client, and only secondarily a non-free client.[45] The *meybyon eyllyon* of Table 1 and some other Ior passages are villeins, but elsewhere in Ior the property of a *mab eillt* is given a higher value than that of a *taeog*.[46]

I have spoken of 'subordinate status' deliberately, because to speak of non-free or unfree status would beg the question of what makes a status free. For *gŵr rhydd* ('free man' [male]) and *dyn rhydd* ('free man' [human]) occur in the lawbooks, and the statements of the Blegywryd Redaction about the ability of wives to give property away suggest that the Blegywryd redactor had a

43 LTMW 110.20–23, translating Ior §87/3,4.

44 Frederick Verinder, *Land and freedom* (London, 1935), p. 33.

45 The General Index of LTWL (p. 557b) has '*Mab aillt* (the son of a villein, a villein)', and on the face of it, *meybyon eyllyon* could mean 'clients' sons', but this is certainly not what is intended. If *meybyon* has any significance, it is in making it clear that the clients are male: *eyllyon* is an adjective qualifying the noun *meybyon*. Bleg 50.24–26 has values for *odyn eillt brenhin* and *odyn eillt breyr* whereas WML 103.1–5, in a very similar passage, has the same values for *odyn tayaa6c brenhin* and *odyn taya6c breyr*. The ordinary word for 'friend', *cyfaill*, earlier *cyfeillt*, can hardly have meant 'fellow-villein'.

46 LTMW 195.30,31, translating Ior §144/14; see also the Glossary at LTMW 310 and the notes there cited.

wider (and more correct) vision of status than those responsible for the Latin redactions. The Latin redactions all contrast the ability of *uxor optimatis* and *uxor villani*,[47] whereas Bleg (62.9,13) speaks of *gwreic gwr ryd* and *gwreic tayawc*. It is conceivable that the wife of a breyr's son had less authority to give property away than a breyr's wife; what is not conceivable is that a breyr's son could not take a wife while his father was alive, or that any limits on his wife's authority should have been left unrecorded. We are put upon inquiry also by LTMW 91.16–18 (translating Ior §77/34) 'it is not right to pay land without status instead of land to which a status is attached, such as the office of cynghellor, or the office of maer, or an immunity', where *immunity* translates *redyt*, and was preferred to *freedom* because it must surely refer to something more than the qualities implied by 'free man'. It seems very likely indeed that it refers to specially generous conditions, such as those of the land held by the family of Ednyfed Fychan, the 'Wyrion Eden' of the records.[48] It is evident that some free men were more free than others, but the lawyers certainly drew a line somewhere between the free and the less than free, and we must try to do the same.

The best answer seems to be that the status of a patron–client relationship is free if the client can insist on giving up the relationship. The terms of a particular free-status relationship may impose conditions on its termination, but that will not matter if the conditions do not amount to a total bar on termination; to make this point clear we can look at the lawbooks' provisions for associating aliens and slaves with the Welsh community. The alien must find himself a Welsh patron, whether king or gentleman or villein, and could move from one Welsh patron to another, on condition of leaving half his property to the deserted patron. The patron had a corresponding liberty to dismiss the client; if, however, the alien and his descendants stayed with the same patron and his descendants, the clientship would become permanent in the fourth generation, and could not thereafter be broken: it would have

---

47 LatA 144.11,14; LatB 221.24,27; LatD 342.23,26.
48 See Glyn Roberts, 'Wyrion Eden' in *Aspects of Welsh history* (Cardiff, 1969), pp. 179–214, especially pp. 181–84; 'Teulu Penmynydd', ibid., pp. 240–74. A footnote on p. 244 refers to J.E. Lloyd, *History of Wales* (London, 1912), ii, 622, n.54: 'The "distain" or steward … held his position by hereditary right', citing VC II.xi.33 [= Ior §78/6]. However, this sentence names the 'King's fee … from land which carries an office, such as the office of chief falconer or steward …' (LTMW 92.8–10), which must mean that anyone who acquired the holding would get the office. In practice, the office would be hereditary if the holding was allowed to descend normally, and in fact the descendants of Ednyfed Fychan were *disteiniaid* for several generations, though the records which set out those generous terms do not mention the office. Dr Paul Russell's words at 284.2–4 of *The Welsh king and his court*, 'The offices associated with the king's court … are often hereditary and are therefore frequently linked with land' seem to me to put the cart before the horse; I would prefer 'The offices associated with the king's court … are often linked with land and are therefore frequently hereditary.' The presence of *Wele Hebbogothion* in Dinlle (*Rec. Caern.* 22–3) may be relevant here.

ceased to be a free-status clientship. Villein clientship, on the other hand, was always unfree: the client was not free to leave, and the patron was not free to dismiss; hence the lawbooks have something to say about runaway villeins.[49]

In Welsh the slave was *caeth*, representing Latin *captus* and implying that the primary source of slave status had been capture in war; the Latin redactions have *captivus*, which may reflect similar thinking, but the lawbooks show that slave status could arise in other ways. For the value (*gwerth*) of a slave varied, not according to the status of the owner but according to the provenance of the slave: a slave from 'this island' was worth less than one from overseas, 'because he himself debased his status by willingly becoming a hireling';[50] and though in some contexts *gwerth* is used for the measure of the wergild payable for a free man (where *galanas* would be more technically appropriate), it is clear enough that the *gwerth* of the slave is the price which was payable to his owner. If the slave struck a free man, his owner was liable, 'for a person has possession of his bondman as of his animal'.[51] If a slave struck a free person, his hand was to be cut off, but his owner had the option of paying the victim's *sarhaed* or handing the slave over to the victim and his kin. Yet it seems that some of the lawyers were not quite at ease in treating the killing of a slave as a matter for compensation to the owner: they will have realised that a 'voluntary' slave would usually have kin. However we explain it, three of the Cyfnerth manuscripts, *W*, *X*, and *Z*, have *galanas caeth telediw*. Manuscripts *V* and *Mk* have *g6erth* for *galanas*, and so does manuscript *U* – but there *gwerth* has been written in a space from which all but the last stroke of a longer word has been deleted; that stroke is so much like the end of an *s* that we can boldly guess that the deleted word was *galanas*.

It is thus easy to see that when non-free status became more significant the lawyers would need a term of art which could not be misinterpreted. They found it in the word which is *villanus* in Latin and *villein* in French and English, and which appears in the lawbooks in two words which are note-worthy both for their form and for their later history. Because native Welsh words do not normally begin with the *v*-sound (which is represented in

---

49 E.g. *tayogeu ffoaduryonn* Bleg 28.17 = *rustici fugitivi* LatD 348.15–16.

50 WML 194.7–9, translating WML 45.16–18. The values were £1·5 and £1.

51 WML 299.34–300.1, translating WML 116.7–8, and giving the reason for the rule that 'the bondman of another person' is one of the 'persons whose worth the king is not to demand, although they shall be killed in his gwlad'. The passage is in manuscripts *Mk* (93.20–23) and *Z* (38b.8–13), but not in manuscript *V*, and this is not because of a lacuna in *V*, for the paragraphs on either side of this passage are in *V*. For the 'possession' of Wade-Evans's translation (Welsh *medyant*), we should probably substitute 'control', which is the basic meaning of the element *medd*, as it is of the essence of the concept of possession: see the references s.v. *medu* in *Drych yr Oesoedd Canol*, ed. Nesta Lloyd and Morfydd E. Owen (Cardiff, 1986), p. 252, and Henry Lewis and Holger Pedersen, *A concise comparative Celtic grammar* (Göttingen, 1937), p. 382.

Modern Welsh by *f*, but in the lawbooks by *f*, *u*, *v*, *w*, and other more exotic forms), borrowed words which begin with a *v* tend to be regularised by treating the *v* as the mutation of a *b* or an *m*, as in a native Welsh word. So the *villanus* became a *bilaen/bilein*, or less often a *milein*; and the latter form has survived into the Welsh of today, with a pejorative meaning (like the English *villain* and its French counterparts): a popular modern Welsh dictionary has as its only definitions 'angry, fierce, savage, cruel'.

The liability of the villeins was not individual. They were organised in units for which the Welsh name is *tref* – and a very troublesome name it is. In modern Welsh it means 'town', as contrasted with 'country', *gwlad*, and with 'village', *pentref*. There is an obvious similarity between the changes in meaning of *tref* and English *tun/town*, but that leaves us with the problem of translating *tref*. The *township* which is sometimes used will not do, for that word has a technical meaning in English law; and it seems to me that *townland*, which is not a term of art in English law, will serve better than any other form, for though the *tref* of medieval Wales does not correspond exactly to the Irish townland, it does seem to me to be a unit of the same order of magnitude. Diffidently, apologetically, I hold on to *townland*. There was no difficulty in Welsh, which produced *taeawctref* and *bileindref*, but there are no corresponding Latin terms. There are English parallels to the *villa rusticana* of LatA and LatD: 'The sources sometimes use the word *rusticus* or something similar, but in many cases it is their modern reader who decides who was a peasant.'[52]

The villein townlands sent men with axe and horse to accompany the hosting, to make *castra* for the king; and here a mistranslation testifies to the Latin source of the Blegywryd version: that version must be translated 'to make his castles', whereas *castra* has here the special sense of 'camps', the *lluest* of the other Welsh versions. *Lluest* is another of those words whose meaning has changed: it came to be applied to the summer shieling, and is now found mainly in the names of holdings in some parts of Wales. My last observation on this set of sentences must point out that the Iorwerth readings do not follow each other as those of the other redactions do, but come from different parts of the redaction: with the contrast between *meybyon eyllyon* and *byleyntref*, they will have been picked up from different sources. The source which gave *byleyntref* may also have had the borrowed *cost* rather than the native *treul* of the other Welsh versions; but that substitution may have been made by the Iorwerth borrower.

With this slight uncertainty about *galanas*, it is the less surprising to find that the slave has a *sarhaed*, an 'insult-price', but comparison of the readings is a complex exercise. The name *sarhaed* comes in its Welsh form at LatB 220.2 and LatD 340.10 as well as at Bleg 59.5, and as *iniuria* at LatE1 464.4,

52 Susan Reynolds, *Fiefs and vassals* (Oxford, 1994), p. 39.

but elsewhere, in Welsh (Cyfn at WML 45.18) and Latin (LatA 138.4, LatE2 464 n.1–1), liability is said to arise if a free man strikes a slave. The payment in all cases is set at so many pence and the pence are to be spent on named goods. According to the fullest form, the slave gets sixpence for three ells of home-made white cloth to make a coat for him when cutting gorse, three for breeches, a penny for brogues and gloves, a penny for a rope and a penny for a hedging-bill or an axe if he is a woodman. Some manuscripts make the total 12*d.*; others make it 13*d.* because they have not realised that the hedging-bill and axe are alternatives. This confusion surely implies that the rule was not of practical importance when the texts were compiled, but the rule does invite an Anglo-Saxon comparison, which Maitland made. In *Domesday Book and beyond* he drew attention to two passages in *Leges Henrici Primi*. At 70§4 L.J. Downer's edition has 'If a freeman kills a slave, he shall similarly pay to the slave's relatives forty pence and two gloves and a capon', translating his text 'Si liber seruum occidat, similiter reddat parentibus xl denarios et ii mufflas et unum pullum mutilatum', and noting the alternative *billum* as found in two manuscripts for *pullum*. Maitland quoted the Cyfnerth provision from *Ancient laws* and went on 'If we read *billum* instead of *pullum* the English rule may remind us of the Welsh. His hedger's gloves and bill-hook are the arms appropriate to the serf, "servitutis arma"; cf. Leg. Hen. 78§2.'[53] In contrast with Leg. Hen. 70§§3,5, which are traced to Ine 74 in Downer's edition, no source is there named for 70§4, and we are left wondering whether we can attribute these gloves to a borrowing from Wales, perhaps through Asser. The *servitutis arma* are to be given to the man who becomes a slave: 'As a symbol of this change of status he shall take up a sickle or a goad or the arms of slavery of this kind'; conversely, a slave who is emancipated is to be given 'a lance and a sword or whatever are the arms of freemen'.[54] The Welsh texts have no expression which echoes 'arms of slavery'.

Anglo-Norman influence is to be seen in the development of procedure, with some evidence for a wish to use trial by jury in preference to compurgation, and a more subtle change by way of modifying compurgation in the direction of the jury. I have examined this in detail elsewhere,[55] and will not pursue it here, but we shall look at a passage in the Blegywryd Redaction whose wording is perhaps best explained as adopting an Anglo-Norman expression from English law. A passage dealing with the loss of property deposited appears in exactly the same words in Cyfn (WML 63.16) and Bleg 46.9–12, where it reads (with editorial punctuation) 'Or cledir y dayar hagen

---

53 F.W. Maitland, *Domesday Book and beyond* (Cambridge, 1897), p. 31 n.9. For the references to 'Leg. Hen.' see *Leges Henrici Primi*, ed. and tr. L.J. Downer (Oxford, 1972).

54 Downer 245, 243.

55 'Towards the jury in medieval Wales' in John W. Cairns and Grant McLeod (eds.), *The dearest birthright of the people of England* (Oxford and Portland, Or., 2002), pp. 17–46.

y dan y ty gwedy gwnel ef y gyfreith y vot yn iach, brenhin bieu dayar, ac ny dyly keitwat uot drosti.' This is translated by Melville Richards 'If the earth however be excavated under the house after he has shown in law that he is clear, (the king owns the earth), the guardian is not to be answerable for it.'[56] This is a possible translation, but I would revise the Bleg punctuation by adding a comma after *ty*, and substituting a semi-colon for the comma after *iach*; this would clear the way for the translation 'If however the earth is dug under the house, after he makes his law he is clear: a king owns the earth and the guardian is not liable for it.' Here 'makes his law' translates the Welsh literally, and corresponds exactly to the *fit/fist sa ley* of an English Year Book.[57] The Latin versions do not help, for they omit the sentence.

From one point of view, the most valuable service rendered by any medieval Welsh jurist was Iorwerth ap Madog's vision of the addition to the Test Book of the values of equipment (Welsh *dodrefn*), for by naming so many items and giving an idea of their relative values he described much of the physical background of his society. The very words used will tell us something: some of them, like the *distain* and *edling* discussed earlier, are taken from Anglo-Saxon to fill a gap in the Welsh lexicon; but a new word may be used because it is for the moment fashionable. It was the social prestige of French in the court of Llywelyn ab Iorwerth and his wife Joan which led to the substitution of *cost* for *treul*, and to the rather surprising *tryzor* (Ior §12/9, from manuscript *B*; the form also appears in manuscript *E*, 10.27) which represents the French sound.

A full study of the vocabulary of the lawbooks is a lifetime's task for a dedicated team; here we will take a single line from *Llyfr Iorwerth* (§142/14–16): 'Hossaneu maur, viii.k'. Duy hvsyaus, vi.k'. Dvy estywaus, iiii.k'.' At LTMW 195.7–8 this is translated 'Long hose, eightpence; a pair of hose, sixpence; a pair of kneeboots, fourpence', but the names raise more than one problem of interpretation. Thus *hvsyaus* may be a 'ghost' form infected by the *-aws* of *ystywaws*, or may represent an early form of French *houseaux* ('Spatterdashes; leggings; long leather gaiters' according to a modern French dictionary). *Hosan* is today the ordinary Welsh word for 'sock' and 'stocking' – but that will not have been quite what medieval *hose* and *hosan* meant.

The third of these *dodrefn* has been harder to run to earth,[58] and has left me with a debt of gratitude to several collaborators. First came Mr Gareth

---

56 *The Laws of Hywel Dda* (*the Book of Blegywryd*), translated by Melville Richards (Liverpool, 1954), p. 56.

57 *Year Books 2 & 3 Ed.2* (1308–10), ed. F.W. Maitland, Selden Society, xix (1904), p. 138; cf. *gagea sa ley*, ibid; *faire sa ley*, *gagea la ley*, *Year Books 3 Ed.2* (1309–10), ed. F.W. Maitland, Selden Society, xx (1905), p. 117.

58 At *Diwylliant Gwerin Cymru* (Liverpool, 1942), p. 42 Iorwerth Peate argued that this third item must be understood as stockings of asbestos. This involved an emendation to *ystinos*,

Bevan, who gave me access to the slips of *Geiriadur Prifysgol Cymru*, and showed me a note which connected the French *estival* and its plural *estivaux* with a Latin *aestivalia* on the one hand and the German *Stiefel* on the other.[59] This led to Grimm's Dictionary, s.v. *Stiefel*: 'aestivalia *erscheinen aber "in geistlichen kreisen als nebenform von der in der Benedikinterregel den mönchen gebotenen fusztracht der* caligae ... *mit höherem, bis an die knie heran reichenden beinleder zum schutz bei sommerlichen arbeiten auszerhalb des klosters und reisen für kloster und stift".*[60] Grimm cites Chapter 50 (*rectius* 55) of the Benedictine Rule, and I took advantage of the late John Sheringham, who laboured hard but in vain in the search for clear authority in that chapter. Quite recently Professor David Trotter responded to my request for information about *estivaux* in Anglo-Norman by a very thorough examination of a wealth of material, which showed uncertainty about the ultimate source of this and other words, but led me to the conclusion that for thirteenth-century Benedictines *aestivalia* might be the same as *caligae*, the 'military boots' which remind us of the Emperor Caligula, or might be longer than those; at any rate they were worn by the monks when they set out in summer to clear up neglected growth. The safest translation seems to be 'summer boots', leaving open the question of how far up the leg they reached.

So when Brother Cadfael pulled on his boots in order to ride out from Shrewsbury Abbey during Stephen's reign, did he think of them in Latin as *aestivalia*, or in French as *estivaux*, or in Welsh as *ystywaws*? A century later, we can believe that the court of Llywelyn ab Iorwerth and Joan would think of them by their French name, and we may wonder about the circumstances in which the legal value of these summer boots could be important. We can at least claim to be repaying our debt to the Anglo-Norman lender, for the Welsh form *ystywaws* is evidence that *estivaux* were known in that corner of Wales by the second quarter of the thirteenth century.

---

not supported by any of the manuscripts, none of which has the –*n*-. If asbestos was used for making garments in the medieval world, the interpretation of *dwy ystywaws* as 'two [garments made of] asbestos' requires too many improbable assumptions to be credible.

59 Adolf Tobler, *Altfranzösisches Wörterbuch*, ed. Erhard-Lommatzsch, iii (Wiesbaden, 1954), 1395–6.

60 *Deutsches Wörterbuch*, X.ii.2772.

The use and adaptation of the action of replevin in Ireland during the reign of Edward I

PAUL BRAND

IN HILARY TERM 1299 Theobald de Verdun appeared in the Dublin Bench to answer Vivian de Donmowe on a plea 'that he replevy to the same Vivian his animals which he had taken', namely two cows each worth four shillings.[1] Theobald justified the distraint he had made. A 'great war' had broken out in his parts with Gillice Roth O'Railly. Theobald had gone to John Wogan, the chief justiciar of Ireland, and had asked him for assistance in defending those parts against the king's enemies. The justiciar had told him to go back and call together the magnates and others and devise a remedy by their advice. When they had met, it had been determined 'by common counsel' that two shillings should be levied from each carucate in those parts. Vivian was one of three named individuals who were the tenants of five carucates in 'Donmowe' who had refused to pay the ten shillings they owed. Theobald had therefore distrained them for the ten shillings by taking their animals. A jury confirmed that war had indeed broken out in those parts, but what had been said by Theobald about carucage having been granted by the common counsel of all the magnates and respectable men of those parts was not true. The grant had been made only by those living closest to the march where the fighting was taking place. Under questioning, however, the jury did agree that it was to the benefit of the whole area that the money be levied in this way for resistance to the 'felons'. Judgment was then adjourned.

This is one of the relatively limited number of surviving pieces of evidence from the reign of Edward I (king of England and lord of Ireland, 1272–1307) for the use of the action of replevin in the lordship of Ireland and is drawn from an early nineteenth-century calendar of a plea roll destroyed in 1922. As has been seen, it is concerned with a specific use of the power of distraint and whether or not that particular use had been justified. But it is also a good example of the way in which a case that appears to be about the seizure of two cows can then lead to a discussion about the working and mechanisms of local taxation and the kind of consent needed to raise a carucage in Ireland. It is disappointing that there is no recorded outcome to the case.

1 NAI, RC 7/5, p. 449.

40

In this paper I want to provide an overview of what is discoverable about the working and utilisation of the action of replevin in the lordship of Ireland during Edward's reign. Since the legal system of the lordship was based on that of the kingdom of England and the starting-point for both its legal procedures and its legal rules was those followed in England, it will be useful to look first, albeit in a fairly summary way, at the working of the action in England during this period. I will then attempt on the basis of the admittedly much more fragmentary evidence that survives for Ireland to discover how far Irish practice in this period followed and how far it diverged from the English model.

I

By the reign of Edward I the action of replevin in England had become a flexible means of challenging the use of distraint (the seizure and impounding of domesticated animals or of chattels) in the variety of different contexts in which the use of distraint was sanctioned by English legal custom and was therefore *prima facie* lawful. Outside those contexts, the appropriate remedy for an improper use of distraint which even on its face was unjustified was the action of trespass. By bringing the action of replevin the person whose animals or chattels had been taken in distraint was denying that the distrainor had on this specific occasion been entitled to exercise that right. An additional incentive for bringing the action was that as part of the initial preliminaries to the hearing the local sheriff was entrusted with the responsibility for ensuring the release of the distresses that had been taken and their return to the person distrained pending the outcome of the hearing. Only if the litigation decided that the distraint had been justified was their 'return' to the distrainor awarded by the court. In all the courts that heard cases of replevin plaintiffs seem to have continued, as a matter of form, to allege not only that they had been unjustly distrained but also that the distresses so taken had been retained by the distrainor despite an offer of 'gage and pledges', the 'gage' apparently being a chattel of nominal value, the 'pledges' sureties to appear in court to answer the claim being asserted by the distrainor. In the Common Bench certainly, and probably in lesser courts as well, this second allegation was of no practical significance and did not need to be maintained or proved, and there is some reason to suppose that already in the later twelfth century it may have commonly been treated as a fiction to give colour to the exclusive jurisdiction of the county court (and the higher courts to which county court cases might be removed) over cases in which the use of distraint was challenged.[2] By the reign of Edward I the most common

2 Paul Brand, *The making of the common law* (London, 1992), pp. 309–10.

context for the use of the distraint challenged in actions of replevin in the Common Bench (and probably in county courts as well) seems to have been a feudal lord's demand for tenurial services from one of his tenants, a context in which the lord was entitled to distrain anywhere in the tenement held of him and thus to seize the chattels of his sub-tenants as well as of the tenant who held directly of him.[3] The next most common context in Common Bench cases was where animals had been seized while 'doing damage' (*damage feasant*), that is while grazing or trampling down crops on arable land belonging to the distrainor or grazing pasture or meadow land where the owner of animals possessed no rights of common.[4] There were, however, a substantial number of other possible contexts as well.

In England, the action of replevin had normally to be initiated in the county court and could be initiated there either by writ or without writ by means of a simple plaint made to the sheriff.[5] From the county court actions of replevin could be removed into the Common Bench by the writ *pone* (if initiated by writ) or the writ *recordari facias* (if initiated by plaint), but there were significant restrictions on the availability of these removal writs, particularly if requested by defendants. It is impossible to tell what proportion of replevin cases were both heard and finally determined in county courts. All that can be said is that a relatively large number of replevin cases (just under 2,300 cases) were pleaded in the Common Bench during the reign.[6] It is also true that a significant number of these cases (particularly after 1290) are the subject of surviving reports: 17 cases before 1290 are reported and no less than 344 from the period 1290–1307. This makes reports of replevin cases much more common than reports of any other form of action (the next most popular type of reported case is dower with 103 reported cases). It also means that more than one in seven of all recorded replevin cases of the period are reported. Replevin could be initiated in some local courts other than the county court, but only by virtue of a franchisal right to do so, for which the franchisee had to to be able to show either a specific royal grant or exercise of the franchise time out of mind, and from the 1230s onwards there is evidence of royal action to stop the unwarranted exercise of such jurisdiction. In practice in England the franchise seems to have remained relatively uncommon: a right exercised by most bishops and older religious houses and by many earls and a few barons, but often only in some and not in all of their lands.

---

3 Brand, *Making of the common law*, pp. 302–03.
4 These account for only about one-third of the number of replevin cases about services. My figures are derived from an unpublished study of the action of replevin in the reign of Edward I.
5 Paul Brand, *Kings, barons and justices: the making and enforcement of legislation in thirteenth-century England* (Cambridge, 2003), p. 96.
6 For the annual totals of replevin cases pleaded in the Common Bench see Brand, *Making of the common law*, p. 299.

A number of significant statutory and non-statutory changes affected the action of replevin during the reign of Edward I and the final years of the reign of his predecessor, Henry III. The most important statutory changes were probably those made by chapter 2 of the Statute of Westminster II (1285).[7] These allowed lords who had distrained for services to remove replevin cases brought against them in the county court into the Common Bench as of right and also liberalised in their favour the rules about the kind of past possession of services they had to show to justify their use of distraint (any seisin by them or any of their ancestors since 1242 would now be sufficient).[8] They also required sheriffs, before securing the release of distresses, to take sureties not just for the prosecution of cases but also for the surrender of the distresses taken, if judgment was given for the distrainor; and provided measures to prevent those distrained from repeatedly securing the releases of their distresses and then failing to appear to prosecute their cases, a second such failure to lead in future to a judgment barring any further release. Non-statutory changes that took place during the reign included one allowing the use of the action to challenge process or final judgment in civil litigation in local courts and also to challenge presentments made at views of frankpledge in such courts and action taken in response to them.[9] A development which also affected the action, but only indirectly, was the development of a number of new forms of action based on or created by statute as alternative ways of challenging distraints. Legislation of 1259 (re-enacted on several occasions and for the final time in 1267 as part of the Statute of Marlborough) created the action of *contra formam feoffamenti* to allow tenants to challenge their lords' use of distraint to enforce the performance of suit of court unless the lord could show the tenant was obliged to perform it by the terms of the enfeoffment creating his tenancy or that he or his ancestors had performed it prior to 1230.[10] The new action did not, however, displace the continued use of replevin to challenge distraints for suit of court: it was a complementary, and not a replacement, remedy.[11] Legislation of 1275 (Westminster I, c. 35) prohibited magnates and others distraining those merely passing through their jurisdictions, but without property there, to answer for contracts made or trespasses committed elsewhere.[12] This led to the creation in 1290 of a special writ specifically based on the statute to enforce it, but it was relatively uncommon. Legislation of 1259 (re-enacted on several occasions and finally as part of the Statute of Marlborough in 1267) made statutory the existing

7   *Statutes of the realm*, i, 72–73.
8   For a discussion of these changes and the background to them see Brand, *Making of the common law*, pp. 288–92.
9   Brand, *Making of the common law*, pp. 295–98.
10 Brand, *Kings, barons and justices*, pp. 43–53 and chapter 8.
11 Ibid., pp. 252–62.
12 *Stat. realm*, i, 35.

common-law rule against making distraints on the highway or (in the case of a lord) outside the lord's fee, and from 1271 onwards there existed another statutory writ to enforce its provisions that was also in relatively common use.[13] Legislation of 1275 (part of the *Districciones Scaccarii* of that year) prohibited the taking of plough animals or sheep in distraint, unless there was nothing else that could be taken in their place or they were taken *damage feasant*.[14] This also led to the creation of a special form of action specifically based on the statute in use from 1276 onwards.

II

Our main source of knowledge about the use and working of the action of replevin in the lordship of Ireland during this period are the various different records which derive (either at first or at second hand) from litigation heard in the Dublin Bench, the Irish equivalent of the English Common Bench at Westminster. Only one original Dublin Bench plea roll survives. This is a roll for Easter term 1290 now in the British Library.[15] There are, however, also quite extensive Latin calendars of a number of the Dublin Bench rolls which were destroyed in 1922 during the Civil War. These are mainly contained in a series of volumes made for the Irish Record Commission early in the nineteenth century and now in the National Archives of Ireland.[16] There is also a calendar of part of a Dublin Bench roll for Trinity term 1282 in the Royal Irish Academy.[17]

There is just enough evidence to demonstrate that in the lordship of Ireland, as in England, replevin was a plea that could be initiated in the county court, and that it could be initiated either by writ or without a writ. One of the Irish Record Commission calendars contains a fairly complete transcript of a Dublin Bench enrolment from Michaelmas term 1298 which records an action of false judgment impugning a judgment that had been given in a plea of replevin in the Waterford county court in a replevin case between William le Rous of Waterford and Walter bishop of Waterford. The recorded argument from the county court clearly indicates that the plea had been initiated by writ.[18] Another calendared version of an entry from the Dublin Bench roll of Michaelmas term 1304 contains a reasonably full record

---

13 Brand, *Kings, barons and justices*, pp. 94–95 and 369–77.
14 *Stat. realm*, i, 197b.
15 BL, Additional Roll 13598.
16 There is a full list in G.J. Hand, *English law in Ireland, 1290–1324* (Cambridge, 1967), pp. 241–42.
17 RIA, MS 12.D.12.
18 NAI, RC 7/5, pp. 383–84. For the eventual reversal of this judgment in Trinity term 1301 see NAI, RC 7/8, pp. 151–52.

of a replevin plea initiated without writ in the county court of Cork and evoked to the Dublin Bench by a writ of *recordari facias*.[19] It seems likely that in Ireland (as in England) replevin pleas had normally to be initiated in the county court and could only reach the Dublin Bench by removal from there. There is also clear evidence from an entry on the surviving Dublin Bench plea roll for Easter term 1290 of the hearing of a replevin case initiated without writ in a seignorial court (that of Joan Butler at Thurles, Co. Tipperary), presumably by virtue of a franchise and of the use of a *recordari facias* to remove that plea into the Dublin Bench issued at the request of the defendant.[20]

There is rather more evidence to show the regular hearing of replevin cases in the Dublin Bench itself: at least fifteen pleas during the course of the reign, a reasonably substantial number, though tiny by comparison with the total from the Westminster Bench. Many more such cases may have gone uncalendared or have been on plea rolls lost before the nineteenth-century calendarers could set to work. As far as our evidence goes, actions of replevin in Ireland, as much as in England, were concerned in this period solely with whether or not a particular use of the power of distraint had been justified. There are no cases that turn, whether in part or in whole, on whether or not distresses had also been detained 'against gage and pledges'. And by far the most common use of the action in Ireland, as in England, so far as our surviving evidence goes, was to challenge the use of distraint to enforce the performance of services to a feudal lord.[21] There are also examples of it being used to challenge the exercise of jurisdictional rights over the plaintiff in a seignorial court (also fairly common in England),[22] and there is the one case with which I started, showing it being used to challenge the levying of local taxation (also occasionally found in England).

It is also possible to track the importation into Ireland and application of various of the statutory and non-statutory changes that affected the action in England and also the use of some of the new statutory actions to challenge the use of distraint that complemented the action of replevin. The purported reason given by c. 2 of the Statute of Westminster II for allowing lords to initiate the removal of replevin cases out of the county court into the Common Bench was to ensure that any disavowal by a tenant of holding of the lord was of record and could be used as the basis for an action of right to recover the tenement in demesne.[23] There are no examples of actions of right

---

19 NAI, RC 7/10, p. 81.
20 BL, Additional Roll 13598, m. 10d.
21 For examples see BL, Additional Roll 13598, m. 5d; NAI, RC 7/3, p. 153; RC 7/5, pp. 440–41; RC 7/7, pp. 151–52, 227–29; RC 7/6, pp. 529–30; RC 7/8, pp. 133–34; RC 7/10, p. 81; RC 7/11, pp. 588–90.
22 For examples see NAI, RC 7/3, pp. 397–98; RC 7/6, pp. 500–02, 517–19, 526–27.
23 Brand, *Making of the common law*, pp. 288–91.

on disavowal in the surviving material derived from the Dublin Bench plea rolls. However, it may be significant that in the only action of replevin without writ removed from a franchisal court (that of Joan Butler of Thurles) it seems to have been the defendant (James Keting) who had procured the removal of the case; that he avowed on the plaintiff (Geoffrey de Salle) for tenurial suit of court, and Geoffrey had disavowed holding of him; and that, as in England, this disavowal was not subject to any kind of investigation but was taken as bringing the suit to an end in favour of the plaintiff.[24] The removal was probably authorised under the provisions of the Statute of Westminster II, c. 2. It is not now possible on the basis of the surviving evidence to prove that there was any significant 'liberalisation' of the rules relating to avowries for service in favour of lords in Ireland. It is, however, possible to show that there arose in Ireland exactly the same sort of conflict over statutory inter-pretation between the rules of c. 2 of the Statute of Westminster II (apparently allowing lords to distrain for any services of which they or their ancestors had been seised since 1242) and the strict application of the terms of a charter of feoffment promising exemption from all services other than those specified (apparently required by part of c. 9 of the Statute of Marlborough of 1267) as was also taking place around the same time in England.[25] Our evidence for this is a case heard in the Dublin Bench in Michaelmas term 1308 (early in the reign of Edward II).[26] Richard Tyrel had avowed a distraint made on the prior of the Hospitallers in Ireland as made in a holding of five carucates in 'Kylmehanok' for one year's arrears of a service requiring the Hospitallers (at Kilmainham) to provide Richard with five loaves of fine wheat each day and five gallons of beer and two meals of three courses each day. Richard based his claim to this on the seisin of his grandfather and father at the hands of the prior's predecessors. The prior in response showed the court the original charter of Richard's ancestor, Hugh Tyrel, granting Chapelizod and the five carucates at 'Kylmehanok' in pure alms and a second charter of Hugh's son Richard confirming that grant. Richard's response was to claim not just that his grandfather had been seised of these services but also his great grand-father and his father and Hugh Tyrel, the *primus conquestor*, thereby demon-strating (as he said) that his ancestors had been seised since the time of the limitation of the writ of novel disseisin (a reference to the standard laid down by Westminster II, c. 2 but in excess of it) and also before. The case was then adjourned for judgment. The earliest evidence I have noted for the appli-cation of the provisions intended to secure that those distrained did not abuse their right to secure the release of their distresses by repeated renewals of non-prosecuted replevin suits comes from 1336 when a judgment of

24 BL, Additional Roll 13598, m. 10d.
25 Brand, *Kings, barons and justices*, pp. 257–62.
26 NAI, RC 7/13/3, pp. 58–61.

'return irreplevisible' is calendared as having been made and recorded on the Dublin Bench plea roll.[27] There is also some evidence of one of the non-statutory Edwardian developments being transferred to Ireland, the use of the action to challenge the exercise of jurisdiction by seignorial courts. In a Dublin Bench case of Michaelmas term 1295 the abbot of Dunbrody challenged the use of distraint by (or more plausibly on behalf of) Roger Bigod, earl of Norfolk, to make him appear in the earl's court at Great Island (*Insula Hervy*) in Co. Wexford to answer a complaint of trespass brought against him by a third party. The abbot said that the land where the distraint had been made (the 'old grange') had been given to his house by Walter Marshal, earl of Pembroke, in pure alms quit of all things except judgment of life and members, and he ought therefore to be exempt from the court's jurisdiction.[28] In two other cases (enrolled in a virtually identical form) in Michaelmas term 1300 Bertram de Troye and William Dyket challenged the use of distraint by the serjeant of Theobald de Verdun to secure their appearance to answer Theobald in his court of Kells, Co. Meath, on a charge of defamation.[29] This was for having allegedly said of Theobald that he was the 'most false man (*falsissimus homo*) and the worst towards his men (*pessimus versus homines suos*) and had unjustly vexed them in various ways'. The challenge was not because such a plea of defamation was outside the jurisdiction of his court, but rather on the grounds that the tenements where the distraint had been made were not held directly by them of Theobald, only on a lease from the abbot of St Mary's Dublin, who held them in free alms by the confirmation of Theobald's ancestor. In a fourth case heard in the Dublin Bench the same term John of Hereford challenged the use of distraint by Henry Marshal to secure John's appearance at his court of Kilcleen to answer a plea of debt brought against him by Luke Chamberlain.[30] John asserted that he had been given his tenement there in frankmarriage with his wife Cecilia by Thomas of Crumlin and that Thomas had been enfeoffed of the tenement by Luke with a specific promise of freedom from suit at his court and exemption from the court's jurisdiction in respect of pleas of trespass or other cases; that Luke had later granted his seignory to Henry; and that Henry was bound by the prior promise of exemption from the court's jurisdiction. All four cases, as has been seen, revolve about the question of whether or not the courts concerned could properly exercise jurisdiction over the cases (and persons) concerned.

There are also at least two examples of the use of the new statutory actions complementing the common law action of replevin. Both of them are on the

27 NAI, RC 8/20, pp. 110–11.
28 NAI, RC 7/3, pp. 397–98. The abbot acknowledged (or asserted) that the lord of Wexford was seised of masses and prayers being performed in the abbey for himself and his ancestors for the land.
29 NAI, RC 7/6, pp. 500–02, 526–27.
30 NAI, RC 7/6, pp. 517–19.

surviving Dublin Bench plea roll for Easter term 1290. One is an action based on the 1275 statute privileging plough animals and sheep. It was brought by Thomas the son of Maurice Barefoot against Hugh of Stradley, the steward of the liberty of Kildare, for seizing animals from his plough.[31] Hugh justified the distraint as made in order to levy debts owed to the king and to Agnes de Vescy, lady of Kildare, by Thomas's father Maurice, contracted prior to the enfeoffment of Thomas by Maurice. The steward had distrained him by animals from his plough because he had been unable to find any other distresses within the liberty. Maurice denied owing any debt and claimed that he had enough elsewhere within the liberty (at Kildare and at Cloncurry) that could have been distrained. When the steward denied this the issue of fact went to a jury. The second case is an action of *contra formam feoffamenti* brought by William fitzRalph against Hugh Tyrel for distraining him to perform suit to his court of Castleknock.[32] As in England, the litigation only proceeded after an initial disregarded prohibition, although this was not part of the process authorised by the statute.[33] In England, a series of cases had established that the action could not be used when it was a sub-tenant who had been distrained.[34] Here, however, the case proceeded despite that fact. All that happened was that Hugh's immediate tenant, the prior of All Hallows Dublin, joined with the plaintiff to counterplead Hugh's avowry for suit and show that Hugh himself had quitclaimed all right to suit and all jurisdiction other than for personal trespasses by a deed made in 1288 (and here quoted in full). After this, the case was compromised for a small further payment by the prior.

III

Thus far, I have been looking at the ways in which the characteristics and the development of the action of replevin in the lordship of Ireland seem generally to have resembled the characteristics and development of the action of replevin in England. I want now to turn to evidence showing what seem to have been some specifically Irish characteristics and some quite distinctive Irish developments in the action.

The earliest known legislation enacted, or perhaps more accurately the minutes of the earliest series of legislative decisions reached, by the Irish parliament survives on a single sheet of parchment now in The National Archives of England at Kew. It was printed by Richardson and Sayles in 1952

31 BL, Additional Roll 13598, m. 5d.
32 BL, Additional Roll 13598, m. 9.
33 Brand, *Kings, barons and justices*, pp. 213–15.
34 Ibid., pp. 220–21.

as one of the appendixes to their book on *The Irish parliament in the middle ages*.[35] Although not dated in the original, Richardson and Sayles argued on the basis of one of its other clauses relating to the native Irish request for a general grant of the Common Law that it probably belonged to the first half of 1278. One of these minutes related to the writ of replevin (*de bref qe est apele replegiari*) and noted a decision made by the *riches hommes*, who occur elsewhere in these minutes as the makers of legislation, but who seem to be distinct from the absentee great lords who are represented by their stewards and bailiffs. The decision was that, if the person who had made a distraint for a rent or a debt was willing to find sureties that he had a better right to retain the distress than the other to secure its release and to allow a good inquest to pass on this at the next county court, the sheriff was to make no release but to take an inquest on this at the next county court without allowing any essoin. Only then was he to do as he saw right required in respect of the release of the distress. The provision is a little opaque as it stands. It seems to relate to the first stage of an action of replevin, when the person who had been distrained had acquired his writ and gone to the sheriff with the writ (or made his plaint to the sheriff) and found pledges to prosecute and asked for the release of his distresses. At this point, apparently, the distrainor was to be given the right to find a kind of counter-surety to appear at the very next session of the county court (without using the normal opportunities for delay offered by the essoin and the possibilities of sitting out mesne process) and plead the case. He was then to be allowed to keep the distresses till the litigation was determined. What is perhaps more puzzling is the reference to the distraint as having been made for 'debt or rent'. 'Rent' is perhaps to be interpreted in a generous sense as meaning any kind of tenurial service. But what about 'debt'? The normal English common law rules did not allow distraint for debt by a creditor against his debtor. This might perhaps be a reference to distraints made for judgment debts adjudged by lower courts (for which distraint was licit) or for amercements adjudged by such courts. One piece of evidence may, however, suggest that distraint for ordinary debt was possible in at least some of parts of the lordship and might then be challenged by a writ of replevin. A false judgment case was brought in Michaelmas term 1298 to challenge a judgment given in the Waterford county court in 1295. The record shows that the count of William le Rous had specified that what had been taken from him in distraint by Walter bishop of Waterford had been twenty-three marks in cash.[36] One of the objections made by the bishop had been that money could not be claimed by a writ of replevin, but only by a writ of debt. William had responded that

---

35 H.G. Richardson and G.O. Sayles, *The Irish parliament in the middle ages* (Philadelphia and London, 1952), pp. 290–93.
36 NAI, RC 7/5, pp. 383–84.

there was no difference between money and chattels and that money could be claimed as chattels in this action.

Geoffrey Hand's discussion of this clause suggests that it 'could hardly have gone further in favour of the lord, since it in fact removed the essential feature of replevin – return of the distress pending the plea in the county court'.[37] In some respects, however, the new mechanism was not that far removed in its overall impact on the distrainee from what the English legislation of 1285 achieved in requiring the distrainee seeking the return of his distress to find sureties for their value in case a 'return' was adjudged. Moreover, under the new procedure authorised by the statute the tenant (or other distrainee) might have indeed have to wait a little longer for the return of his distress if he succeeded in his action, but he did apparently secure in return the assurance of a much quicker disposition of his action and might indeed have considered this a price worth paying. Nor is it entirely clear that the ability to secure the preliminary release of what had been taken in distraint was the absolutely essential feature of replevin. What litigants may have considered more essential was the impartial determination of whether or not a particular use of distraint had been justified. If I am right in supposing that the balance of advantages between lord and tenant was not nearly so much upset by the measure as Hand suggests it may not be quite so necessary to invoke the strength of the magnates in the 'councils of the lordship' as an explanation for the measure. Hand also suggests 'official anxiety to ease the burdens of sheriffs and serjeants' may be part of the explanation. This does not seem a plausible motive for a measure that added to the complications of their work rather than simplified it. Nor is there any other legislation of the period that can be explained by a like motivation.

Hand also doubts whether or not the legislation was ever carried into effect. The evidence suggests that it was, though not perhaps in every case. The legislation after all allowed, but did not require, this alternative process. The record of the case heard in the county court of Waterford in 1295 already mentioned shows as the final judgment of the county court in favour of the plaintiff (William le Rous of Waterford) not that he was to retain the twenty marks at stake in the case but that he was to 'recover' them plus damages of ten pounds, suggesting that the bishop of Waterford had retained them until then.[38] So, too, in the case removed by *recordari facias* from the Cork county court and determined in the Dublin Bench in 1304 the final judgment was that the plaintiff (Robert de Caunteton) was to have delivery of his animals or their value with damages assessed by the justices, suggesting that the defendant (David son of Alexander de Roche) had retained them until then.[39]

37 Hand, *English law in Ireland*, p. 160.
38 NAI, RC 7/5, pp. 383–84.
39 NAI, RC 7/10, p. 81.

There are other judgments in favour of plaintiffs given in the Dublin Bench that likewise suggest that the defendants had remained in possession of the distresses until that point: a judgment in 1306 that the plaintiff have his animals returned or their value;[40] a judgment in 1328 that the plaintiff was to have his animals released plus damages;[41] a jury verdict in 1336 in favour of the plaintiff where the jurors were asked the value of the animals taken in distraint.[42] Something similar is suggested by at least two of the judgments given in favour of defendants in cases of 1299 and 1300. In both the judgment was that the plaintiffs take nothing by their writs but nothing at all was said about the defendants getting a 'return' of the distresses.[43]

The wording of the legislation of 1278 talks of the distraint having been made for 'rent or debt'. What it does not mention is distraint for *damage feasant*. One of the puzzling features of the recorded replevin cases from Ireland in this period is that none of them (so far as I have seen) involve distraints or avowries of distraints made for animals taken *damage feasant*, and so none of the underlying disputes seem to be about rights of common. I am uncertain why this should have been the case. Were distraint and replevin not used in such disputes in Ireland? Or were there no rights of common to be disputed?

As we have seen, the franchise of hearing replevin pleas was fairly closely guarded in England and the general principle always maintained that only the king could grant the franchise to any franchisee (or the franchisee enjoy the right by virtue of having exercised it time out of mind). Here lies another contrast with Ireland. The very earliest evidence in Ireland referring to the hearing of such pleas comes from *c*. 1262–70 and is in the form of a charter which exists in two versions (a short and a longer one) granted by Geoffrey de Joinville, lord of the liberty of Meath in right of his wife Maud. This confirmed to the magnates of Meath (his immediate tenants) various rights which had been granted to them by the conqueror Hugh de Lacy and his son Walter, including the right to hear pleas of replevin (*placita namii vetiti*) for all tenants in their lands.[44] The longer version adds, however, that if a plea was brought against any of the said magnates by the complaint of another magnate who was his neighbour, such a plea was to be determined in Geoffrey's court or that of Maud or Maud's heirs. This suggests that in Meath at least the hearing of replevin pleas goes back to the earliest days of the colony. It also shows the franchisal right to hear such pleas passing to the

40 NAI, RC 7/11, pp. 588–90.

41 NAI, RC 8/15, pp. 187–89.

42 NAI, RC 8/20, pp. 48–51.

43 NAI, RC 7/5, pp. 440–41; RC 7/6, pp. 529–30.

44 The shorter version is in *Calendar of the Gormanston register*, ed. James Mills and M.J. McEnery (Royal Society of Antiquaries of Ireland extra volume: 1916), pp. 176–77. The longer version is in *Cart. St Mary's Dublin*, I, 275–77; *Reg. Tristernagh*, pp. 52–54.

next level down beyond the holder of a greater franchise and through the grant of the franchise holder, not that of the lord of Ireland, and with no apparent thought that this might need any kind of confirmation from him. What we do not know is if any similar process of sub-delegation of juris-dictional rights to the franchise took place in any of the other great liberties.

There is one last difference between the recorded replevin pleas in the Westminster Bench and the recorded replevin pleas in the Dublin Bench. This does not so much tell us about differences between the two juris-dictions' treatment of the action of replevin as about the relative skills of the lawyers available for hire in the two jurisdictions. This is the relatively high proportion in all the surviving records of enrolments that show fairly basic errors in the pleading of cases. The calendar of the Dublin Bench plea roll for Easter term 1282 shows the steward of the liberty of Kildare excepting to the count made against him by or for William of Thornborough on the grounds that William had not produced suit in his count or mentioned the production of suit in it. The 'suit' mentioned in the count were the supposed witnesses to the matters of complaint the plaintiff had once been required to bring with him to court. The English evidence suggests that they had normally only to be produced when the defendant waged his law in denial; and one English plaintiff lost his case as late as 1260 for failure to produce them when the defendant had offered to wage his law.[45] But it seems that by 1282 they had become nominal in all actions other than the actions of naifty and debt: something that had to be mentioned, but did not in reality have to be produced. William lost his case in this instance, as has been seen, not because he did not have any suit (there seems no reason to suppose that this was required in Ireland any more than it was in England) but because he or his lawyer failed even to mention his willingness to produce them: a technical fault in pleading rather than a matter of real substance. In two other cases the mistakes made were not in the count but in that rather more complicated object of the lawyer's skill, the defendant's avowry of his distraint. In a Dublin Bench plea brought by William son of Alexander of Clogher against the prior of Downpatrick in Trinity 1301 the defendant avowed for a rent owed to his church and showed that his predecessor had been seised of it at the hands of a prior tenant of the land (master Nicholas of Clogher) and avowed a distraint on William without showing how the tenement had come to him. When the plaintiff objected on what amounted to these grounds, judgment was given for the plaintiff.[46] In a third case heard in the Dublin Bench in Trinity term 1306 and brought by the chancellor, master Thomas of Quantock, against Maurice le Ercedeken, Maurice avowed for arrears of a rent which had been sold to him and counted on his seisin of the rent at the

---

45 TNA:PRO, KB 26/164, m. 16d: *Gilbert Chittynho* v. *William le Folur.*
46 NAI, RC 7/8, pp. 133–34.

hands of the guardians of Thomas the son of Aeneas son of Odo.[47] Since such a seisin was not the proper basis for an avowry (since a guardian's actions could not prejudice his ward) judgment was given for the plaintiff. Both of these were fairly elementary mistakes on the part of the defendants or more likely the lawyers acting on their behalf.

IV

The surviving material in the form both of plea roll enrolments and reports makes it possible to know an enormous amount about the working of the action of replevin in England, at least at the level of the Westminster Bench, though rather less about the way in which the action worked in the courts which probably continued to determine the vast majority of such cases, the county courts. Much less evidence survives for the working of the action in the lordship of Ireland. I hope that I have nonethless managed to demonstrate that this surviving evidence shows the ways in which the action in Ireland continued in general terms to resemble its counterpart within the English system, concerned only with the justice of distraints and not with 'detention against gage and pledge', and most commonly concerned with distraints made for feudal services, and that it continued to develop in ways that reflected the statutory and non-statutory changes in England. But I hope I have also shown the ways in which the Irish action also went its own way, reflecting the different conditions of the lordship and also the ability of the lordship's parliament to make significant changes in the functioning of this basic common-law action. The history of the Common Law in Ireland, even in the Middle Ages, is not just a story of the adoption of English legal institutions and legal rules; it is also the story of their creative adaptation to suit Irish conditions, to make it truly an Irish Common Law.

47 NAI, RC 7/11, pp. 588–90.

The Danes and the marriage break-up of Philip II of France

FREDERIK PEDERSEN

ON 14 AUGUST 1193 the illustrious king Philip II of France repudiated his queen, Ingeborg, the daughter of the Danish king Valdemar I, during her coronation ceremony in Amiens cathedral. The events that followed merited twenty-four papal letters and the comment and speculation of several chroniclers across Europe. Shortly after the defeat of the Danes by the Germans in 1864, the Danish historian A. Fabricius wrote a scholarly study of Ingeborg's fate. However, this study was marred by the author's highly wrought romantic writing style,[1] and was quickly superseded by a study of the incident by the German historian Robert Davidsohn.[2] Since then the marriage of Philip II and his Danish queen has not seen a full-length scholarly study, but in the twentieth century the incident has formed a significant part of studies by Tenbrock in 1933,[3] by Helene Tillmann in 1953,[4] by Georges Duby in 1978,[5] in 1986 by John W. Baldwin (in his study of the government of Philip Augustus) and by Christopher Brooke around 1990.[6]

But with its heady mixture of sex, international politics, and papal intervention, the story has almost been an embarrassment to Danish historians, though some feminist historians have tried to put the story to new use.[7] Hal Koch in his history of the Danish church dismisses the twenty-year struggle

---

1 A. Fabricius, *Ingeborg, Philip Augusts Dronning* (Copenhagen, 1870).
2 Robert Davidsohn, *Philipp II. August von Frankreich und Ingeborg* (Stuttgart, 1888).
3 R.H. Tenbrock, *Eherecht und Ehepolitik bei Innocenz III* (Dortmund, 1933).
4 Helene Tillmann, *Papst Innocenz III*, Bonner Historische Forschungen (Bonn, 1954).
5 Georges Duby, *Medieval marriage: two models from twelfth-century France*, trans. Elborg Forster, foreword by John Baldwin, The Johns Hopkins Symposia in Comparative History, vol. 11 (Baltimore, 1978), pp. 3–15.
6 Christopher N.L. Brooke, *The medieval idea of marriage* (Oxford, 1989), p. 124; John W. Baldwin, *The government of Philip Augustus: foundations of French royal power in the middle ages* (Berkeley, 1986).
7 Nanna Damsholt, 'Medieval women's identity in a postmodern light: the example of Queen Ingeborg,' in Brian P. McGuire (ed.), *The birth of identities: Denmark and Europe in the middle ages* (Copenhagen, 1996), pp. 225–42.

in a single paragraph,[8] while Kai Hørby in the Gyldendal History of Denmark only comments on the case when it affects internal Danish developments.[9] More recently, the same embarassment is visible in Ole Fenger's contribution to the eighteen-volume History of Denmark.[10] So it is worth repeating its main points, not only for its value as an entertaining vignette of the realities of political marriages, but also for the insight it offers into the reception of legal knowledge across Europe in the late twelfth to the early thirteenth century and the way in which the incident came to be subservient to Innocent III's larger imperial policy.

THE PRELUDE TO THE CONFLICT

The events of the case unfolded as follows. On 14 August 1193 Philip II of France took a new wife. His bride, the eighteen-year-old Ingeborg, the daughter of King Valdemar I and sister of the Danish king Canute VI, had only arrived in France the previous day in the company of two men who had the mastery of the French language which it was hoped Ingeborg would soon acquire, Master William of Æbelholt/Paraclete, a former canon of Sainte Genevieve in Paris, and the bishop of Roskilde, Peder Sunesøn, a former Danish law graduate in Paris. In the evening Philip and Ingeborg, who had never set eyes on each other before, retired to consummate their marriage. The following day, the two spouses attended a mass celebrated by the arch-bishop of Rheims in the cathedral in Amiens, as had been the custom of the French monarchy since the days of Clovis, and Ingeborg was crowned queen of France. During the ceremonies, Philip grew pale and restless and showed every sign that he could hardly wait for the service to be over. Upon its conclusion, Philip approached the Danish party and requested that they take Ingeborg back to Denmark with them. He announced that he intended to seek an annulment of the marriage. When told, Ingeborg rejected the sug-gestion out of hand, crying loudly and in rather simple Latin: '*Mala Francia: Roma, Roma* (Bad France: to Rome to Rome)'. Philip took no heed of her distress and dispatched her to the monastery of Saint-Maur-des-Fossés not far from Paris. This was the beginning of a conflict between Philip and his legal wife that would not only be an embarrassment for the French king and the papacy for the next twelve years but that would also poison their relationship until Philip's death in 1223.

8 Hal Koch, *Den ældre middelalder indtil 1241*, vol. 1 of *Den danske kirkes historie*, ed. Hal Koch and Bjørn Kornerup (Copenhagen, 1950).

9 Kai Hørby and Michael Venge, *Tiden, 1340–1648*, vol. 2 of *Danmarks Historie*, Første halvbind, exec. ed. Axel E. Christensen, et al. (Copenhagen, 1980).

10 Ole Fenger, '*Kirker rejses alle vegne*', *1050–1250*, vol. 4 of *Gyldendal og Politikens danmarks-historie*, exec. ed. Olaf Olsen, reprint, 1989 (Copenhagen, 2002).

Philip's unusual behaviour after his wedding caused widespread comment among contemporary chroniclers. Virtually all of them agree that Philip had no grounds for complaint about Ingeborg's beauty or virtue. Whatever his reasons were, the one night that he spent with Ingeborg left such a strong impression on him that he refused to meet her face to face for the next seven years and led him to keep her incarcerated, first in Saint-Maur outside Paris and later in Cysoing near Lille.

PHILIP'S FIRST MARRIAGE

Ingeborg was not Philip's first wife and it was not the first time Philip had demonstrated a worrying disregard for his married partner. One presumes that the Danes had not heard of his treatment of his first wife, Isabelle of Hainault. Shortly before his fifteenth birthday, Philip had married Isabelle on 28 April 1180 at Bapaume near her native Flanders. The ceremony was celebrated by the bishops of Senlis and Laon with only a relatively small number of French nobles present, despite the fact that a royal wedding should have been a state occasion. Adding insult to injury, Philip had the coronation of Isabelle as his queen performed at Sens rather than at Amiens, which was the traditional place for such a ceremony. Apart from this slightly odd beginning, Philip's married life with Isabelle was relatively calm for four years. Isabelle's parents were staunch supporters of Philip's policies in Flanders, but two years after their deaths in 1182, and four years after his marriage to Isabelle, the seventeen-year-old Philip suddenly announced in March 1184 that he was going to divorce her. He refused to reveal any reasons, but this astonishing move could be (and was taken by many to be) a disavowal of his relations with the Flemish party at court. Philip may have had political intentions for this move. It might also be conjectured that his reaction to Isabelle was due to his alleged homosexuality. Like so much else in this case, his motives can only be guessed at. But, this was the first sign of a general fear of women which was to so poison his later relationship with Ingeborg of Denmark.

Like Boccaccio's Patient Griselda, Isabelle of Hainault humiliated herself and pleaded with the king to be restored to the queenship. She publicly sought his mercy, walking barefoot through the streets of Senlis dressed in a penitent beggar's robes. Her actions gathered a huge crowd who followed her to the castle in Senlis. This demonstrated to Philip that Isabelle had the support of his people. So he took her back. What role she played in Philip's life after this is unclear, but it is certain that she maintained the title and honour of queen. She also clearly had sexual relations with Philip. These relations may have been rather infrequent for it took another three years before she gave birth to a son, whom they called Louis (who ruled as Louis VIII, 1223–1226). This son was to be the only heir produced by the couple.

In the intervening years Philip had become increasingly friendly with Richard, prince of England – indeed they were virtually inseparable – and he spent most of his time with Richard. Many historians have argued that their relationship went beyond mere friendship, quoting the contemporary chronicler Roger of Howden, who claimed that they shared everything: the same plate, the same food, even the same bed. Marital relations between Philip and Isabella continued, though, for Isabelle died in childbirth in 1190. The same year Philip went to the Holy Land to participate in the Third Crusade together with King Richard. The crusade was a disappointment to Philip. He fell out with Richard and returned to Paris on 27 December 1191.

DENMARK AND FRANCE IN THE TWELFTH CENTURY

Soon Philip was once again paying full attention to the matters arising from the governance of his realm. One of these was the pressing question of how to secure the succession to the throne. Louis had been seriously ill while Philip was in the Holy Land and his son's continued ill-health and the prospect of his death must have made the matter an urgent concern for Philip and may to a certain extent explain his apparent rush into a marriage with a princess, any princess, from Denmark.

It is customary to consider Denmark a country at the periphery of Europe in the high middle ages and we can only speculate why Philip made contact with the Danes. Counting in favour of a Danish marriage was the fact that the French remembered the Danes as mighty warriors and the empire of Canute the Great: Canute's Viking empire and previous Viking incursions are frequently mentioned in the letters that passed between clerics in France and Denmark. However, since the death of King Canute IV in 1086, the Danish kingdom had lurched from crisis to crisis and had most recently been wracked by civil war from 1137 to 1157. But the country was now in the ascendancy. The current ruling dynasty had re-established the kingdom as a force to be reckoned with in European politics: the current king, Canute VI, was the grand-son of Duke Canute Lavard, who was canonised in 1170. At the translation feast at Ringsted that year, the six-year-old Prince Canute had also been crowned king of Denmark and the legitimacy of his kingship was thus intimately connected with the sainthood of his grandfather. Canute's father, Valdemar I, had pursued an expansionist policy in the Baltic under the guise of a crusade, which had received strong support from Bernard of Clairvaux and had been authorised by Pope Alexander III in 1168. Canute was now pursuing his father's policies and like Philip he regarded himself as a crusader. Under Canute's leadership, Denmark had recently enjoyed military successes in Pomerania and had declared its independence from the Holy Roman Empire after the death of Frederick I Barbarossa. His new-found confidence is also clear in his dynastic policies. In the period from the end of Canute II's Northern Empire, when Danish princes and princesses had married into the most prestigious families in Europe, the Danish royal family did not marry their sons and daughters outside Scandinavia and Russia. Danish society had stabilised by the late twelfth century. The Danes then began to increase their sphere of influence through marriage alliances: Canute VI had married the daughter of the Welf Henry the Lion and his sister, Sophie, was promised to the son of Frederick I, the Hohenstaufen Henry VI. However, the latter marriage was never celebrated. It was preceded by a political meltdown in which Valdemar Knudssøn, the bishop of Schleswig, who was aligned with the Hohenstaufen family and had a claim to the Danish throne[11] organised a rebellion against Canute, and Sophie eventually married Count Siegfried of Orlamünde, a relatively unimportant player in the European political theatre. Added to the rising importance of Denmark was the fact that Philip had gathered together an invasion fleet in Wissant to take advantage of the perceived weakness of the kingdom of England during the incarceration of Richard the Lionheart. William of Newburgh, an English chronicler, suggests that Philip's interest was motivated by his desire for the English crown and a wish to join the Danish fleet and army to his own forces in an invasion attempt. To the modern historian, such motives cannot be entirely dismissed, as the final release of Ingeborg from captivity in 1213 coincided with Philip's plans for an invasion of England, but William of Newburgh emphasised that such services were categorically refused during the marriage negotiations. King Canute and the Danish kingdom were thus a wild card in European politics: through his sister's marriage to the powerful king of France he was clearly hoping to gain from the weakness of the Hohenstaufens who had forced his predecessors to pay homage for Denmark in 1134 and 1152.[12] However, Canute had aligned Denmark with the Welf party in the struggle for imperial succession. He thus stood in opposition to the Hohenstaufens whom Philip favoured, but the fact that another sister had been espoused to Henry VI did offer the tantalising possibility that the Danes might swing behind Philip's favoured candidate for the imperial throne.

Intellectual and social connections between Denmark and France were also lively. The colleges and monastic centres of learning in the city of Paris attracted Denmark's brightest students and Danish nobles in appreciable numbers. The integration of the Danes into European centres of learning is clear from earlier events such as an eleventh-century papal letter urging the

---

11 He was the illegitimate son of Canute Magnussøn who had been king of Jylland, 1146–1157 and who had been a co-regent with Canute VI's father Valdemar I, 1154–1157. The period 1146–1157 is one of political unrest in Denmark.

12 Ole Fenger, '*Kirker rejses alle vegne*', *1050–1250*, vol. 4 of *Gyldendal og Politikens danmarks-historie*, exec. ed. Olaf Olsen, reprint, 1989 (Copenhagen, 2002), pp. 112 and 130.

king of Sweden to follow the example of the king of Denmark in sending Swedish scholars to Rome to be trained in canon law.[13] The head of the church in Denmark at the time of the marriage negotiations was the king's chancellor, Archbishop Absalon of Lund, who had also studied in Paris, and it was he who had endorsed the invitation of Master William of Æbelholt to come to Denmark.[14] Among the most illustrious Danes in Paris were the Sunesøn brothers, the younger of whom, the future archbishop of Lund, Anders Sunesøn, may even have been a friend of an Italian nobleman called Lothario de Segni, who was later to become Pope Innocent III.

In the twelfth century there was no university at Paris, but the monastery of St Genevieve was one of its first centres of learning. From it at least two Danish bishops, the brothers Peder and Anders Sunesøn, had graduated as masters of arts sometime before the events we are now recounting. Around 1165 a certain Master William was invited to leave Paris to come to Denmark to reform the wealthy, but embarrassingly undisciplined, monastery on Eskilsø in Roskilde Fjord. William accepted the invitation. There is a certain whiff of scandal around William, who admits to having been the subject of a papal investigation in one of his letters, but his life in Denmark was to be exemplary.[15] William later transferred this monastery to the parish of Tjæreborg in northern Sjælland, taking the opportunity to rename the monastery *Paracletus*, probably in imitation of Abelard's monastery in northern France. This new monastery became the largest hospital in Scandinavia and a series of miraculous cures ascribed to William after his death led to his canonisation in 1224, only twenty-one years after his death in 1203. William of Paraclete/ Æbelholt was not only the head of one of the proto-colleges of the University of Paris, but also an old friend of Philip's close adviser, Bernard de Vincennes.

13 E.g. the letter from Gregory VII to the Norwegian King Olav Kyrre dated 15 December 1078, in which Gregory explained that he had exhorted the king of the Danes to send young high-born men to the curia to be taught the holy and divine laws and to return to their country and bring the mandates of the apostolic see to the king. Lauritz Weibull, ed., *Diplomatarium danicum 1053–1169*, vol. 2 of *Diplomatarium danicum, 1. Række*, in collaboration with Niels Skyum-Nielsen, Det Danske Sprog- og Litteraturselskab (Copenhagen, 1963), p. 37. Later events, such as the endowment of several scholarships for Danish students to Paris by Bishop Jens Grand (1291–1302), a century after the events narrated here, show that there was a strong continued interest in the canon law in the country.

14 As mentioned before, William was a close friend of King Philip's ecclesiastical adviser, Bernard de Vincennes, who was probably the one to put the idea of an alliance with Denmark to the king in the first place. Certainly, judging from William's letters, he seems to have taken the responsibility for this misalliance upon himself. C.A. Christensen, Herluf Nielsen, and Lauritz Weibull, eds., *Diplomer 1170–1199 & Epistolæ abattis Willelmi de Paraclito*, vol. 3 of *Diplomatarium danicum, 1. Række*, Det Danske Sprog- og Litteraturselskab (Copenhagen, 1976–77) [hereafter *DD 1. Rk., 3. Bd.*], pp. 567–68.

15 We do not know why William came to be investigated. The only reference to the case comes from his own collection of letters (see below, p. 62).

However one looks at it, it is clear that Ingeborg was an unknown entity to Philip, for he had requested marriage to a sister – *any sister* – of the Danish king! Philip's bride turned out to be the eighteen-year-old Princess Ingeborg, Canute's sister. My guess is that the personal friendship between Bernard of Vincennes and William of Æbelholt/Paraclete had something to do with Philip's decision, but, like so much else in this case, his motivation for choosing Ingeborg still remains obscure.[16] Be that as it may, Ingeborg arrived in France on the day of the wedding in the company of Master William of Æbelholt and Peder Sunesøn, who was now bishop of Roskilde. William and Peder had mastery of French, but Ingeborg was ignorant of the language. (She was, however, acquainted with Latin, as her response to Philip's repudiation demonstrates).

THE WEDDING NIGHT

We know virtually nothing about what happened on the wedding night. However, we do know that the spectacular dislike for Ingeborg that Philip later displayed did not affect his performance in bed. According to her statement he had intercourse with her. He argued that he had ejaculated outside her vagina. You may take this fact as an indication that, like a recent American president, he 'did not have sexual intercourse with that woman', a spin that Philip's lawyers were to put on the event in 1205 in order to argue (unsuccessfully and somewhat anachronistically) that the marriage had not been properly consummated and was therefore not valid. However, regardless of the spin, there is one fact that stands out. Ingeborg may have been stubborn, but her stubbornness was matched by Philip's obstinacy, and his dislike for his Danish queen made him disregard the recently introduced rules of canon law regarding what constituted a valid marriage. There is a certain irony in the fact that history has come to ascribe these rules to a 'Parisian school'.

INGEBORG AND PHILIP, 1193–95

So, despite the fact that Ingeborg had invoked the support of the law of the church, and of Canute, the king of Denmark, of William, a former master of a Parisian college, and of Bernard de Vincennes, one of Philip's own advisors, Philip persisted in his attempts to get rid of her. He tried to cover his actions with a varnish of canonical respectability. He argued rather feebly that he was

---

16 Bernard's repeated complaint that he was responsible for the calamities that followed and William's disgrace with the Danish king lend some support to this idea.

related to Ingeborg within the degrees of affinity forbidden by the church: Ingeborg was related by blood to Philip's first wife Isabelle within four degrees.[17] On 5 November 1193 a council consisting of fifteen bishops, counts and knights, most of whom were either kinsmen of the king or members of his household, was convened by his uncle, the archbishop William of Rheims, at Compiègne. To the consternation of the Danes, this French council dissolved the marriage, a decision that should not surprise anybody given its composition.

In the following years Philip ignored papal censure and found a woman whose family would allow him to marry her. It had not been an easy task as his history of problems in his first marriage and the obviously irregular end to his marriage with Ingeborg dissuaded several likely candidates. In the end, he married Agnes of Meran, a woman whose family, like Philip himself, were staunch supporters of the Hohenstaufen. The marriage was celebrated in June 1196, almost in defiance of the pope, immediately after the first attempt at reconciliation at a council convened under papal authority in Paris. Over the next five years Agnes would bear two children, a daughter, Marie, and a son, Philip, before her death in 1201.

WILLIAM OF PARACLETE AND ANDERS SUNESØN IN ROME AND FRANCE

This, the dynastic aspect of the case, is well known. But there is another side to the early part of this story. Even though the argument may ostensibly have been about spiritual matters, the two main Danish canon lawyers involved in the case, William of Paraclete/Æbelholt and Peder Sunesøn's younger brother, Anders (who was now the chancellor of Canute VI) learnt through personal experience that being involved in politics at this level was not without personal danger. The Danes had not accepted Philip's plea of affinity at the Council of Compiègne. Master William of Æbelholt set to work compiling an alternative genealogy and, together with King Canute's chancellor, Anders Sunesøn, William travelled to the Curia in Rome to persuade Pope Celestine III to overturn the decision of Philip's council. Anders was destined to become one of the great men of the Scandinavian church. Although he was in his early thirties he had already been William's pupil, taught philosophy at Paris and (presumably) law at Bologna and travelled to Oxford, where he probably also taught law. He was now the royal chancellor, but would become the archbishop of Lund and thus primate of Scandinavia

17 Marie-Bernadette Bruguière, 'Le mariage de Philippe Auguste et d'Isambour de Danemark: aspects canoniques et politiques,' in *Mélanges offerts à Jean Dauvillier* (Toulouse, 1979), pp. 135–56.

within the next decade. In this capacity he is said to have inspired a Catalan friar called Dominic Guzman to found an order of monks aimed at the conversion of heretics in Europe, rather than the Holy Land.[18]

William and Anders arrived in Rome in the autumn of 1194. The pope, Celestine III, only slowly responded to their pleas. After a year and a half, in May 1196, Celestine dispatched two legates to investigate the case. Having joined William and Anders, they convened a council in Paris. But the legates found that they were powerless in the face of royal opposition.

In France a compilation of letters from William survives in seventeenth and eighteenth-century transcripts from a single, now lost medieval manuscript.[19] In one of these letters, William, writing as Anders Sunesøn, apologises to Cardinal Octavian of Ostia for having left his presence without asking leave.[20] He explains that he (i.e. Anders) had to cut short his stay in Rome soon after obtaining letters for a commission for the two cardinals to go to France owing to certain developments.

> It was the opinion of many, and the assertion prevailed, that snares had been extended in many places to capture me, nor could I escape them unless I had committed myself to the danger of the sea.

Anders had thus fled Rome in an imperial ship carrying papal letters and instructions to the papal legates. Meanwhile, William travelled overland to Pisa where the two Danes met up again. Krarup suggests that the 'snares' were assassins dispatched by Philip, but is probably going too far.[21]

It is more likely that Anders and William were in danger of being incarcerated and their papal letters stolen. And indeed this was what happened. As William and Anders were to meet with the papal legates in France, they considered it safer to continue from Pisa overland towards Paris. But when they reached Burgundy, Count Odo III of Burgundy had them imprisoned, if not at the behest of King Philip, then definitely to his advantage. Though it was standard procedure to detain foreign diplomats until their credentials could be checked, the prisoners were only released after seven days and after the intercession of the abbots of Citeaux and Clairvaux, Garnier and Guido.

18 Alfonso IX, king of Castile, chose Diego d'Azevado, bishop of Osma, to go to Denmark in 1205 as his ambassador for the marriage of Alfonso's son. St Dominic accompanied him as a member of the episcopal household.

19 The collection consists of 'epistolas uidelicet, quas ad personas diuersas emisimus uel sub aliorum nomine scripsimus': Christensen, Nielsen and Weibull, *DD 1. Rk., 3. Bd.*, pp. 429–575.

20 Christensen, Nielsen, and Weibull, *DD 1. Rk., 3. Bd.*, pp. 524–25.

21 Multorum erat opinio, et invalescebat assertio, quod michi multis in locis ad me capiendum laquei tenderentur, nec possem euadere, nisi maris discrimini commissem. Hoc igitur, soli domino papæ comminicato consilio, de nocte consurgens nauem conscendi de exercitu imperatoris uenientem pasasque tendentem: sic nullo interuallo posito die secunda apud Pisas applicui. Christensen Nielsen and Weibull, *DD 1. Rk., 3. Bd.*, p. 525.

The quick resolution came about in no small part due to the fact that the monastery of Cîteaux, the hugely influential mother house of the Cistercian order, was only four miles from Dijon and that the Danish church had historically good relations with the order through the persons of the archbishops of Lund, Eskil and Absalon. However, Odo was still a useful ally for Philip: when Anders and William left Dijon it was without 16 papal letters they had been carrying when they arrived in Dijon.[22]

William and Anders were released into the protection of the order and sent to Clairvaux near Champagne. After their release from the care of the order six weeks later they turned towards Châtillon-sur-Seine outside Paris where they met the two papal legates before 1 March 1195. But they had to wait until 7 May 1196 before the legates were able to convene a council in Paris at which Philip would answer his accusers. The long wait was a good indication of the disdain in which Philip held the papal commission, and the legates found that they were powerless in the face of royal opposition. Their case was not helped by the fact that Celestine had instructed them not to put pressure on the French king. Once again, Ingeborg's party had been thwarted by the sheer determination of Philip. But the death of Pope Celestine brought new hope to the Danish party.

A NEW HOPE

The Council of Compiègne of 1193, which had ruled that the marriage of Philip and Ingeborg was tainted by affinity, and the ineffectual Council of Paris in 1196 had hardly increased the authority of church. This is particularly surprising since the memory of Pope Alexander III and his concern about the reform of Christian marriage must have been live among laity and royalty alike. But this was to change with the election of a man who is universally acknowledged as one of the most able and committed lawyer popes of the Middle Ages. Not only was Count Lothar de Segni, who took the papal name Innocent III, a friend of Denmark, but he exhibited a strong desire to impose the rule of law and was thoroughly familiar with the legal and theological implications of marriage.[23] And indeed, Innocent's concern

22 Fabricius, *Ingeborg*, 58; Christensen, Nielsen, and Weibull, *DD 1. Rk., 3. Bd.*, pp. 557–58.
23 While still a cardinal, Lothar de Segni had composed a treatise on *The four kinds of marriage* in which he confronted the human elements of marriage and related them to the divine, thus giving the human elements of marriage a fuller and richer meaning. 'All that happens on the physical, the psychological and the psychosociological level is thus sublimated ... marriage becomes a means ... of sharing in the love of God in Christ: God saves us in espousing us and helps us to understand his love for us through our own love. United to God, man and woman ... can deploy all their affective energies.' Jean Leclercq, *Monks on marriage: a twelfth-century view* (New York, 1981), p. 37. Reading his treatise we are reminded that preserving the sanctity of marriage would clearly be a prime concern for this cardinal as pope.

for the sanctity of marriage became one of the biggest obstacles to cordial relations between the papacy and Philip. Although demonstrably sometimes influenced by political circumstances, Innocent would time after time urge Philip to regularise the union and end his cohabitation with Agnes of Meran and to treat Ingeborg, if not with marital affection, then at least with grace.

Innocent took up office on 22 February 1198 and his first business-like letter to Philip, informing him of his appointment, was dispatched soon afterwards. However, he soon focused his attention on Philip's marriage. In a letter dated 19 May 1198 Innocent rejected the annulment granted to Philip because of his alleged affinity to Ingeborg and exhorted Philip to put his marriage in order by taking back Ingeborg (whom Innocent had heard was 'of rare devotion and honesty'[24]) into his 'conjugal grace' and repudiating Agnes. This, Innocent insisted, was a prerequisite before the papacy would even consider re-examining the question of Philip's and Ingeborg's ties of affinity. When this and subsequent letters had no effect, Innocent pronounced an interdict over France to commence on 13 January 1200.[25]

The threat of the interdict forced Philip to the negotiating table. Both parties were keen to find a solution: Philip for obvious reasons, Innocent because of the reprisals suffered at the hands of royal officials by priests in France who obeyed the interdict. A compromise was reached. As she was pregnant with her second child by Philip, Agnes of Meran was allowed to stay within the boundaries of France and Philip agreed to meet publicly with Ingeborg, the papal legate Peter of Capua and other ecclesiastics. The reconciliation can hardly be said to have been an auspicious occasion, though. It took place in a royal manor outside Paris and Ingeborg was kept by the king under virtual house arrest. But the meeting in 1200 did pave the way for a council to be held at Soissons in March 1201 where the king's complaints would be heard before a tribunal whose authority was acknowledged by both parties.

THE EMPIRE STRIKES BACK

The realities of European politics asserted themselves at this point. The turn of 1200/1201 was a time when Philip's support for Innocent's favourite for the German crown, the Welf Otto of Brunswick, would have been especially welcome. Octavian, the papal legate, showed himself to be a man of business and, contrary to Innocent's instructions, Octavian agreed to hear Philip's case at once instead of waiting for six months to evaluate the reality of the reconciliation. What he may have thought in private we do not know, but in public Innocent sternly rebuked Octavian for his actions and instructed him to

24 Mira sanctitatis et honestatis.
25 Baldwin, *Government*, 85.

disregard political advantage and proceed in the matter according to canon law. Innocent reiterated these instructions on another two occasions and seems thus to have held to his own principles. However principled Innocent's stand may have been, it had disastrous consequences for Ingeborg. Seeing that the council was not going to be favourable to him, Philip relinquished the right he had claimed to have a new decision made by the council and dispatched Ingeborg to the royal manor in Étampes where she spent the first six years as a prisoner in the cellars and the following six years above ground under house arrest.

Philip soon tried to turn the outcome of the Council of Soissons to his advantage. He argued that Ingeborg had foregone her right to its decision because she had not produced any witnesses at the proceedings, and added a new objection: Ingeborg had cast a spell on their wedding night to make him impotent. Innocent intimated that he was willing to oblige Philip. In a letter of July 1202 Innocent set two preconditions for dissolving the marriage. Ingeborg must be given an opportunity to defend herself and her case must be heard by a disinterested judge. Innocent was clearly shaken by Philip's obstinacy and offered to send his own legates to Denmark to interrogate witnesses there. In a further gesture towards Philip, Innocent finalised the legitimisation of Philip's and Agnes's children in the same letter.

Philip had reached an important point in his case. The succession had been secured and he allowed himself some delay in getting the pope's permission for the dissolution of his marriage. The unforeseen death of Agnes of Meran in July 1201 afforded Innocent the possibility of legitimising her two children without having to resolve the thorny question of the legality of the union, since the children were arguably born under the presumption of a legal marriage. Thus, Innocent avoided having Philip actively working against his candidate in the election of the German emperor, Otto of Brunswick. The succession of Ingeborg's other brother, Valdemar II ('the Victorious') to the Danish throne also meant a change in the Danish outlook. Valdemar, Anders Sunesøn (who had now become archbishop of Lund) and Peder Sunesøn (who had taken over from Anders as Valdemar's chancellor) realised that the best outcome they could hope for was that the case did not jeopardise their crusading and empire-building in the Baltic.[26] Thus, the case of Ingeborg came to take a back seat by comparison with larger European imperial concerns.

Philip was therefore no longer in a hurry. His new strategy focused on an attempt to break Ingeborg's spirit and on forcing her to take the veil or simply leave France. For the next six years Ingeborg was kept in isolation in Étampes under appalling circumstances. She described her plight in a letter which was smuggled out to Innocent in 1203:

26 Phillip Pulsiano and Kirsten Wolf, eds., *Medieval Scandinavia : an encyclopedia* (New York, 1993).

Let it be known, Holy Father, that I have no relief here in my prison, but that I suffer under innumerable and unbearable insults. For no one dares visit me here, nor does any ecclesiastic offer me solace, nor am I allowed to hear the Word of God from anyone to strengthen my soul or confess my sins to a priest. Often I fast involuntarily, but daily I enjoy the bread of sorrow and the drink of want. I am offered no medicine for the infirmity of my body and I am not allowed to bathe. If I wish to be bled I cannot and therefore I fear for my eyesight and for the infirmity of my body. There are not many clothes, and those that can be found are not fit for a queen. I cannot recount my troubles in detail, because those things which should not be denied to any Christian woman are denied to me. Because of these and other things which I cannot make myself reveal to you, Holy Father, I am in such a state, that I am now disgusted with life.[27]

Innocent wrote to Philip in June 1204 demanding that his legate, the abbot of Casamari be given access to the queen, and pointed out that Philip would be held responsible and not be allowed to marry again if anything should happen to Ingeborg. The pope also demanded that the queen should be allowed to read his letters which had previously been kept from her. Before he had received an answer, Innocent wrote to Philip again in December after a meeting with a Danish delegation in Rome. In veiled tones the pope threatened further sanctions against Philip unless there was some let-up in his treatment of Ingeborg.

Contrary to this firm public stand on the issue, Innocent seems secretly to have tried to persuade Ingeborg to accept a separation in 1205. On 5 July he wrote to her that he would not be able to refuse the king's action for annulment if he proved his grounds of *maleficium*, affinity and consanguinity.[28] Innocent explained that he had tried, but failed, to persuade the king to treat Ingeborg with marital affection and he expressed his concern that the two should no longer suffer under their miserable situation. One must also consider that the charge of sorcery was a serious one and perhaps Innocent was concerned about the consequences of Philip's proving the charge: at the very least, Philip might use a successful sentence against her to confiscate her dower. Be that as it may, considering Philip's frame of mind, it is likely that Innocent's continued official insistence on a renewed attempt to consummate the marriage was the main obstacle.

27 Damsholt, 'Women's identities,' pp. 236–38; Niels Skyum-Nielsen, ed., *Diplomatarium danicum 1200–1210*, vol. 4 of *Diplomatarium danicum, 1. Række*, Det Danske Sprog- og Litteraturselskab (Copenhagen, 1958), pp. 162–65.
28 Constance Rousseau, 'The spousal relationship: marital society and sexuality in the letters of Pope Innocent III,' *Mediaeval Studies*, 56 (1994), 89–109.

Finally, sometime before May 1207, Philip agreed to the pope's conditions and to try and have intercourse again with Ingeborg.[29] But once again Philip changed his mind as soon as Innocent sent his legate to France. Philip objected that the legate's authority was insufficient, because he was not empowered to make a final decision in the case which could not be appealed to Rome. In his letter Philip implied that the queen was now ready to take the veil and to leave him to live separately by himself. But Innocent stood firm. He quickly replied with two letters in succession. In one he admonished the king to renounce the case and to consider the scandal that would arise from his suggested course of action. And in the other he rejected Philip's suggested compromise, that Ingeborg should enter a nunnery and that he be allowed to marry after swearing an oath that the marriage was unconsummated. Innocent rejected this suggestion since Ingeborg had explained that the king had repeatedly attempted intercourse with her, despite his claims to have failed in his endeavours.[30] We learn some further details of what had happened on 14 August 1193 from the final letter in the case dated 9 June 1212. In this letter the pope clarified his definition of sexual intercourse. Philip had said that he could swear that there had been no sexual intercourse because he had not deposited any semen in the womb of his wife. Philip seems to have admitted, however, that he had placed his penis in her vagina, and that in the eyes of Innocent III constituted *carnalis copula*.[31] In his final instructions to the papal legate, Innocent authorised him only to proceed to a final decision if the parties were agreed on the outcome. Philip, once again, despatched the papal legate since he was not willing to grant a final separation.

This was the closest the matter came to a resolution. A number of letters passed between Innocent and Philip in the following years. Usually, it was Innocent who initiated a dialogue with Philip and usually the letters were despatched at times that show a disregard for any considerations of political advantage. In 1212 the matter reached its final conclusion as far as the papacy was concerned. Innocent's confidential agent, Master Robert Courçon, concluded enquiries that showed that the marriage had been consummated

---

29 August Potthast, editor, *Regesta pontificum romanorum inde ab anno post christum natum 1198 ad anno 1304* (Berlin, 1873), no. 3359.

30 Potthast, *Regesta pontificum*, no. 3557.

31 ... sit errorem inductus ut credat se licite posse jurare quod reginam uxoram suam carnaliter non cognovit, pro eo forte quod etsi commistio sexuum in eorum carnali commercio intercesserit, commistio tamen seminum in vase muliebri non exstitit subsecuta, nos confessiones ejusdem reginae sub jurejurando factas subtiliter atendentes, et salutem ipsius regis paterno zelantes affectu, per nostras eum litteras exhortamur ut suum de caetero ab hujusmodi falsis insaniis avertat auditum et praefatem reginam pro Deo et propter Deum habeat commendatam, quae pro servata lege conjugii. J.-P. Migne, *Patrologiae cursus completus series latina.*, vol. 216 (Paris, 1800–75), pp. 618–19.

on 14 August nineteen years previously and Innocent declared that he could
not in conscience separate the two. The king was told to cease his litigation
before the papacy and the following year Philip released Ingeborg from her
captivity. When he had shown any inclination to ease her situation in the past
the reason had been political and this was true in this instance as well. The
Holy Roman Emperor, the Welf Otto of Brunswick, was an enemy of
France, but he had also become an enemy of Danish interests in the Baltic
region. Ingeborg's brother Valdemar II (*Sejr* [the Victorious]) had pursued
an ambitious programme of conquest in the Baltic and was threatening
imperial interests in Northern Germany and Pomerania. Otto of Brunswick
did what he could to stop Danish expansion and Valdemar found that he
stood to gain more by switching his allegiance to the Hohenstaufen. Philip,
on the other hand, was preparing to invade England following Innocent's
interdict of King John and in this game his Danish queen strengthened his
claim to the English throne. Although she did not see much of Philip,
Ingeborg seems to have been accepted by the rest of his family and for the
remaining twenty-seven years of her life was for all intents and purposes a
free woman. When Philip died in 1223 she even received her dower and was
given the honour that was due to a widowed queen. She used her new wealth
among other things to contribute to the ransom of her brother when he was
captured on the island of Rügen and to found a priory for the knights of St
John in Corbeil. Ingeborg died in 1236 and was buried in the priory church
of St John under a copper effigy which remained in place until 1736 when it
was removed to make way for a new altar.

CONCLUSION

The story of the conflict between Philip and Ingeborg is complex and full of
surprising twists and turns. Ingeborg was an unusual woman by any stretch
of the imagination. At the age of eighteen she found herself in a foreign
country, fighting to preserve her marriage to a man who took an instant and
spectacular dislike to her. On the face of it and according to the letter of the
law, the Danish monarchy had an open and shut case. Not only that, but the
Danish princess came from a holy family, and had the support of some of the
best legal minds of the twelfth century. Their case was also strengthened not
only by her sainted grandfather, but also by the presence of William of
Paraclete/Æbelholt who was soon to gain sainthood for himself. However,
the conclusion that must be drawn from this story is a depressing one for a
lawyer: the law of marriage in the Middle Ages could only reach so far. In
this case, Ingeborg, despite all her support and despite clearly having right
on her side, became the helpless pawn in a game of high politics: despite his
well-documented concern for the sanctity of marriage, Innocent III could

only pursue the case subject to the realities of European politics. Not only did Philip dislike the Danish princess he had met only once, he also knew that Innocent had to rely on his support in imperial matters and he used this leverage to spectacular effect. The Danes also realised that they had met their match and that they needed the active or at least the passive support of the French. The accession of Valdemar II in 1202 confirmed this accommodation: under the rule of her second brother, the Danes concentrated their efforts in securing their freedom from the German empire and their new conquests in the Baltic.

So, in a word, the law of the church could only reach so far. When it came up against a determined ruler it had to acknowledge defeat. The outcome of this accommodation is the sad story of the Danish princess who spent twenty years of her life paying the price for one night with a husband whose motives for his rejection of her remain as murky now as they were then.

Birlaw courts and birleymen

W.D.H. SELLAR

'BIRLAW COURTS AND BIRLEYMEN' may seem an obscure title, but the birlaw was a well-known and widespread institution in Scotland for many hundreds of years.[1] It was once known in England also, although apparently not in Ireland.[2] This is certainly the story of an adventure of the law; although one might also call it the adventure of a legal historian. My own interest in birlaw courts was first aroused by a short appendix entitled 'The Burlaw Men' in Croft Dickinson's classic study of barony courts in Scotland, *The court book of the barony of Carnwath* (1937).[3] That appendix still remains the essential starting point for anyone interested in the history of the birlaw in Scotland. In fact, apart from the occasional reference, little has been written since about this long-standing institution, and the birlaw court and its history remains largely unknown even to Scottish legal historians and record scholars. This is partly no doubt because birlaw courts in Scotland have left little by way of written record of their proceedings, subject to one or two exceptions to be noted later.[4]

Dickinson noted the presence of birleymen (*Birlawmen; berla men; barle men*) in the Carnwath record, all at Whitsun courts. These courts were particularly concerned with economic matters and the keeping of 'good neighbourhood'. The birleymen helped to enforce the 'styles and statutes' of the court, and might act on occasion as arbiters in matters concerning neighbourhood. Dickinson pointed to references to the birlaw in the medieval treatise *Regiam majestatem*, and in Sir John Skene's *De verborum significatione* of 1597. He gave several examples of birlaws and birleymen on the record from 1479 onwards. He noted that in the barony of Forbes in the seventeenth century birleymen were appointed for each parish, and in the burgh of Peebles for each 'quarter' of the town. The system, he believed, 'was an ideal

---

1 The variant spellings of 'birlaw' and 'birleymen' are legion (below, note 16), with no agreed modern form. I have chosen to use 'birlaw' and 'birleymen', rather than Croft Dickinson's 'burlaw' and 'burlaw men', as a matter of convenience. I also sometimes refer to 'the birlaw', rather than 'the birlaw court', for the reasons given below, pp. 77, 84.

2 I am most grateful to both Fergus Kelly and Kenneth Nicholls for advising me that they are not aware of references to birlaw courts or birleymen in Irish sources.

3 *The court book of the barony of Carnwath 1523–1542*, ed. W. Croft Dickinson (Scottish History Society, Edinburgh, 1937), Appendix A, 'The burlaw men', pp. cxiii–cxvi.

4 Below, pp. 76–78. For the position in England see below, pp. 81ff.

one for preserving the peace of the community and for ensuring that each tenant paid a proper regard to the welfare of his neighbours'.[5] He refers to the nine birleymen [Bourlawmen] appointed in the barony of Stitchill in 1655, 'to desyde all matters questionable and debaitable among neybors ...', and to the 'birly men' of the barony of Forbes in 1668, concerned with the 'keiping of guid nightbourheid'.[6] Birleymen might be concerned with, for example, the maintenance of hedges and ditches to prevent animals from straying into the corn, disputes as to pasturage, questions as to boundaries, and the assessment of compensation.

Dickinson believed that birlaw courts had at first been independent of the barony court but were later subsumed into it. 'Undoubtedly,' he wrote, 'burlaw courts were at first held by and among the tenants themselves, but before long we find the baron and his baillie choosing the burlaw men, whilst in the barony of Skene, in 1615, the burlaw court ("barla court") was presided over by the laird and the baillie'.[7] He cited the record of the barony court of Stitchill as evidence that baron courts might uphold the decrees of the birleymen, or of the birlaw court, and interpone authority to them: all tenants were to 'obey the Sentences and Decreits to be pronounced be the Bourlawmen in tym cumeing and that non oppose them neither be word nor deid nor scold, raille, nor outcry against ther proceedings in tym cumeing utherwyas nor be order of Law and justice under the paine of five punds and personall punishment at the Lairdis pleasure ...'.[8] The etymology of 'birlaw' suggested by Dickinson was particularly intriguing. Following the Oxford English Dictionary, he wrote that, 'the word is probably derived from the Old Norse *býjar-lög*, that is "law community" or "law district", and so came to mean the local law governing small townships or villages'.[9] Dickinson, however, did not suggest how the name or the institution came to Scotland.

Professor Archie Duncan, in a passage which clearly draws on Dickinson, wrote that our knowledge of the village community in medieval Scotland is 'shadowy'. He notes the role of the 'burlaw men' in the keeping of good neighbourhood in the later medieval period, then adds these challenging

5 Dickinson, 'Burlaw men', p. cxv.
6 Ibid., pp. cxiv–cxv, citing C.B. Gunn (ed.), *Records of the baron court of Stitchill* (Scottish History Society, Edinburgh, 1905), p.2, and J. Maitland Thomson (ed.), 'The Forbes baron court book, 1659–1678' in *Miscellany iii* (Scottish History Society, Edinburgh, 1919), pp. 205–321 at p. 275. The editor of *Stitchill* notes that the term 'stent maisters' is used elsewhere rather than birleymen.
7 'Burlaw men', pp. cxv–cxvi, note 8;'Extracts from the court books of the baronies of Skene, Leys and Whitehaugh, 1613–1687' in John Stuart (ed.) *Miscellany v* (Spalding Club, Aberdeen, 1852), pp. 215–38 at 218.
8 Ibid., pp. cxiv–cxvi; *Barony court of Stitchill*, p. 24.
9 Ibid., p. cxiii, citing *Oxford (new) English dictionary* (1934), s.v. *burlaw*. Dictionaries generally are an invaluable source of reference on this subject: see, for example, below, pp. 78–80.

comments: 'The antiquity of this institution is uncertain but the derivation of its name from Old Norse suggests that it developed between the ninth century and the twelfth. We must be chary of assuming that it arose among the peasantry rather than by the landlord's command, but nonetheless it is the nearest we shall get to a "popular" institution in Scottish society.'[10] This article explores the history of the birlaw and birleymen in Scotland further, and seeks to answer a number of questions. When did birlaw courts first appear in Scotland? What type of business was transacted in birlaw courts? How long did birlaw courts and birleymen continue to function? Finally, if the etymology of 'birlaw' is indeed Scandinavian, how and when did that Scandinavian influence arise?

As Dickinson noted, the first known reference to the birlaw appears in the treatise *Regiam majestatem*, now generally believed to have been compiled in the first half of the fourteenth century. The chapter *De effusione sanguinis* ('On the shedding of blood') sets out a tariff calculated in cows for the shedding of blood, according to the rank of the victim: nine cows for shedding of blood from the head of an earl or king's son, six for the son of an earl, or for a thane, and so on down the scale:

> *Item sanguis de capite unius comitis aut filii Regis sunt novem vaccae. Item sanguis filii comitis aut unius thani sunt sex vaccae. Item de sanguine filii thani tres vaccae. Item de sanguine nepotis thani duae vaccae et duae partes unius vaccae. Item de sanguine unius rustici una vacca.*

The chapter then deals with blood drawn below the breath (*subtus anhelitum*), the rights of unmarried women, and a blow not causing the shedding of blood, before concluding with the sentence:

> *Cetera omnia et singula quae currunt in curiis dominorum secundum auxilium et favorem terminantur, exceptis legibus de Burlawis quae per consensum vicinorum erunt.*[11]

This may be translated as 'All other matters brought before lords' courts are determined in accordance with the strength and favour enjoyed by the parties excepting the laws of Burlaw which are determined by the consent of neighbours'.[12]

---

10 A.A.M. Duncan, *Scotland, the making of the kingdom* (Edinburgh, 1975), pp. 349–50.

11 The edition of *Regiam majestatem* now in general use is that of the Stair Society, edited by Lord Cooper (Stair Society, Edinburgh, 1947), in which this chapter appears as iv, 39. In the edition of the *Regiam* in the *Acts of the parliaments of Scotland*, T. Thomson and C. Innes (eds.) (12 vols., Edinburgh, 1814–75) [*APS*], the chapter appears as iv, 58 (*APS* i, 641), and the relevant clause reads *exceptis burlawis que per consensum vicinorum concurrunt*.

12 I am grateful to Paul Brand for advice on this translation, which differs from that of Lord Cooper.

In his English edition of *Regiam majestatem*, published in 1609, Sir John Skene translates the same sentence as follows: 'All other and sundrie things, quhilk occurres in Barone courts, are determined at the discretion and will of the Lord of the court. Except Birlaw courts, the quhilkis are rewled be consent of neighbours.'[13] In his Latin edition, published in the same year, Skene glosses the sentence thus:

> *Apud Germanos* Baur *rusticum significat* & Lauch vel law *lex dicitur, hinc* Burlaw, *rusticorum leges, de re rustica latae. Nos hodie* Birlaw *courtis*, & Birlawmen, *dicimus.*

The chapter on the shedding of blood is one of four chapters not originally part of *Regiam majestatem*, as noted by both Lord Cooper and Sir John Skene. These chapters constitute a tract long referred to, on grounds which are not quite clear, as *Leges inter Brettos et Scotos*, 'the Laws of the Bretts and the Scots', and of which French and Scots versions also survive. The core text of 'the Laws of the Bretts and the Scots' awaits a modern editor. It is older, perhaps much older, than the main body of *Regiam majestatem*, although the passage on the birlaw appears to be an addition to the original core text.[14] However, even if this passage was added to the original provisions on the shedding of blood, it seems reasonable to conclude that the birlaw was already old and well established by the early fourteenth century.

Sir John Skene's *De verborum significatione* of 1597 contains this entry:

> BURLAW, *Byrlaw.* lawes of *Burlaw* are maid, and determined be consent of nichtbors, elected and chosen be common consent, in the courtes, called the *Byrlaw* courts. In the quhilk, cognition is taken of complaints betuixt nichtbour & nichtbour ... The quhilk men sa chosen, as judges and arbitrators to the effect foresaid, are commonly called *byrlaw* men. It is an dutch word [that is, German], for *baur* or *baursman* in dutch, is *rusticus*, an husbandman. And sa *byrlaw* burlaw or baurlaw, *leges rusticorum*: Lawes maid be husbandmen, concerning nichtbour-heid to be keeped amangs themselues.[15]

This entry tallies with Skene's gloss on the sentence in the *Regiam*. It is valuable also as giving Skene's own contemporary comment on birleymen and birlaw courts. Again there is an emphasis on neighbours, neighbourhood

---

13 Sir John Skene, *Regiam majestatem, the auld lawes and constitutions of Scotland* (Edinburgh, 1609), and *Regiam majestatem Scotiae veteres leges et constitutiones* (Edinburgh, 1609).

14 The final sentence, including the reference to the birlaw, does not appear in the version of the *Leges* given in *APS* i, 665 from the late thirteenth-century Berne manuscript.

15 Sir John Skene, *De verborum significatione* (Edinburgh, 1597).

and on common consent. Skene's etymology, echoed in his comments on *Regiam majestatem*, is plausible enough, though not correct. His three variant spellings could be multiplied many times over.[16]

It is indicative of the poverty of the Scottish record, as compared with the English, that the first known reference to birlaw courts in practice occurs 150 years after *Regiam majestatem*: the Cupar-Angus example of 1479 cited by Dickinson. The rental book of the Abbey of Cupar-Angus requires that a leaseholder 'sal kepe gud nychtburhede ... And owkly [weekly] he and his nychtburis sal halde a byrlay courte amang thame self, for commown profit of the town [that is, of the farmtown or 'township'] and correccioun of al fautis'.[17] Again, the emphasis is on neighbours, neighbourhood and the common weal. A few years later, from 1488–1492 inclusive, 'birlawmen' are among the burgh officials appointed at the Michaelmas head court of the burgh of Dunfermline.[18] Later head courts there refer to 'the haill comonis', *communitatem dicti burgi*, and 'the nychtbouris'. Even for the sixteenth century few references survive. In addition to the examples from *Carnwath*, the Forbes rental of 1532 shows joint tenants being bound to keep good neighbourhood 'at the sight of umpires called "birleymen," chosen by themselves'.[19] Sir James Balfour in his *Practicks*, referring to a case decided in 1552, notes of 'landis lyand togidder in rin-rig' that 'everie ane of thame may be compellit at the instance of ane uther, to concur in keiping of gude nichtbourheid ane with the uther, in tilling, labouring, sawing, scheiring, pastouring, and dykeing, and in all uther thingis pertening to gude and thriftie nichtbourheid'.[20]

After 1600, however, references become more frequent, both in the surviving record and in non-legal sources. This is so throughout Scotland, Highland and Lowland, although Lowland examples predominate. Some further examples may be added to those given by Dickinson. In 1660 the bailie of the regality of Melrose upheld a decision of the 'birlawmen' of Darnick: 'The bailie absolves the defenders, and interpones his decreit to the said condescendence and stent agreed on in the said birlaw court.'[21] Dr Athol

---

16 Variants include birlaw, birlawe, burlaw, byrlaw, bourlaw, boorlaw, bierlaw, byerlaw, byrlaw, berlaw, baurlaw, birley, birla, barla, and birlie; also birlaw-man, byrlaw man, birleymen, berla men, barle men and barleymen! See also *OED* under 'birlaw', 'birlie', 'bourlaw', 'burley' and 'byrlaw'.

17 Charles Rogers (ed.), *Rental book of Cupar-Angus* (2 vols., Grampian Club, London, 1879–80), i, 230 (*Carnwath*, p. cxiv).

18 Erskine Beveridge (ed.), *Burgh records of Dunfermline* (Edinburgh, 1917), pp. xvii, 4, 16, 22, 30, 39.

19 The reference and the quotation are from Cosmo Innes, *Scotch legal antiquities* (Edinburgh, 1872), p. 254.

20 P.G.B. McNeill (ed.), *Balfour's practicks* (2 vols., Stair Society, Edinburgh, 1962–3), ii, 536–37. I owe this reference to Robert A. Dodgshon, 'Farming in Roxburghshire and Berwickshire on the eve of improvement' in 1975 *Scottish Historical Review*, pp. 140–54 at p. 151.

21 C.S. Romanes (ed.), *Records of the regality court of Melrose, 1547–1706* (3 vols., Scottish History Society, Edinburgh, 1914–17), i, 311. There are further references to birlaw courts

Murray has drawn my attention to a declaration made by the birlawmen of the barony of Fintry in 1685 and by those of the barony of Buchanan in 1719.[22] In Kintyre in 1672, four named 'birlawmen' were appointed for each of nine parishes by 'Acts of Bailyierie ... made & sett doun be ane Noble Earle Archibald [9th] Earle of Argyll'.[23] These birleymen were drawn from the local gentry, including, for example, the laird of Ralstoun, the laird of Sanda and Lachlan MacNeill of Tirfergus. The 1672 Acts followed earlier 'Acts of Neighbourhood' for Kintyre, promulgated by the 9th earl's father, the marquis of Argyll, in 1653 'for the better settling the condition of the countrey; and for keeping good neighbourhood ...'.[24] In Erskine's *Institute* there is a reference to the role of birleymen in valuing or apprising the value of a debtor's goods in the execution of poinding [impounding].[25] The *Balgair court minutes* – the court of a landowner in Stirlingshire, but apparently not a baron court – record the laird presenting two 'Birlawmen' to his court in 1709, birleymen conducting a perambulation and division of lands in 1713, and one James Whyte being fined fifty pounds Scots in 1726 by Balgair's bailie 'for refusing to be a birlaman'.[26] In the island of Islay, references to 'two sworn birleymen' for the assessment of damage done to grass or corn became standard in leases granted by Campbell of Shawfield in the island of Islay from 1724 onwards.[27] However, I have not yet found any references to birlaw courts or birleymen in the Outer Hebrides, Orkney and Shetland, all areas of intensive Scandinavian settlement, despite the suggested Scandinavian etymology.[28]

The great nineteenth-century record scholar and legal historian Cosmo Innes wrote of the birleymen in his *Scotch legal antiquities* in 1872, 'Let me say something of this rural officer chosen by the people. I think he is not yet extinct in some northern districts – not forgotten anywhere in Scotland. The birleymen were the arbiters – the referees in rural differences – between tenants of the same estate'. He added that, 'In the old time, to dispute the award of the birleymen left a stain on a man's character'.[29] Innes believed that

held in the Borders in the eighteenth century in Dodgshon, 'Farming in Roxburghshire and Berwickshire'.

22 National Archives of Scotland [NAS], GD220/6/693/25 and 220/6/1790/7.

23 A.I.B. Stewart, 'Regulation of agriculture in seventeenth century Kintyre' in W.M. Gordon (ed.), *Miscellany iii* (Stair Society, Edinburgh 1992), pp. 220–21.

24 A.I.B. Stewart, 'Regulation of agriculture', pp. 216–17.

25 John Erskine, *An institute of the law of Scotland* (Edinburgh, 1773), III, vi, 23. I am indebted to Professor Bill McBryde for this reference.

26 Jean Dunlop (ed.), *Court minutes of Balgair 1706–1736* (Scottish Record Society, Edinburgh, 1957), pp. 8, 10–11, and 24 (see also pp. 26, 27, 28 and 30). I am most grateful to Athol Murray for these references.

27 Freda Ramsay (ed.), *The day book of Daniel Campbell of Shawfied 1767 with relevant papers concerning the estate of Islay* (Aberdeen, 1991), pp. 6 (1724), 73 (1748), 71 (1752) and 223 (1777).

28 An explanation for this is suggested below, p. 84.

29 Innes, *Scotch legal antiquities*, p. 254.

the institution had spread north from England. Elsewhere, when discussing 'constant quarrels' about the souming of cattle and sheep in the forfeited estate of Robertson of Struan in 1755, which had been referred by the baron-bailie to the birleymen of the district to resolve, Innes commented, 'You see how far the Saxon institution had penetrated into the Highlands'.[30]

Most references to the birlaw and birleymen are of a secondary nature, actual records of Scottish birlaw courts and their proceedings being extremely rare. One record of birlaw enactments which does survive is 'The Boorlaw Book of Yester and Gifford' in East Lothian, written in the later eighteenth-century.[31] This sets out 40 acts of the birlaw in the form of 'Act anent ...'. The last act is dated the 19th of July 1780, and the 38th the 24th of June 1761. The first 37 acts are written in the same hand as the last three, which are preceded by the note, 'The above 37 Acts has been time Immemorial the Boor law or commonly pronounced the Birla of Yester'. The first two acts read as follows:

1. Act anent over Soumes. If any person dwelling in the neighbourhood holding sumes above their stent [allowed number] being warned by the Birlamen to remove them of the ground, for ilk twenty four hours they shall keep them after the command of the Birlamen they shall pay Twenty shillings scots.

2. Act anent Night Lairs. Whosoever shall have a beast lying out of the house betwixt the 3rd of may & the corns being all shorn & led home to the barn yard, for ilk night lair shall pay to the birla twelve shillings scots and they shall pay to the complainer what damage the corn is comprised to.

Several acts are concerned with the digging and use of turf and peat. For example, the seventh act reads: 'Act anent Casting [digging] of Elding. Whosoever shall cast Peits, truffs, diviots or Faill upon their Neighbours ground, they shall pay to the Birla Twenty Shillings for breaking the ground...'[32]

Other acts seek to uphold the authority of the birleymen and the birlaw court:

---

30 Ibid., p. 268. 'Souming' refers to the number of beasts which a tenant was allowed to put on the common grazings.

31 Records of the feuars of Gifford, NAS GD/1/16/2. See further, Marquis of Tweeddale, 'The boorlaw book of Yester and Gifford' in *Transactions of the East Lothian Antiquarian and Field Naturalists Society*, vii (Haddington, 1958), pp. 9–17 and John H. Simpson, *The feuars of Gifford, 1750–1980* (Edinburgh, 1986), chapter 1, 'The eighteenth century'.

32 'Fuel, feal and divot' is one of the rural servitudes recognised by Scots law: the right to cut peat for fuel and turf for walling.

11. Act anent abusing of the Birlawmen. Whosoever shall revile scold or abuse the Birlemen ... with base or unbecoming words or speeches they shall for each fault of that nature pay to the Birlaw Twenty shillings scots.

17. Act anent Absenting from the Birla. Whosoever absents himself from the Birla being in health and at home and sends others in his stead for ilk absence they shall pay to the Birla half a merk.

Other matters covered by the acts include the tethering of horses, 'wanton Staigs [young horses] in the harigg', wrongous complaints about neighbours, and 'Blowen Pease in the Harvest time'.

The vocabulary used might repay further study. Much of it is now impenetrable without the aid of a good Scots dictionary, and it would be interesting to know how common it was in the eighteenth century. The use of the phrase 'the Birla' – 'commonly called the Birla of Yester' – rather than 'the Birlaw court' at the beginning of the record and in several of the acts is also a point of interest.[33]

This birlaw, which had earlier been closely associated with the barony of Yester, merged into, or was assimilated by, a body known as 'the Feuars of Gifford', which emerged in the mid-eighteenth century and survives to the present as a trust with charitable status. The last entry in the Boorlaw Book, dated 22 August 1793, concerns a general meeting of the Feuars of Gifford.

New birlaw courts were still being set up as late as the eighteenth century. In 1715 farmers in and around Edinburgh and Leith petitioned Leith Town Council to have 'Burlay Baillies [that is, birleymen] chosen and elected' to make the necessary 'acts and statutes'.[34] The petition was granted and the Council appointed 'the said byrlaw Court to commence from Lammas next'. The court was to be maintained by the members, rather than at public expense. From 1724 there is a record of the proceedings of this birlaw court – perhaps the only reasonably full record of the proceedings of a Scottish birlaw court to have survived.[35] The emphasis is again very much on neighbours, neighbourhood and common consent. An entry for 20 July 1724 notes that:

The persons hereto subscryving being admitted and entered Members of the Burlaw Court of Leith Doe hereby bind and oblidge themselves

33 See below, p. 84.
34 David Robertson, 'The burlaw court of Leith' in *Book of the Old Edinburgh Club* xv (Edinburgh, 1927), pp. 165–205 at 166–67, citing the minutes of Edinburgh City Council. This informative article was known also to Croft Dickinson.
35 Edinburgh Council Archives, SL 86/11/1–3 (Leith Burlaw Court, 3 vols.). These three Sederunt Books cover the period 1724–1750. The first volume also contains (loose at end) an 'Alphabeticall Indix of the Bourlaw Court Acts' by subject matter for the period 1715 to 1729.

to stand to abyde by and fulfill all the Acts and statutes of the said
Burlaw Court Made and to be Made for the better regulation of the
neighbourheid and Members of the said Court, and oblidgs them to
obey the sentences of the said Burlaw Court in all tyme coming.[36]

The court met weekly or fortnightly from spring until autumn. At first it
met in the open air at the 'Ducatt yeard' (Dovecote yard) by Leith links, but
soon the birlaw bailies petitioned the bailies of South Leith to be allowed to
sit inside in a house when the weather was 'foull, stormy or rigidly cold'![37]
The birlaw's activities were not confined to Leith, but ranged widely over
farmland around Edinburgh, including Broughton, Canonmills and Inverleith.

This birlaw too had its own acts and statutes, some in language almost
as impenetrable as that of the Boorlaw of Yester; for example, an act of
28 September 1719 concerned the liability of persons setting out 'Scabbed
or Colded horses on the Grass Stanks or Seughs of the Ground'.[38] The index
to the acts discloses many about animals, as one would expect – cows, 'duks',
dogs, fouls, geese, hens, horses, sheep and swine. One intriguing entry indexed
under 'Bullets' refers to a complaint by Thomas Sheills, tenant at Broughton,
that 'Severall people when playing att the Bullets on [Broughton loan] Upon
pretence of Seeking for their Bullets, Trade doun and Spoil his growing
Corn'. The birlaw ordained that any person so transgressing should pay a
fine of one pound scots and empowered Thomas Sheills 'to Seize the bullets
of the transgressors And to Detain them till the said One Pund be paid'.[39]
The reference is evidently to the game of bullets, once widely popular, which
involved pitching a rounded stone (the 'bullet') from point to point in as few
chucks or throws as possible.[40]

The Leith birlaw court ceased to function about the middle of the
eighteenth century.

As Cosmo Innes suggests, the birleyman remained a familiar figure in
rural Scotland until well into the nineteenth century. Already in 1602 John
Colville, attempting to reconvert his countrymen to Roman Catholicism, wrote
of the ecumenical councils of the Church 'as far in maiestie and authoritie
exceding your Synods as a gret parlament doth exceid a poor birla court'.[41] Sir

---

36 SL 86/11/1–3, vol. 1, loose paper; see Robertson, 'Burlaw Court', p. 171.
37 SL 86/11/1, petition at end of vol.1; Robertson, 'Burlaw Court', p. 172.
38 SL 86/11/1, 'Alphabeticall Indix': 'Colded'; and see Robertson, 'Burlaw Court', p. 181.
39 SL 86/11/1–3, vol. 1, 27 May 1728.
40 The game of 'lang bullet' also figures in *Mathiesone* v. *Anderson*, a case of accidental
    slaughter in 1640, in which stones had been rolled down the 'bank or bra[e] of the castell of
    Edinburgh' with fatal consequences (J. Irvine Smith, ed., *Selected Justiciary Cases*, ii (Stair
    Society, Edinburgh, 1972), p. 395).
41 John Colville, *The Paranaese or admonition of Io. Colville … unto his cuntrey men* (Paris 1602).
    epistle, 23. Colville also wrote (ibid.) that the General Assembly of the Church of Scotland

Walter Scott wrote in *Waverley* of 'Jamie Howie, wha's no fit to be a birlie-man, let be a bailie'.[42] In 1866 it was noted that 'Birley Court, in the tradition of the Borders, [was] a name for any particularly stormy meeting'.[43] The birleyman, or burlaw-bailie, even has his place in verse, although the words are not flattering and the verse is not good. Allan Ramsay's 'The Lure: A Tale' contains this stanza:

> This Falconer had tane his Way
> O'er *Calder* –moor; and gawn the Moss up,
> He there forgather'd with a Gossip:
> And wha was't, trow ye, but the Deel [the devil],
> That had disguis'd himsell sae weel
> In humane shape, sae snug and wylie;
> *Jude* took him for a Burlie-baillie.[44]

Birlaws and birleymen gradually disappeared in the course of the nineteenth century, although some were remembered well into the twentieth. For example, it was said in Banffshire in 1928, 'I min' fin the vailyations for an oot-gyaan [out-going] tenant wis deen [was done] by the birley man'.[45] One late example is to be found at St Boswells, near Melrose, where an annual birlaw court was held by the proprietors of the undivided common green. The court's function was restricted to letting the green, dividing the income, and appointing 'Birlymen'. The existing record begins in 1823 – surprisingly late. The last description of the meeting as a 'Birly Court' is in 1840; but the meeting continued to be held for many more years, appointing named birleymen until 1873. The record of lettings continues in scrappy fashion until 1969.[46]

One set of birleymen survive to the present day in the Border town of Selkirk where they remain an integral part of the annual and highly symbolic 'Selkirk Common Riding', the riding of the marches of the burgh. 'Burleymen' are now appointed by a trust set up in 1975 after the old town council disappeared in local government re-organisation. An attractive leaflet on the history of the Common Riding provides yet another misleading etymology of 'birleymen': that they are so called because their function was to carry out the burgh law.[47]

in relation to Ecumenical Councils was 'in proportion as a flee is to ane Elephant'! See also *Dictionary of the older Scottish tongue* [*DOST*], 'Birlaw'. An electronic edition of both *DOST* and the *Scottish national dictionary* [*SND*] went online in 2004: www.dsl.ac.uk.

42 Sir Walter Scott, *Waverley*, chapter xlii (otherwise ii, xiii).

43 *Proceedings of the Berwickshire Naturalists Club*, 1866, p. 261, *per OED*, 'birlie'.

44 Allan Ramsay, *Poems II* (Edinburgh, 1728), p. 238. Allan Ramsay the poet (1686–1758) was the father of Allan Ramsay the painter (1713–1784).

45 *Scottish national dictionary* [*SND*], 'Birlie'.

46 NAS, GD1/1152/1.

47 *Selkirk common riding history – alive in the present*, published by *Selkirk Chronicles* (nd).

How did the birlaw come to Scotland? As already noted, Cosmo Innes believed that it had come from England, describing it as 'the Saxon institution'.[48]

A check through the Oxford English Dictionary reveals that the birlaw was indeed once common in England.[49] The main entry (under 'byrlaw', of which 'birlaw' is said to be an obsolete form) describes 'byrlaw' as, 'The local custom or "law" of a township, manor, or rural district, whereby disputes as to boundaries, trespass of cattle, etc., were settled without going into the law courts; a law or custom established in such a district by common consent of all who held land therein, and having binding force within its limits'. These definitions, it will be seen, fit well the Scottish birlaw also. The earliest form of the word given, 'Birelag', comes from the record of Furness Abbey in Lancashire in 1257; and the second, 'Birlawe', from Devon in 1292. The suggested etymology is given as 'apparently' ON [Old Norse] from a hypothetical '*býjar-lög, f. býjar gen. case of bý-r (= BY n.)', a dialect variant of baer, a village, town or farm, plus 'log (pl. of lag) law, "law community, communion, also a law district"'; with a note cautioning that the existence of *býjar-, baejar-lög in Old Norse has scarcely been proved.

A separate entry under 'by-law' describes 'by-law' as 'apparently the same as BYRLAW; occurring in the thirteenth century as the name of a custom (in Kent) according to which disputes were settled outside the law courts, on the testimony of neighbours, by official or specially deputed arbitrators'. The earliest forms given here are 'bilage' in 1283 and again in 1303, both from Kent. The suggested etymology notes that the word appears to be a doublet of byrlaw in sense, the difference in form being perhaps explicable by 'the derivation of bylaw from the stem instead of the genitive case of ON. bý-r, Sw. and Da. by, dwelling-place, farm, village, township, town'. However, it is also noted, with a view to the earliest examples of the word, that 'the difficulty of assigning a Scandinavian etymology to the local name of a Kentish custom is obvious, but cf. quot. 1292 under BYRLAW from an assize held in Devonshire ...'. The more recent Danish and Swedish forms bylag and byalag, both describing a village community, are also noted.[50]

This short excursus has been necessary to show that although the ultimate Scandinavian etymology of the word birlaw is not in doubt, some details remain unclear, not least the exact relationship between 'birlaw' and 'by-law'. OED also notes, under 'byrlaw', here following place-name scholars, that the Yorkshire place-names Brampton Bierlow, Eccleshall Bierlow and Brightside Bierlow, appear to incorporate the word 'birlaw'.[51]

---

48 Above, p. 76.
49 I have used *OED Online*, which for 'byrlaw' etc. is based on the 1989 edition updated. The ongoing new edition started with the letter 'M' and, unfortunately, has not yet reached 'B'.
50 Below, p. 85.
51 See, for example, Armitage Goodall, *Place-names of south-west Yorkshire* (Cambridge, 1914),

There can be little doubt that the name 'birlaw', and probably the institution also, came to Scotland from England. Given the Scandinavian derivation of the word the most likely area of origin within Britain is the Danelaw. Although surprisingly little has been written about the birlaw in studies of the medieval village community or in general works on English legal history, there is ample evidence for the functioning of birlaw courts throughout England from the late thirtienth century onwards.[52] Particularly relevant here is an article published in 1965 by Warren O. Ault on open-field husbandry, the village community and agrarian by-laws in medieval England.[53] Ault noted that Vinogradoff had pointed to the existence of village by-laws already in the fifteenth century, and had suspected that there must be some from an earlier date.[54] Through the study of the rolls of manorial courts, courts baron and courts leet, Ault was able to point to the existence of such village by-laws already in the late thirteenth and fourteenth centuries. These regulated a wide variety of matters, including conservation of grain, gleaning and reaping, protection of sheaves against theft, peas and beans, stubble, right of fallow, tethering of animals, pasturing of sheep, control of pigs, fencing of fields, ploughs and ploughing, rights to hay, boundaries, access and rights of way.[55]

The regulations are typically described as 'statutes', 'ordinances' and 'customs'. Examples given by Ault include the phrases *statutum ville* (1290, Newington, Oxon.), *statute et ordinaciones autumpnales* (1290, Great Hornwood, Bucks.), *sicut statutum fuit per le byrlawe* (1317, Abbot's Ripon, Hunts.), *birlawe* (1322, Burwell, Cambs.), *ordinacio bilegis* (1325, Littleport Manor, Cambs.) and *consuetudines vocate belawes* (1379, Heyford, Oxon.).[56] There is regular emphasis on common consent and assent. Ault discusses the various phrases used by way of description and notes as the 'simplest of all, most frequent, and least informing' *ordinatum est ex commune assensu*, a phrase which occurs more than fifty times in the rolls of Durham's halmotes.[57] More informative are phrases such as *per communitatem tocius villate* (1324, Newington, Oxon.), *ex commune assensu tocius villate* (*c.*1425, Wimeswold,

---

'Bierlaw'; and Allan Mawer (ed.), *The chief elements used in English place-names* (Cambridge, 1924), '*byarlog*'.

52 A notable exception is Angus Winchester whose work on birlaw courts is noticed below, pp. 82–83.

53 Warren O. Ault, 'Open-field husbandry and the village community: a study of agrarian by-laws in medieval England' in *Transactions of the American Philosophical Society*, new series, 55, pt.7 (1965), pp. 5–102. I am most grateful to Paul Brand for alerting me to this article some years ago. See also W.O. Ault, *Open-field farming in medieval England: a study of village by-laws* (London and New York, 1972).

54 Ault, 'Open-field husbandry', p. 12.

55 Ibid., pp. 12–40.

56 Ibid., pp. 40–41. Ault gives 'le bye-lawe' for the 1317 entry in the main text, but 'le byrlawe' in the documentary appendix (p. 59, no.34).

57 Ibid., p. 41.

Leics.) and *ex commune assensu omnium vicinorum* (1383, Durham Halmote).'[58]
Ault notes and disagrees with Maitland's comment on the community of the
vill being, 'generally a body of men whom the lawyers call serfs' and shows
that, on the contrary, they were usually freemen.[59] He emphasises that, 'when
it comes to the statutes of autumn the assent of the whole community – lord,
freemen, and villains – was essential'.[60] Ault calls those responsible for the
observance of the laws, termed in the record *custodes, conservatores* and *prepositi*,
'wardens' or 'overseers'. He describes them as being usually 'among the more
substantial and responsible members of the farming community', and notes
that they were elected: 'In general, then, it may be said that the wardens of
the by-laws were elected by the same authority that enacted the by-laws.'[61]

The courts were freestanding inasmuch as they were not an integral part
of the feudal structure: 'The wardens of the village by-laws ... performed no
services for the lord as such. They were not subject to inquest in his court as
to the discharge of their duties. They were not officers of the manor but of
the community that chose them and they served without pay.'[62] If vill and
manor coincided, then the manor court might act as a forum. However, Ault
notes that evidence of non-manorial meetings is plentiful in the sixteenth
century, adding that, 'For evidence of such non-manorial meetings we have
to rely on inference in the earlier centuries, but it is clear and inescapable'.[63]
Ault does not mention Scotland, nor does he speak of 'birlaw courts' or
'birleymen'. Yet it is clear that he is describing the same institution, and we
may suspect that in some instances at least the vernacular word which lies
behind *custodes* and *conservatores* and the like is not 'warden' but 'birleyman'.
Ault's descriptions of the 'wardens' as being 'among the more substantial and
responsible members of the farming community' tallies with the later
Scottish evidence.

The institution of the birlaw seems to have disappeared, or to have been
subsumed into other bodies, rather earlier in England than in Scotland. Birlaw
courts and birleymen perhaps survived longest in north-west England, where
their survival is attested to by dialect dictionaries. Angus Winchester has
recently described rural life in northern England and the Scottish Borders
between 1400 and 1700.[64] His work is based on a detailed study of manorial

---

58 Ibid., p. 41.
59 Pollock and Maitland, i, 624.
60 Ault, 'Open-field husbandry', p. 43.
61 Ibid., pp. 44, 46.
62 Ibid., p. 49.
63 Ibid, p. 54.
64 Angus Winchester, *The harvest of the hills: rural life in northern England and the Scottish
   borders*, 1400–1700 (Edinburgh, 2000). I am grateful to Andrew Humphries, a fellow
   participant in a 'Commons Old and New' Workshop in Oslo in March 2003, for alerting me
   to Angus Winchester's work.

courts, occasionally including birlaw courts, in the northern counties of England (Cumberland, Westmorland, Northumberland, Co. Durham, and the North and West Ridings of Yorkshire) in the sixteenth and seventeenth centuries. He provides the best account to date of the functioning of the birlaw in England.

In a chapter entitled 'Law, Custom and Good Neighbourhood' Winchester notes the antiquity of manor courts. He speculates that they 'represent the incorporation into the manorial system of the village folk-meeting, assumed to be an ancient institution common to much of rural Europe'.[65] He notes Ault's work and the emphasis placed in the records which Ault studied on agreement 'by the community of the vill', and 'by agreement of all the neighbours'. 'Byrlaw' courts, writes Winchester, sometimes described in Latin as *plebiscitum*, were known over much of northern England and in Scotland.[66] He is aware of Dickinson's appendix and the suggested Scandinavian derivation. Two documents in Winchester's own appendix set out articles laid down by sixteenth-century birlaw courts in Yorkshire and Lancashire.[67] These documents, he believes, 'bring us as close as it is possible to come to decision-making in the hill farming hamlets. Both are brief statements of local byelaws, apparently drawn up by hamlet communities and enrolled in the record of the manor court of which the hamlet in question was a member'.[68] These by-laws are reminiscent of the acts of the birlaws of Yester and of Leith already noticed. Thus the first of the by-laws from Halton Gill in Yorkshire in 1579 reads: 'Imprimis that no habitator ther shall kepe any riggold tuppes to com emonges ther ewes in ryding tyme, peyn [under pain of a fine of] iiis.iiiid.'; and the fifth that, 'every inhabitant shall kepe ther stint both winter & somer in field and pasture in peyn of iiis.iiiid'. The other regulations, from Outhwaite in Lancashire in 1580, are headed, 'A byarley and orders maide by the tenants of Hulthwatt as is hereunder sett downe in articles the xiith daie of October by the consentes of all the said tenantes'. Winchester emphasises the role of customary law, the regulation of rights in commons and the preservation of 'good neighbourhood' in the work of the birlaw and manorial courts.[69] Spellings of birlaw range from 'byrlaw' and 'byarley' to *curia sive birelagium* (in Millom, South Cumbria), 'court barron or byerlaye', 'bierlays', 'birelag', 'bierlow', 'byerlay' and 'barley jury'.[70] Birleymen, 'burlawmen' or 'barleymen' appointed by manorial courts are also in evidence.

65 Ibid., p. 42.
66 Ibid., pp. 34, 42. For the use of *plebiscitum* see also Ault, 'Open-field husbandry', p. 41 (*plebiscitum* [1433], *plebeicitum et bilages villate* [1494]), and p. 43 (*plebiscitum*).
67 Winchester, *Harvest of the hills*, Documents 5 and 6 at pp. 172–75.
68 Ibid., p. 172.
69 See especially ibid., pp. 45–48.
70 Ibid., pp. 174, 43, 44 and 48.

Detailed consideration of the reasons for the decline and disappearance of the birlaw is beyond the scope of this article. Writing on the Leith birlaw court in 1927, David Robertson singled out the Heritable Jurisdictions Act 1746 as an agent of change, and pointed also to new agricultural methods of draining, dyking and especially enclosure as bringing to an end the usefulness of the court.[71] In fact, the agents of change were well under way by the mid-eighteenth century, and earlier legislation, such as the Winter Herding Act 1686, the Division of Commonties Act 1695 and the Runrig Act of the same year had already made an impact. Angus Winchester also considers the reasons for the decline of manorial courts, including birlaw courts, in northern England. He regards the centuries covered by his book as 'the heyday of manorial regulation of common land', partly brought about by the increasing enclosure of pasture in the sixteenth and seventeenth centuries.[72] He sees the forces of agricultural change gaining momentum in the eighteenth century as part of a long transition towards individual as against communal ownership, involving 'an assault on the ideals of "ancient custom" and "good neighbourhood" which underpinned the workings of the manorial courts'.[73] The decline of the birlaw, then, is intimately connected with 'the tragedy of the commons', the gradual disappearance of commons or commonties before a more aggressive private ownership.

What more can be said of this adventure of the law? And what of the apparent Scandinavian provenance? I was fortunate enough to be in Oslo for much of the academic year 2002–3 and was able to discuss the birlaw with Scandinavian scholars. There seems no doubt that the Scandinavian etymology is correct. Indeed it was pointed out to me that to talk of birlaw *courts* is otiose as the notion of a court or assembly is implicit in the second element of the word 'birlaw'. One thinks here of 'the Boor Law or commonly pronounced the Birla of Yester', and of the payment of fines 'to the birla'.[74] It also seemed agreed that the etymology of the word is likely to be Old Eastern Scandinavian rather than Old Western Scandinavian. This supports the conclusion already reached that the institution is likely to have spread to Scotland from the south, from England, the Danelaw being the obvious source, rather than from Norwegian settlements in the north and west. Either route is, in principle, quite credible: another Scandinavian legal institution, the 'ting', is commemorated in several Scottish placenames, particularly in Orkney and Shetland; while the ceremony of 'fencing the court', once a

71 Robertson, 'Burlaw court of Leith', pp. 169–70 and 204–05.
72 Winchester, *Harvest of the hills*, ch.7, 'Manor courts in a changing world, 1400–1700', and at p. 148.
73 Ibid., p. 148.
74 Above at p. 77. A further possible instance is the text of *Regiam majestatem* in *APS*, which gives *exceptis burlawis* rather than *exceptis legibus de Burlawis* (above, p. 72).

regular feature of Scottish court procedure, is found also in Scandinavia and the Isle of Man.[75]

It seems probable then that the institution spread north to Scotland from the Danelaw at some time well before the fourteenth century.[76] It is suggested that the birlaw is equally likely to have spread south to other parts of England at an early date, some considerable time before the name was first recorded in the thirteenth century, and that the hesitation of the compilers of *OED* regarding the etymology of the word 'by-law' is unjustified.[77]

The case for origin in the Danelaw is further strengthened by the fact that the birlaw, or an institution very similar, can be found in both Denmark and Sweden, in early modern times at least, and quite possibly earlier, under the name of *bylag* and *byalag*, whereas there seems to be no corresponding nomenclature in Norway. Village communities have been studied extensively in Scandinavia over recent years, following similar studies in Germany and England. Professor Michael Jones of the University of Trondheim has studied institutions for local self-government at what he terms 'the lowest regional level', that is, the 'village', 'farm community' or 'neighbourhood unit'. Building on the work of the Danish legal historian Poul Meyer and others, he has compared such institutions in Ostrobothnia, Sweden, Denmark and Norway.[78] He notes, in particular, the existence of village by-laws termed *byordning* and village leaders termed *byamän* in Ostrobothnia, and the institution of the *byalag* in Sweden. The *byalag* still functions in the south of Sweden in Skåne or Scania (formerly an integral part of Denmark) where membership of the body can be considered a mark of esteem.[79] Given the astonishing longevity

75 For the 'ting', see *inter alia*, *SND*; G. Fellows-Jensen, 'Tingwall, Dingwall and Thingwall' in *Twenty-eight papers presented to Hans Bekker-Nielsen on the occasion of his sixtieth birthday* (Odense, Denmark, 1993), pp. 53–67; and Stefan Brink, 'Law and legal customs in Viking age Scandinavia' in Judith Jesch (ed.), *The Scandinavians from the Vendel period to the tenth century: an ethnographic perspective* (Center for Interdisciplinary Research on Social Stress, San Marino (R.S.M.), 2002), pp. 87–117. 'Fencing the court' marked the official constitution of the court, latterly by a mere form of words, but originally, no doubt, by some kind of physical barrier: see W. Croft Dickinson (ed.), *The sheriff court book of Fife 1515–1522* (Scottish History Society, Edinburgh, 1928), Appendix A, 'The procedure of the court' at p.309; *Balfour's practicks*, i, 273, 'Of courtis' c.viii; and *DOST*, 'Fens, Fence'. The procedure of 'fencing the court' does not appear to be recorded in Anglo-Saxon law, although the possibility cannot be entirely ruled out. I am most grateful to the late Patrick Wormald for assistance on this point.

76 Barbara Crawford makes the same suggestion in 'Scandinavian influence II: historical background', a paper given in 2002 in Perth on Scottish urban origins, p. 4 of 6, which can be accessed on the net at www.tafac.freeuk.com/perthcon/scandinavian2.htm. I am grateful to Dr Crawford for drawing this paper to my attention.

77 Above, p. 80.

78 Michael Jones, 'Landscape – morphology or community? The role of land rights, customs and local institutions for shaping the land in Nordic agrarian societies,' unpublished paper. Professor Jones also spoke to this theme at a Landscape Law and Justice seminar in Oslo. I am most grateful to him for permission to refer to his article in advance of publication.

79 I am grateful to Dr Wilhelm Ostberg of the National Museum in Stockholm for this information.

of the birlaw in Scotland, and to an extent in England also, it would not be surprising if the *byalag* in Denmark and Sweden had an equally long history.

My initial assumption had been that the birlaw had travelled from Scandinavia, probably Denmark, to the Danelaw, and from there to Scotland. However, Professor Stefan Brink of the University of Uppsala, who has made a study of early Scandinavian institutions, while accepting the link between the birlaw and the Danelaw, questioned whether this adventure of the law had begun life in Scandinavia. Rather, he suggested, the borrowing might have taken place in the other direction, from the Danelaw to Scandinavia. Whichever is correct, the reign of Cnut, king of both Denmark and England (1016–35), would seem as likely a period as any.[80] The suggestion that the birlaw was forged in England raises further intriguing questions which cannot be followed in any detail here. Could the institution have evolved on an Anglo-Saxon base, but with an added Scandinavian dimension and a Scandinavian name? The 'Wantage Code' of Ethelred II (978–1016) and the laws of the West Saxon king Ine (688–726) may be relevant here. It is entirely possible that in Scotland too, the birlaw may also have drawn on an existing native institution such as the *comhdhail*. Professor Geoffrey Barrow has suggested, in particular, that the reference to 'Couthal' [for *comhdhail*] in an Arbroath agreement of 1329 'is used in such a casual manner as to suggest that in Angus at least it was a well-known term applied to a species of birlie or burlaw court, so humble indeed that Abbot Geoffrey speaks somewhat contemptuously of its dealing with the "innumerosis actibus inter semetipsos tantummodo contingentibus"'.[81]

The story of the birlaw in Scotland provides a remarkable example of survival. Always a low-key institution, but one with extraordinary staying power, the birlaw continued to function, little altered in its essentials and seldom keeping a formal record, for upwards of half a millennium. At its heart, even after the institution had been subsumed into other bodies, notably the courts of feudal lords, lay the consent and active participation of the community concerned. The birlaw and the birleymen must have impinged on the daily lives of those living on the land in a way that better recorded superior courts never did. It seems clear that the institution, in the form in which we know it, came to Scotland from the Danelaw before legal records begin, perhaps in the tenth or early eleventh century. Whether it originated in the Danelaw, or came from Scandinavia, it may already have had hundreds of years of history behind it. Warren Ault writes of the open-field system so closely associated with the birlaw that, 'Some scholars are able to discern

---

80 Crawford, 'Scandinavian influence', p. 3, suggests that the institution might have travelled north with Malcolm Canmore in 1054.

81 G.W.S. Barrow, *Scotland and its neighbours* (London & Rio Grande, 1992), 'Popular courts', pp. 217–45 at 220.

elements of it in what Tacitus wrote about the Germanic tribes ...'. In addition to Tacitus's *Germania*, Ault also points to the laws of King Ine; while Angus Winchester, as noted above, writes of 'the village folk-meeting, assumed to be an ancient institution common to much of rural Europe'.[82] Altogether a quite remarkable adventure of the law!

I have acquired debts over the years to audiences in Edinburgh, Durham, Dublin and Oslo, and also to the many friends who have generously supplied me with information and references to the birlaw and to birleymen in Scotland. I trust that it does not seem invidious to single out Athol Murray, formerly Keeper of the Records of Scotland, and Alan Borthwick of the National Archives of Scotland by name. I am grateful also to the staff of the National Archives of Scotland for general assistance at a time before the existence of a computer index. My thanks too to Stefan Brink and Doreen Waugh for advice on questions of etymology. Finally I should like to record my gratitude to the Senter for Grunnforskning in Oslo for supporting the Landscape Law and Justice programme in 2002–3, and to Michael Jones of the University of Trondheim for inviting me to participate in it.

82 Ault, *Open-field farming*, p. 16; and above, p. 82.

The role of exceptions in Continental civil procedure

C.H. VAN RHEE[1]

EXCEPTIONS ARE A COMPLICATED phenomenon in the history of European civil procedure. The concept is known not only on the European Continent, but also in the British Isles. In his *An introduction to English legal history*, for example, Professor J.H. Baker mentions dilatory and peremptory exceptions in the context of pleading.[2] Although the relationship between exceptions in England and on the Continent will not be discussed in this paper, it is important to note that the terminology at least coincides in Civil Law and Common Law jurisdictions. A similarity in terminology may indicate a relationship. Although such a relationship needs to be proven as regards exceptions, it is clear that in respect of other aspects of civil procedure more than nominal relationships do exist, for example as regards the 'essoins' of the medieval Common Law,[3] which were also to be found in Continental civil procedure.[4] I think that this needs to be emphasised for it shows that the 'approximation' of English and Continental civil procedural law is not a recent phenomenon. It started long before the introduction of the Civil Procedure Rules of Lord Woolf in 1999.[5] This being stated, let us now return to the exceptions on the European Continent.

In Continental Europe, different opinions have been voiced regarding the definition of *exceptiones* and their role in civil litigation. Even though they

1 The author would like to thank Jan Hallebeek (Amsterdam) and Eric Pool (Amsterdam) for their critical remarks on a draft version of this paper. The present paper is a slightly revised version of an article that was published in L. de Ligt, J. de Ruiter, E. Slob, J.M. Tevel, M. van de Vrugt, L.C. Winkel (eds.), *Viva vox iuris romani: essays in honour of Johannes Emil Spruit* (Amsterdam, 2002), pp. 297–313.

2 J.H. Baker, *An introduction to English legal history* (London, 2002), p. 77.

3 J.H. Baker, op. cit., p. 58; P. Brand, 'Delay in the English common law courts (twelfth to fourteenth centuries)' in C.H. van Rhee (ed.), T*he law's delay: essays on undue delay in civil litigation* (Antwerp/Oxford/New York, 2004), pp. 36–37.

4 E.g. C.H. van Rhee, *Litigation and legislation. Civil procedure at first instance in the Great Council for the Netherlands in Malines (1522–1559)* (Brussels, 1997), pp. 290–91 (the act of casting the 'essoins' was called 'sinnen' or 'sumen' in Dutch). See also P. Hyams, 'The common law and the French connection' in R.A. Brown (ed.), *Proceedings of the Battle Conference on Anglo-Norman Studies*, II (Ipswich etc., 1979), p. 77.

5 On this subject see also: C.H. van Rhee, 'Civil procedure: A European ius commune?' in

form a problematic area of the law, recently promulgated legislation continues to make use of them. An example is the Spanish Code of Civil Procedure.[6] We also encounter them in the recently modernised Dutch Code of Civil Procedure.[7] The decision to retain *exceptiones* is remarkable in the light of recurrent pleas to have them abolished. These pleas have been voiced in the Netherlands for at least a century.[8]

The present article focuses on aspects of the historical development of exceptions, more specifically on an important division of *exceptiones* introduced by Gaius in his Institutes (IV, 120). The central theme of this article is the role of this division in determining the point at which particular defences had to be introduced in the proceedings. I will conclude by tracing the process by which this long significant distinction between different types of exception has disappeared from modern Dutch civil procedure. I shall start my inquiry at the time of the Roman formulary procedure, for this is the procedure where the concept of *exceptiones* (most probably)[9] first appears in history; according to Gaius, they were unknown in the older procedure of *legis actiones*.[10] Subsequently, I will make some remarks with reference to developments in the medieval *Ius Commune*. The history of exceptions in France is the next stop. Finally, Dutch law in the nineteenth, twentieth and the beginning of the twenty-first centuries will be discussed.

European Review of Private Law (2000), 589–611; C.H. van Rhee, 'Towards a procedural ius commune?' in J. Smits, G. Lubbe (eds.), *Remedies in Zuid-Afrika en Europa* (Antwerp, 2003), pp. 217–32; C.H. van Rhee, 'English and Continental civil procedure: similarities today and in the past' in J. Sondel et al. (eds.), *Roman law as formative of modern legal systems. Studies in honour of Wieslaw Litewski* (Krakow, 2003), pp. 201–16.

6 Ley 1/2000, January 7, de Enjuiciamiento Civil, Article 405.

7 Articles 11, 110, and 128.

8 In a legislative proposal dating from the start of the twentieth century, the distinction between defence on the merits and *exceptiones* had actually been removed. However, this proposal was not promulgated. See below and also C.H. van Rhee, '"Ons tegenwoordig sukkelproces". Nederlandse opvattingen over de toekomst van het burgerlijk procesrecht rond 1920' in *Legal History Review*, 68 (2000), 344. More recently W.D.H. Asser, then Advocate-General at the Dutch Supreme Court (*Hoge Raad*), claimed that the concept of *exceptiones* should be struck from the statute book. See HR 22 October 1993, NJ 1994, 374. See also W.D.H. Asser, 'Rechtsvordering, de geschiedenis voorbij?' in M.E. Franke et al. (eds.), *Historisch vooruitzicht. Opstellen over rechtsgeschiedenis en burgerlijk recht* (BW-krant jaarboek 1994) (Arnhem, 1994), pp. 46–48.

9 E.g. H. Seelig, *Die prozessuale Behandlung materiellrechtlicher Einreden – heute und einst –* (Cologne etc., 1980), p. 14.

10 Gai. Inst. IV, 108.

ROMAN LAW

The formulary procedure

In an often discussed paragraph in his *Institutes* (IV, 116), Gaius explains why *exceptiones* were introduced. He writes: 'Exceptions have been provided for the protection of defendants, since it is often the case that, though a man is liable at *ius civile*, his condemnation in an action would be inequitable.'[11] On the basis of this paragraph one may conclude that Gaius considered *exceptiones* to operate as 'equitable' corrections of the *ius civile* (they could, of course, also operate as corrections of the *ius honorarium*). They had either a procedural character, for example, when it was claimed that the judge lacked jurisdiction, or were based on grounds derived from substantive law.[12] *Exceptiones* took the guise of a clause inserted in the *formula* of remedies (actions) of strict law granted to the plaintiff at the request of the defendant. If proven, they resulted in the plaintiff losing his case, even though he himself had also succeeded in proving the necessary facts.

Exceptiones are divided by Gaius into two groups. He distinguishes *exceptiones dilatoriae* and *exceptiones peremptoriae*.[13] As regards the former *exceptiones*, Gaius remarks that they are defences *quae ad tempus valent*, i.e. defences which can only be advanced for a (limited) period of time. An example of a situation in which they could be used is when it had been agreed that something would not be claimed within a specific period. If, nevertheless, an action was brought within the agreed period, a dilatory exception could be introduced.[14] Gaius also further distinguishes *exceptiones dilatoriae ex persona*. The author gives as an example the *exceptio cognitoria*, which could be requested if the opposing party had appointed a representative in an action without having the power to do so, or if a representative had been appointed who was not allowed to undertake representation.[15] *Exceptiones peremptoriae* are, according to Gaius, defences 'that are available at any time and cannot be evaded'.[16] By virtue of them the defendant argued that the plaintiff could never succeed in his claim, for example, because judgement had already been pronounced on the same issue (the defence of former adjudication or *res iudicata*).[17]

11 'Conparatae sunt autem exceptiones defendendorum eorum gratia cum quibus agitur. Saepe enim accidit, ut quis iure civili teneatur, sed iniquum sit eum iudicio condemnari.'
12 Kaser/Hackl, *Das römische Zivilprozessrecht* (Munich, 1996), pp. 242 and 261.
13 Gai. Inst. IV, 120. See also D 44,1,3. On the latter text, see D. Simon, *Untersuchungen zum Justinianischen Zivilprozess* (Munich, 1969), p. 96: '[…] eine mit ziemlicher Sicherheit überarbeitete Stelle, in der aber die ursprünglich gaianische Vorstellung noch zu fassen ist […].'
14 Gai. Inst. IV, 122.
15 Gai. Inst. IV, 124. On the *exceptio cognitoria* (and the *exceptio procuratoria*), see D. Simon, op. cit., pp. 66ff.
16 'quae perpetuo valent nec evitari possunt.'
17 Gai. Inst. IV, 121.

The above division probably did not have any significance in regard to the point in the proceedings a particular exception could be introduced (a role performed, as will be seen below, by this division in later periods). After all, in principle the insertion of all *exceptiones* in the *formula* had to be requested before *litis contestatio* (joinder of issue), i.e. in the initial phase of the procedure (*in iure*): this was the time when the magistrate established by which *formula* the *iudex* would have to decide the case.[18]

The real significance of Gaius's division becomes clear if one realises that Gaius made his classification from the perspective of the plaintiff, who in the initial phase of the proceedings (*in iure*) had to decide whether or not to continue the action.[19] If at this stage the plaintiff came to the conclusion that the defendant could successfully plead one or more *exceptiones dilatoriae*, he was advised to postpone the action until the grounds for that exception had disappeared.[20] If he nonetheless continued his action, he would lose his case. Additionally he would lose the possibility of starting new proceedings after the period of time during which the dilatory exception could be invoked had passed. If the plaintiff decided that the defendant could invoke one or more *exceptiones peremptoriae*, a postponement of the action was of no use, since these exceptions did not disappear as a result of lapse of time. This also explains why Gaius categorises the above *exceptiones ex persona* as *dilatoriae*. After all, even though they did not disappear as a result of lapse of time, they could be neutralised by a postponement of the action until, for example, instead of the original 'representative', a representative who was allowed to act as such had been appointed.[21]

On the basis of the above one may conclude that in the first centuries of the Christian era, the role of *exceptiones* in civil litigation was tightly linked to certain peculiarities of the Roman Law of that period. As a result, a change in the concept of the exception was unavoidable following later developments in Roman Law. As will appear below, these developments are of great significance for a study of the modern concept.

---

18 M. Lemosse, 'À propos du régime des exceptions dans le procès postclassique' in *Studi in onore di Cesare Sanfilippo*, I (Milan, 1982), p. 244. Some doubt as to the relevance of the division for the moment of introduction of defences is caused by Gaius IV, 125. There it is stated that *exceptiones peremptoriae* could be requested later in the proceedings on the basis of *restitutio in integrum*. At the same time, Gaius claims that it was an open question whether this was possible as regards *exceptiones dilatoriae*. The reason for his uncertainty is not clear. On this text, see F. Eisele, *Zur Geschichte der processualen Behandlung der Exceptionen* (Berlin, 1875); M. Amelotti, *La prescrizione delle azioni in diritto Romano* (Milan, 1958), pp. 78ff.

19 D. Simon, op. cit., p. 94.

20 Gai. Inst. IV, 123.

21 D. Simon, op. cit., pp. 95–97.

The cognitio procedure

The concept of *exceptio*[22] changed when the formulary procedure was relegated to the background. This development resulted eventually in the formal abrogation of this type of litigation in AD 342. As a result, the *cognitio* procedure was the only procedure left.[23] This procedure is the root from which medieval Romano-canonical process developed and is therefore the distant ancestor of modern continental systems of civil litigation. It was not confined by the 'forms of action' of the formulary procedure. An exception in this procedure may be defined as a preliminary defence which aims at having the claim dismissed on grounds other than the substance of the claim.[24] These grounds can have either a procedural character or be derived from substantive law.[25]

The distinction between *exceptiones dilatoriae* and *exceptiones peremptoriae* continued to apply. However, regarding their definition, the perspective changed. Gaius had stressed that dilatory exceptions could only be advanced for a certain period of time. Justinian in his *Institutes* added, that they were exceptions *quae [...] temporis dilationem tribuunt*,[26] i.e. defences by means of which the defendant obtained a postponement of the action. With reference to peremptory exceptions, Gaius had stressed that they were valid for an indefinite period of time and, consequently, could not be evaded. Justinian, however, states that they could always be brought against the plaintiff's action and could at all times block the case (*quae semper agentibus obstant et semper rem de qua agitur peremunt*).[27] This change in perspective was related to the formulary procedure being replaced by the *cognitio* procedure.

As stated above, the original division was based on features of the formulary procedure. After all, in the formulary procedure it was important for the plaintiff to distinguish dilatory from peremptory exceptions during the initial phase: *exceptiones dilatoriae* could be avoided by a postponement of the action at that stage. Such a postponement was crucial, since otherwise dilatory exceptions would acquire peremptory force.[28] In the *cognitio*

---

22 In the *cognitio* procedure the term *praescriptio* was used as a synonym for *exceptio*. See Kaser/Hackl, op. cit., p. 487.

23 On the *cognitio* procedure, see e.g. L. Wenger, *Institutes of the Roman law of civil procedure*, translated by O.H. Fisk (New York, 1940).

24 Inst. 4,13pr, which replaces the above cited Gai. Inst. IV, 116, may be mentioned in support of this interpretation. After all, it does not present the *exceptiones* as corrections of the *ius civile* (or the *ius honorarium*) anymore, but as defences against an in itself justifiable action.

25 Kaser/Hackl, op. cit., p. 487.

26 Inst. 4,13,10.

27 Inst. 4,13,9.

28 For this reason, Gaius's division of preliminary defences into dilatory and peremptory exceptions has been criticised. After all, dilatory exceptions were at the same time potential peremptory defences. See S. Solazzi, 'Sulle classificazioni delle "exceptiones"' in *Archivio Giuridico 'Filippo Serafini'*, CXXXVII (1949), 3ff. See also M. Lemosse, op.cit., pp. 244–45.

procedure dilatory defences retained their temporary character even if the plaintiff decided to continue the action: in this procedure the plaintiff could always bring a new case on the same issue after having his action dismissed following a successful dilatory defence.[29] Nevertheless, the distinction between the two types of preliminary defences remained important in the initial stages of the proceedings, but now mainly from the perspective of the defendant: it played a significant role with respect to the moment particular defences had to be introduced and proven. This appears from the rules governing these aspects of the proceedings, which were closely linked to the traditional division of defences.[30] Of course, the distinction remained relevant for the plaintiff as well, but now only because it allowed him to decide whether or not a new action could be brought on the same issue after his action had been dismissed as a result of a successful preliminary defence (this subject will not be investigated in depth in the present article).

It was laid down that *exceptiones dilatoriae* had to be advanced and proven before *litis contestatio* (it should be noted that *litis contestatio* in the *cognitio* procedure, even though it was situated in the initial phase of the procedure, differed from the highly technical concept of *litis contestatio* in the formulary procedure).[31] Later a distinction was made between *exceptiones* having a procedural character (whether these defences should be classified as dilatory or should be viewed as a separate class of defences is subject to discussion)[32] and *exceptiones dilatoriae*. The former group of exceptions had to be advanced and proven before *litis contestatio*. Regarding the latter type of exceptions, however, it was determined that they only needed to be proven after the plaintiff had proven the facts advanced by him.[33]

Originally, *exceptiones peremptoriae* needed to be advanced in the initial phase of the proceedings as well.[34] By the time of Justinian, however, it seems to have been possible to introduce peremptory defences at any stage in the proceedings.[35]

29 M.A. von Bethmann-Hollweg, *Der Civilprozess des gemeinen Rechts in geschichtlicher Entwicklung* III: *Der römische Civilprozess* III (Cognitiones) (Bonn, 1866), p. 267; Kaser/Hackl, op. cit., 491.
30 See also M. Lemosse, op. cit., pp. 246–48. Cf. P. Collinet, *La procédure par libelle* (Paris, 1932), p. 198.
31 C 8,35,12; H. Seelig, op. cit., p. 27; Kaser/Hackl, op. cit., p. 489.
32 According to M.A. von Bethmann-Hollweg, *Der römische Civilprozess* III (Cognitiones), pp. 264ff, procedural exceptions fell outside the traditional division of dilatory and peremptory defences. This seems to be the opinion of most modern authors too. See, e.g., Kaser/Hackl, op. cit., p. 584; D. Simon, op. cit., pp. 65ff and 93ff; H. Seelig, op. cit., p. 27. P. Collinet, op. cit., pp. 197ff, is of the opinion that at least part of the procedural exceptions are dilatory *ex persona*.
33 C 4,19,19; Kaser/Hackl, op. cit., p. 584; D. Simon, op. cit., p. 97; M. Lemosse, op. cit., pp. 243ff.
34 Kaser/Hackl, op. cit., p. 489.
35 C 7,50,2pr. and C 8,35,8; Kaser/Hackl, op. cit., p. 585; P. Collinet, op. cit., pp. 306–07 and pp. 358–59; D. Simon, op. cit., pp. 99–101. See also the literature referred to by M. Lemosse, op. cit., 245, note 6. For detailed information on exceptions at the time of Justinian, see

THE MEDIEVAL 'IUS COMMUNE'

In medieval legal treatises preliminary defences were dealt with at length. The medieval *Ius Commune* adopted the division of exceptions into *exceptiones dilatoriae* and *exceptiones peremptoriae*.[36] This distinction continued to play a role from the perspective of the defendant who had to decide as to the moment when defences were to be introduced and proven. A notable development in the period under consideration was the consolidation of the preliminary procedural defences of the late *cognitio* procedure under the heading of *exceptiones declinatoriae iudicii* (also *exceptiones declinatoriae fori*). Since these declinatory exceptions were viewed as falling within the larger group of dilatory exceptions, the terminology *exceptiones dilatoriae solutionis* was coined in order to refer to the non-declinatory *exceptiones dilatoriae*.[37]

With reference to the *exceptiones dilatoriae* (including the procedural defences now termed *exceptiones declinatoriae*) the rules of the late *cognitio* procedure continued to apply.[38] However, deviations from these rules can be found. In Canon Law, for example, we find a flexible approach to the introduction of dilatory defences if the defendant only gained knowledge of circumstances justifying such defences at a late phase of the proceedings.[39] Also dilatory defences which would result in the judgement being void (e.g. the defence of lack of jurisdiction *ratione materiae* or the defence that the judge or plaintiff was excommunicated) could be introduced at any stage in the proceedings.[40]

Exceptiones peremptoriae continued to be subject to the Justinianic rule that their introduction was not linked to a particular phase of the proceedings.[41] We also find deviations from this rule, where Canon Law distinguished a peculiar kind of peremptory exception, the so-called *exceptiones litis ingressum*

P. Collinet, *La nature des actions, des interdits et des exceptions dans l'oeuvre de Justinien* (Paris, 1947), pp. 487ff. On the time for the introduction of peremptory exceptions in practice, see U. Zilletti, *Studi sul processo civile giustinianeo* (Milan, 1965), p. 168: 'Ora in tanto ciò è possibile, in quanto vi sia una tendenza che sul concreto piano processuale unifichi le eccezioni dilatorie sostanziali e le eccezioni perentorie in una più generica categoria di "difese" spettanti al convenuto, favorita anche dall'emergere di *praescriptiones* di incidenza puramente istruttoria.'

36 A. Engelmann et al., *A history of Continental civil procedure* (Boston, 1927), p. 467.
37 P. Fournier, *Les officialités au moyen age* (Paris, 1880), p. 161; A. Engelmann et al., op. cit., p. 468; H. Hoehne, 'Pilii Medicinensis Summula' in *Ius Commune*, IX (1980), pp. 161ff; W. Litewski, *Der römisch-kanonische Zivilprozess nach den älteren ordines iudiciarii*, I (Kraków, 1999), pp. 305 and 309ff.
38 P. Fournier, op. cit., p. 167; W. Litewski, op. cit., p. 309.
39 X 2,25,4. P. Fournier, op. cit., pp. 162–63; W. Litewski, op. cit., pp. 307–08.
40 X 2,25,12. See also VI 2,12,1; Clem. 2,10,1; P. Fournier, op. cit., p. 163; W. Litewski, op. cit., p. 308.
41 See above and W. Litewski, op. cit., p. 308.

impedientes. To this class belong the exceptions of former adjudication (*res iudicata*), settlement out of court (accord) and submission to arbitration. These defences could be introduced before the dilatory exceptions. Since they did not necessarily bar the plaintiff from bringing a new action on the same issue, their classification as peremptory exceptions is not always justified (they may have been classified as such for historic reasons).[42]

THE FRENCH ORDINANCE OF 1667

The important French Ordinance on civil procedure of 1667[43] was, to a large extent, reproduced in the 1806 *Code de procédure civile*. Since the 1667 Ordinance incorporates many medieval developments in civil procedure, it may rightly be viewed as the link between medieval and nineteenth-century civil procedure. The Ordinance also serves this purpose for Dutch procedural law, since the Dutch Code of Civil Procedure (1838) was to a certain degree a copy of the French 1806 Code. The 1667 Ordinance is discussed extensively by Pothier in his *Traité de la procédure civile*, which will be used together with the Ordinance as the point of departure in discussing preliminary defences in French law before codification.[44]

The Ordinance mentions the usual categories of preliminary defences: declinatory (these were also known as *fins de non procéder*)[45] (Article VI.3), dilatory (*titre* 9), and peremptory (Article V.5) exceptions. As regards peremptory defences, Pothier introduced a distinction not expressly to be found either in the 1667 Ordinance or in Roman or medieval sources:[46] they concern either 'la forme' or 'le droit'.[47] According to Pothier, the former 'tendent à faire renvoyer le défendeur de la demande contre lui donnée' because of defects in the writ of summons or its service. These defects could, for example, arise when the claim was omitted from the writ ('parce que l'exploit de demande n'est pas libellé') or when in his report the bailiff (*huissier*) did not mention the place where he was registered.[48] Peremptory defences concerning 'la forme', if successful, ended an action without

---

42 On the particular character of the *exceptiones litis ingressum impedientes*, see J. Kohler, *Prozessrechtliche Forschungen* (Berlin, 1889), pp. 88ff. See also A. Engelmann, op. cit., p. 469; P. Fournier, op. cit., p. 168.

43 F. Isambert et al. (eds.), *Recueil général des anciennes lois françaises, depuis l'an 420 jusqu'à la Révolution de 1789, XVIII* (Paris, 1829), pp. 103ff.

44 I consulted *Oeuvres de R.-J. Pothier contenant les traités du droit français*, VI (Brussels, 1832).

45 R.-J. Pothier, op. cit., I.II.IV.I. The following defences were considered to be declinatory in character: the defence 'pour cause d'incompétance', the defence 'pour cause de privilège', and the defence 'pour cause de litispendence' (R.-J. Pothier, op. cit., I.II.IV.I).

46 The distinction certainly does not coincide with the medieval distinction between ordinary peremptory defences and *exceptiones litis ingressum impedientes*.

47 R.-J. Pothier, op. cit., I.II.II.

48 R.-J. Pothier, op. cit., I.II.II.I.

barring the plaintiff from bringing a new case on the same matter. It is therefore hard to see why these defences were classified as peremptory other than for historical reasons. The *exceptiones peremptoriae* which concerned 'le droit' were also known as *fins de non recevoir*. They were defences 'qui, sans entrer dans le mérite de la demande, tendent à prouver que le demandeur n'a pas le droit de la former, n'y est pas recevable [...]'.[49]

On the basis of the above distinctions, the following rules applied concerning the moment particular defences had to be introduced. As was usual, declinatory defences had to be advanced before the other preliminary defences.[50] If successful, they could result in a referral (*renvoi*) of the case to the competent court (Article VI.1 of the 1667 Ordinance). Next came, according to Pothier, peremptory defences concerning 'la forme'.[51] Subsequently, dilatory exceptions had to be introduced. According to Article IX.1 of the 1667 Ordinance a defendant who wished to advance several dilatory defences needed to propose them simultaneously.[52] An exception was made for the *exception pour délibérer* (i.e. a preliminary defence available to presumptive heirs who could thereby postpone the action in order to allow a decision about their acceptance of the succession), which could be introduced separately before the other dilatory exceptions (Article IX.2). Only peremptory defences concerning 'le droit' could, according to Pothier, be advanced at any stage prior to final judgement (to this end Pothier refers to C 8,35,8). However, Pothier limits this rule to cases where the defendant was unaware at earlier phases of the proceedings of grounds for introducing such defences. If he was aware of them, he ought to have advanced his peremptory defences during the initial stage of the proceedings. Nevertheless, a defendant who chose to introduce defences later without good cause was not barred from doing so: if he knowingly failed to advance defences before *litis contestatio*, he did not lose the right to advance them; he would, however, not be awarded the expenses of the proceedings on the merits which, retrospectively, appeared to have been unnecessary due to the success of a peremptory defence (he would, of course, recover his other expenses because of the successful outcome of the case).[53]

---

49 R.-J. Pothier, op. cit., I.II.II.II.
50 R.-J. Pothier, op. cit., I.II.III.
51 R.-J. Pothier, op. cit., I.II.II.I.
52 Attempts to concentrate the introduction of dilatory defences date from medieval Canon Law. See X 2,25,4; P. Fournier, op. cit., 162; A. Engelmann, op. cit., p. 468. Whether E. Deroy was right when he claimed that the concentration of the introduction of dilatory defences was an innovation of the 1667 Ordinance may therefore be doubted. See E. Deroy, *Des exceptions dilatoires* (Paris, 1898), p. 7.
53 R.-J. Pothier, op. cit., I.II.II.II.

THE CODE DE PROCÉDURE CIVILE (1806)

In 1811 the French *Code de procédure civile* came into force in the Low Countries as a result of the annexation of the Netherlands to the French Empire. It remained the law in this area long after the Netherlands had regained their independence: the *Code* was only replaced by a native product in 1838. Since this article is also concerned with the antecedents of preliminary defences in the Netherlands, the point of departure here (in addition to the *Code*) is one of the rare Dutch handbooks on the French *Code* by W.IJ. van Hamelsveld, published in 1823.[54]

Van Hamelsveld distinguishes the usual categories of preliminary defences, including the two types of peremptory defences introduced by Pothier.[55] It should be noted, however, that the terminology 'peremptory defence' does not occur as such in the *Code*.[56]

We do not find many deviations from the 1667 Ordinance in regard to the timing of the introduction of exceptions. Declinatory exceptions, which, if successful, resulted in the remanding of the case to the competent court (*renvoi*), had to be advanced before all other defences. This is determined by Articles 168 and 169 of the *Code*. It should, however, be noted that in these Articles the term 'declinatory defence' is not used. Nevertheless, it appears that declinatory defences are meant where Article 168 refers to 'la partie qui aura été appelée devant un tribunal autre que celui qui doit connaître de la contestation'. This phrase was interpreted as comprising defendants who could introduce the defence of lack of jurisdiction *ratione personae* (Articles 168 and 170), as well as the defences of *lis pendens* and *connexité* (Article 171).[57]

Dilatory defences had to be introduced simultaneously, before a defence on the merits (Article 186).[58] According to Van Hamelsveld, the simultaneous introduction of dilatory exceptions was justified by the fact that as a result only a single postponement of the action was necessary. Allowing the separate

---

54 W.IJ. van Hamelsveld, *Manier van procederen in burgerlijke regtszaken volgens de thans nog bestaande wet van burgerlijke regtspleging*, 2 vols. (Amsterdam, 1823).

55 W.IJ. van Hamelsveld, op. cit., I, 83–84.

56 Cf. J. ten Brink, *De exceptiën en hare wettelijke regeling* (Leiden, 1901), pp. 39–40.

57 See F.R. Pennink, *Aanteekeningen op verschillende artikelen van het Wetboek van Burgerlijke Regtsvordering* (Zutphen, 1853), p. 69. See also E. Pigeau, *La procédure civile des tribunaux de France*, I (Paris, 1807), pp. 130ff.

58 According to E. Deroy, op. cit., pp. 8, 159 and 168, this rule was difficult to apply. In his opinion the *Code* only recognised two defences which could be classified as dilatory, whereas it was exactly these two defences which, also according to the *Code*, could be introduced separately. By way of explanation Deroy suggests that Article 186 was a direct copy of the equivalent rule in the 1667 Ordinance, which recognised more than two dilatory exceptions. See also C.W. Star Busmann, *De exceptio plurium litisconsortium in het burgerlijk procesrecht* (Utrecht, 1902), pp. 49–50, who notes that Article 159 of the Dutch Code of Civil Procedure of 1838, in its turn, was a direct translation of Article 186 of its French counterpart.

introduction of dilatory defences would have caused multiple postponements and, consequently, additional delay.[59] According to Article 187, the *exception pour délibérer* was exempt from this rule and could be introduced separately, before the other dilatory defences.[60] According to E. Pigeau, who played a prominent role in the preparation of the *Code de procédure civile*, dilatory exceptions could also be advanced separately, if the necessity of their introduction only became clear after the introduction of earlier dilatory defences.[61] This rule, which originated in medieval Canon Law, was, however, not expressed in the *Code*, nor is it mentioned by Van Hamelsveld.

The time for introducing peremptory defences is unclear due to the fact that the *Code* does not use the terminology 'peremptory defence'. It is not certain whether such defences were recognised at all, and if so, which defences should be classified as peremptory. As stated above, Van Hamelsveld claimed that Pothier's distinction between peremptory defences concerning 'la forme' and 'le droit' continued to apply. As regards peremptory exceptions concerning 'la forme',[62] Van Hamelsveld maintained that they had to be introduced before all other preliminary defences except for the defence based on lack of jurisdiction (*ratione personae*; as stated above, the defences of *lis pendens* and *connexité* should also be brought under this heading) (Articles 168–171).[63] As regards peremptory defences concerning 'le droit', Van Hamelsveld suggested applying the Roman rule that they could be introduced at all stages in the proceedings (C 7,50,2).[64] Pigeau, however, was of the opinion that a defendant who proposed a defence on the merits before a peremptory defence concerning 'le droit' should have his exception denied. More generally, Pigeau held that according to the *Code* the following order should be observed in introducing defences: declinatory defences, peremptory defences concerning 'la forme', dilatory defences, peremptory defences concerning 'le droit', and, subsequently, defences on the merits.[65]

Exceptions based on lack of jurisdiction *ratione materiae* could be advanced at any stage of the proceedings (Article 170; cf. Article IV.1 of the 1667

59 W.IJ. van Hamelsveld, op. cit., I, 89.

60 The wording of Article 187 makes it doubtful whether the defence *pour délibérer* can be classified as a dilatory defence ('L'héritier [etc.] pourront ne proposer leurs exceptions dilatoires qu'après l'échéance des délais pour faire inventaire et délibérer'). Most authors do, however, classify this defence as such.

61 E. Pigeau, op. cit., p. 188.

62 The following defences were considered to be peremptory concerning 'la forme': the defence that the claim was void due to irregularities in the service of the summons or otherwise, the exception that preliminary conciliation had been omitted, and exceptions concerning the person of either the plaintiff or the defendant ('incapacité' or 'défaut d'intérêt') (E. Pigeau, op. cit., p. 141). Cf. Article 173 of the *Code*.

63 See also E. Pigeau, op. cit., p. 129.

64 W.IJ. van Hamelsveld, op. cit., I, 84–85. See also E. Pigeau, op. cit., p. 129.

65 E. Pigeau, op. cit., pp. 129 and 194.

Ordinance). According to Van Hamelsveld and French textbook writers this was because such lack of jurisdiction had to be taken into consideration *ex officio*, i.e. even if it was not introduced by way of a defence. This was because jurisdiction *ratione materiae* was considered to be a matter of *l'intérêt public*.[66]

DUTCH PREDECESSORS OF THE 1838 CODE OF CIVIL PROCEDURE

The Dutch Code of Civil Procedure (1838) was not the first code drafted in the Netherlands containing procedural rules. In this section I will discuss four earlier (draft) codes dating from 1799,[67] 1807/1808,[68] 1809,[69] and 1820[70] respectively (the 1820 draft is a draft of a Civil Code).[71] Regarding preliminary defences, each code proposed a decisive break with the past.

The first three codes follow a similar pattern. They abolished the classification of preliminary defences into declinatory, dilatory and peremptory exceptions. Instead they determined that only eight named defences were to be introduced preliminarily. These defences had to be advanced simultaneously. All other defences were to be introduced at the same time as the defence on the merits. An advantage of these rules was that differences of opinion regarding the category of exceptions to which a particular defence belonged were prevented. As a consequence, the time for introducing specific defences was very clear.

The 1820 (draft) code approached preliminary defences from a slightly different angle. It reintroduced the familiar subdivision into declinatory, dilatory and peremptory defences. This division was significant for various reasons, for example, as regards the ruling the court had to give when a defence of a particular type was successfully introduced. The division was also important in order in establishing whether or not a plaintiff could start

---

66 W.IJ. van Hamelsveld, op. cit., I, 86. See also E. Pigeau, op. cit., p. 130.

67 *Algemeene manier van procedeeren* (The Hague, 1799). Articles 60–66 on preliminary defences are to be found in the section *Manier van procedeeren in civiele zaaken, zoo voor de burgerlyke rechtbanken als voor de departementaale gerechtshoven.*

68 I consulted J. van der Linden, *Ontwerp Burgerlijk Wetboek 1807/1808*, ed. J.Th. de Smidt (Amsterdam, 1967). Articles 21–32 on preliminary defences are to be found in book 4, title 6.

69 *Wetboek op de regterlijke instellingen en regtspleging in het Koningrijk Holland* (The Hague, 1809), Articles 600–07.

70 I consulted *Ontwerp van het Burgerlijk Wetboek voor het Koningrijk der Nederlanden aan de Staten-Generaal aangeboden den 22sten November 1820* (2nd ed., Leiden, 1864), Articles 3277–93.

71 The 1815 draft of a Civil Code also contains rules on preliminary defences. Unfortunately, I did not have the opportunity to consult a copy of this unpublished draft. See, however, J. ten Brink, op. cit., p. 38.

a new action on the same matter after he had lost his original case due to a successful exception. Surprisingly enough, the division did not play a role with reference to the time for introducing defences. Article 3292 contains a rule, which may be compared with the provisions concerning preliminary defences in the preceding (draft) codes. The Article lays down that nine specifically named exceptions could be introduced before the defence on the merits (most likely they had to be introduced at the same time, although this was not expressly stated in the 1820 draft); all other exceptions had to be joined with this defence.

THE DUTCH CODE OF CIVIL PROCEDURE (1838)

The 1838 Code of Civil Procedure was, to a large extent, based on the French 1806 Code. The innovative Dutch ideas in regard to preliminary defences, reflected in the (draft) legislation from the period 1799–1820, did not leave many traces. The role of the traditional division in determining the moment particular defences had to be introduced, which was absent in the Dutch rules from 1799–1820, was again present in 1838 (at least, to a certain extent; see further below). Nevertheless, the 1838 Code was not an exact copy of its French counterpart. Differences between the Dutch legislation and the French 1806 *Code* in the area of preliminary defences can, to a large extent, be attributed to deliberations in the Dutch Parliament.[72]

The important role played by the traditional division of exceptions as regards the moment of introducing defences does not appear directly from the Code itself. After all, like its French counterpart the Code only explicitly refers to dilatory exceptions in this respect (Article 159). However, parliamentary history shows that the legislator had the traditional division at the back of his mind when drafting the Code. This appears from Article 160, which in its final version determined that all 'other' preliminary defences, i.e. defences which had not been assigned a particular time for their introduction, were to be advanced together with the defence on the merits. Originally 'other' read 'peremptory', but because it was doubted whether all defences one wished to bring within the ambit of Article 160 did have a peremptory character, the term 'peremptory' was replaced by 'other'.[73] Consequently, the Code made it necessary to determine whether a particular defence was dilatory in nature, or belonged to the category of 'other' exceptions.

72 See J. van den Honert, *Handboek voor de burgerlijke regtsvordering in het Koningrijk der Nederlanden* (Amsterdam, 1839), pp. 274ff; J.J.F. Noordziek, *Geschiedenis der beraadslagingen gevoerd in de Kamers der Staten-Generaal over het ontwerp van Wetboek van Burgerlijke Regtspleging*, I (The Hague, 1885).

73 J. van den Honert, op. cit., pp. 280–81.

In conformity with the French *Code*, Article 155 of its Dutch counterpart determined that the defence of the judge lacking jurisdiction *ratione personae* had to be advanced separately before the other defences. This defence was to be followed by defences based on *lis pendens* (Article 158), on *connexité* (also Article 158)[74] and on the nullity of the summons (Article 93). It was unclear whether the last defence had to precede or to follow the former two defences; the Code was ambiguous on this particular point.[75] Although the French *Code* of 1806 was also ambiguous on the point, it was generally held that the defence based on *lis pendens* and *connexité* should precede the exception based on nullity of the summons, since the former two defences were declinatory in nature, whereas the latter could be classified as peremptory concerning 'la forme'.[76] This approach was of no help for Dutch procedural law, since Dutch procedure did not recognise peremptory defences concerning 'la forme' as a separate class of exceptions.[77]

Dilatory defences came next in line. They had to be introduced simultaneously[78] with the exception of the defence *pour délibérer*, which could be advanced separately before the other dilatory defences (Article 159). Subsequently, three peremptory exceptions could be introduced separately: the defence of former adjudication (*res iudicata*), settlement out of court (accord) and the defence concerning the person of either the plaintiff or the defendant (Article 160). We do not find this rule in the French Code.[79] All other defences (except for the defence that the judge lacked jurisdiction *ratione materiae*, which could be advanced at any stage of the proceedings (Article 156) had to be joined with the defence on the merits (Article 160). The latter rule was also absent in the French *Code* of 1806. As stated above, commentators on the *Code* made a distinction between peremptory defences concerning 'la forme' and peremptory defences concerning 'le droit' and referred to Roman law regarding the time for introducing the latter type of peremptory defences.

---

74 In a defence based on *connexité* it was stated that the action should be brought before another court of law where a related lawsuit was pending.

75 F.R. Pennink, op. cit., pp. 68–69.

76 E. Pigeau, op. cit., p. 141.

77 R. van Boneval Faure, *Het Nederlandsche burgerlijk procesrecht*, I (Leiden, 1893), 326.

78 According to A. de Pinto it was different if the ground for a dilatory defence only came to the notice of the defendant at a late stage in the proceedings. F.R. Pennink, op. cit., pp. 71–72, was, however, of the opinion that such a rule (which, as should be noted, originated in Canon Law, see above) was not recognised by the Dutch Code.

79 The defence concerning the person of the plaintiff or the defendant could, according to Pigeau (op. cit., p. 141), be introduced before the dilatory defences, since this defence could be classified as peremptory concerning 'la forme'. The defence of *res iudicata* and the exception of settlement out of court belong to the group of *exceptiones litis ingressum impedientes* of medieval Canon Law. According to Canon Law, these defences had to be submitted in the initial stages of the procedure.

LEX HARTOGH (1897)

An important moment in the history of preliminary defences in the Netherlands was the reforms in the Code of Civil Procedure produced by the *Lex Hartogh* (1897).[80] The *Lex Hartogh* aimed at reducing delay in civil procedure. It removed any reference to the traditional division of preliminary defences. In a new Article 141(2), which has been reproduced in a slightly modernised form in Article 128(3) of the present Code, we find it stated that all preliminary defences are to be introduced jointly with an initial defence on the merits. Preliminary defences that are omitted at this time cannot in principle be introduced later. Conversely, if the defendant initially limits his defence to preliminary defences, he is not allowed to introduce a defence on the merits at a later stage. Originally, the only exception to this rule was to be found in Article 141(3), which states that the *exception pour délibérer* may be advanced separately before all other defences (currently the defence of lack of jurisdiction *ratione personae* may also be advanced separately; see below).[81]

Even though the traditional division was evidently absent, it continued to play a role. Soon after the introduction of the *Lex Hartogh*, for example, the Dutch Supreme Court determined that peremptory defences were to be treated as equivalent to a defence on the merits.[82] This meant that their introduction was not limited to the initial phase of the proceedings (at least, if at this stage an initial defence on the merits had been introduced). As a result, the only *exceptiones* left within the ambit of Article 141 were declinatory or dilatory in nature. As regards declinatory exceptions, Article 141(2) originally also applied to the defence of lack of jurisdiction *ratione personae*, as a result of which this defence had to be joined with the defence on the merits. In 1954, however, a change in the Code of Civil Procedure was introduced (Article 154) which allowed the defendant to advance the defence of lack of jurisdiction *ratione personae* before all other defences.[83] It was not made clear whether this defence should precede or follow the *exception pour délibérer* (a defence which, as was stated above, can also be introduced separately during the initial stage of the proceedings). Another novelty introduced in 1954[84] was the rule that a successful defence of lack of jurisdiction *ratione personae* would result in a referral of the case to the court

80 7 July 1896 (Stbl. 103).
81 It should be noted that as a result of the *Lex Hartogh* some of the former preliminary defences (especially those with a procedural character; see J. ten Brink, op. cit., p. 78) are not classified as defences any more, but as 'preliminary requests'. As regards these requests Article 141 (now Article 128(3)) is not applicable.
82 HR 6 May 1904, W 8063; J.A.H. Coops, *Grondtrekken van het Nederlands burgerlijk procesrecht* (Zwolle, 1966), p. 76. See also C.W. Star Busmann, op. cit., pp. 42–45.
83 21 January 1954 (Stbl. 27).
84 21 January 1954 (Stbl. 27).

competent to hear the action (Article 157a(1) Rv). In the nineteenth century the legislator had expressly decided not to adopt a similar rule from the French *Code* (see above). At that time the rule was considered to be wrong, since it was felt that the judge lacking competence also lacked jurisdiction on the issue of remand, and that the judge to whom the case was remanded was not bound by the decision of his colleague without competence in the case.[85]

RECENT DEVELOPMENTS

The *Lex Hartogh* remains the main landmark in the development of preliminary defences in the Netherlands up to this very day. This would have been different if a legislative proposal, drafted at the beginning of the twentieth century, had been implemented.[86] In this proposal, *exceptiones*, apart from the *exception pour délibérer* and the preliminary defence of lack of jurisdiction *ratione personae* (both of which, under the proposal, had to be introduced at an early stage), stopped playing a role. As a general rule, according to the proposal all defences could be brought at any phase of the proceedings. The court would, however, be given a wide measure of discretion in this respect: if it was held that a particular defence could have been proposed earlier, the judge could refuse to allow the defence, at least if the late defence was considered to be detrimental to expediency or to the interests of the parties. Since, however, the proposal was not introduced the provisions on preliminary defences of the 1838 Code as modified by the *Lex Hartogh*, remained applicable.

With reference to the interpretation of these provisions, an important judgement was rendered by the Dutch Supreme Court in 1993.[87] At stake was the question whether a certain defence (the defence that the action had been brought by the wrong person) could be classified as a preliminary defence in the sense of the above-mentioned Article 141(2). The Supreme Court decided that this was not the case. It was held that only defences which on procedural grounds prevent the court from taking cognisance of the case on the merits can be classified as preliminary within the ambit of this Article. An example is a defence based on defects in the summons (a defence classified as peremptory concerning 'la forme' in French law, but as declinatory in Dutch law).[88]

The 1993 ruling is also important under the present revised Code of Civil Procedure. As stated above, the revised Code has not introduced important changes as regards preliminary defences. Paragraphs 2 and 3 of Article 141

---

85 J. van den Honert, op. cit., p. 277.
86 See C.H. van Rhee, 'Ons tegenwoordig sukkelproces', op. cit.
87 HR 22 October 1993, NJ 1994, 374.
88 R. van Boneval Faure, op. cit., III, 140.

of the old Code, although modernised, are reproduced in Articles 128(3) and 128(4) of the revised Code, whereas the rule of Article 154(2) is to be found in Article 110(1).

CONCLUSION

It was Gaius who introduced the division of exceptions into *exceptiones dilatoriae* and *exceptiones peremptoriae*. Within the formulary procedure this division was relevant mainly for the plaintiff, who, when confronted with a dilatory exception, could avoid definitively losing his case by postponing the action. Only in the *cognitio* procedure did this distinction gain relevance for the defendant. After all, it was in this procedure that the question to which class an exception – now to be viewed as a preliminary defence – belonged became relevant in respect of the time when it had to be introduced and proven. It was also in the *cognitio* procedure that we find first traces of a third category of exceptions, i.e. procedural ones, termed declinatory exceptions in the Middle Ages.

Medieval law showed great interest in the theory of preliminary defences. Apart from giving procedural preliminary defences their specific name (i.e. declinatory exceptions), it introduced further distinctions. This occasionally led to conceptual unclarity. The same can be said about distinctions introduced in later times, for example, Pothier's distinction between peremptory defences concerning 'la forme' and peremptory defences concerning 'le droit'. It is therefore no surprise to witness attempts to abolish the traditional distinction completely. In the Low Countries we find these attempts in draft legislation from the period 1799–1820. The draft legislation opted for an enumeration of specific defences that could be introduced preliminarily. Unfortunately, the Dutch Code of Civil Procedure promulgated in 1838 did not follow this approach, but introduced a system by and large based on the French 1806 *Code*. In the French *Code* and, therefore, in the Dutch Code the traditional categories of preliminary defences continued to play a role.

In 1897 the Netherlands witnessed an attempt to reduce delay in civil proceedings. In that year, the *Lex Hartogh* came into force. It determined that all but one preliminary defence (in 1954 an extra preliminary defence was added) had to be introduced jointly with an initial defence on the merits. Since, however, additional defences on the merits could be introduced at a later stage, it was necessary to draw a strict line between defences on the merits and preliminary defences. In doing so, the traditional categories of preliminary defences played a significant role.

Shortly after the introduction of the *Lex Hartogh* the Dutch Supreme Court determined that peremptory defences should be considered equivalent to a defence on the merits. As a result, these preliminary defences did not have to be introduced at an early phase of the proceedings any more, at least if some defence on the merits had been introduced initially. Some 90 years later, the same Court determined that only defences having a procedural character were to be considered as having a preliminary character. Even though this was not stated explicitly, the ruling meant that the category of dilatory defences lost much of its relevance in Dutch civil procedure. As a result, the main type of preliminary defences left were the ones first distinguished as a separate class in the late *cognitio* procedure, i.e. the ones termed 'declinatory exceptions' by medieval lawyers. In the future, these exceptions will continue to play a role in Dutch procedural law. However, Gaius's division of preliminary defences into *exceptiones dilatoriae* and *exceptiones peremptoriae* has to a large extent been put to rest.

Sir William Petty and the Court of Admiralty in Restoration Ireland

KEVIN COSTELLO

ONE OF THE MORE neglected aspects of the career of the celebrated political economist, demographer, scientist, landowner and public administrator, Sir William Petty, has been that of Petty's career as a judge. Yet for a significant period of his career, between the years 1676 and 1683, Petty occupied judicial office, albeit on the margins of the Irish judicature, as judge of the Irish Court of Admiralty. Petty was only really active as judge for the first four years: in 1680 Petty left Dublin for Piccadilly, from where he operated the Court of Admiralty, at one remove, through a surrogate. Petty's appointment was not a success. The Irish Court of Admiralty faced similar conflicts with rivals for admiralty jurisdiction as those faced by the English High Court of Admiralty during the post-Restoration period, in particular from the courts of common law, but also from the courts of the municipal corporations, from manorial jurisdictions, and from the Commissioners of Customs in Ireland. Petty was unable to make a successful defence of the court against this opposition. He had also seriously underestimated the difficulties involved in judicial office, and his lack of technical competence was embarrassingly exposed. Petty was also capable of falling short of expected standards of judicial neutrality; this was particularly so where his own financial interests were concerned.

THE IRISH COURT OF ADMIRALTY AT THE RESTORATION

A court of admiralty was first established in Ireland in the 1570s.[1] The court appears, in part at least, to have been established in order to extend the benefits of the unique *in rem* process to the wider Irish maritime industry.[2] However, the court, which never attracted a great volume of business and whose judges had a reputation for venality,[3] did not perform with distinction.

1 J. Appleby and M. O'Dowd, 'The Irish Admiralty: its organization and development, c. 1570–1640,' *Irish Historical Studies*, 24 (1985), 299.

2 Dr Ambrose Forth, the first judge of the court, in correspondence with Dr Julius Caesar in 1592, referred to 'my Lord Admiral having to that purpose for the ease of the subject his admiralty court established there [in Ireland]'; 13 July 1592 (BL, Caesar papers, Add. MS 12,503, f. 398).

3 Two of the pre-Civil War Irish admiralty judges, Sir Lawrence Parsons (judge between

The court appears to have ceased functioning by the early 1640s and was suspended in 1643.[4] In 1660, on the eve of the Restoration, the General Convention of Ireland recommended the re-establishment of the system of provincial vice admiralties (though not of the central Court of Admiralty).[5] Ten years after the other principal courts of justice had been restored, the central Court of Admiralty of Ireland was, on the recommendation of the English Privy Council, eventually re-established, in June 1670.[6] The first appointment to the restored Irish Court of Admiralty was Sir William Glascock. William Glascock had been MP for Newport in the Isle of Wight since 1661[7] and had been enlisted as a parliamentary supporter of the court faction based around the duke of York, the lord admiral, an association to which he probably owed his appointment to the Irish court. Although he was well qualified for civilian office (having spent the Civil War studying civil law at Leyden) his tenure at the Irish court was characterized by long periods of absenteeism, with the office being filled by a surrogate. The Act Book of the English High Court of Admiralty records appeals from Ireland in 1674[8] and 1675.[9] In both of these cases Dr John Topham, who also served as Master in Chancery,[10] is recorded as acting as surrogate judge of the Irish court. Earlier in the 1670s, the vacuum caused by Glascock's absence may have been filled by the continued availability of the Court of Vice-Admiralty of Leinster to discharge ordinary admiralty business. However, Glascock's abuse of office appears to have been intolerable to the lord lieutenant who, in 1676, engineered his dismissal from office. In his *Autobiography*[11] Sir John Bramston described the career of his friend:

1619 and 1629) and Sir Adam Loftus (who served as judge 1610 to 1619, and 1628 to 1643), had both been suspected of low-level corruption.

4 Sir Adam Loftus, the last pre-war appointee, died in 1643. In practice the court seems to have been in abeyance for several years prior to that date.

5 A. Clarke, *Prelude to Restoration* (Cambridge, 1999), p. 269.

6 The privy council decreed on 10 June 1670: 'Upon consideration of the papers and other matters this day offered concerning the settlement of a Court of Admiralty in Ireland as hath been done in former time; in regard the Board were satisfied the Lord High Admiral of England hath in his power an authority to settle there one or more Courts of Admiralty as he shall see fit for that Kingdom, as hath been done in former times, the Council do not think fit to give any further direction but to leave it to his Royal Highness the Lord High Admiral of England to settle with speed one Court of Admiralty as he shall judge most convenient, that there be no failure of justice there.' TNA:PRO, PC/2/62, f. 185.

7 B.D. Hemming (ed.), *The House of Commons, 1660–1690, Members C–L* (London, 1983), pp. 396–97.

8 *Hackett v. Alnon* (TNA:PRO, HCA 3/52, f.130).

9 *The Unity of Salem* (TNA:PRO, HCA 3/52, f.433).

10 In 1673 Dr Topham replaced Dr Dudley Loftus as master in chancery, following the imprisonment of the latter for defiance of the new rules for the regulation of the Corporation of Dublin (*Cal. S. P. dom., 1673*, pp. 591–92); during the 1670s Topham also served as advocate general of the Army (*Cal. S.P. dom., 1673*, p. 186.)

11 *The autobiography of Sir John Bramston, K.B.*, Camden Soc., 1st ser., vol.32 (1845), p. 313.

After the Restoration of the King he was by his kinsman and friend, the Earl of Portland, Governor of the Isle of Wright procured to be elected burgess, and served the King industriously. His Majesty made him Judge of the Admiralty in Ireland, and granted him a salary of £100 per annum; but his employment in the Parliament not suffering him attend there, the Earl of Essex, Lieutenant of Ireland, put another into that office, and his salary was by that means lost.

Sir William Petty succeeded to the judgeship of the Court of Admiralty in July 1676. The appointment was not an obvious one. Why did Petty, who was, after all, not even a lawyer, let alone a civilian, want this unpromising office? Firstly, the position was, naively, imagined by Petty to be an office of prestige. Somewhat embarrassingly, after his elevation, he wrote enquiring as to the diplomatic precedence of the judge of the Court of Admiralty and whether the judge of the Court of Admiralty was entitled to a place on the Privy Council.[12] His relationship with the new lord lieutenant, the duke of Ormonde, had, during the 1660s, become strained, but the position of judge provided him, so he thought, with an opportunity to restore good relations. He made his first attempt with a sycophantic verse which, having sought clearance from Samuel Pepys as to whether he should proceed with the gesture,[13] he presented to the duke of Ormonde upon his arrival at Skerries in 1667.[14]

But there were also less self-promoting concerns. Petty was genuinely interested in maritime affairs. In 1663 he had made his first disastrous attempt at a catamaran design. While he did not prove a success as judge his principal interest, in maritime administration, continued after he left the court. In 1685 he was at work preparing a projected 'Treatise of Navigation' and investigating inventions for de-salinating seawater.[15]

It is unclear who secured with the duke of York the sanction for the appointment of Petty. He enjoyed an extensive range of contacts both in the Admiralty and in the duke of York's circle. He could count amongst his contacts Sir William Glascock, Sir Robert Southwell, Sir Peter Pett (the King's Advocate in Ireland), Sir John Werden (secretary to the duke of York), Sir Allen Apsley, and Samuel Pepys, secretary to the Admiralty. Petty himself pointed to the influence of Sir George Cartaret, Treasurer to the Admiralty. Relations with Cartaret were poor; the two men had fallen out in a dispute

12 Petty to Gamble, 1 Aug. 1676, McGill University Library, Petty letterbook, MS 7,614, f. 199.

13 Petty to Southwell, 22 Aug. 1677, *The Petty-Southwell correspondence, 1676–1687* (hereafter *Petty-Southwell corr.*), ed. Lansdowne (London, 1928), p. 33.

14 'A Naval Alegory; By the Register of the Admiralty of Ireland; To His Grace James Duke of York as Grand Pilot of the good ship Ireland, upon his fourth expedition on that bottom'; *Petty papers*, ed. Lansdowne (London, 1927), ii, p. 248.

15 BL, Petty papers, Add. MS 72,893, ff.30–31v.

about land, and in a moment of neurosis, when he began to find the office of judge a source of stress, Petty analysed his appointment as having originated in a complicated design by Cartaret to humiliate him. Writing to Sir Peter Pett he traced his nomination to Cartaret, accusing Cartaret of prevailing upon Glascock and Pett to induce him into accepting the office: 'Sir George Cartaret and others promoted this business and made William Glascock the instrument of their revenge; but who would have thought you would have co-operated? In fine I am so laughed at I dare not put on my gown.'[16]

THE JUDICIAL BUSINESS OF THE IRISH COURT OF ADMIRALTY IN PETTY'S TIME

Prize

The highpoint of Irish prize jurisdiction in the later seventeenth century occurred during the period of the Second Anglo-Dutch War (1665–67). A high volume of Dutch vessels were condemned by the Courts of Vice Admiralty of Connaught, and, especially, of Munster.[17] The income generated by these condemnations was considerable. It was a measure of the extent of prize income that when the proceeds were allowed by the King to the Irish administration, it was understood that they would make a substantial con-tribution towards the cost of maintaining the army in Ireland.[18] The exercise by the Irish courts of admiralty of a prize jurisdiction during the Second Anglo-Dutch War had a clear constitutional basis. In June 1665, Charles II, acting upon the advice of the Commissioners for Prizes, promulgated for Ireland a scheme for the administration of prizes equivalent to that which operated in England. It was decreed that Irish courts of vice-admiralty would exercise prize jurisdiction; that they would comply with the same rules and directions as regulated the High Court of Admiralty in England and that there be an Irish Commission of Appeals in Prize Cases (with further appeal to the High Court of Admiralty in England).[19] However, during the Third Anglo-Dutch War (1672–74), and thereafter until 1745, prize jurisdiction was withdrawn from Irish admiralty courts. The cancellation of Irish prize jurisdiction may have been a reaction to a scandal in the Connaught Court of Vice Admiralty in 1667 arising out of the allegedly corrupt administration of a Genoese prize case, the *Sacrifice of Abraham*, when it was alleged that the

---

16 Petty to Pett, 26 Aug. 1676 (McGill U. Lib., Petty letterbook, MS 7,614, ff.199 and 208).
17 17 Dutch vessels were condemned by the Vice-Admiralty Court of Munster; 11 by the Vice-Admiralty Court of Connaught: report by king's advocate, Peter Pett, 26 Dec. 1667 (Bodl., Carte MSS, vol. 35, f. 766).
18 Order of 14 Aug. 1667 (Bodl., Carte MSS, vol. 52, f. 155).
19 Instructions to the Lord Lieutenant, 26 June 1665 (TNA:PRO, PC/2/58).

Vice-Admiral of Connaught, Sir Oliver St George had carried off to his country house valuable luxuries looted from the captain's cabin.[20] In the periods of war that followed no grant of prize jurisdiction equivalent to that in 1665 was entrusted to an Irish court. Instead an arrangement was set in place under which sub-commissioners acting on behalf the English Commissioners of Prizes operated in Ireland with the function of collecting prizes taken into Ireland prior to their condemnation in England. Sub-commissioners acting on behalf of the English Commissioners of Prizes were established at Kinsale, County Cork. The instructions issued to the sub-commissioners in 1674 required them to take measures in respect of prizes taken into Munster ancillary to their ultimate condemnation in London: they were to detain and preserve the vessel, to administer standard-form interrogatories to the crew, and to seize and preserve the ships' papers.[21] The Admiralty in Ireland was entrusted with a purely ancillary administrative function, with no role in the judicial process leading to prize condemnation allowed to it.

In 1677 the *Golden Salmon*, a Dutch whaling vessel whose entire crew 'had forsaken her and escaped on long boats', was found drifting on the Atlantic by a French privateer [22] and was taken into Youghal. Petty, apprised of the arrival of the captured French vessel, decided that the case was one of piracy and had the French captor charged with piracy (a strange manoeuvre since the court of admiralty had no jurisdiction over piracy).[23] In his defence the captor alleged that he was a privateer acting under licence of the French government. Accordingly, prize condemnation proceedings were opened. These resulted in a sentence in favour of the captor. Following condemnation, the *Golden Salmon* was purchased by a Youghal merchant, Walter Galway, who bought nine-tenths of her from the French privateer, and the remaining ten per cent from the officers of the Admiralty. Sir William Petty, seeking reassurance from his superiors, and, in particular, the duke of York and Sir John Werden, described the proceedings in correspondence with Sir Robert Southwell:[24]

> There came into Youghal, a French man in a Dutch ffluit,[25] without a commission, and without bringing with him any of the taken ship's company. Hereupon we accuse him of a piratical act. He (as the readiest way to clear himself) claims from us the adjudication of his prize. We, upon discussion of the matter, clear him of piracy and adjudge the said ffluit unto him as lawful prize, and demand of him the tenths, in right of

---

20 Report of Jenkins, Wiseman, Turner and Walker, 1668 (TNA: PRO, SP 79/1(3)).
21 Instructions to sub-commissioners at Kinsale (BL, Harleian MS 1511, f. 341).
22 BL, Leoline Jenkins papers, Add. MS 18,206, f. 127r.
23 The Piracy Act, 1612 (11, 12 & 13 Jas I, c. 11) had transferred piracy jurisdiction from the Court of Admiralty to specially appointed piracy commissioners.
24 Petty to Southwell, 10 Nov. 1677, *Petty-Southwell corr.*, p. 38.
25 The editor of the *Petty-Southwell corr.* suggests that the word may be Petty's rendering of the Dutch word *vloot*.

the Admiral of Ireland. He denies these tenths to be due. The expedient we used is that he pay or secure the said tenths and have given him six weeks time to solicit a remittal of the same from His Royal Highness. Now you being Vice Admiral of Munster (unto which Province this matter relates) must acquaint his Royal Highness, or Sir John Werden herewith. We here are the blind leading the blind.

Petty's sense of panic was well founded. Firstly, there was the obvious question of the jurisdiction of the Irish court to condemn a prize to a captor who acted under a letter of marque granted by a foreign state (the king of France), and not by the crown of England. Secondly, even if the Irish court did have such jurisdiction, it could hardly have condemned the vessel now that hostilities between France and the United Provinces had ceased. Petty's errors were soon exposed. The Dutch proprietor, Cornelius Thenispeck, sought the intervention of the Commissioners of Admiralty in London. As an interim measure, Ormonde by order in council directed the mayor of Youghal to prevent Galway disposing of her. Sir Leoline Jenkins, the judge of the High Court of Admiralty, was called upon to sort out the constitutional and diplomatic imbroglio. Jenkins identified two grounds of exception to Petty's sentence: firstly, the fact that there was now a cessation of hostilities between France and the United Provinces, and, secondly, that article 21 of the Treaty at Breda of 1667 forbade England from providing assistance to privateers from third party states attacking vessels belonging to the United Provinces. As to the first objection, Jenkins wrote: 'The cessation of hostilities between France and the Estates General is not a thing that His Majesty's subjects are concerned with, or govern themselves by, being exclusively a matter between foreign states, and His Majesty no party to it.'[26] However, Jenkins pointed out, Petty's sentence had precipitated an infringement of the duty, prescribed in article 21 of the Treaty of Breda, requiring England not to lend assistance to the privateers of a third state attacking the vessels of the United Provinces:[27]

> all of your majesty's subjects are bound by [the Treaty of Breda] and are bound to take notice of it, and it was therefore an error to lend or interpose your majesty's authority in a judicial way by condemning of this ship. Besides such proceedings are contrary to a fundamental maxim in neutrality: for a neutral ship being in peace when his neighbours are at war, ought not to weaken the condition of one neighbour better than that of another, and hence the French man of war hath the help and benefit of a court of law, and an open free market for his prize – which is as great a privilege an any of His majesty's subjects may have.

26 BL, Leoline Jenkins papers, Add. MS 18,206, f. 127r.
27 Ibid.

Sir Robert Southwell had, with the best of intentions, and in order to help his friend, circulated Petty's letter to two leading English civilians, Dr Bradford and Dr Trumbell. This can only have further aggravated Petty's embarrassment. Both expressed astonishment at Petty's assertion of international prize jurisdiction:[28]

> As to Sir William's letter, I cannot but wonder that he should take upon himself to adjudge a prize to the French which no one can do but such as are empowered by the French King to reside within our King's territories and with her leave as our Commissioners did in Gallicia in the late war against the Dutch which Dr Trumbell instances to you in his letter to you. I see the good gentleman hath not been well versed in the practical part of admiralty proceedings. I fear the matter will be complained of both by the French and the Dutch, the latter may expect that we should not ever arrest their ships in point of property when brought into His Majesty's ports. The French would not like it if we would pretend to a 10th of their prize. The French captors are permitted to take their prize from any part of His Majesty's seas.[29]

While both Jenkins and Bedford agreed that Petty's sentence was illegal, they disagreed as to the proper disposal of the case. Bedford's analysis was premised upon the view that the prize proceedings were void (and that therefore the provisional title to the vessel had not passed from the French captor): the sentence 'was erroneously given by an incompetent judge and therefore void and the French should be permitted to carry away their prize unless the laws of Ireland are different from these here'.[30] Jenkins, on the other hand, concerned about the diplomatic consequences of infringement of the Treaty of Breda, concluded that the vessel should be returned to the original Dutch proprietor. That, however, could be effected only under the force of an executive direction, and not by order of the Irish Court of Admiralty, since the court had no jurisdiction over transactions made *infra corpus comitatus*. Jenkins advised that:[31]

> the Petitioner be entitled to have the sentence reversed, and ship and lading restored. As to the reversal of the sentence, that can be legally done. But as to restoration ... it is probable that the bargain was made on land, and therefore jurisdiction will be prohibited to the Court of Admiralty. The result is that if there were a good sale by the captors to

28 Bedford to Southwell, 11 Apr. 1678 (BL, Petty papers, Add. MS 72,852, ff.152, 153r).
29 Dr Bedford refers to the proclamation of 26 May 1676.
30 BL, Petty papers, Add. MS 72,852, f. 153r.
31 BL, Leoline Jenkins papers, Add. MS 18,206, f. 127r.

Walter Galway, the petitioner would have no remedy. Yet this would be interpreted by the Dutch as a breach of the Treaty and may for ought I know run up as high as to reprisals against us.

Following Jenkins's advice the sentence was countermanded by order of the Privy Council given on 20 February 1680, and Galway directed to restore the vessel to Thenispeck. The king then compensated Galway with a gift of forfeited lands in Munster acknowledging, in a sharp official rebuke to Petty, that 'if there was an error in him [Galway], he was led into it by the Court of Admiralty which condemned her notwithstanding any articles to the contrary'.

This was not the only international diplomatic incident caused by Petty's exercising an unconstitutional prize jurisdiction. In the spring of 1676 the Swedish envoy to England, Baron Sparr, had granted a letter of marque to an Irish privateer, Terence Byrne, as part of Sweden's war effort against Denmark. Within months the Swedish envoy then tried to revoke the commission on the ground that Byrne had failed to comply with the necessary formalities, but particularly because it was concerned to secure observance of a proclamation issued by the crown forbidding English subjects serving under commissions granted by other states. Byrne, who had ignored the instruction to return his commission, then captured a vessel, the *Christian Albert*, belonging to subjects of the town of Eckenförde in Holstein-Gottorp, a former ally of Sweden which had been invaded by Charles V of Denmark. In December 1676 Byrne sailed his capture into Kinsale, where he had the ship arrested by virtue of a warrant from the Court of Admiralty. There then commenced before Petty what the Swedish envoy to England described as a 'tedious and chargeable lawsuit at the Court of Admiralty'.[32] Prize condemnation proceedings had during the Second Anglo-Dutch War usually been disposed of within a few days. This action, however, dragged on from January to October 1676. The legality of the capture depended on the single issue of whether the territory of Holstein-Gottorp was in hostility to Sweden (in which case the capture was legitimate), or an ally of Sweden (in which case the claimant was entitled to return of the vessel). The claimant, Peter Tam, master of the *Christian Albert*, argued that the people of Holstein continued to be allies of the king of Sweden. This view was supported by the Swedish government which contended that occupation by the Danes did not make the people of Holstein subjects of Denmark: 'yet can such an inrode and usurpation by no legal means assert and make ye Duke's subjects to be ye King [of Denmark's] subjects.'[33] The captor Byrne, on the other hand, attempted to prove, by calling witnesses and presenting documentary evidence, that the

32 'Memorial of the Envoy of Sweden touching a ship of Holstein, Peter Tam Master', 15 Apr. 1678 (TNA:PRO, SP 95/11, ff.31,32).
33 Ibid.

people of Holstein had submitted to allegiance with the kingdom of Denmark, and that the seizure was justified by his Swedish commission. Petty never finally determined this question. In October 1677, Petty worriedly reported that he had heard 'that Tam hath caused Monsr Leyinburg to write something to my Lord Lieutenant reflecting upon my Justice, which is totally untrue in matter of fact'.[34] Following an order to Petty from the lord lieutenant this matter was taken out of the hands of the Court of Admiralty to be decided before the Irish Privy Council (which then tried but, again, failed to resolve the issue).[35] Petty was, as in the *Golden Salmon*, overreaching himself; the Irish Court of Admiralty was not an international court. It had no jurisdiction to process captures under Swedish letters of marque, or to determine complex disputes of North European politics or nationality arising from the terms of foreign commissions.

Having his lack of technical competence exposed so publicly in the proceedings in the *Golden Salmon*, Petty's lack of self-confidence must have been reduced even further in the next prize-related case to come his way: *Fleming* v. *McDonnell* in 1679. The *Fleming* case was probably the most intricate case to come before the Irish Court of Admiralty in the late seventeenth century; Petty confessed to having been 'almost frightened with the trouble and perplexity of the business'.[36] A sizable privateering business was generated by commissions granted by the duke of Ormonde in the late 1640s against the parliamentary forces,[37] and acting under one of these commissions, the marquis of Antrim seized a ship, laden with wines, belonging to a Scottish merchant, Thomas Fleming, en route from St Malo to the port of Leith in Edinburgh. The vessel was taken into Dunkirk where the prize was divided between the captors, Lynch, Antrim, and Vanderkipp. Fleming petitioned Charles Stuart, then in exile, and he, in turn, established a special admiralty court sitting at Brussels presided over by two members of his entourage, Sir Henry Downing and Sir Thomas Cunningham. The sentence of the ad hoc court at Brussels directed the captors to make restitution of the vessel to Fleming. Fleming spent nearly thirty years attempting to execute that order; he appears never to have succeeded. The first proceedings opened in Galway before the Court of Vice Admiralty of Connaught in August 1667.[38] Fleming lost before Colonel Spencer (the judge of the Vice Admiral of Connaught) and an appeal was taken before the High Court of Admiralty in March 1667.[39] However, the appeal appears to have

---

34 Petty to Southwell, 10 Nov. 1677, *Petty-Southwell corr.*, p. 38.

35 *Cal. S.P. dom.*, *1678*, pp. 74, 75.

36 Petty to Williamson, 18 July 1678, *Cal. S.P. dom.*, *1678*, p. 300.

37 J.H. Ohlmeyer, 'Irish privateers during the Civil War, 1642–1650,' *Mariner's Mirror*, 76 (1990), 119.

38 TNA: PRO, HCA 15/13.

39 30 Mar. 1667, TNA: PRO, HCA 3/51, ff. 79r, 109, 122, 135, 140v, 152v, 155, 205, 219.

been discontinued without being determined.[40] A successful appeal would have had limited strategic benefit. It would only have been good for the province of Connaught, and would not, were the vessel removed, have enabled Fleming to secure enforcement outside the province. A decade later Fleming revived the matter before the Court of Admiralty in Dublin, 'the scope of the libel' again being to put the Brussels sentence into execution.

The case (a re-possession suit) was tried before Petty in the Irish Court of Admiralty in 1679. At the trial, the proctor for the marquis of Antrim pleaded seven peremptory exceptions to the Brussels sentence: (i) that the Brussels court was a tribunal not known to the law; (ii) that the defendants had not been called upon to appear; (iii) that the sentence did not 'conform to the solemnity of the law'; (iv) that the sentence was not 'certain or liquid' but 'vague and uncertain'; (v) that the Brussels sentence was given against Vanderkipp, and not against the defendants who were not in partnership with Vanderkipp; (vi) that the defendants were immunized against prosecution by the Treaty of Galway; (vii) that the defendants were entitled to the benefit of the Act of Free and General Pardon, Indemnity and Oblivion, 1660.[41] Sentence was 'after much contest and the ordinary delays of court'[42] pronounced by Petty in favour of Fleming. Petty held that the defendants were within the range of the Brussels sentence, and were not entitled to the benefit of the Act of Oblivion, on the ground that a proviso in the 1660 Act did not extend to acts of piracy.[43]

The marquis of Antrim, as he had in the Connaught case, then moved an appeal to the High Court of Admiralty in London, and, on lodging the appeal, was granted an inhibition suspending the sentence of the Irish Court of Admiralty. However, the defendant failed to comply with the order to give bail to abide the judgment of the court (the 'usual course'),[44] and the inhibition was discontinued. The defendants then initiated, but did not pursue, an appeal against the revocation of the inhibition to the Court of Delegates. The inhibition being revoked, the Irish Court was free to put the Brussels sentence into execution. However, before it could do so, the marquis of Antrim had recourse to the Irish Court of King's Bench for an order of prohibition. The King's Bench granted the writ. A report, which was subsequently prepared by the Irish King's Bench for the lord lieutenant, outlined the grounds upon which the prohibition was granted: firstly, that the Brussels sentence

---

40 The final reference to *Fleming* v. *Lynch* in the Act Book of the High Court of Admiralty is 3 Oct. 1670 (TNA: PRO, HCA 3/51, f. 219).

41 12 Chas. II, c. 11 (Eng.).

42 Petty to Williamson, 18 July 1678, *Cal. S.P. dom. 1678*, p. 300.

43 S. 10 of the Act of Oblivion exempted murder and piracy at sea from the application of the indemnity.

44 *The life of Sir Leoline Jenkins*, ed. W. Wynne (London, 1724), ii, 788.

was void and, secondly, that the Irish Court of Admiralty had acted in breach of natural justice:[45]

> That the Lord Marquis of Antrim, Ambrose Lynch, Gregory Lynch and Arthur French had exhibited a suggestion in the court of King's Bench setting forth that by the law of the land no judgment or sentence ought to be given against any person, till they be by due process of law summoned to appear and answer, notwithstanding which Mr. Fleming had impleaded the said Lord Marquis and the others in the Admiralty Court of Ireland upon a sentence against one Cornelius Claizen Vanderkipp and his partners at Brussels the 11 August 1650; whereupon the said sentence is void in law and of no force against the said Lord Marquis and others and that they were never named or parties that they did offer the same to the Court of Admiralty and prayed ye Benefit of the Act of Oblivion. But the said Court of Admiralty refuse to admit of the said allegations, but proceeded to sentence against the said Lord Marquis and the others.

The Court of Admiralty had been successfully outmanoeuvred. Fleming, having exhausted his legal remedies, was forced to petition Charles II seeking a royal letter directed to the lord lieutenant to have the prohibition lifted. An opinion was sought from Sir Leoline Jenkins, who advised that an executive order of the type petitioned for was inappropriate: 'this prayer is not regular; for a writ of consultation upon the prohibition would be the proper mode of proceedings.' However, despite Jenkins's suggestion that Petty resist the prohibition by means of a writ of consultation, it appears either that no such writ was sought, or if sought, that the prohibition was not rescinded. In 1681 the King wrote to the lord lieutenant, encouraging him to persuade the defendants to submit to 'arbitration by such judges as his Grace shall appoint to determine the matters in difference'.[46] While Petty had managed to avoid the extravagant jurisdictional errors which he had committed in the *Golden Salmon* and the *Christian Albert*, Jenkins's assessment that Petty's sentence 'look[ed] suspiciously,' and Petty's inability to react effectively when checked by the writ of prohibition from the King's Bench, suggest that, despite a greater cautiousness, Petty was still struggling.

Instance jurisdiction

The Irish Court of Admiralty was not a court of general maritime jurisdiction. By statutes of 1389[47] and 1400[48] (extended to Ireland by Poynings's

---

45 Ibid.
46 Charles II to Ormonde, 23 Aug. 1681, *Cal S.P. dom., 1680–1681*, p. 248.
47 13 Rich.II, st. 1, c.5.
48 2 Hen. IV, c.11.

Law, 1495) jurisdiction over disputes relating to contracts entered into, or wrongs committed, on land was expressly prohibited to it. 13 Rich. II, st. 1, c. 5 provided:

> Forasmuch as great and common clamour and complaint hath been oftentimes made before this time and yet is, for that the admiral and their deputies hold their sessions within divers places within the realm as well within franchise as without, accroaching to them greater authority than belongeth to their office in prejudice of our lord the King and the common law of the realm, and in diminishing of divers franchises, and in destruction and impoverishing of the common people. It is accorded and assented, that the Admirals and their deputies shall not meddle from henceforth of any thing within the realm but only of a thing done upon the sea, as it hath been used on the time of the noble prince King Edward, Grandfather of our lord the King that is now.

In the sixteenth century admiralty jurisdiction in England had expanded considerably beyond the limits of the fourteenth-century statutes, and the court had begun to develop into a court of general maritime jurisdiction. That, in turn, led to a reaction on the part of the common law courts in the late sixteenth century and into the seventeenth century, as they drove back the jurisdiction of the High Court of Admiralty. The statutes of Richard II were deployed by the courts of common law, and particularly the Court of King's Bench under Coke C.J. (whose treatment of the court of admiralty in chapter 22 of the Fourth Part of *The Institutes* provided the principal source of anti-admiralty argument) with the objective of suppressing the growing civil maritime jurisdiction of the English court of admiralty. Most of the principal categories of civil litigation undertaken by the court (the relief to unpaid suppliers or fitters, and suits involving breach of contracts of lading or of charterparties) were withdrawn from admiralty jurisdiction.

In 1633, Charles I, on the petition of the judge of the English High Court of Admiralty, Sir Henry Marten, assembled a judicial conference to settle the claims for immunity from prohibition claimed by the Court of Admiralty over categories of litigation then being withdrawn from the court by prohibition: seamen's wages disputes; suits by unpaid suppliers or fitters of ships; breach of charterparties and contracts of lading, and in cases arising from the court's exercise of regulatory jurisdiction over abuses committed in navigable rivers.[49] The conciliar conference resulted in an order in council of 1633 which defined the instance matters over which the English Court of

---

49 See the detailed discussion in M.J. Prichard and D.E.C. Yale, *Hale and Fleetwood on Admiralty jurisdiction* (hereafter *Hale and Fleetwood*), Selden Society, vol. 108 (1992), pp. xciv–cviii.

Admiralty was to have jurisdiction and to be free from prohibition from the courts of common law.[50] The four areas conceded to the admiralty court were: (i) contracts made upon the sea or in a foreign jurisdiction; (ii) disputes involving breach of contracts for mariners' wages, freight or charterparties (despite the fact that the contract had been made upon land); (iii) suits for non-payment for work done in the repairing or fitting out of vessels (again despite the fact that the contract had been made upon land); and (iv) the court was to have jurisdiction 'to make enquiry of, and to redress all annoyances and obstructions in navigable rivers beneath the first bridges that are any impediments to navigation, or passage to, or from the sea; and also to try personal contracts and injuries done there, which concern navigation upon the sea, and no prohibition is to be granted in such cases'.

In the early seventeenth century the permissive grant of prohibitions against the admiralty court had been as significant a problem in Ireland as it had been in England.[51] The settlement of 1633 was then directed to be observed in Ireland in order to curtail the exercise by the courts of common law of the use of writs of prohibition against the Court of Admiralty in Ireland.[52] Records of the Irish Court of Admiralty for the Restoration period do not survive. However, the evidence supplied by Petty's papers, suggests a depression in business, and that the order in council of 1633 did not succeed in suppressing intervention by prohibition against the Court of Admiralty in Ireland. Firstly, the case load was very slight. In his address to the admiralty sessions held at Ringsend, County Dublin, in October 1677 Petty mentions that there were only five items of business currently before the Court of Admiralty.[53] Second, of the three categories of litigation permitted by the order of 1633 it was modest seamen's wages cases which made up the principal business of the court. In 1677, Petty in a letter to Southwell complained that 'this Court increases apace, I mean the trouble and business of it which chiefly concerns poor men'.[54] But even this limited authority was further compromised by the existence of three techniques by which instance matters might be withdrawn from the court: by appeals to the High Court of Admiralty, by writs of prohibition from the superior courts, and by *replevins* obtained from the municipal sheriff.

50 *Cal. S.P. dom., 1631–1633*, pp. 539–40.
51 In the mid-1630s the judge of the Admiralty Court of Leinster sent over a schedule (which no longer survives) listing prohibitions issued against the Irish courts of admiralty to the Lords of the Admiralty in London; Alan Cooke to the duke of Northumberland, 23 Aug. 1638 (Alnwick Castle, Northumberland MSS, vol. 14, f. 170).
52 In 1637 the king transmitted the Privy Council declaration of February 1633 to the lord deputy with an instruction that it 'be communicated to our judges on that side, and to be in like manner ordered and settled there'; Charles I to Wentworth, 7 Aug. 1637: *Cal. S.P. dom., 1637*, p. 359.
53 BL, Lansdowne MS 1,228, ff. 38–56v.
54 Petty to Southwell, 10 Nov. 1677, *Petty–Southwell corr.*, p. 39.

Early in 1679 Petty complained that 'an appeal had been brought into the Admiralty of England in a case of poor seaman's wages where so much as a probable tale could not be told in prejudice of the sentence given here for these poor seamen'. The case to which Petty (almost certainly) refers was that of *Pippard* v. *Fleming*,[55] a seaman's wages case, and the only case to come to London by way of appeal from the Irish court during the period that Petty held office. The use of the device of appeal may have provided a means of evasion for some masters seeking to avoid claims in the Irish court.[56] But Petty appears to have exaggerated the extent of the actual use of the appeal to London. During the period that Petty served as judge there was only one such appeal: that in *Pippard* v. *Fleming*. From the beginning, Petty had expressed strong constitutional hostility to the exposure of the Irish court to appeal. In Petty's view there was no jurisdiction to subject the Irish court to appellate review. The argument was an attractive one. Before the Test Act of 1673[57] the Irish Court of Admiralty derived its title from the Lord High Admiral of England and Ireland. Since the High Court of England also derived its title from the Lord High Admiral, the Admiral was competent to entrust an appellate jurisdiction from his Irish court to the High Court of Admiralty. However, in 1673, following the refusal of the duke of York to subscribe to the test, the Admiralty divided: James duke of York became Admiral of Ireland and Prince Rupert became Lord Admiral of England.[58] When the duke of York resigned the office of Admiral of England he ceased, according to the Petty theory, to have competence to direct the High Court in England. It followed that he had no jurisdiction to entrust admiralty jurisdiction, including an appellate competence to the High Court of Admiralty in England. There is, however, no evidence that this, at least stateable, constitutional argument was ever debated in Doctors' Commons; the argument would, however, have ceased to have relevance when the Admiralty became, once again, vested in the Lord High Admiral of both kingdoms.

55 TNA: PRO, HCA 24/119.
56 There were, however, techniques available to the Irish court to frustrate exploitation of appeals in seamen's wages cases. Following the appeal in *Pippard*, advice was sought from Doctors' Commons on the problem of appeals to England in wages cases. Dr Bedford (in an opinion dated 11 April 1677) recommended that, where the court apprehended an appeal it ensure that the wages were, prior to the final sentence, given to the plaintiffs upon bail to repay in the event of their claim not succeeding rather than withholding wages until the determination of the appeal. Where this was done, he argued, the master would very rarely take the trouble of an appeal (BL, Petty papers, Add. MS 72,852, ff.152–154 v).
57 'An Act for Preventing Dangers which may happen from Popish Recusants', 25 Chas II, c. 2 (Eng.). Failure to take the prescribed oaths disqualified the recusant from any office in England, but not (until 1704) in Ireland.
58 J. and S. Shaw 'Admiralty administration and personnel, 1619–1714', *Bulletin of Institute of Historical Research*, xiv (1936/37), 166.

The other, more common, sources of interference derived from the process of *replevin* and writs of prohibition. Petty, in an account written in 1679, described five writs of prohibition which had recently been directed against the court.[59] In addition to harassment by prohibitions, the device of *replevin* enjoyed a particular popularity in Ireland as a means of frustrating admiralty process. It had one particular advantage over the writ of prohibition in that it could be obtained of right from the sheriff attached to the municipal corporations. These, of course, were officers who, given the corporations' own claims to admiralty jurisdiction, were likely to be particularly receptive to interposing themselves against the Court of Admiralty. The clearest record of the deployment, in Petty's time, of *replevin* occurred in the *Jacob of Dublin* in 1682.[60] The *Jacob* had lain under arrest in the custody of deputies of the marshal of the Court of Admiralty. It was re-seized under process issued out of the Recorder's court in Dublin. The recently appointed marshal of the Court of Admiralty, Captain Francis Robinson, then retaliated: the vessel was re-seized from the officers of the mayor of Dublin, Sir Humphrey Jervis (who had a longstanding grievance against the admiralty court) and the sheriff's officials were committed to prison for contempt by Petty's surrogate, the notoriously troublesome Dr Dudley Loftus. While the use of *replevin* was probably common, the retaliatory use of the contempt power by the Court of Admiralty was rare, legally dubious and highly provocative. The intensity of the violence of the inter-curial conflict in Dublin became a matter of national political concern. Sir John Werden, secretary to the duke of York, requested the lord lieutenant to investigate the conflict.[61] The earl of Arran, Ormonde's son and personal secretary, provided his father with the following assessment of the conflict:[62] 'Sir John Werden, the Duke's secretary gave me notice of some disorder in something belonging to the Admiralty between ye officer of the court and the Lord Mayor who by virtue of a charter lays claim to a jurisdiction. The right must no doubt be judged according to law if the parties have a mind to it but care ought in the meantime to be taken to prevent violence.'

Dublin's Elizabethan charter of 1582[63] entrusted the office of admiralty and all matters pertaining to it to the mayor of Dublin, and the *Jacob of Dublin* appears to be one of a number of cases in the 1670s where interven-

---

59 Petty to Southwell, 4 Jan. 1679, *Petty-Southwell corr.*, pp. 63–67.
60 BL, Petty papers, Add. MS 72,893, ff.87–88v.
61 Duke of York to Arran, 25 Nov. 1682 (Bodl., Carte MSS, vol. 39, f. 614).
62 Arran to Ormond, 5 Dec. 1682 (Bodl., Carte MSS, vol. 144, f. 406).
63 *Calendar of the ancient records of Dublin in the possession of the municipal corporation* (hereafter *Cal. anc. rec. Dublin*), ed. J.T. Gilbert (Dublin, 1889–95), i, pp. 36, 37.

tion upon admiralty proceedings was justified by reference to the provisions in the charter of 1582. While the *Jacob of Dublin* provides the fullest record of this technique to survive from the period of Petty's tenure, intervention by *replevin* appears to have been a common wrecking instrument against the work of the court. In 1698 the judge of the Court of the Munster Vice Admiralty, Thomas Farren, described the extent to which the procedure was used as a means of frustrating admiralty process in seventeenth-century Ireland:[64]

> long before the late troubles it was customary and usual throughout the kingdom for the sheriffs of the several cities therein to grant *replevins* against ships and goods taken by virtue of warrants out of the several admiralty courts in ye Kingdom when ye property of them have been claimed by others and that the granting of the *replevins* is grounded on ye common laws of this Kingdom and that no sheriff can deny such *replevins* upon good security offered them to return the said ships and goods if return of them shall be awarded and if any sheriff should refuse granting them an action on the case would lie against them for their refusal.

The Court of Admiralty was allowed to exercise jurisdiction in suits for enforcement of bottomry bonds, where the master hypothecated or pledged the vessel in order to obtain credit for the provisioning of the vessel. This was the only form of hypothecation which the court was permitted by the courts of common law to enforce, and the common law courts were, in the Restoration period, reducing the category of bottomry bond enforceable by the admiralty court.[65] A court of admiralty did not have until the mid-nineteenth century jurisdiction to enforce mortgages for the purchase of vessels. However, in the *Orrery* in 1678 Petty's court exercised jurisdiction in a suit concerning the enforcement of a maritime mortgage, subject-matter well off the limits allowed to the court. It was also a suit in which Petty was disqualified by a substantial material interest. The story of the *Orrery* began in 1677 when Petty lent £1100 to a London merchant, Mathew Elliston, in return for which Elliston provided and accepted bills of exchequer, and as security for the loan oppingorated his share in the *Orrery*, a ship which Elliston was in the course of building on the Kenmare river. Elliston then failed to meet his liabilities under the bills of exchequer. Petty who had lost considerably by reason of Elliston's bankruptcy, wrote: 'I hoped to have spent

---

64 Affidavit of Thomas Farren, 21 Sept. 1698 (TNA:PRO, HCA 13/18).
65 G.F. Steckley, 'Bottomry bonds in the seventeenth century Admiralty Court,' *American Journal of Legal History*, 45 (2001), 256.

this money with my friends in London this summer, but now?'[66] On 28
December 1677, Tom Coggs, a collaborator with Petty in the venture, began
proceedings in the Irish Court of Admiralty. A monition was entered, and
upon the non-appearance of the defendants, a sentence was decreed under
which the *Orrery* was directed to be delivered to Coggs. However, at night
the defendants re-seized the *Orrery* as it lay under arrest on the Kenmare
river: sails were procured and the rudder re-attached. After a violent
confrontation with the marshal and his assistants, the *Orrery* set sail,
delivered from the authority of the Irish Court of Admiralty.

Petty, rather than maintaining discretion about his participation in
litigation in which he was interested, pestered the Admiralty with petitions
and affidavits. He unabashedly pressurised Southwell to intervene directly,
or indirectly, with the judge of the English High Court of Admiralty, Leoline
Jenkins: 'Sir William Temple, Sir William Godolphin, Mr Pepys and Mr
Cooke, I think have all interests in Sir Leoline, and I hope you have likewise.
For God's sake use some means that wee be not run down violently against
the Cryes and Clamours of our right.'[67]

Gerald Aylmer, the historian of the seventeenth-century English administrative system, in accounting for Petty's relatively mediocre public career, has
assessed Petty as an individual whose defects of personality outweighed his
altogether exceptional talents.[68] The proceedings in the *Orrery* illustrate one
of Petty's principal personality failings, a tendency to pursue personal
financial disputes in a way which compromised his integrity and retarded his
public career. Not for the first time in Petty's judicial career, the proceedings
had to be taken to the notice of government. A petition to the Irish Privy
Council was submitted by one of Elliston's colleagues, Zacharai Stilgo, complaining about the proceedings taken by Petty and Coggs in the Court of
Admiralty. The petition was referred to the lord chief baron and the chief
justice of the Court of King's Bench who directed that the proceedings in
the Court of Admiralty be terminated and that Petty be left to whatever
common law remedy might be available.[69] Petty, blind to his own misconduct,
suggested that the council was influenced by the fact that the defendants were
English, and by a concern to promote the shipbuilding industry in Ireland. He
seems to have had no conception of the degree to which he had been at fault.
It is more likely that the advice to the Privy Council was necessitated by two

---

66 Petty to Southwell, 4 Jan. 1678, *Petty-Southwell corr.*, p. 62.
67 Petty to Southwell, 18 Oct. 1679, *Petty-Southwell corr.*, p. 80.
68 'Patronage at the Court of Charles II' in E. Cruickshanks (ed.), *The Stuart courts* (Stroud,
    2000), pp. 191, 195.
69 BL, Petty papers, Add. MS 72,856, f. 108. An attempt in November 1679 to have the
    sentence of the Irish court in these proceedings enforced by the English court was
    dismissed, the court holding that it had no jurisdiction to enforce the sentence of the Irish
    Court of Admiralty: *Pilkington* v. *The Orrery* (1679) Burrell 253, 167 Eng. Rep. 560.

compelling constitutional considerations: that Petty's acting as judge in
litigation which concerned his own interests was unsupportable; and that the
subject-matter of the dispute fell outside the permitted zone of admiralty
instance jurisdiction.

Admiralty droits

The admiralty perquisites side of the court's jurisdiction concerned those
maritime casualties, royal fish (whales and porpoises), unclaimed vessels, and
cargo (flotsam, jetsam and ligan) which, in default of a claim being made by
the original owner, fell to the crown. The court's function was to determine
whether property fell within the definition of admiralty perquisite, and
whether any other person had a superior right to the property. By an
arrangement of longstanding the Irish court was allowed retain for itself all
admiralty perquisites of under £20 value. However, the extent of *droit*
business being transacted by the Irish court fell well below its potential level.
Petty's papers indicate that the jurisdiction was being undermined from
three sources, all intercepting property so that it could not be taken to the
notice of the court. The principal source of rivalry for the jurisdiction came
from lords of manors adjoining the coastline who claimed title to *droits* found
on their coastline as part of their wider manorial grant; a second source
of tension was by acts of pure theft by local people taking admiralty
perquisites for themselves; a third source of interference derived from the
Commissioners of Customs in Ireland whose officers withheld admiralty
perquisites from the admiralty courts.

In December 1678, a whale was washed up on the Wicklow coast. Having
issued a precept to his marshal to empanel a jury, Petty travelled from Dublin to
hold a court of admiralty. On arrival he found that the most valuable parts of the
creature had been extracted by servants of the local manorial lord, Sir Richard
Parsons, while other pieces had been taken as souvenirs by local people:

> Upon Tuesday last there came a rumour to this town that a whale of
> great bigness (and consequently worth) was cast up in Wicklow about
> 17 miles from this place; soon after Col. Dillon (the Vice Admiral) sent
> his servant to look after it upon Wednesday. I also sent a precept by the
> marshal, who empanelled a jury upon the place in order to enquire not
> only into the value of this fish but in ye propriety also; for that several
> lords of manors especially Sir Richard Parsons pretended to this fish,
> but before I could hear from the Vice Admiral's agent or the marshal of
> the court another rumour came to this town (together with some small
> parts of the fish itself) that the whale was all cut in pieces and carried
> away by the country people but more especially by a principal tenant of
> the said Richard Parsons. Hereupon the vice admiral and myself went

down in person on Thursday and the next morning (being Friday the third instant) we held a court of inquiry whereupon we found as follows: 1. That this whale having offered at two other places did upon Sunday the 29th past at 3 in the afternoon (and at one hours flood) come aground on the place where she last rested and where the people began to break her up and divide her together with the names of the persons with whose hands ropes, boats and anchor she was stayed in that place. 2. We found that upon Monday the 30th several persons by the direction of Sir R. Parsons's said tenant opened her belly to rid it of the entrails and then cut off as many big pieces as they could carry and with horses and oxen drew them to Sir Richard Parsons's land, housing some part of it within said tenants outhouses.

3. We found her dimension to be 16 yards and a half long and by the best estimation we could make about seven yards in compass and the fat and skin to be about 3 inches thick and the gills placed at the mouth to consist of about 200 small flakes of the matter which we commonly call whale bone one side whereof was fringed with a stuff like small pack thrid of which flakes many persons took one or two a piece out of curiosity being of no real value or use we reason of. 4. We found that about three quarters of the said whale did lie collected in the places aforementioned and the rest carried away by hundreds of country people as a novelty.

A further source of interception came from the Commissioners of Customs. The Commissioners with their more expansive apparatus, were usually first to seize potential admiralty perquisites. There are a number of references to the Commissioners either refusing to release admiralty *droits*, or else re-seizing *droits* until duty on the goods was paid. In 1682 Petty raised this problem with Sir John Werden, the secretary to the duke of York. Petty reported to Southwell that he had asked Werden to 'procure an instruction to the new Commissioners for Ireland that ye Vice Admirals officers when they seize floating goods may be allowed to keep them in their custody whereas of late farmers' officers have still refused them for their duty and I put that point to be now determined, whether such goods shall be liable to duty or no'.[70] It is unlikely that Petty's intervention was effective. A report compiled by the registrar of the Munster court in 1688 indicated that the problem persisted. The report listed a quantity of barrels of wine abandoned at sea which had been seized by customs officers in the remoter parts of the province, and which they refused to release to the marshal of the court of admiralty until payment of customs' duty had first been made:[71]

70 Petty to Southwell, 19 Oct. 1682, *Petty-Southwell corr.*, p. 109.
71 Southwell to Pepys, 2 July 1688 (Bodl., Pepys papers, Rawlinson A. 186, p. 49).

The reason why several gills of wine contained in the within account are not appraised is because they lie in several remote parts of this county and the officers appointed to appraise them have no security for their charges in going to ye several places where the wine lies and are unwilling upon their own costs and charges and having no security to be reimbursed to travel so far, the wines being all taken account of by ye officers of the customs house or into their custody and they affirm that no wine will be delivered until order from ye commissioners who have already ordered that what money ye wine is sold must be delivered into their several collectors.

The criminal jurisdiction of the Irish Court of Admiralty in the Restoration period

The criminal side of the court's business followed an annual 'court of enquiry' held, usually, in late August or September. A jury was empanelled, and following a charge from the judge, was directed to make presentments identifying offences of navigational obstruction or irregular fishing in the port of Dublin. The procedure by way of presentment jury was intended to elicit the observations of the vocational group best acquainted with the state of the port; accordingly, the tradition was that the grand jury was composed of the 'gabbardmen' and fishermen of the port of Ringsend. A note taken by Petty's register, James Waller, described the charges found by the Ringsend jury, and returned to the court, in 1680:[72]

Mr Martin saith:
1. That boats of gabbards do bring sand to sell to the builders and lay down their sand upon my Lord Santry's wall and other places upon ye Wood Key and Merchants Key so as by leaving it store great part of it falls upon ye river and they neglect to remove it.
2. There is house upon ye Merchants Key falling down and rebuilding. The rubbish whereof is thrown or let fall into the river.
3. Inquiry as to stores and other thrash thrown out at Salmon Poole to the prejudice of shipping.
4. Take notice of ye sand that grows up upon ye East side of ye new bridge.

The practice was to hold these sessions at Dublin's principal port town, Ringsend, or at nearby Lazy Hill, with the judge, following the practice of the English admiralty sessions, making a long formal address to the jury, followed by dinner[73] for an invited group, and an afternoon's drinking for the

72 4 Aug. 1680 (BL, Lansdowne MS 1,228, f. 56).
73 See the entry in Pepys's *Diary*, 17 Mar. 1663, for a description of a charge by the judge of the English Court of Admiralty, Dr Exton, at the criminal sessions: 'To St. Margaret's Hill in Southwark, where the Judge of the Admiralty came and the rest of the Doctors of Civil

jury. Two of Petty's Ringsend grand jury addresses survive.[74] Those addresses
were, following the contemporary practice of the judges of the English High
Court of Admiralty, divided into two sections: the first, following the English
convention, was a highly rhetorical eulogy on the Lord High Admiral, the
Court of Admiralty, and the maritime industry. The second part, 'the
articles', described the offences over which the court had jurisdiction, and
invited the jury to report whether there was, in respect of the various subjects
over which the court had jurisdiction, anything amiss. Grandiloquence was
conventional in the admiralty judge's sessions address; Petty's adapted that
form in order to satirise his own court, and crack in-jokes:[75]

> Don't you see what a noise and tumult is in all land courts? What
> armies of barristers and attornies are drawn up against each other?
> How their registers are confounded with orders? How tedious suits are
> there! And with what reluctancy the condemned party obeys those
> courts? Whereas in ye High Court there is no noise at all, our criers
> need not Sir Samuel Moreland's trumpet to make his oyez with. He
> can whisper it, and be heard sufficiently. With this beard (that you see
> him wear) he can made such waves as may sufficiently signify the
> pleasure of ye court without words. If a fish were our crier his voice
> may be sufficient. Lord! what Morose have given to have been judge of
> this quiet court? And how unhappy was Glascock that he had not dealt
> with him, rather than me. We have no *strepitus forensis* amongst us, Sir
> Peter Pett's absence can make no famine of our law; 'tis true, that
> sometimes a pair of proctors do thunder and lighten a little, at each
> other, but all ends in a shower, and they soon find liquor wherewith to
> quench their hottest ebullitions. Our court is almost arrived at that
> quiet and perfection, that ye High Court of Chancery of England was
> in, when Sir Thomas More was Chancellor, for then there was no
> causes depending, and we haven't above five; we sit and adjourn chiefly,
> to represent ye ebbing and flowing of sea, which does ye same. I know
> no courts so spiritual as ours, the courts that are so called are carnal to
> ours; the officers of our courts are poets, and write songs and allegories
> and spiritual fancies.

Law, and some other Commissioners, whose Commission of oyer and terminer was read,
and then the charge given by Dr Exton, which methought was somewhat dull, though he
would seem to intend it to be very rhetorical, saying that justice had two wings, one of
which spread itself over land, the other over the water, which was this Admiralty Court.
That being done, and the jury called they broke up, and to dinner in a tavern hard by, where
a great dinner and I with them.' *The diary of Samuel Pepys*, ed. Latham and Mathews
(London, 1971), iv, 76.

74 BL, Lansdowne MS 1,228, ff.38–56v
75 Ibid.

The second part of the address described the jurisdiction of the jury, and detailed the subject matter of the inquiry it was to make. Thus, Petty describes the jury's jurisdiction over navigational obstruction:

> In ye care of ports and harbours, that is to say that no obstruction or impediments of passages navigation, be neither made or suffered to be in navigable waters if they can possibly be removed or prevented, and therefore ye good men of ye jury are to enquire what persons do cast out of any ship or other vessel within any haven, creek river or channel, flowing, running to any town, any manner of gravel, ballast rubbish or other filth, whereby such rivers are annoyed clayed or made unfit for navigation and passage and you are to have a special care that in no navigable rivers or ports within ye admirals jurisdiction there be suffered any broken anchors, timbers, stakes, riddles or other misdemeanors to lie in any vessel's way towards any town, wharf, key whereby ye passage of such vessel may be hindered or endangered and you are to see that no inhabitant dwelling upon or near the shore, beneath the bridges do cast out of their houses, yards, wharfs or quays, any rubbish, soil, sea coal, dirt to ye ends aforementioned and forasmuch as there be many impediments and dangers of navigation as barrs, rocks, shelfs, sands flats, shole waters and ye like which are all covered by one smooth face of the water, it is ye care of ye admiral to appoint not only landmarks, beacons, light houses, buoys and perches to serve as dead and dumb pilots, but also to appoint living pilots where there is occasion, as where the sand do remove and where channels do change their course, and tides set different ways, upon such odd and irregular causes as strangers cannot take notice of wherefore gentlemen you are to present what ye find amiss upon this head, that is to say in short, all things that do hinder or endanger navigation.

The grand jury was then required to make a return to the Court of Admiralty within seven days of the original address. Following the return of the grand jury presentment those identified could be cited and tried. The primary sanction was by way of a fine, usually only a few shillings; imprisonment lay only in default of payment of the fine.[76]

Again, this useful, local jurisdiction was highly fragile and under attack from the primary rival for admiralty jurisdiction in late seventeenth-century Ireland, the municipal corporations. In a note to Sir Robert Southwell,[77] who,

---

76 In 1663, in a legal opinion prepared for the duke of York for the benefit of the Court of Vice Admiralty of Leinster, it was stated that 'ye judge hath power to impose fines upon offenders and to commit them to prison for non payment of those fines'. Duke of York to Cooke and Wentworth, 10 Dec. 1663 (TNA:PRO, ADM 1755). The opinion was drafted by two senior civilians, Doctors William Turner and David Budd.

77 Petty to Southwell, 4 Jan. 1677, *Petty-Southwell corr.*, p. 66.

in turn, distributed a copy to Samuel Pepys,[78] Petty described four writs of prohibition which had been issued against the Irish Court of Admiralty. The cause of one of these prohibitions was a charge, prosecuted at the 1679 session, which intruded deeply into Dublin municipal concerns. It involved the newly constructed Essex Bridge. In November 1677 Petty had written to Southwell:[79] 'You may have heard that there is a new bridge lately built at Dublin, below the old one without leave of the Admiral. This Bridge I allow to be a good work, but have questioned the builders for passing by the Admiral.' The promoter of the new Essex Bridge,[80] Sir Humphrey Jervis, the Dublin entrepreneur and ship owner, who frequently crossed swords with Petty during his period as admiralty judge, then retaliated with a writ of prohibition; Petty wrote: 'a bridge hath been made across a navigable river, without the Admiralty leave; and a prohibition brought to the suit commenced thereon.'[81] The grounds upon which the prohibition was sought, do not survive. It is unlikely that Petty could have succeeded in resisting the prohibition. The proposition that the judge of the Court of Admiralty was competent to act as administrative regulator of bridges in navigable rivers was one for which there is no authority in the seventeenth-century literature on admiralty law, or in the Admiral's patent. His claim to do so is symptomatic of a more general fault. Petty generally appears to have assumed that he had a jurisdiction far wider than that which the court was, by the late seventeenth century, considered to possess. In his 1677 address[82] to the grand jury, he asked it to report on the operation of ferry services; to report on the immigration of fugitives or persons bringing seditious books, and to report on the emigration of persons in the king's pay; to report on infringements of the customs laws; and to present persons building houses or quays on the seabed without special licence of the Admiral.

Records of three further prohibitions appear in Petty's notes: 'a prohibition hath been brought after an execution in the case of using unlawful ways of fishing'; '[A] prohibition in a suit for stopping and annoying a navigable river. The like in the case of a pilot condemned to pay damages for casting away a ship in a gross manner.'[83] The precise jurisdictional grounds upon which these prohibitions were being sought can only be a matter of conjecture. It may be that prohibitions were grounded on claims that the jurisdiction of the court did not operate within the admiralty jurisdiction entrusted to Dublin by the charter of 1582; or it may be that the fourteenth-century statutes of

---

78 Petty's account is preserved in Pepys's papers: Bodl., Pepys papers, Rawlinson A 172, f. 13.
79 Petty to Southwell, 10 Nov. 1677, *Petty-Southwell corr.*, p. 39.
80 M. Craig, *Dublin 1660–1860* (London, 1992), p. 25.
81 Petty to Southwell, 4 Jan. 1679, *Petty-Southwell corr.*, p. 66.
82 BL, Lansdowne MS 1,228, ff.38–56v.
83 Petty to Southwell, 4 Jan. 1679, *Petty Southwell corr.*, p. 66.

Richard II[84] which forbade the exercise of admiralty jurisdiction in *corpore comitatus* were being invoked. The fourth article of the Resolutions of 1633 had conceded to the court of admiralty its customary criminal jurisdiction to correct navigational abuses committed in navigable rivers beneath the first bridges. It is well known that in England, following the Restoration, the Resolution of 1633 ceased to be observed by the courts of common law, which resumed its pre-1633 campaign to push back further the jurisdiction of the admiralty.[85] What Petty's letters indicate is that in post-Restoration Dublin, the courts of common law had found a way around the fourth article of the Resolutions of 1633, and that, contrary to the injunction that no prohibitions be granted in cases of 'annoyances and obstructions of navigable rivers' the courts of common law in Ireland were doing precisely that.

The Navigation Act, 1671

Between 1671 and 1680 Irish trade and national revenue were weakened by the effects of the Navigation Act, 1671.[86] The Navigation Act, 1671 required that merchandise shipped from America first be landed in ports in England, Wales, or Berwick on Tweed. Failure by a vessel setting out from the Americas to give the statutory security to comply with the legislation, or landing directly in Ireland, and not at one of the authorized ports, constituted a ground of forfeiture. The legislation indicated, though only somewhat obliquely, that the enforcement of the legislation, through power of seizure and condemnation, was entrusted to courts of admiralty. The only reference to the issue of what courts were to have jurisdiction was found in section 1, which directed that, upon forfeiture, there be distributed 'one moiety to the King's Majesty, his heirs and successors, and the other moiety to him that shall seize and sue for the same in any of the said plantations, *in the court of the High Admiral of England, or any of his vice admirals, or in any Court of Record in England*'. It was questionable whether the Irish Court of Admiralty fell within any limb of the description of courts with jurisdiction; the Irish Court of Admiralty was not 'the court' of the High Admiral of England; neither was it, unlike the four provincial courts of vice-admiralty, a court of any of 'his Vice Admirals', and it obviously was not a court of record 'in England'. Nonetheless, it appears that from the mid-1670s the Irish Court of Admiralty was assisting the enforcement of the Navigation Acts in two ways: firstly in executing processes issued out of the English Court of Admiralty; and, secondly, by exercising its own independent enforcement jurisdiction.

---

84 13 Rich. II., st.1 c.5 (1389); 15 Rich. II., c. 3 (1391).
85 See *Hale and Fleetwood* at pp. cxvii-cxxix.
86 22 & 23 Chas. II, c. 26.

The Irish Privy Council, following representations by high-profile Dublin merchants whose vessels had been arrested, protested about the harassing of Irish trade by warrants issued out of the High Court of Admiralty in England into Ireland. By reference to the constitutional theory which prevailed in Doctors' Commons – that the Court of Admiralty was the court of the Lord High Admiral of England and Ireland, and that, since the Lord High Admiral had jurisdictional competence over both kingdoms, that the Court had jurisdiction in Ireland – the High Court of Admiralty was quite entitled to have its warrants executed in Ireland. Following the complaint of the Irish Privy Council, the judicial surrogates at the High Court of Admiralty, Doctors Exton and Lloyd, were summoned to a conference with the Committee of Trade and Plantations, where they informed the Committee that Irish ship owners were, in collusion with the Irish customs' farmers, fraudulently exploiting the proviso in the Navigation Act, 1671 which allowed for landing in Ireland in cases of shipwreck. The Committee for Trade, by way of response to the petition of the Irish Privy Council, informed it that the Navigation Act, 1671 was being evaded in Ireland, and directed the co-operation of the Irish Privy Council in the enforcement in Ireland of the orders of the High Court of Admiralty:[87]

> and by them we are informed that it is not without good cause that so strict a hand is kept for hindering the irregular trade of the merchants of Ireland to your excellencies plantations who have of late ventured upon pretence of shipwreck and other fraudulent devices to elude the several acts of parliament here which expressly provide that this kingdom be made a staple of the commodities of your majesty's plantations for the supply of other countries in which unlawful practices they have been encouraged and abetted by the farmers of your majesty's revenue that they thereby may defraud your majesty's customs in England and draw into themselves a benefit from the customs in Ireland arising by this irregular trade; so far are they from being damnified ten thousand pounds as in the said papers is alleged by them. In consideration whereof our humble advice is that we see no reason why any seizures of this kind should be forbidden or discontinued. Your majesty's Lord Lieutenant and Council of Ireland may receive your royal order to take care, as much as in them lies, that the method of law now practiced in that Kingdom according to the powers of your majesty's Court of Admiralty here may have due course and effect which is necessary for securing our customs in England pursuant to the several acts of Parliament made in this behalf.

The cases which had been the subject of the complaints to the privy council were the *Providence of London*[88] (owned by John Rogerson), the *Dublin*[89]

87 Coventry to Ormonde, 19 June 1679 (Bodl., Carte MSS, vol. 39, f. 55).
88 Affidavit of Patrick Little and John Murphy 8 Jan. 1679 (TNA:PRO, HCA 15/9).
89 Affidavit of Patrick Little, 3 July 1679 (TNA:PRO, HCA 15/11).

and the *America*[90] (owned by Petty's old enemy, Humphrey Jervis). Petty's court entered enthusiastically into conflict with these powerful Irish trading interests. There were violent engagements as Petty's marshals, usually greatly outnumbered, attempted to execute warrants for the arrest of vessels, or to seize goods landed in breach of the Act of 1671. In the case of the *Dublin* the master, following the arrest, came aboard, and having been informed that the marshal had arrested the ship by virtue of a warrant out of the Court of Admiralty of England he replied that was 'a foolish thing, meaning the broad arrow, and contemptuously with his own hand rubbed it'. The proprietors also sought the assistance of the common law (particularly the notoriously anti-admiralty municipal) courts. Following the arrest of the *Dublin*, a bill of indictment was laid against the deputy marshal, Patrick Little, before the Dublin sessions of the peace, charging him with several thousand pounds' worth of damage. On his refusal to give bail, William Davis, recorder of Dublin, remanded Little in custody where he remained for six days.

The Navigation Act, 1671 entrusted enforcement powers to the English High Court of Admiralty. Although it is less certain whether the Irish Court of Admiralty had enforcement jurisdiction, in at least two cases, warrants were issued directly out of the Court of Admiralty of Ireland. In the *Dublin* two warrants were issued, the first from the Irish court, and the second from the English. The *Providence of London*[91] was alleged to have imported 460 hogsheads of tobacco from Virginia directly into Dublin in breach of the Navigation Acts. A warrant had issued from the English Court of Admiralty for the arrest of the vessel. Accordingly, two deputy marshals of the Irish Court of Admiralty went on board the vessel, drew the broad arrow and removed its sails as it lay at anchor in Salmon Pool. Rogerson, allegedly, had the tobacco taken off the vessel, and Petty, at his own initiative, issued a second warrant of attachment. Rogerson, however, refused to permit Petty's men to enter his premises:[92]

> The 5th or 6th [December] about one of the clock in order to serve and execute another warrant or attachment from the said High Court of Admiralty of Ireland upon the said tobacco he demanded entrance into the said Rogerson's cellars or warehouses where the said tobacco lay but was not suffered to enter there into though the said Patrick showed the said attachment unto the said Rogerson and told him the contents thereof the said Rogerson answering and confessing that there was in his hands certain quantities of tobacco which he had from the said *Providence of London* but withal refusing to give an obedience unto the said attachment.

90 Ibid.
91 Affidavit of Patrick Little and John Murphy, 8 Jan. 1679 (TNA:PRO, HCA 15/9).
92 Ibid.

THE ORGANISATION OF THE IRISH COURT OF
ADMIRALTY IN PETTY'S TIME

Like all courts of vice-admiralty, the Court of Admiralty of Ireland was constituted of three officers: the judge, the registrar and the marshal. The office of judge was supplemented by the office of judge's surrogate. Petty's warrant of appointment authorized him to appoint a surrogate to act in his place; Petty's surrogate was Dr Dudley Loftus. The formal condition necessary to constitute a surrogate was an instrument of deputation. There appears to have been a view in circulation that Petty had made that appointment in a manner which was technically defective. In the mariners' wages case, *Pippard* v. *Fleming*, the ground of appeal to the High Court of Admiralty in London was that Loftus had been irregularly appointed, and had acted without 'any legitimate deputation having been made, signed and signified'.[93]

From 1681, when Petty withdrew to his London residence in Piccadilly, the court was effectively left in the hands of Loftus. Loftus's association with the Court of Admiralty stretched back to 1654 when he had been appointed judge of the Commonwealth Court of Admiralty.[94] Following the Restoration he had served as deputy to Carey Dillon in the Vice-Admiralty Court of Leinster,[95] and he continued to serve as surrogate to Sir Paul Rycaut right up to the mid-1690s.[96] While Loftus was, unlike Petty, a trained civilian, his principal failing was a confrontational and troublesome personality: in the 1660s he had been dismissed from his office as judge of the Court of Prerogative; in 1673 he had been incarcerated in Dublin Castle[97] and stripped of his office as master in chancery for agitating against government-instigated reforms of the corporation of Dublin. It was this side to his personality which underlay the most dramatic incident during his period as Petty's surrogate, the imprisonment, described earlier, in the *Jacob of Dublin* of the officials of the mayor of Dublin, for their alleged contempt in executing the process of *replevin* against a vessel arrested by the Court of Admiralty.

The two administrative officials of the court were the registrar and the marshal. The registrar (with responsibility for recording the proceedings, sealing processes and maintaining moneys paid in) was Petty's brother-in-law,

93 TNA:PRO, HCA 24/119.

94 Loftus is referred to as judge of the Irish Court of Admiralty in the Commonwealth civil list of 1654 (BL, Betham papers, Add. MS 19, 833, f. 4). Loftus was stated to be in receipt of a salary of £100.

95 TNA:PRO, HCA 3/51, ff. 327, 596.

96 Dr Loftus served as surrogate to Sir Paul Rycaut who, during a disastrous period for the court, served as absentee judge from 1689 to 1698, while simultaneously serving as resident to Hamburg. Rycaut considered Loftus 'a very unfit man for the place but I know no other to employ' (BL, Rycaut papers, Lansdowne MS 1,153 C).

97 1 Sept. 1673 (TNA:PRO, SP 63/334, f. 107).

and a member of Petty's wider entourage, James Waller. It is not clear to what extent Waller possessed the technical skills required to perform the office of registrar of a civil law court, and his functions appear, in practice, to have been undertaken by a deputy,[98] the Dublin notary Thomas Wilkinson (described by Petty as 'a man well versed in these affairs')[99] who would continue to serve for the next forty years, until he died in 1718. Petty's job description of the office of marshal was as a position suitable for 'some stout, active fellow'.[100] The office of marshal was officially shared between two officers, Charles Sturt and George Pigott.[101] It is unclear to what extent Sturt and Pigott personally discharged any of these functions; it would seem that they acted as overseers and that the function was, in practice, discharged by an array of deputies. When, in July 1682, Sturt died, the office of marshal was, on the duke of York's direction, filled by Captain Francis Robinson, an army officer who had fallen on hard times. There were doubts over Robinson's judgment, and when a few months later the fight over the *replevin* proceedings in the *Jacob of Dublin* broke out, Ormonde's son, Richard, earl of Arran, who had served with Robinson,[102] held the new Admiralty marshal partly responsible for the resulting inter-jurisdictional tension. 'The person employed by the judge', he wrote to his father, 'is liable to mistakes and to do extravagant things. I found him so when he was in the army, and it may be doubted whether his civil employment will reform him. I believe it will always be so when poverty is the best qualification a man has for an office.'[103]

In addition to the central Court of Admiralty based in Dublin, Petty also established a series of satellite courts operating in Munster. In September 1677 he had drawn up a commission for Thomas Palmer to act as deputy judge for the coastline from Bantry to Valencia, while a Mr Brown was deputed to serve for the area from Valencia to Smerwick.[104] Thomas Meade, the Kinsale lawyer who represented the interests of the Perceval family, was appointed deputy judge with a commission entitling him to act in Kinsale and the coast of Cork to the west of Kinsale.[105] However, objections were raised in Munster circles that Meade's Catholicism disqualified him from office. Petty recounted: 'Since I gave Mr. Mead his Commission I have been peppered with Letters accusing him to be Puritan Papist, devoted to the

---

98 See, for instance, an affidavit of 14 Dec. 1678 attested by Thomas Wilkinson, where Wilkinson is described as deputy register (TNA:PRO, HCA/15/9, f. 41).

99 Petty to Werden, 4 Aug. 1683 (McGill U. Lib., Petty letterbook, MS 7,612, f. 459).

100 Petty to Werden, 3 Mar. 1677 (McGill U. Lib., Petty letterbook, MS 7,612, f. 288).

101 Peter Pett to Southwell, 12 July 1676 (BL, Petty papers, Add. MS 72,852, f. 119).

102 Arran had been Colonel of the King's Regiment of Guards of Ireland.

103 Bodl., Carte MSS, vol. 144, f. 400.

104 Petty to Crookshank, 15 Sept. 1677 (McGill U. Lib., Petty letterbook, MS 7,612, ff. 354, 355).

105 'I doubt T. Meade grumbles inwardly that he is not judge of all Munster, whereas I design him but for Kinsale and all the coast of Cork westward thereof'. *Petty-Southwell corr.*, p. 40.

French, and that his name is Myagh and not Mead; with such other circumstances as envy and prejudice uses to accumulate.'[106] There was, by contrast with the position in England following the Test Act, 1673, no statutory prohibition on Catholic appointments to vice admiralty offices, and the religiously indifferent Petty refused to compromise: 'as for our friend Mr. Mead, I ever thought him only a papist and free of any imprudent biases. Born in the town of Kinsale among the English, restored by the Court of Claims, with all other circumstances that might occur in one that was not a Protestant, and being otherwise not obnoxious either in behaviour or ill life, I believe as you do, that 'tis either personal malice, or indignation of the common law that any justice but their own should be upheld.'[107]

The office of judge of the Court of Admiralty of Ireland was, unlike the judges of the four courts of common law, not on the civil establishment. The judge depended entirely on his fees. Of course, the nature of the work undertaken by the judge of the Irish Court of Admiralty, largely involving seamen's wages' complaints, and, after the Second Anglo–Dutch War, deprived of prize business, meant that the level of fees generated by the office must have been negligible. Petty in an affidavit submitted to the Court of King's Bench valued the profits of the office 'as somewhat under two perches of oysters'.[108] Indeed, Petty claimed that his postage costs exceeded his income from fees, and directed Sir Robert Southwell to see if he could (as his predecessors had been) be exempted from postage. The principal source of the admiralty judge's income derived not from his judicial work but from a peculiar and legally dubious duty extracted by the Court of Admiralty in Ireland: fees for fishing licences. The legal justification for this appeared to derive from the terms of the patent granted to the Lord High Admiral. The traditional patent entrusted the Lord High Admiral in vague terms with authority over fishermen.[109] Petty argued that since his patent designated him commissary of the Lord High Admiral, it followed that the admiralty judge acquired the administrative powers of the Admiral. In a letter to Sir Allen Apsley, Petty wrote:[110] 'I am not only judge of ye admiralty, but also commissary of his Royal Highness in all maritime matters, and particularly of fishing and as doth ye Judge of Admiralty of Scotland take himself as appears.' However, the admiralty fishing licence was unknown in England, and there were considerable doubts about the legality of a power which

106 Petty to Southwell, 19 Mar. 1678, *Petty-Southwell corr.*, p. 49.
107 Petty to Southwell, 30 Mar. 1678, *Petty-Southwell corr.*, p. 53.
108 Petty to Pett, 26 Jan. 1677 (McGill U. Lib., Petty letterbook, MS 7,614, f. 263).
109 The Lord Admiral's patent of 1611 provided: 'He is simply the officer of the greatest power and strength in the kingdom, having at his command all the shipping, mariners, seamen, fishermen.' J. and S. Shaw, 'Admiralty administration and personnel, 1619–1714', *Bulletin of Institute of Historical Research*, xiv (1936/37), 166.
110 Petty to Apsley, 9 Sept. 1676 (McGill U. Lib., Petty letterbook, MS 7,612, f. 209).

interfered with the right of the subject to fish in tidal waters and high seas.[111] Challenges by the Corporation of Dublin to the legality of the tax appear to have been contemplated in Petty's time.[112] However, it was not until 1752, when a writ of *replevin* designed to challenge the legality of the measure, was initiated in the Court of Common Pleas, that the Irish Court of Admiralty ceased the practice.[113] However, so long as the measure was allowed to continue it provided the judge's principal source of revenue.[114] The licence could also, it appears, be purchased by payment in kind. In a note to his friend Sir Peter Pett, Sir William proudly disclosed that 'we hath gotten 6 shillings and 8d. for a license to dredge oysters and are promised half a hundred of oysters for granting it a little before the piscine day under colour of helping a poor old seaman'.[115]

The Court of Admiralty of Ireland did not, in the reign of Charles II, have a settled, official place of business. It discharged its annual criminal 'court of inquiry' at the Dublin port district of Ringsend. The rest of the business appears to have been conducted from Sir William's home in George's Lane.[116] Nor did it possess that traditional symbol of admiralty authority, a silver oar. In 1662 the duke of York waived the income generated by the sale of oil from a whale condemned by the Leinster Vice-Admiralty in order to allow the court acquire a silver oar. But it is not clear whether such an oar was ever manufactured.[117]

111 *Warran* v. *Mathews* (1703) 1 Salk. 357, 91 Eng. Rep. 312.
112 It can be inferred that it was resistance to the regulation of fishing by the Court of Admiralty within its chartered admiralty area which underlay the following resolution by Dublin Corporation in October 1677: 'it is ordered and agreed upon, by the authority of this present assembly, shewing that the fishing of Salmon Poole, and within the city liberty, anciently belonged to the Sheriffs of this city, and that the Court of Admiralties of late pretend a right thereunto, the petitioners therefore humbly prayed this present assembly that the sheriffs of this city may be justified in their ancient right as to the said fishing, and that the said privileges may not be lost: it is therefore ordered and agreed upon , by the authority of the said assembly, that the Sheriffs, with the advice of the Lord Mayor and recorder, do take care to effect the cities right in the premises, and that the same be done at the cities charge, on the Lord Mayors warrant to the city.' *Cal. anc. rec. Dublin*, v, p. 147.
113 TNA: PRO, ADM 2/1052, f. 68.
114 In 1680 Thomas Dance, recorded 'The reckoning made between Sir William and Patrick Redmond about the Herring Licenses. There appears to be due to Sir William the sum of forty five shillings to complete the sum due for the season 1679 and before'; 4 Aug. 1680 (BL, Petty papers, Add. MS 72,893, f. 56r).
115 Petty to Pett, 26 Aug. 1676 (McGill U. Lib., Petty letterbook, MS 7,612, f. 208).
116 Georges Lane is described as the address of the Court of Admiralty in Petty's 1677 grand jury speech (BL, Lansdowne MS 1,228, ff.36–58v).
117 A subsequent judge of the Irish court, Dr William King, on taking up office in 1701 wrote 'There is a seal of the Admiralty. But neither oar nor any certain place or court to which any person may be cited' (King to Ellis, 13 Nov. 1701, BL, Ellis papers, Add. MS 28,887, ff. 389–390).

More serious a problem than its weak physical apparatus was the court's want of intellectual resources. The London civilian Dr Bedford, noting that 'Sir William Petty grows weary under the difficulty in proceedings and that it is improbable to discharge his office without others frequently arising' suggested that he hire 'some understanding proctor'. However, he did concede that that 'would be difficult to do unless about £100 be secured which is improbable the profits ever will afford'.[118] Petty probably attempted to compensate for his lack of legal training, and the lack of the assistance of professional expertise in Dublin, by building up a small library of admiralty legal literature. Soon after his appointment Petty was reminding his predecessor to provide him with his collection of admiralty texts:[119] 'Pray Sir William Glascock to send me ye books and papers he promised and particularly *Les uses et coustumes de la mer*.'[120] Petty also owned a copy of the systematically-organised account of admiralty practice, *Praxis curiae admiralitatis Angliae*, prepared by the Elizabethan civilian, Francis Clerke.[121] Clerke's book functioned as the vademecum of the 'part-time, sometimes honorary, and rather amateurish judiciary'[122] of the courts of vice-admiralty in the late seventeenth century (men such as Petty), and Petty highly recommended it.[123] Indeed, the publication in Dublin of the first edition of Clerke's manuscript was Dublin's principal contribution to seventeenth-century admiralty literature.[124] Clerke's Elizabethan manuscript was first edited for publication by Dr Thomas Bladen, dean of Ardfert, and chaplain to the duke of Ormonde.[125] In addition to texts on admiralty law, Petty's library would have included copies

---

118 Bedford's opinion, Doctors' Commons, 11 Apr. 1678 (BL, Petty papers, Add. MS 72,852, ff.152–54v).

119 Petty to Pett, 1 Aug. 1676 (McGill U. Lib., Petty letterbook, MS 7,612, f. 200).

120 Etienne Cleriac, *Uses et coustumes de la mer divisées en trois parties* (Bordeaux, 1661).

121 The text was first published in Dublin in 1666, and in London in 1667.

122 D.M. Derrett, 'The works of Francis Clerke, proctor,' *Studia et Documenta Historiae et Juris*, 40 (1973), 52.

123 'Now as to ye Admiralty proceedings these rules are comprehended in a small book called Clerk Practice which is not unlike the little book in England and Ireland, wherein ye rules of their respective Chanceries are contained;' Memorandum by Petty on admiralty law, undated, BL, Lansdowne MS 1228.

124 The text was first printed in Dublin in 1666, and later, in London in 1667; E.R. Dix, *Dublin printed books* (Dublin, 1898), i, 132. The following account of the publishing history of the book is supplied in A. Wood, *Athenae Oxonienses: an exact history of all the writers and bishops who have had their education in the university of Oxford* (London, 1813), i, 658: '*Praxis admiralitatis angliae*. Dubl. 1666, qu. published by the said doctor [Bladen]. But the copy from whence that edition was published, being, as was pretended, false in many matters, a better copy was published at London, 1667, in oct. ... by E.S. "who was one Edward Stephens of Glocester-hall."' No copy of the Bladen edition survives.

125 During the interregnum Bladen had 'fled to a quiet retreat, and employed himself in the study of civil and cannon law': see the dedicatory note to Clerke's *Praxis in curiis ecclesiasticis* (London, 1684); H. Cotton, *Fasti ecclesiae Hiberniae* (Dublin, 1857), i, 442.

of treaties and proclamations. In 1676 Petty requested 'from ye Lords Commissioners of Admiralty or Mr Pepys a collection of all proclamations and other acts of state which they act by in England'.[126]

WITHDRAWAL AND DEPARTURE, 1680–1683

Petty had entered office with hopes of prestige and executive power. However, upon assuming office he discovered the position quite the reverse. The job was comparatively low-grade. The court was constitutionally weak. He found himself technically out of his depth. On the occasions that he did exercise authority his orders were countermanded by writs of *replevin* or prohibition, or by orders of the Privy Council. Business was negligible, and the office was unrewarding. In a letter to his confidente, Peter Pett, Petty confessed:[127]

> The Admiralty Power is now in its neape tide, if you can send us any paper to blow wind in its arse. Enim mihi magnus Apollo Carey Dillon vacua dominatur in aula[128] is mighty busy where there is nothing to do. Our register's inkhorne is quite mouldy and our marshal's oar all chaps for want of moisture. Lord how many years will Sir George Cartaret rue the longer for his exploitation of his friend Sir William.

By 1680, however, Petty had begun to withdraw from active involvement in the Court of Admiralty. During the following three years he directed his talents to other concerns, the reform of revenue administration, his Kerry estates, the Royal Society and, his experiments with the double-bottomed ship.[129] During this period Dr Dudley Loftus served as Petty's surrogate, administering judicial functions on his behalf and keeping Petty apprised of developments in the court.

In the end it was Dublin college politics which appears to have determined the timing of Petty's departure, and his choice of successor. Dr Henry Styles was a Senior Fellow at Trinity College Dublin and Regius Professor of Law. In addition to holding the Regius Professorship he had served as vice provost

---

Bladen also produced a first edition of Clerke's other civilian text, *Praxis in curiis ecclesiasticis*. The reliability of the Bladen transcription of the ecclesiastical law work is assessed critically by J.H. Baker in *Monuments of endlesse labour: English canonists and their work, 1300–1800* (London, 1998), p. 75.

126 Petty to Gamble, 1 Aug. 1676 (McGill U. Lib., MS 7,612, ff.198–200). In 1677 Petty was still complaining that he did not have 'the late treatis between his Majesty and other princes for our direction'. Petty to Southwell, 10 Nov. 1677, *Petty-Southwell corr.*, p. 39.

127 Petty to Peter Pett, 26 Jan. 1667 (McGill U. Lib., Petty letterbook, MS 7,612, f. 263).

128 'The great Apollo Carey Dillon is lord and master in an empty chamber'.

129 Fitzmaurice, *The life of Sir William Petty* (London, 1895), pp. 250–58.

of Trinity, and was, when the provostship of Trinity fell vacant in 1683, considered the leading candidate. The earl of Arran reported that while everyone with whom he had discussed the matter 'thought him the fittest man,' Archbishop Michael Boyle, who rated him morally deficient, was determined that he not succeed.[130] Arran correctly, as it turned out, calculated that unless Styles made his peace with the Primate, an appointee would have to be translated from Oxford. This is what happened: in July the Oxford-based theologian, Dr Robert Huntington, was appointed in preference to Styles. In the meantime Petty, who was now dividing his time between Ireland and England, had become preoccupied with another project: obtaining the commission for the administration of licences for wine, beer and strengthened wines.[131] The timing of Petty's resignation, occurring just after Styles's failure to be appointed provost,[132] suggests that he was obliging Styles with an escape route from Trinity, while providing himself with cover with which to disengage. In August 1683 Petty wrote to the secretary of the duke of York a dispirited letter of resignation, identifying the lack of judicial business as his ground of resignation. This letter, probably Petty's last official act as judge of the Irish Court of Admiralty, was entrusted to Dr Styles to bring with him to an interview with the Admiralty Commissioners in London:[133]

> I troubled you lately with a letter of ye 4th inst. about ye Passes and ballastage. This is to desire your assistance for the bearer, Dr Stiles to succeed me in the place of judge of the admiralty, which I doe not quit because it affords me no wages, but because it gives me no such work as I expected, and have been glad to have bestowed my time upon, even without recompense or reward, than the satisfaction to have done well.

It is likely that as Petty concluded this particular chapter of his public career, he must have done so without having fulfilled even that minimum condition of the 'satisfaction to have done well'.[+]

---

130 Arran to Ormond, 29 Jan. 1683 (Bodl., Carte MSS, vol. 168, f. 79). See also McDowell and Webb, *Trinity College Dublin, 1592–1952* (Cambridge, 1982), pp. 25–27.

131 Arran to Rochester, 18 October 1683 (Bodl., Carte MSS, vol. 169, ff.14–16).

132 Robert Huntington, a fellow of Merton College, Oxford, was appointed Provost in September 1683; C. Maxwell, *A history of Trinity College Dublin, 1592–1892* (Dublin, 1946), p. 76.

133 Petty to Werden, 4 Aug. 1683 (McGill U. Lib., Petty letterbook, MS 7,612, f. 459).

+ This paper was written during the period of a Government of Ireland Senior Research Scholarship granted by the Irish Research Council for the Humanities and Social Sciences. The author wishes to acknowledge the support of the IRCHSS, as well as assistance provided by: Sonia Anderson (then of the Historical Manuscripts Commission), Toby Barnard (Hertford College, Oxford) and Lynda Mulvin (University College Dublin).

The value of judicial independence: evidence from eighteenth-century England

DANIEL M. KLERMAN AND PAUL G. MAHONEY[*]

JUDICIAL INDEPENDENCE IS GENERALLY regarded as a worthwhile feature of a legal system. This paper tries to provide empirical support for that view by examining stock market reactions to improvements in judicial tenure and salaries in eighteenth-century England. We find that tenure during good behaviour, as granted by the 1701 Act of Settlement, is associated with an eight percent rise in stock prices. Other improvements in judicial tenure and salary increases are associated with positive, but small increases in equity prices.

Prior scholars have tried to measure the impact of judicial independence through cross-sectional studies. That is, they have compared how countries with varying degrees of judicial independence perform in terms of economic growth, human rights, democracy, political liberty, and similar measures. They have generally found that countries with more independent judiciaries do better.[1]

These studies have the same drawbacks as most cross-sectional studies – the number of countries is small, the number of potentially relevant variables

* The authors thank Aaron Edlin, Bernie Black, Hamilton Bryson, Lance Davis, John de Figueiredo, John Donohue, Thomas Gallanis, Elizabeth Garrett, Joshua Getzler, Chris Hoag, Philip Hoffman, Timur Kuran, Hazel Lord, Jacob Klerman, John Langbein, Ed McCaffery, Bentley MacLeod, Mike Macnair, Matthew McCubbins, Charles Miller, Larry Neal, Mitch Polinsky, Renee Rastorfer, Andrei Shleifer, Eric Talley, Barry Weingast, Mark Weinstein, participants in the 2004 American Law & Economics Association conference, the 2003 American Society for Legal History conference, the 2003 British and Irish Legal History conference, the Caltech/University of Southern California Modeling the Constitution conference, the Harvard History of Capitalism seminar, and the 2003 NBER Law & Economics Summer Institute, and workshop participants at Dalhousie Law School, Northwestern University Law School, Stanford Law School, UCLA Law School, the University of Southern California Law School, and the University of Virginia School of Law for assistance, comments, and suggestions.

1 P. Mahoney, 'The common law and economic growth: Hayek might be right', *Journal of Legal Studies*, xxx (2001), 503–25; L. Feld and S. Voigt. 'Economic growth and judicial independence: cross country evidence using a new set of indicators', *European Journal of Political Economy*, xix (2003), 497–527; R. La Porta, F. López-de-Silanes, C. Pop-Eleches, and A. Shleifer, 'Judicial checks and balances', *Journal of Political Economy*, cxii (2003), 445–70.

is large, and it is difficult to develop a valid cross-cultural measure of judicial independence. In addition, it is always possible that the correlation between judicial independence and economic performance is not causal, but rather reflects the influence of some other factor or factors.

We accordingly apply an alternative test of the importance of judicial independence by examining change over time within a single country. Judges gained formal independence in England in a series of steps starting in 1701 and continuing through the eighteenth century. Fortunately, during this period there was a functioning stock market in London for which continuous daily prices are available starting in 1698.

We accordingly test for abnormal returns[2] on publicly traded stocks around the time of events changing the degree of judicial independence. These events include key dates in the passage of statutes granting judges security of tenure and increasing judicial salaries. Any abnormal returns associated with these events measure traders' perceptions of the impact of judicial independence on publicly traded companies. There is ample reason to think that market participants would have recognized a link between the status of the judiciary and private rights after witnessing royal interference in judicial proceedings during the seventeenth century.

Empirical results are consistent with the view that participants in the financial markets viewed judicial independence as beneficial. Abnormal equity returns around the time of every event we examined have the correct sign. Individually, however, only the abnormal returns around key dates surrounding the 1701 Act of Settlement are statistically significant. The Act of Settlement mandated that judges enjoy tenure during good behaviour rather than at the pleasure of the crown. As we discuss in detail below, it appears likely that the proposal to include provisions for judicial independence in the bill, and a later attempt by King William III to have them removed, were unexpected.

We obtain similar results using two different approaches. In the first, we compare price movements on the London market in the three days surrounding various events affecting judicial independence to their long-term averages. The second uses the fact that the principal English stocks were traded in Amsterdam as well as London, and that price changes were highly correlated between the two markets.[3] News from England generally took

2 The 'abnormal' return on a security over some time period is the actual return less the return that investors anticipated for that time period. Those expectations are not directly observable, and there is accordingly a large literature within financial economics that attempts to determine the expected return for a share of stock. For purposes of this paper, we take the expected return simply as the long-run average. Thus, if prices were rising an average of 1% per day, then a 1% increase in stock prices on a particular day would be a zero abnormal return, but a 5% increase would be a 4% abnormal return. Despite its simplicity, this specification has performed well in prior empirical studies.

3 L. Neal, 'The integration and efficiency of the London and Amsterdam stock markets in the eighteenth century', *Journal of Economic History*, xl, no. 1 (1987), 97–115.

three days to reach Amsterdam, but news from the Indies or France should have reached Amsterdam and London at about the same time on average. Thus, it would be predicted that the London market would react first to changes in judicial independence and that the Amsterdam market would react a few days later. This delay allows us to infer that price movements on the London exchange reflected changes in judicial independence (or other events in England), rather than military or commercial happenings elsewhere.

This time-series approach is a useful supplement to the prior cross-sectional analyses because it avoids many of the drawbacks mentioned above. We can isolate the effect of mandating that judges gain tenure during good behaviour or increasing salaries, holding other aspects of the legal system constant. Our analysis focuses on a single country, thereby avoiding the problem of correlations between legal system design and other political and cultural differences among countries.

We must acknowledge, however, that our approach also has significant limitations. Our results measure market participants' predictions about the benefits of judicial independence, rather than its actual effects. Nevertheless, we believe that these predictions transmit important information. Many eighteenth-century stock traders would have had personal experience or second-hand information about the extent of corruption and royal inter-ference, issues about which historians today can only guess. Thus, contem-porary traders would have had both the information and the pecuniary incentive to make securities price movements a good predictor of actual effects. This assessment is bolstered by Neal's work on the informational efficiency of the London market.[4]

The late seventeenth and early eighteenth centuries were a time of extreme political ferment in England. Events of considerable importance to financial markets, including the War of the Spanish Succession, were ongoing during 1701. We try to avoid the confounding effects of these incidents by focusing on narrow event windows around important legislative events and by looking at contemporary diaries and press accounts for other major news around the same times. There are also important data limitations. Only a handful of securities were publicly traded during the period of interest, making it difficult to draw strong inferences from standard event study procedures. Despite these limitations, however, the time series evidence is a useful supplement to cross-sectional studies of judicial independence.

In assessing the impact of the Act of Settlement and related events, this paper also contributes to an ongoing debate about the economic impact of the Glorious Revolution. Financial historians contend that Parliamentary control over borrowing and expenditure increased the government's credibility

4 L. Neal, *The rise of financial capitalism: international capital markets in the age of reason* (Cambridge, 1990).

and ushered in a revolution in public finance.[5] North and Weingast further claim that the government's increased credibility 'was part of a larger commitment to secure private rights,' which led to growth and financial innovation in the private sector.[6]

Both claims have been disputed. Sussman and Yafeh provide evidence that the risk premium on government debt remained high until the mid-eighteenth century, contradicting the claim that the government's credibility improved immediately after 1688.[7] Relying on similar evidence, Stasavage contends that the balance of power between owners of land and owners of capital was more important than institutional change in creating policy stability and credibility.[8] The relationship between the Glorious Revolution and the private economy is also controversial. Wells and Wills show that threats to the constitutional arrangements inaugurated by the Glorious Revolution, primarily heightened probabilities of a Jacobite invasion, led to lower share prices.[9] Clark examines land returns, rents, and prices and finds little change around 1688.[10] Quinn notes that while the risk premium on government debt declined in the 1690s, interest rates on private debts increased.[11] Our paper provides support for the North and Weingast view that institutional changes that followed the Glorious Revolution had an impact on private economic activity.

We first discuss theoretical arguments suggesting that judicial independence might matter, as well as some reasons to be sceptical. The next section describes the historical background and the events which will be tested for market impact. We than describe the data and methodology. Results are then presented and discussed.

5 P. Dickson, *The financial revolution in England: a study in the development of public credit, 1688–1756* (London, 1967); L. Neal, 'How it all began: the monetary and financial architecture of Europe during the first global capital markets, 1648–1815', *Financial History Review*, vii (2000), 117–40.

6 D. North and B. Weingast, 'Constitutions and commitment: the evolution of institutions governing public choice in seventeenth-century England', *Journal of Economic History*, xlix (1989), 824.

7 N. Sussman and Y. Yafeh, 'Constitutions and commitment: evidence on the relations between institutions and the cost of capital' (unpublished 2002).

8 D. Stasavage, *Public debt and the birth of the democratic state: France and Great Britain, 1688–1789* (Cambridge 2003).

9 J. Wells and D. Wills, 'Revolution, restoration, and debt repudiation: the Jacobite threat to England's institutions and economic growth', *Journal of Economic History*, lx, no. 2 (2000), 418–41.

10 G. Clark, 'The political foundations of modern economic growth', *Journal of Interdisciplinary History*, xxvi (1996), 563–88.

11 S. Quinn, 'The Glorious Revolution's effect on English private finance: a microhistory, 1680–1705', *Journal of Economic History*, lxi (2001), 593–615.

THEORY

A government that can credibly commit to repay its debts, enforce private contracts, and protect property rights will likely foster economic activity. As North and Weingast point out, however, it is difficult for governments to so commit.[12] There are often large, short-run gains to be made by defaulting on sovereign debt, expropriating property, or favouring certain parties in private disputes. A crucial factor in economic growth, therefore, is the development of institutions by which governments credibly commit to sound policies. North and Weingast suggest that England devised just such institutions in the late seventeenth century, following the Glorious Revolution of 1688–89. In particular, they single out 'a Parliament with a central role alongside the Crown and a judiciary independent of the Crown'.[13]

Parliament's power of the purse, coupled with its practice of earmarking specific revenues for the repayment of particular loans, led to a sharp increase in the government's capacity to borrow. Judicial independence should not have added significantly to the credibility of the government's promise to repay its debts because a court cannot ensure enforcement against the government. Even if a court ruled in favour of government creditors, as one did in a famous case at the turn of the eighteenth century, payment still required the cooperation of Parliament.[14] Nevertheless, a judgment by a neutral arbiter in favour of a government creditor could increase the reputational cost of a default and thus contribute somewhat to the credibility of the government's promises.

North and Weingast suggest that these institutional changes also made it more difficult for the government to engage in opportunistic interference with private property and contract rights. Here we expect judicial independence to play a central role. One of the principal functions of the judiciary is to adjudicate property and contract disputes between private parties. There is a risk that wealthier or politically powerful litigants will subvert lawsuits by bringing financial or political pressure to bear on the judge. Judicial independence helps insulate judges from such pressures. It thus increases the potential returns to contracting and investments in property and reduces the returns to lobbying, thus creating more of the former and less of the latter.

If judicial independence improves the security of property and contract rights, then increases in judicial independence should have a positive impact on the value of long-term assets, including corporate equities. This should be true even for politically well-connected firms like the Bank of England and the East India Company. It may be that those firms viewed their political

---

12 North and Weingast, 'Constitutions'.

13 Ibid., 804.

14 J. Horsefield, 'The "stop of the exchequer" revisited', *Economic History Review*, xxxv, no. 4 (1982), 511–28.

connections as the primary guarantor of their own property and contract rights, including repayment of debts owed them by the government. But their shareholders, suppliers, and customers, would have also been concerned about judicial partiality. This fear would have led shareholders to invest less, customers to offer lower prices, and suppliers to demand higher prices. Neutral adjudication would protect the rights of those who dealt with the firm and thereby increase the value of the firm and of a non-controlling stake.

Testing the impact of judicial independence on the private economy is complicated by the fact that, during the relevant period, all of the major publicly traded firms held sovereign debt. If judicial independence increased the government's credibility but had no effect on the security of property and contract rights generally, we might still observe a positive impact on equity prices. Although our primary objective is to determine whether judicial independence resulted in increases in asset values, we also try to determine whether any such increases can be explained solely by changes in the value of outstanding government debt.

Although it is usually assumed that freeing judges from external pressures will help ensure the rule of law, this is not necessarily so. Unconstrained judges might lazily refuse to decide cases at all, or they might impose personal preferences at odds with contractual and property rights. While this is possible, it is important to note that English judges had earned a reputation as defenders of the rule of law during the constitutional struggles of the seventeenth century. The reasons for this judicial proclivity are something of a mystery, although it probably reflects judges' concerns for their reputations, the interest of the legal profession as a whole, and the large property holdings of the judges themselves.

Although the importance of judicial independence is generally acknowledged, there are also reasons to doubt that changes in judicial independence will strongly affect the value of long-term assets. Judicial independence can usually be revoked. During the relevant period, it would have taken only an ordinary statute to do so in England. The monarch retained the unilateral power to appoint judges, and used that power to appoint judges whose careers of public service could be thought to assure subservience.[15] In addition, no institutional mechanism, including high salaries, can completely ensure that judges will not be swayed by bribes, pensions, or promotion. In fact, high judicial salaries can have the perverse effect of making judges more attentive to the government's desires, because they increase the negative consequences of dismissal. Perhaps most importantly, judges require assistance from other governmental actors to enforce their judgments.

---

15 D. Lemmings, 'The independence of the judiciary in eighteenth-century England' in P. Birks (ed.), *The life of the law* (London, 1993), p. 125.

HISTORICAL BACKGROUND AND KEY EVENTS

Before the late seventeenth century, English judges were essentially servants of the king. The king appointed them and could remove them. They were paid by the king in amounts and at intervals that he saw fit. During the mid-seventeenth century, Charles I and Charles II were, for part of their reigns, pressured into appointing judges 'during good behaviour,' but these were aberrations, and when circumstances changed, Charles II resumed the tradition of appointing judges to serve 'during pleasure'. He also forced the retirement of judges who displeased him.[16]

In spite of their formal dependence, some English judges exhibited substantial de facto independence. Chief Justice Coke famously defied King James I on numerous occasions, although his eventual dismissal from office showed the limits of his power. On the other hand, especially in the mid-seventeenth century, during the reign of the Stuarts, the baleful consequences of judicial dependence were vividly demonstrated. King Charles II defaulted on his debt with impunity. James II removed twelve judges in four years, primarily because they refused to recognize his power to 'dispense' or suspend the operation of law in specific cases or against specific individuals. Similarly, the trial of Algernon Sidney and others exposed the degree to which a dependent judiciary could produce dubious convictions in politically sensitive cases. A century earlier, Henry VIII, in his quest for increased revenue, pressured the judges to issue a judgment in *Lord Dacre's Case* which threw in doubt the ownership of any lands which had passed by will – probably most of the land in England.[17]

In 1688, the Glorious Revolution deposed the despotic James II and invited William III from the Netherlands. Although Parliament at this time instituted a number of important institutional reforms, it did not protect judicial independence. A provision in the Bill of Rights giving security of tenure was deleted in committee. Two similar statutes were rejected by William III or blocked by his Parliamentary allies in 1692. William III did appoint judges with commissions specifying tenure 'during good behaviour,' but, as under Charles I and II, he retained the right to resume appointments 'during pleasure'.[18]

Continuous daily share price data become available in 1698. The rest of this historical background will therefore highlight key dates whose market impact can be measured. These key dates are organized around two aspects of judicial independence – security of tenure and judicial salaries. Table 1 identifies these dates and their predicted impact on equity markets.

16 J.H. Baker, *An introduction to English legal history* (4th ed., London, 2002), pp. 166–68.
17 Ibid., pp. 167, 254–55.
18 D.A. Rubini,' The precarious independence of the judiciary, 1688–1701', *Law Quarterly Review*, lxxxiii (1967), 343–45.

Table 1. Judicial independence in England: key events

Date	Description of Event	Predicted impact
11 March 1701	Amendment to Act of Settlement providing tenure during good behaviour	Positive
10 May 1701	Attempt to remove amendment	Negative
3 March 1761	Proposal that judicial tenure survive demise of crown	Positive
8 March 1779	Proposal to increase judicial salaries	Positive
12 June 1799	Proposal to increase judicial salaries	Positive

Security of tenure

On 11 March 1701, the House of Commons first discussed and drafted an amendment to the Act of Settlement relating to judicial independence.[19] The Act of Settlement was a bill clarifying the succession to the crown after the death of William III and Princess Anne. The amendment provided '[t]hat Judges commissions be made *quamdiu se bene gesserint* [during good behaviour], and their salaries ascertained and established; but upon the address of either house of Parliament, it may be lawful to remove them.' That is, it provided for life tenure, fixed salaries, and removal only by a vote of either the House of Commons or House of Lords.

This event is almost ideal for testing the hypothesis of the effect of judicial independence on asset prices for several reasons. As noted above, the House of Commons had, on several prior occasions during the early 1690s, attempted to enact a statute giving judges life tenure. In each instance, William III opposed the measure. The fear of encountering similar opposition to a stand-alone bill presumably led the Commons to insert the provision into the proposed Act of Settlement. Both the crown and Parliament were eager to secure the Protestant succession, so the bill was likely to receive royal assent. Moreover (and also likely because of the fear of royal opposition), there is no prior evidence of the Commons' plan to add such an amendment, so news of it probably was a surprise to the markets.

Several other amendments to the Act of Settlement were also first discussed and drafted on 10 March or 11 March. Among those amendments

19 N. Luttrell, *A brief historical relation of state affairs from September 1678 to April 1714* (6 vols., Oxford, 1857), v, 26.

were provisions requiring the new sovereign to be in communion with the Church of England, requiring him or her to procure Parliamentary consent for foreign wars or to leave the country, and barring those receiving royal offices or pensions from serving in the House of Commons.[20] We cannot, of course, separate the market impact of these provisions from that of the judicial independence provision. Nevertheless, we believe that these other amendments would not have surprised the market. They were further expressions of Parliamentary power over the king, a power that was already well established by 1701. Moreover, these provisions were different from the judicial independence provision in one critical respect. The latter was a matter of governmental structure with which William III disagreed. The other provisions implied not merely disagreement, but rebuke. William III viewed them as such, and (unlike the judicial independence provisions) they angered him sufficiently to raise concerns that he or the House of Lords might reject the entire bill.[21] The possibility that the bill might be rejected would create uncertainty as to succession of a Protestant to the crown. This, we predict, would have upset the market. Thus, the fact that the other amendments would most likely have had a negative impact strengthens the inference that a positive market reaction would actually represent reaction to the amendment providing for security of tenure.

On 10 May 1701, parliamentarians allied with the crown introduced an amendment to allow removal of judges only upon the vote of both the House of Commons and the House of Lords. The supporters of judicial independence wanted the House of Commons to have unilateral removal power and therefore opposed the amendment. In response, the amendment's sponsors moved to delete the judicial independence provisions from the bill altogether. The crown and its supporters apparently believed the House of Commons would reject a provision that did not give that house unilateral removal power. However, the Commons voted in favour of the newly amended bill.[22]

On its face, the change increased judicial independence, as it made it more difficult to remove a sitting judge. It is more plausible, however, to interpret the amendment as a setback to judicial independence for two reasons. First, as described by Rubini, the amendment was a last-ditch attempt by the crown to secure removal of the judicial independence provision from the Act of Settlement.[23] As such, this would have been bad news, assuming that judicial independence is good news. Even though the attempt failed, it left some doubt as to whether the bill might be rejected either in the House of Lords or by William III. Second, the original bill, which gave the Commons the

20 Ibid.
21 H. Horwitz, *Parliament, policy and politics in the reign of William III* (Newark, 1977), p. 284.
22 *Journals of the House of Commons* (London, 1803), xiii, 524–25.
23 Rubini, 'Precarious independence of judiciary'.

unilateral power to remove a judge, effectively gave the Commons (and therefore the legislative supporters of secure property rights) a veto over the appointment of new judges. The amended bill, however, allowed removal only when the Commons and Lords concurred. We therefore predict a negative reaction.

The Act of Settlement passed the House of Lords in late May and was given royal assent on 12 June. We cannot, however, interpret any positive effect on stock prices around those dates as reflecting the importance of judicial independence. The Act also advanced two central post-Glorious Revolution policies, the Protestant succession and Parliamentary power, and should therefore have had a positive impact apart from the judicial independence provision.

Although the 1701 Act of Settlement provided security of tenure, it was understood to apply only during the life of the appointing sovereign. That is, when the king or queen died, the commissions of all sitting judges expired, and the new monarch had the right to appoint an entirely new bench.[24] Queen Anne took advantage of this power in 1702 and failed to reappoint several of William's judges. Similarly, in 1714 and 1727, George I and George II failed to reappoint several of their predecessors' judges.[25] On 3 March 1761, George III addressed Parliament and requested legislation allowing judges to continue in office indefinitely after the death of the monarch and reiterating that judges could only be removed upon a vote of both Houses of Parliament.[26] Since the bill encountered no opposition and was assured royal assent, 3 March 1761 is the only date which is predicted to have had a market impact, and, of course, it should be positive.

Judicial salaries

We hypothesize that increases in judicial salaries reduced the likelihood of bribery or other financial subornation, thereby making private rights more

---

24 Baker suggests that this aspect of tenurial insecurity was partially remedied by a 1707 statute which allowed judges to remain in office for six months after the monarch's death. Baker, *Introduction*, p. 168. We do not believe the statute meaningfully increased judicial independence. It was, instead, part of a set of technical provisions meant to assure governmental continuity between Queen Anne's death and her successor's arrival from Germany. The new king, whenever he arrived in England, was free to dismiss Anne's judges.

25 J. Sainty, *The judges of England, 1272–1900: a list of judges of the Superior Courts* (Selden Society Supplementary Series, vol. x (1993)), pp. 35–36, 50, 127–28. We do not test the effect of these removals on stock prices because we lack evidence of the baseline expectation. Obviously the removals were 'news' only to the extent they diverged from what the markets expected. Given the new monarch's right to remove any and all judges, the fact that some were removed was news only to the extent there was an expectation that the right would not be exercised. We lack sufficient information to determine whether that was the case.

26 *Journals of the House of Commons*, xxviii, 1094.

secure. Parliament increased judicial salaries on three occasions during the eighteenth century.

On 8 March 1779, a committee of the Commons was instructed to consider a £500 increase in the salary of the Chief Baron of the Exchequer and £400 increases in the salaries of the barons of Exchequer and puisne judges of King's Bench and Common Pleas. That same day, the king communicated his disposition to assent.[27] Twenty years later, on 12 June 1799, a committee of the Commons was instructed to consider a further round of salary increases. The Chief Baron of the Exchequer's salary would rise by £500 to £4000, and the salary of the puisne judges and barons would rise by £600 to £3000. The king communicated his support on the same day.[28] In both cases, the measure was not controversial, and the king's endorsement made enactment into law a foregone conclusion. We therefore believe these dates are the only relevant ones.

The other eighteenth-century salary increase occurred in 1758–59, and unfortunately we do not have a similarly obvious candidate for the event date. On 16 June 1758, the Commons requested that the king give judges a rise in salary and undertook to allocate tax revenues to reimburse the king during the next legislative session.[29] On 19 June 1758, the king agreed to the request.[30] On 9 May 1759, the king requested reimbursement, and on 14 May, Commons proposed, and the king agreed, to introduce a bill making the salary increases permanent.[31] It is not obvious which of these dates, if any, generated new information. In the event, abnormal returns on 16 June and 19 June 1758 and 9 May 1759 are modestly positive, and on 14 May 1759 modestly negative. Given the uncertainly about which dates are most relevant, we do not further consider the 1758–59 salary increase.

There is good reason to suspect that the market impact of the events in the period 1759–1799 would not be as substantial as those of 1701. The permanence of the post-Revolution changes in English government was still in doubt in 1701, but not by mid-century. The marginal impact of these changes, therefore, must have been less than that of the hotly-contested issue of security of judicial tenure. We nevertheless include these measures because they affected the status of the judiciary. If impartial judges are good, the additional security of tenure and remuneration should have had some impact on equity values.

27 Ibid., xxxvii, 207.
28 Ibid., liv, 620.
29 Ibid., xxviii, 313.
30 Ibid.
31 Ibid., 578, 584.

DATA AND METHODOLOGY

We use a data set derived from *The course of the Exchange*, a sheet published by John Castaing, a London merchant, and successors from 1698 to 1809, as our principal source for London prices. The Castaing publication and its competitors are described in detail by Neal.[32] For 1700–01, the data set contains daily prices for the Bank of England, the Million Bank, the Old and New East India Companies, and the Royal African Company. For the period 1759–99, the set contains daily prices for the Bank of England, the United East India Company, and the South Sea Company. The Castaing publication occasionally contains prices for other companies, but these traded infrequently and are not included in the data set.

The Castaing publication contained information about dividend payments, but the information is not complete, particularly in the early period. We accordingly supplement Castaing with dividend information compiled by Scott for early joint-stock companies up to the year 1720.[33]

We construct an equally-weighted market index consisting of the average of the returns for each stock traded on a particular day, that is

$$M_t = \frac{1}{n} \sum_{i=1}^{n} \left(\frac{P_{i,t} - P_{i,t-1}}{P_{i,t-1}} \right),$$

where $P_{i,t}$ is the price for stock i on date t, n is the number of stocks with prices for day t, and M_t is the index for date t. We do not know the number of shares outstanding for all relevant periods and so cannot construct a value-weighted index. We do have this information for 1701, however. As a check, we create a market capitalization-weighted index for that period, with consistent results.

There are many days on which not all of the stocks traded. Some of these reflect the fact that shares had to be deposited with a registrar or paying agent around the time of dividend payments and elections of directors. Thus, there are sometimes gaps of a week or more in the price series for a particular company. There are other days on which no trades occurred in a particular stock, and these are particularly common after the bubble period of 1720 and the consequent decline in stock market investment.[34] The number of

32 Neal, *Rise of financial capitalism*. The data set is available from the Inter-University Consortium for Political and Social Research at the University of Michigan, www.icpsr.umich.edu. We looked at microfilm of the originals to determine ex-dividend dates.

33 W.R. Scott, *The constitution and finance of English, Scottish and Irish joint-stock companies to 1720* (New York, 1951).

34 We compared the distribution of the daily values of the index to those of an alternative index that is defined only for days for which a price is reported for each stock. The mean and standard deviation of daily values for both indexes over our estimation periods are almost identical.

observations for the South Sea Company for the 1770s and 1790s is so small that we omit it from the index for those periods.

We use a conventional event study to look for abnormal returns around the time of key dates in the movement towards greater judicial independence. We first employ a constant expected-return model. We predict that changes in judicial independence affected all securities traded on the London exchange and therefore lack an unaffected market portfolio to use as a factor for predicting returns. Brown and Warner, however, note that a constant-return model performs well in short-run event studies with daily data.[35] We accordingly take the expected return on the market index for day τ, M_τ, to equal the average daily return on the index over a 100-trading day estimation period ending 5 trading days prior to the relevant event. Where there are two or more events in a short time period, such as our March 1701 and May 1701 events relating to the Act of Settlement, we use a single estimation period ending before the first such event. The abnormal return for each day τ is the observed return minus the expected return on that day. We calculate cumulative abnormal returns over 3-trading day event windows centred on the relevant events and use the standard deviation of daily returns during the estimation period to assess the statistical significance of the abnormal return. Table 2 provides descriptive statistics for daily returns during each of our estimation periods.

Table 2. Descriptive statistics for equity returns during estimation periods

Estimation Periods

	10/26/1700 to 3/4/1701	8/11/1760 to 2/20/1761	9/26/1778 to 3/1/1779	12/22/1798 to 5/31/1799
Average	-0.28	-0.04	0.03	0.01
Median	-0.20	0.00	0.00	0.09
Standard deviation	1.24	0.37	0.54	0.73
Maximum	3.69	1.44	1.92	1.71
Minimum	-4.23	-1.65	-1.28	-3.57

All amounts represent daily total returns, in percents, on an equally-weighted portfolio of all stocks contained in the data set. The estimation period from 26 October 1700 to 4 March 1701 excludes the run on the Bank of England during the period 29 January to 6 February inclusive.

35 S.J. Brown and J.B. Warner, 'Using daily stock returns: the case of event studies', *Journal of Financial Economics*, xiv, no. 1 (1985), 3–31.

The estimation period prior to the introduction of judicial independence provisions into the Act of Settlement runs from late 1700 through the end of February 1701. This period includes a major political event – the invasion of the Spanish Netherlands by Louis XIV of France, one of the provocations that led to the War of the Spanish Succession. The invasion prompted a run on the Bank of England. Our market index shows a few days of very large negative abnormal returns upon news of the invasion, followed by a sharp but partial correction. We exclude the week following the invasion from our estimation period, given the existence of several extreme outliers in the index. In principle, the effect of excluding the data is unclear. All but one of the returns during that week are negative, which would bias the expected return in a negative direction, thus increasing the apparent abnormal return around the time of the 11 March event. On the other hand, inclusion of those observations would increase the standard deviation of returns, which would reduce the likelihood of rejecting the null hypothesis of zero abnormal return. In fact, the effects offset; none of the inferences described below is sensitive to the exclusion of the late January 1701 data.

A final methodological concern is that with only 3 to 5 traded stocks, the daily returns on our market index are not normally distributed, which should lead to over-rejection of the null hypothesis of zero abnormal returns. We discuss this issue in more detail in connection with our results.

We also carry out tests where possible using an alternative expected-return model. Neal notes that shares of the three main English joint-stock companies, the Bank of England, the East India Company, and the South Sea Company, were traded in Amsterdam.[36] Van Dillen provides prices every two weeks for the period 1723 through 1794.[37] Neal compares these to the prices of the three companies on the London Stock Exchange for the same dates.[38] He notes that both the levels and the first differences of the two price series are highly correlated.

Using the Van Dillen data, we construct an equally-weighted index of the three English companies traded in Amsterdam and compare it to our London market index on the same dates. We calculate two-week holding period returns (rather than first differences of prices). Consistent with Neal's analysis, we find that the two-week returns for the entire period 1723 through 1794 are highly correlated (Pearson correlation coefficient = .654, p < .01).

This close correspondence between the London and Amsterdam markets provides an alternative test of the importance of legislative events occurring in

36 Neal, 'Integration and efficiency'.
37 J.G. van Dillen, 'Effectenkoersen aan de Amsterdamsche beurs 1723–1794', *Economisch-historisch Jaarboek*, xvii (1931), 1–34. These data are included in Neal's data set described in footnote 32 and accompanying text.
38 Neal, 'Integration and efficiency', Table 1.

London. Much of the news bearing on the future profitability of the trading companies would come from Asia and the Americas and should have reached London and Amsterdam at the same time on average. Returns on all shares were highly sensitive to diplomatic and military news from throughout Europe, which again would on average have arrived at approximately the same time in London and Amsterdam. In contrast, the proceedings of the British Parliament occurred literally within walking distance of the City of London, but news took three days on average to reach Amsterdam from London.

To the extent there exist prices from Amsterdam for dates falling within our three-day event windows, then, we can be reasonably confident that those prices do not yet reflect the Parliamentary actions of interest. Thus, we can take the Amsterdam return as the expected return for the London stocks, and any abnormal return in London can plausibly be attributed to events occurring there that were not yet reflected in Amsterdam prices.

Two of our events – the 1779 judicial salary increase and the 1761 provision for tenure after the demise of the monarch – fall within the time period for which Amsterdam data are available. Unfortunately, van Dillen's data set does not always include an observation within our event window. We accordingly supplement van Dillen's data by going to his original source, the *Amsterdamsche Courant*, which typically published stock prices two or three times a week. Using this source, we are able to obtain prices during both event windows. We calculate a two-week holding period return for each of the three stocks in Amsterdam and in London and define an abnormal return as the London return minus the Amsterdam return. For purposes of assessing statistical significance, we derive the abnormal return in the same way for each two-week period covered by van Dillen's data and compute the standard deviation of abnormal returns.

RESULTS

The first column of Table 3 reports abnormal returns based on the constant-return model for the events described in the previous section. We first calculate abnormal returns for three-trading day event windows around 11 March 1701 and 10 May 1701. These are the dates on which the Act of Settlement was amended to include a provision for judicial tenure during good behaviour and on which there was an attempt to delete that provision.

The cumulative abnormal return for the market index for the period centred on 11 March is 8.41% and is significant at the 1% level. There is a similarly large price decline in the 3 trading days surrounding 10 May 1701. The cumulative abnormal return of –8.74% is also significant at the 1% level. The magnitude of the abnormal returns is obviously large. In assessing statistical significance, however, we must keep in mind the small number of traded stocks and the consequent non-normality of daily returns on our index.

Table 3. Cumulative Abnormal Returns

Event	Equities		Bonds	Correlation of equity and bond returns
	3-day CAR	2-week CAR (Amsterdam)	3-day CAR	
11 March 1701. Amendment providing tenure during good behaviour.	8.41%** (2.15) [0.00]			
10 May 1701. Attempt to delete amendment providing tenure during good behaviour	-8.74%** (2.15) [0.00]			
3 March 1761. Proposal that tenure survive demise of crown.	0.83% (0.64) [0.19]	3.95% (3.89) [0.31]	0.47% (0.85) [0.58]	0.42
8 March 1779. Proposal to increase judicial salaries by £400–£500.	1.35% (0.94) [0.15]	7.84%* (3.89) [0.04]	1.13% (0.95) [0.23]	0.25
12 June 1799. Proposal to increase judicial salaries to £2000–£3000.	0.33% (1.03) [0.75]		-0.19% (0.82) [0.82]	0.06

*, ** = significant at the 5%, or 1% level, respectively.

Standard errors in parentheses. P-values in brackets.

In columns one and three, abnormal returns are defined as the return in excess of the mean daily return during a 100-trading day estimation period ending 5 trading days prior to the event (or prior to the first event, where two events fall within the same six-month period) and are cumulated over a 3-trading day event window. Standard errors are calculated as the standard deviation of daily returns during the estimation period times the square root of the number of days in the event window.

In column two, abnormal returns are defined as the difference in returns on the relevant stocks on the London and Amsterdam stock exchanges over a two-week holding period. Standard errors are calculated as the standard deviation of abnormal returns over the period 1723–1794.

In order to alleviate the problem of non-normality, we employ a bootstrap procedure as an alternative method of assessing the statistical significance of cumulative abnormal returns. Specifically, we draw 10,000 resamples of size $b=3$, with replacement, from the 100 days of pre-event return data and calculate 3-day cumulative abnormal returns for each sample. We then take these CARs as an approximation of the distribution of CARs under the null hypothesis of zero abnormal return. The standard deviation of the 10,000

Figure 1. Equity Index Daily Returns, October 1700–June 1701

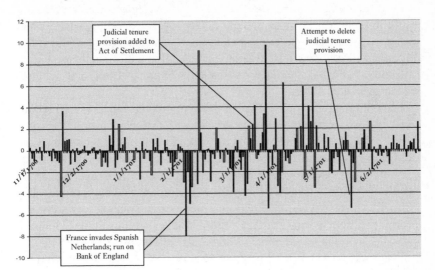

CARs (2.14) is almost identical to the standard error calculated directly from the estimation period (2.15), indicating that our rejection of the null hypothesis is not simply a consequence of the non-normality of daily returns.

We also consider the possibility that our estimation period is atypical. Figure 1 shows daily returns on our equity index for every trading day from the beginning of the estimation period (26 October 1700) through the end of June 1701. Looking only at the estimation period prior to the 11 March event (the left two thirds of the figure), it seems very unlikely that rejection of the null hypothesis of zero abnormal return is an artifact of the non-normality of the pre-event data. The daily return on the index for the single day 12 March 1701 (4.13%) is greater than all but one day during the estimation period, and the day in question is the aftermath of the January run on the Bank of England. Indeed, the average return for the three days 10, 11 and 12 March (2.52%) is in the 96th percentile of daily returns for the estimation period. Similarly, the daily return on the index for 9 May 1701 (−5.79%) is lower than any day during the estimation period apart from the January run on the Bank of England.

The volatility of the return series, however, increases substantially in the period immediately following 10–12 March, probably as a result of uncertainty about war with France. Beginning on 18 March 1701, debate in Parliament was dominated by William III's negotiations with France. The King wanted to avoid war by allowing France to keep some of the territory it had recently invaded, whereas some parliamentarians argued for a sterner line. Parliament also impeached several ministers on charges connected with their conduct of diplomacy. It is not surprising, therefore, that the resulting political turmoil and uncertainty about whether England would go to war would lead to swings in equity prices. By the end of the Parliamentary session in June, the uncertainty had largely been resolved, as William had responded to Parliamentary pressure by adopting a more bellicose policy, Parliament had voted supplies for war, and the House of Lords had acquitted the impeached ministers.

The critical issue, then, is whether the more volatile period of mid-March through April, or the less volatile period from October through February should be taken as 'normal' for the purpose of analyzing the 11 March and 10 May events. We note that the period after June 1701 saw a return to the relatively lower volatility characteristic of our estimation period. We carried out the event study using a post-event estimation period beginning in July 1701 with consistent results. Even were we to extend our estimation period through the more volatile March to June period, our results for the 11 March and 10 May events would remain statistically significant.

There was no war-related news during either of our two event windows that could explain the large moves in equity prices. There is one potentially confounding event – on 9 May, the House of Commons lodged formal impeachment charges against the earl of Orford. The formal impeachment charges, however, would not have been news. Commons had already, on 1 April, declared its intent to impeach Orford and three other ministers. We examined returns during 3-day windows around the days on which articles of impeachment were filed against the other ministers. In each case the abnormal return was positive, small in magnitude, and statistically insignificant.

The large and statistically significant results for the Act of Settlement are particularly noteworthy, because the provisions relating to judicial independence were not to take effect immediately. Rather, they came into force only 'after the said Limitation shall take Effect,' that is after the death of Anne, who at the time was only 36. Nevertheless, she had suffered several miscarriages and was not in good health.[39] In fact, she lived only thirteen more years. At five percent interest (the early eighteenth-century market rate), the present discounted value of $1 in thirteen years was 53¢. Thus, if the market had a reasonable sense of Anne's life expectancy, one should almost double the cumulative abnormal returns noted above. So it could be inferred that the market thought security of tenure would increase stock values by 16%.

None of the remaining incremental improvements in judicial independence are associated with statistically significant positive abnormal returns. The 1761 statute providing security of tenure surviving demise of the crown (i.e. tenure which survived a monarch's death) is associated with a 3-day cumulative abnormal return of 0.83%. The two salary increases for which we have

---

39 E. Gregg, *Queen Anne* (New Haven, 2001), pp. 100, 106–07, 120.

reasonable event dates are associated with cumulative abnormal returns of 1.35% and 0.33%, respectively.

As discussed above, a natural interpretation of the modest size of these effects is that the principle of judicial independence was no longer contested by the mid-eighteenth century. The provision for tenure notwithstanding the demise of the crown, moreover, was certainly not an issue of any immediate importance. King George III, the current monarch, was only twenty-two and in good health. In the event, he reigned for nearly fifty-nine more years.

An alternative possibility is that our 3-day event windows are too short for these later time periods. In the aftermath of the South Sea bubble of the 1720s and the Bubble Act, there was a noticeable decline in liquidity for stocks traded on the London Stock Exchange. Bekaert, Harvey, and Lundblad note that the proportion of trading days on which a particular stock does not trade at all is a natural proxy for liquidity in developing markets.[40] We can easily compare this measure throughout the eighteenth century for the Bank of England, which was listed for the entire period. From 1688 through 1719, Bank of England shares failed to trade on approximately 10% of trading sessions. For the period 1721 through 1799, by contrast, the figure is approximately 27%. We would expect information to be more slowly reflected in prices in a less liquid market. We note that there is a large and persistent rise in our stock index over the 2-week period following each of the three post-1720 events. The 2-week abnormal returns beginning 2 March 1761, 6 March 1779, and 11 June 1799 are 3.47%, 6.23%, and 7.02%, respectively, and each is significant at the 1% level. Clearly the selection of 2 weeks is arbitrary and we do not, therefore, take these results as strong evidence in favour of the importance of judicial independence. We do, however, note that our failure to find large effects in the 3-day event windows could be a consequence of the relative illiquidity of the market during the period between enactment and repeal of the Bubble Act.

The results for our alternative expected-return model based on Amsterdam prices are shown, where available, in the second column of Table 3. In each case, the abnormal return has the expected sign. The abnormal return around the time of the 1779 salary increase is positive and significant at the 5% level, and that around the time of the 1759 salary increase is positive and marginally significant (p=0.07). Abnormal returns during the estimation period have mean and median very close to zero, but have thick tails, which again complicates the assessment of statistical significance. The abnormal return for the 1779 event, however, is in the 97th percentile of 2-week abnormal returns for the period 1723–1794, and that for the 1759 event is in the 95th percentile. These results add further evidence that legislative moves to increase judicial independence were responsible for increases in equity prices.

40 G. Bekaert, C.R. Harvey and C.Lundblad, 'Liquidity and expected returns: lessons from emerging markets', Working paper, Duke University (2003).

Table 4. Cumulative returns on individual stocks for 1701 events

Stock	Trading days	
	10, 11, and 12 March	9, 10, and 12 May
Bank of England	1.00%	-5.86%
Million Bank	4.66%	-11.08%
New East India Company	6.53%	-8.65%
Old East India Company	11.28%	-13.89%
Royal Africa Company	10.20%	-8.52%
Average	6.73%	-9.60%

The returns in the Amsterdam market after our London events are also consistent with the results from London. In both instances for which we have Amsterdam prices, there is a positive (but insignificant) abnormal return on the London stocks traded in Amsterdam for the holding period beginning during our event window and continuing until the next available observation. We also note that the abnormal returns for our London Stock Exchange index are positive on average just before our two-week event windows. This provides some assurance that the higher returns in London during our two-week holding periods reflect good news in London at the end of the periods, rather than bad news in London just prior to the beginning of the periods.

Is it possible to determine whether these positive reactions resulted from increases in the value of outstanding government debt securities held by the traded companies, the expectation of an improved climate for private economic activity, or both? In 1701, there were no publicly-traded government debt securities. However, we can compare the market reaction of firms that held relatively more government debt with those that held relatively less.

The assets of both the Bank of England and the Million Bank consisted principally of government debt, so much so that returns on their stock are sometimes used as proxies for the yield on government debt.[41] Like the Bank of England, the New East India Company in effect purchased its charter by making a large loan to the government. The New East India Company lent the government £1.7 million at the time of its formation in 1698 and had a market capitalization of approximately £2.3 million in early 1701. By contrast, the Royal African and Old East India Companies held smaller amounts of government debt.[42]

41 Sussman and Yafeh, 'Constitutions and commitment'.
42 Scott, *Constitution and finance of ... joint-stock companies*.

As discussed above, judicial independence could have affected equity returns in three ways. By marginally boosting the credibility of the government's own promises, it could increase the value of government debt. By increasing the impartiality of adjudication, it could better secure property and contract rights generally and lead to greater investment. Finally, impartial adjudication would also help alleviate manager-shareholder agency problems. The last of these should be relevant to all publicly-traded companies. The first would be relatively more important for the Bank of England, the Million Bank, and the New East India Company, while the second would be relatively more important for the Royal Africa Company and the Old East India Company.

Table 4 shows the returns on the five stocks individually around the March and May 1701 events. Interestingly, the increases in value around 12 March are inversely related to the amount of government debt held by the five companies. The Bank of England and the Million Bank, which held the most government debt, experienced the smallest gains, followed by the New East India Company, which also held a substantial amount of government debt. The two companies that were engaged principally in trade experienced the largest rise.[43] The relationship is not as strong around 10 May, but the average decline for the two trading companies is greater than that of the three that held more government debt. These results are consistent with the notion that judicial independence had an impact not merely on the reliability of government debt, but on the private economy generally.

We also look at returns on government debt instruments during our event windows from later in the eighteenth century. The Castaing data include prices for consols, or perpetual government debt securities, beginning in the 1750s. We again use a simple constant-return model based on the same 100-day estimation periods used for equity returns. We also calculate the correlation between equity and government debt returns during the estimation periods as a rough measure of the extent to which stock and government debt markets moved in tandem generally.

The results are shown in the third and fourth columns of Table 3. There is little relationship between the abnormal returns on the stocks and bonds during our event windows. In particular, in some instances the abnormal bond returns are negative. While we cannot read too much into this, given the lack of statistical significance of the abnormal returns, it does provide additional evidence that the positive reactions of equity-market returns did not arise solely from increases in the value of government debt held by the traded companies, but reflected anticipated improvements in the private economy.

43 The Bank of England's shares were deposited for payment of a dividend beginning on 12 March, so there are no transactions in the Bank's stock on that date. If we take the next observation for the Bank of England, its 3-trading day return would be 3.42%, still the smallest increase of the five companies.

CONCLUSION

Analysis of securities prices around the time of moves to increase (decrease) judicial independence supports the idea that increases (decreases) in judicial independence increase (decrease) the value of financial assets. All abnormal equity returns have the predicted signs. The magnitudes, however, are typically modest, and only the returns around the time of the Act of Settlement are statistically significant.

We believe, however, that the results, read in connection with modern cross-country studies, lend support to the proposition that judicial independence is one of the key features of the design of a high-quality legal system. It is remarkable that incremental changes in the security of judgeships are so persistently associated with abnormal returns in the direction that we would expect if market participants viewed judicial independence as a good thing.

The rule of law in the settler-colonial encounter: the case of Western Australia

IN SWAN RIVER IN 1841 the governor wrote to the Colonial Office requesting approval to suspend the ordinary procedures of law in relation to Aboriginal peoples across the vast colony now known as Western Australia. He was refused permission on the grounds that the principle of 'strict legal equality' must apply to all British subjects, both settler and indigenous. By the end of that decade, however, permission had been granted and for certain infringements of the criminal law Aborigines collectively became subject to summary justice. This essay attempts to understand this transformation, which authorised such exceptional procedures, within the analytical framework of the rule of law, whose fundamental principles the British government had initially upheld. While events in this colony provide the focus for discussion here, the essay introduces at the outset the concerns of the larger project on which it draws.

THE RULE OF LAW

The rule of law is the opposite of the 'rule of men', a legal counter to tyranny and the arbitrary use of force. The idea of the rule of law in both its procedural and rhetorical forms is to prevent and redress injustice. But its complex ancestry, including how its installation has been made possible by the very actions it abhors as well as by the principles and values it defends, belies the possible innocence or simplicity of its authority.

The broader project which frames this essay reflects on that history, by analysing the meaning of the rule of law in British colonies in the nineteenth century but in a way that engages, too, with its heritage and operations within the metropolitan centre. It attempts to add a colonial dimension to historical and jurisprudential accounts of the development of the rule of law, which has

1 This research has been supported by an Australian Research Council postdoctoral fellowship. I thank Patrick Wolfe for his critical reading.

traditionally been represented as a purely internal product of European historical processes.

Informed by the work of Peter Fitzpatrick and others, the theoretical framework understands the rule of law to be not simply an abstract ideal but like the law itself actively constitutive of the nation-state it presupposes, both at home and abroad.[2] Although the rule of law has become the jurisprudential standard for assessing the 'success or desirability of a general theory of law',[3] the historical record unsettles the apparent neutrality of the doctrine. Looking closely at the rule of law in the critical formative stages of colonial rule helps identify its particularity as certain sections of the population, despite being equal subjects, were deemed to fall outside its full protection. Significantly, these initial exclusions in the colonies – like those that occurred elsewhere, including the metropole – would not be confined in their immediate time and place but would set the pattern for discriminatory policies and practices that continued throughout the nineteenth and twentieth centuries.[4] In becoming embedded in the constitutions and the founding legislation of the new nations that would eventually emerge, such exclusions cannot be dismissed simply as examples of historical injustice or misguided racism. Rather, such structural discrimination demonstrates how the rule of law represents the interests of a demographically narrow group of people posited universally.

Discussing the rule of law in relation to ideas and practices that openly contravene its civilising role points, of course, to the paradox experienced more broadly throughout the nineteenth century when doctrines of universal liberty and equality commonly correlated with repression and exclusion, quite overtly in the colonies but in ways that were apparent, too, within Britain itself.[5] The broader context of this project therefore draws on the contradiction between the inequalities necessary to sustain the liberal social and economic order and the universalist political rhetoric that championed it.

In specific terms, the project focuses on the law's relation to indigenous peoples in colonies of settlement and methodologically tests the rule of law in its contradiction, that is, through investigating instances of martial law and other more mundane forms of summary justice. Drawing on postcolonial scholarship, the project is located at the intersection between law, history, race and colonialism.

2   See, for example, in P. Fitzpatrick (ed.), *Nationalism, racism and the rule of law* (Aldershot, 1995); P. Fitzpatrick, *Modernism and the grounds of law* (Cambridge, 2001) and R. Guha, 'Dominance without hegemony and its historiography', in R. Guha (ed.), *Subaltern studies vi: writings on South Asian history and society* (Delhi, 1994), pp. 210–309, esp. 274ff.

3   Hugh Collins, *Marxism and law* (Oxford, 1982), p. 14.

4   For further consideration of these issues in Australia, New Zealand, Canada and South Africa, see J. Evans, P. Grimshaw, D. Philips and S. Swain, *Equal subjects, unequal rights: indigenous peoples in British settler colonies, 1830–1910* (Manchester, 2003).

5   See, for example, E.P. Thompson's classic *Whigs and hunters: the origin of the Black Act*

THE RULE OF LAW AND COLONIALISM

Perceived as a quintessentially English notion, the rule of law encapsulates the long struggle against tyranny evident in the Magna Carta, the Petition of Right, the Habeas Corpus Acts, the Bill of Rights, and the Act of Settlement. Brian Simpson claims that the idea permeated Blackstone's *Commentaries on the laws of England* long before it was formally expressed by Dicey more than a century later.[6] Certainly by the nineteenth century the concept of the rule of law had become one of the principal ideological justifications of the British empire.[7] Its extension to the dominions, in particular, has been seen as one of the great achievements of British colonialism as *all* of the Crown's subjects, whether coloniser or colonised, were theoretically equally amenable to its force and protection.

Recent scholarship has identified how the procedural expression of the rule of law in the colonies deviated somewhat from its English model, reflecting the particular issues and conflicts characterising the fledgling societies it supported. David Neal and John McLaren, among others, have demonstrated how in Australia and Canada different settlers variously appealed to an inherited (or 'transported') understanding of the rule of law as the disinterested arbiter of justice to advance their legal and political rights in the colonies.[8] In attending to the law's engagement with indigenous populations, Martin Chanock, Bruce Kercher and Martin Krygier address my own concerns a little more directly.[9] Krygier focuses explicitly on the differential treatment accorded indigenous peoples in Australia compared with settler subjects. While even those who came to the colonies as convicts benefited from the rule of law, Aborigines, Krygier argues, were regarded as

(London, 1975) and D. Hay, P. Linebaugh, J. Rule, E.P. Thompson & C. Winslow (eds.), *Albion's fatal tree: crime and society in eighteenth-century England* (New York, 1975).

6   A.W.B. Simpson, *Human rights and the end of empire: Britain and the genesis of the European Convention* (Oxford, 2001), pp. 25–27. See also W. Blackstone, *Commentaries on the laws of England*, 4 vols. (Oxford, 1765–1769) and A.V. Dicey, *Introduction to the study of the law of the constitution*, 9th edition by E.C.S. Wade (London, 1952) (1st ed.: 1885).

7   Simpson, *Human rights and the end of empire*, pp. 22–37.

8   D. Neal, *The rule of law in a penal colony: law and power in early New South Wales* (Cambridge, 1991) and J. McLaren, ' Reflections on the rule of law: the Georgian colonies of New South Wales and Upper Canada, 1788–1837' in D. Kirkby and C. Colebourne (eds.), *Law, history, colonialism: the reach of empire* (Manchester, 2001), pp. 46–64. See also A. Atkinson, *The Europeans in Australia, the beginning*, vol. i (Melbourne, 1997).

9   M. Chanock, *The making of South African legal culture, 1902–1936: fear, favour, and prejudice* (Cambridge, 2001); B. Kercher, *An unruly child: a history of law in Australia* (Sydney, 1995) and M. Krygier, 'The grammar of colonial legality: subjects, objects, and the Australian rule of law', in G. Brennan and F.G. Castles (eds.), *Australia reshaped: 200 years of institutional transformation* (Cambridge, 2002), pp. 220–60. See also A. Castles, *An Australian legal history* (Sydney, 1982) and H. Reynolds, *The law of the land* (Melbourne, 1987).

objects rather than subjects of the law due largely to settler greed, government inaction, and 'a failure of moral imagination'.[10]

Krygier identifies certain salient features of colonial society, which effectively denied Aborigines impartial justice, but we understand their purpose or provenance mainly in sociological terms. In accordance with western jurisprudence more generally, Krygier's argument continues to rely on the rule of law – albeit meticulously defined – as the ultimate test of justice. The internal critique adopted here, on the other hand, in outlining the structural imperatives of the settler-colonial formation that supported discriminatory practices in the Australian colonies, interrogates the nature and function of the rule of law itself. The intention of this essay is to provide a conceptual overview of the analytical field and to introduce certain terms and categories through which its problems might be considered. In so doing, it insists on the centrality of colonialism to the development of two of law's constitutive concepts – sovereignty and property. The discussion then illustrates this approach with reference to a specific settler-colonial context to demonstrate the role of the rule of law in upholding the partiality that inheres in these fundamental elements of the liberal order.

RECIPROCITY IN LAW'S ADVENTURES

In the conference from which this collection arises, participants were invited to consider the penetration of the law into new lands or to engage with examples of its doctrinal inventiveness. To some extent this essay speaks to both of these aspects of English law's adventure. But it seeks to qualify at the outset the common underlying assumption of a pre-existent law that arose in England alone and was then available for export as a coherent entity, with due recognition of the local divergences mentioned above, to colonial situations. The discussion suggests, rather, that the relationship between metropole and colony was reciprocal, and that the law, including the rule of law, developed in articulation with Britain's colonial enterprise. Far from being an autochthonous English notion, it is argued that the rule of law, as one of the central underlying ideologies of English liberalism, is centrally bound to colonialism. That is, together with events in Britain, the colonial enterprise helped constitute, as much as it was constituted by, the rule of law.

A number of scholars have recently questioned the customary separation of imperial and domestic histories. David Armitage, for example, in *The ideological origins of the British Empire*, argues that theories of property, liberty and political economy must be put in imperial perspective and that metropolitan state building cannot be viewed in isolation from empire

10 Krygier, 'The grammar of colonial legality', p. 255.

building. In his detailed account of the continuities between developing national and imperial concerns, Armitage observes that those European states that accumulated the earliest overseas empires were also the first to consolidate their states: 'Empires gave birth to states, and states stood at the heart of empires.'[11]

Barbara Arneil further specifies such reciprocity. In explaining the influence of the colonisation of the Americas on John Locke's ideas, Arneil demonstrates how his *Two treatises of government* reconciled traditional English conceptions of property as defined by occupation (until the end of the seventeenth century) with England's colonial ambitions in the New World. According to Locke – and those he would influence such as Blackstone, Vattel and Paley – the natural right to property was authorised or, rather, 'created' on the basis of enclosure and of mixing labour with land, a definition which Arneil asserts 'necessarily ... exclude[d] non-Europeans from being able to exercise it'.[12] Arneil draws on this more comprehensive historical framework to explain why English liberalism, as developed by J.S. Mill and others, continues to be 'plagued by the powerful colonial interests within which it is rooted'.[13]

With his eye more finely focused on the law, Brendan Edgeworth also alerts us to the importance of understanding the co-productive nature of colonialism.[14] Edgeworth argues that the retrospective imposition in England of an enlarged doctrine of feudal tenure effectively elided earlier distinctions between sovereignty and property.[15] While not according with history 'at the time of the Norman conquest and for a long time thereafter,' this legal fiction nevertheless operated to enhance royal authority by citing the Crown as 'absolute beneficial owner of all lands over which dominion was exercised'.[16] Edgeworth makes the important additional observation that while this 'invented tradition' operated ideologically in England to foster modern notions of absolutism, its belated adoption also related directly to contemporary imperial expansion and the very practical concern to maximise economic gains by

11 D. Armitage, *The ideological origins of the British Empire* (Cambridge, 2002), p. 15
12 B. Arneil, *John Locke and America: the defence of English colonialism* (Oxford, 1996), p. 209.
13 Ibid., pp. 210–11.
14 B. Edgeworth, 'Tenure, allodialism and indigenous rights at common law: English, United States and Australian land law compared after *Mabo* v. *Queensland*' in *Anglo-American Law Review*, 23 (1994), 397–434. For related scholarship on the metropole/colony relationship as reciprocal see, among others, M. Peters, 'Sovereignty: a British and New Zealand issue' in W. Prest (ed.), *British studies into the 21st century* (Melbourne, 2001), pp. 96–107 and S. Dorsett, '"Since time immemorial": a story of common law, native title and the case of Tanistry', *Melbourne University Law Review*, 26 (April 2002), 32–60.
15 Edgeworth notes that this 'invented tradition' was recognised by Blackstone and that A.W.B. Simpson, *A history of land law*, 2nd ed. (Oxford, 1986), p. 47, confirms that the feudal 'attitude of mind' would not have endorsed lords or kings *owning* land: Edgeworth, 'Tenure, allodialism and indigenous rights at common law', pp. 428–29.
16 Edgeworth, 'Tenure, allodialism and indigenous rights at common law', pp. 426, 431.

legally facilitating dispossession. Quoting McNeil, Edgeworth observes that in consequence, both in the English context and in the overseas colonies, 'the law supposes that all lands were at one time vacant and that the Crown took them as occupant'.[17] As sovereignty was increasingly understood (and effected) as centralised and exclusive – both at home and abroad – colonial and metropolitan interests were less easily cast as distinctive.

In the nineteenth-century settler colonies, the subject of our concern here, similar legal fictions concerning the Crown's universal and originary title would be relied upon to uphold Britain's claims to (exclusive) sovereignty as indigenous landholdings were variously subordinated to particular colonial imperatives.[18] By this time, too, the enclosure movement of the late eighteenth century that signalled the dispossession of the rural poor in England – and the superseding of pre-capitalist communal forms of landholding – would have its counterpart in the dispossession of native landholders abroad, including in the colony of Western Australia to which we will soon turn our attention.[19]

Formulated within both imperial and domestic concerns, the very concepts of sovereignty and property would uphold particular interests in the developing liberal social, economic and political order at home and abroad, especially through their entrenchment in international and domestic law. As Anthony Anghie and others have demonstrated, the development of international law, with its pervasive privileging of European civilization, must also be situated within early inter-state rivalries over the appropriations of the Americas.[20] As the following discussion suggests, while it would be international law that would deliver distant lands and their peoples to the judgement and rule of European civilisation, it would be the colonisers' domestic legal systems that would secure their hegemony and underwrite the road to nationhood.

17 Ibid. Edgeworth cites Kent McNeil, *Common law Aboriginal title* (Oxford, 1989), p. 106.

18 See, among many others, Edgeworth, 'Tenure, allodialism and indigenous rights at common law' and G. Simpson, 'Mabo, international law, *terra nullius* and the stories of settlement: an unresolved jurisprudence' in *Melbourne University Law Review*, 19 (June 1993), 195–210.

19 A.R. Buck, '"Strangers in their own land": capitalism, dispossession and the law' in A.R. Buck, J. McLaren and N.E Wright (eds), *Land and freedom: law, property rights and the British diaspora* (Aldershot, 2001), pp. 39–56, 47. See generally E.P. Thompson, *Whigs and hunters* and D. Hay, 'Property, authority and the criminal law' in D. Hay et al. (eds.), *Albion's fatal tree*.

20 A. Anghie, 'Finding the peripheries: sovereignty and colonialism in nineteenth-century international law' in *Harvard International Law Journal*, 10, pt. 1 (Winter 1999), 1–80. Anghie explains how sovereignty became associated with particular sets of cultural practices to the exclusion of others so that, within this framework, colonialism can no longer be accounted for as the application of sovereignty. Sovereignty, rather, is constituted and shaped through colonialism. See A. Pagden, *Lords of all the world: ideologies of empire in Spain, Britain and France, c. 1500–c. 1800* (New Haven, 1995) and R. Williams, *The American Indian in western legal thought* (New York, 1990) and J. Malbon, 'Natural and positive law influences on the law affecting Australia's indigenous people' in *Australian Journal of Legal History*, 3 (1997), 1–39.

For while being legally determined under international law, sovereignty still had to be practically secured in the colonies. In the early stages of colonial rule, especially where Europeans were outnumbered or where significant infrastructure had yet to be established, legal assertions of sovereignty over the lands of others could mean little in practical terms. Where outright violence in the face of resistance could not be justified as warfare, colonial legal systems were called upon to support settler interests.

In sum, then, the idea of the rule of law not only anticipated but enabled in the colonies the formation of nation-states, which, in Europe, had in turn been constituted through histories of conquest, coercion and colonialism. Although its rhetorical claims were more clearly subverted by colonial conditions, the rule of law operated ideologically throughout the nineteenth century as if the colonies were already the (homogenous and unified) nation-states they would become. Within this broader framework, the idea of the rule of law could promote universal liberty and justice while overseeing the establishment and protection of the developing normal order.

The discussion now turns to investigating the process of achieving that normal order in the colony of Western Australia where, as elsewhere in the empire, certain British subjects were accorded the full protection of the rule of law while others would fall comprehensively outside its umbrella. In outlining these developments, the argument highlights the unsuitability of the rule of law to colonial conditions in certain times and places and seeks to lay bare what the rule of law needs to secure before it can come into its own: exclusive sovereignty, private property and a market economy.

WESTERN AUSTRALIA AS A SETTLER-COLONIAL FORMATION

As stated at the outset, the rule of law was suspended in relation to Western Australia's indigenous population from the late 1840s. Although the rule of law had yet to be formally expounded, its invocation was frequent in helping justify Britain's colonial interests.[21] By 1885 when Dicey finally unified it as a single doctrine, the rule of law was well on the way to being rendered canonical.[22] We therefore encounter the rule of law here in its early formulation in the Australian colonies, in times and places when it was most susceptible to breaking down.[22a]

---

21 Simpson, *Human rights and the end of empire*, p. 38, and chapter 2.
22 A.V.Dicey, *Introduction to the study of the law of the constitution*.
22a I originally discussed the Western Australian material in 'The formulation of privilege and exclusion in settler states: land, law, political rights and indigenous peoples in nineteenth-century Australia and Natal' in M. Langton, M. Tehan, L. Palmer and K. Shain (eds.), *Honour among nations? Treaties and agreements with indigenous people* (Melbourne, 2004), pp. 69–82.

It is important to state at the outset that these Australian sites are charac-teristic of a very particular colonial formation, that of settler colonialism. As distinct from franchise colonies, like India, or the slave colonies of the Caribbean where resource value was maximised through extracting the surplus value of the *labour* of the colonised, economic interest in settler colonies was vested primarily in the *land*. Although their labour was called upon in certain times and places, in purely structural terms, indigenous peoples were superfluous to colonial interests and in fact stood in the way of the primary objective of securing permanent control of the land and con-verting it to alienable private property. Patrick Wolfe explains that, unlike in colonies of exploitation, the settlers had come to stay, literally *replacing* the indigenous inhabitants on the land by segregating onto reserves those who survived the initial devastation precipitated by disease, dislocation, violence and dispossession. Later, where demographics allowed, settler governments would pursue assimilation policies that placed further barriers in the way of indigenous peoples maintaining social, cultural and political autonomy.[23]

It is hardly surprising, then, that indigeneity assumed, and continues to assume, a heightened significance in colonies of settlement as native peoples' alternative claims to the land threatened, and continue to threaten, the colonisers' assertions of exclusive sovereignty. In Australia, indigenous peoples were deemed to have no proprietorial interest in the land.[24] While Britain thus claimed sovereignty under international law, it was a far cry from having practical meaning in the early days of settlement, especially where colonisers were outnumbered, settlements were few and far between and infrastructure had yet to be laid down. The central significance of the quest to control the land in settler colonies will become increasingly clear as the discussion unfolds.

So it is in this very particular context of settler colonialism that the discussion investigates the rule of law in the colonial encounter – that is, in terms of its meaning and installation *in the lands of others*. The argument suggests that the installation of the rule of law for the settlers was dependent in part upon its abrogation in relation to the indigenous peoples whose lands were in the process of being transferred. The instances of summary justice considered below (as elsewhere in the broader project) might not have attracted the notoriety that came to surround events at Morant Bay or Amritsar or in other parts of Britain's vast empire. But their very mundanity, perhaps, intensifies the already horrifying catalogue of atrocities and coercion

23 See P. Wolfe, 'Nation and miscegeNation: discursive continuity in the post-Mabo era', in *Social Analysis*, no. 36 (October, 1994), 93–152. In the South African case, where settlers remained vastly outnumbered, segregation rather than assimilation remained the primary mode of control.

24 Recently acknowledged as a legal fiction in *Mabo* v. *Queensland* (*No. 2*) (1992) 175 CLR 1.

that, as Brian Simpson has recently observed in *Human rights and the end of empire*, commonly characterised colonial rule.[25]

THE EXCEPTION

There are many ways of demonstrating the partiality of law but I have chosen, methodologically, to chart the limits of the rule of law by investigating its partial or complete suspension in times of perceived crisis in the colonies. In other words, I chart the rule of law in its extraordinary rather than its ordinary mode.[26]

It is helpful in this regard to consider Carl Schmitt's critique of the liberal state. Within this analytical model, exceptions to the rule are regarded as intimately related to, rather than separate from, its regular form. Schmitt quotes Kierkegaard to explain this further:

> The exception explains the general and itself. And when one really wants to study the general, one need only look around for a real exception. It brings everything to light more clearly than the general itself ... If [exceptions to the rule] cannot be explained, then neither can the general be explained. Usually the difficulty is not noticed, since the general is thought about not with passion but only with comfortable superficiality. The exception, on the other hand, thinks the general with intense passion.[27]

As philosopher Giorgio Agamben paraphrases Schmitt, 'What is at issue in the ... exception is ... the creation and definition of the very space in which the juridico-political order can have validity'.[28] Within this model, the exception is not simply the suspension of ordinary law but is actively constitutive of it, creating and defining 'normal times' when the rule of law can come to the fore and the state recede. In the state of *exception*, on the other hand, as Schmitt observes, the *state* remains but the *law* recedes.[29] As Peter Fitzpatrick applies Schmitt's framework to the rule of law: 'With the rule of law, the form of national authority, the state, cannot be exempt from this imperative [being subject to the law], but law will provide the

25 See Simpson, 'The mechanisms of repression' in *Human rights and the end of empire*: pp. 54–90. Simpson demonstrates that official mechanisms of repression were authorised all over the British empire as well as domestically and most of them under the rule of law.

26 For a study of colonial India which adopts a related theoretical and conceptual approach, see N. Hussain, *The jurisprudence of emergency: colonialism and the rule of law* (Ann Arbor, 2003).

27 Schmitt, cited in G. Agamben, *Homo sacer: sovereign power and bare life* (Stanford, 1998), p. 16.

28 Ibid., p. 19.

29 C. Schmitt, *Political theology: four chapters on the concept of sovereignty* (Cambridge, 1988, orig. 1922), p. 12.

"exception" allowing for an almost uncontained exercise of the state's political power where this is deemed by authority to be necessary.'[30]

SUSPENSIONS OF THE LAW AND THE TRANSFER OF THE LAND – LINKING MATERIAL AND IDEOLOGICAL INTERESTS

As befits the structural characteristics of settler colonialism, suspension of the law – in the form of outright martial law or targeted summary justice – correlated specifically with the transfer of the land in the Australian colonies. While proclamations of martial law elsewhere in the empire tended to be associated with chronic or acute civil disturbances involving riotous attacks on courthouses, officials or other symbols of state authority,[31] in the Australian colonies extraordinary measures were generally considered in relation to sparsely-populated rural areas.

Various calls to supersede the ordinary procedures of law usually followed a collection of individual episodes of sheep or cattle theft, attacks on isolated stockmen on station outposts or on overlanders seeking land in unexplored regions.[32] In one case, an appeal to the principles of martial law followed the alleged murder of survivors of a shipwreck off the remote South Australian coast.[33] It is difficult to see any of these actions as constituting a threat to state authority unless this was represented in individual settlers attempting to make manifest the state's exclusive sovereignty in their assertions of claims to private property in the lands of others. It was certainly during this period of pastoral expansion in each of these colonies that demands for extra-ordinary procedures to deal with Aborigines appeared.

But while isolated settlers expressed fear for the safety of their families and stock, local colonial officials had to negotiate more complex concerns. British governments required them to treat Aborigines as equal British subjects who were entitled to the equal force and protection of the law.[34] Given this theoretical commitment to one of the most basic principles of the rule of law, extraordinary practices that targeted designated sections of the population were frowned upon by the Colonial Office.

30 P. Fitzpatrick, 'Introduction' in P. Fitzpatrick (ed.), *Nationalism, racism and the rule of law*, p. xvii.
31 Simpson, *Human rights and the end of empire*, pp. 64–71.
32 See, for example, Report of R.H. Bland, protector of natives, *Government Gazette*, 29 January 1847, encl. in Irwin to Grey, no. 4, 18 February 1847 (TNA: PRO, CO 18/44).
33 I discuss this South Australian case in J. Evans, 'Colonialism and the rule of law: the case of South Australia', in G. Dunstall and B. Godfrey (eds.), *Global and local: comparative histories of crime and criminal justice across Europe and Empire c.1800–1940* (Cullompton, Devon, 2005).
34 The term 'British subject' signified Britain's theoretical commitment to upholding the rights and freedoms not only of British settlers but also of the indigenous peoples they

But officials in the colonies were also receiving reports of settlers shooting those Aborigines they suspected of encroaching on their property, stealing cattle or sheep or otherwise inhibiting settlement, something the Colonial Office could equally not condone. To some extent, then, in the face of these conflicting concerns, consenting to such appeals to extraordinary powers attempted perhaps to *regularise*, if not to regulate, this unlawful force, by bringing it within a putatively legal framework.

THE SWAN RIVER COLONY: EMBODYING DISCRIMINATION IN LAW

In April of 1841, British Secretary of State for War and the Colonies, Lord John Russell, disallowed a bill originating from Swan River which included special summary procedures to be applied in the case of the Aboriginal population alone.[35] Western Australia had been declared a separate colony some twelve years earlier and Governor Stirling had proclaimed the equality of Aborigines before the law.[36] But as pastoral expansion extended away from the original settlement near Perth to encroach on the outer regions, more and more so-called 'collisions' were taking place between settlers and indigenous peoples. The official correspondence states that these conflicts arose mainly in the form of attacks on settlers' stock or provisions.

In such circumstances, the law's relation to Aborigines was brought more clearly to the fore. In the context of widespread concern about settlers 'taking the law into their own hands' rather than pursue costly and time-consuming prosecutions in Perth, Governor Hutt had argued that adopting exceptional summary provisions would allow a fairer and more efficient means of bringing indigenous peoples before British law. Under the proposed legislation, local magistrates (who were themselves prominent settlers and landowners) would have the power to charge and sentence Aborigines suspected of crimes other than murder, rape and arson to up to 12 months' imprisonment, with the option of hard labour and whipping. Punishment would thereby be seen to be immediate and clearly connected with the offence.

It is important to observe at this stage that the bill's origins did not lie simply in settlers and administrators wanting legal recourse to coercion – although this was no doubt the case for some of them, especially as settlement expanded. In addition to serious colonial and metropolitan concern about

dispossessed, appearing to reconcile the classically incompatible ideas of liberty and empire. As such, the term operated ideologically to encompass opposing interests through a notion of individual equality but, in tolerating exceptions, practically facilitated the installation of privilege and exclusion from settlement to nationhood.

35 The proposed bill also sought to admit Aboriginal testimony in criminal cases.

36 See Stirling to earl of Aberdeen, no. 12, 10 July 1835 (TNA: PRO, CO 18/15).

unlawful settler violence, there was at least one other compelling argument that the absence of such procedures actually did discriminate against Aborigines. Given the vastness of the colony, being charged with an offence and being unable to raise bail would potentially subject Aborigines to several months' incarceration before their cases could be brought before the Quarter-sessions hearings.[37] It seemed clear that the rule of law, in applying or not applying, might do little to favour them.[37a]

In responding to the proposal, Secretary of State Lord Russell sympathised with the difficulty of Hutt's position and acknowledged his 'spirit of humanity and zeal for [Aboriginal] welfare' but regarded such discriminatory application of the law as 'dangerous in its tendency, as well as faulty in principle':

> By thus establishing an inequality in the eye of the law itself between the two classes, on the express ground of national origin, we foster prejudices, and give a countenance to bad passions, which unfortunately need no such encouragement. It is wise to sacrifice some immediate convenience with a view to maintain the general principle of strict legal equality ... [38]

In not according with the ordinary procedures of the law, the exercise of such discriminatory summary power had then proved unacceptable to the Crown. For the time being, at least, a commitment to a non-discriminatory rule of law would prevail over the desire of settlers and colonial administrators to secure a more expeditious means of dealing with Aboriginal peoples whose criminalised behaviour was inhibiting settlement.

But by 1847 another Secretary of State, Earl Grey, approved the summary jurisdiction Russell had disallowed, observing that there was ' great danger of abuse either from the absence of such a power, or from the undue exercise of it'.[39] Grey sought to stem unlawful violence and ameliorate Aboriginal disadvantage given the 'peculiar circumstances' of the colony, but nevertheless remained anxious about 'dispensing in the case of the natives, with a portion of those safeguards of criminal justice which are so highly and justly valued by men of British extraction'.[40] He recommended certain safeguards

---

37 Hutt to Russell, no. 2, 20 January 1842 (TNA: PRO, CO 18/31).

37a I thank Anthony Anghie for clarifying this point.

38 Russell to Hutt, no. 64, 30 April 1841 (TNA: PRO, CO 397/5).

39 Grey to Irwin, no. 52, 12 September 1847 (TNA: PRO, CO 397/7). Permanent under-secretary Sir James Stephen had given this advice in a minute on Irwin to Grey, no. 4, 18 February 1847 (TNA: PRO, CO 18/44), but had also observed that 'I do not see why, in mixed cases between Europeans and Aborigines, [summary jurisdiction] should not extend indifferently to both'.

40 Grey to Fitzgerald, no.11, 2 June 1848 (TNA: PRO, CO 397/7). See also Report of the

in the composition of the Bench and a reduction in the sentence to six months.[41] Henceforth, the Aboriginal peoples of Western Australia, purely on the basis of belonging to the category indigenous rather than settler, were made legally subject to the arbitrary procedures of summary justice in place of the right to be brought before a court of law. Section VI of the Ordinance got to the heart of the matter, stating that convictions under these summary powers would stand

> without setting forth the name of any witness, or the place where the offence was committed, and without setting forth any part of the evidence, or stating the facts or the offence in any more particular manner than shall be necessary to shew that the offence was one triable under this ordinance.[42]

The 1849 Ordinance inaugurated a much harsher period of colonial rule in Western Australia as the Colonial Office's previous commitment to upholding strict equality of individuals under the rule of law gave way to the tolerance of exceptional provisions.[43] Tellingly, the maximum 6-month penalty was extended to 3 years in 1859. Although in 1874 sentences were again reduced to 6 months, the requirement that one of the justices had to be a protector or resident magistrate was dropped and the scope of jurisdiction was extended to those deemed 'half-caste'.[44] By 1883, when the northern

legislative council of Western Australia appointed to inquire into and report upon expenses connected with the aborigines (TNA: PRO, CO 18/45, pp. 316–20).

41 Grey recommended – but did not make mandatory – the attendance of the protector to guard against justices who might be 'disposed to exercise their authority oppressively towards the Aborigines'. See Grey to Fitzgerald, no.11, 2 June 1848 (TNA: PRO, CO 397/7).

42 *An ordinance to provide for the summary trial and punishment of Aboriginal native offenders in certain cases*, 12 Victoria, no. 18, 1849. Cases could be tried by any two or more Justices of the Peace 'not interested in the subject matter of the complaint', and one of whom should be a guardian or sub-guardian of natives or a resident magistrate. Under s. XII, the Governor in Council could in certain cases remit or mitigate sentences on consideration of reports of conviction. Male offenders could receive up to two dozen lashes of the whip. Locally, Colonial Secretary R. R. Madden angrily protested against the bill, especially its provision for flogging. He objected that under the ordinance, 'the natives are deprived of the laws which ensure the protection of the settlers, and the regular judicial tribunals, at which alone there is the slightest chance of any adequate means of defence on which depends the due administration of justice.' See encl. Fitzgerald to Grey, no. 33, 21 December 1848 (TNA: PRO, CO 18/48).

43 See generally P. Hasluck, *Black Australians: a survey of native policy in Western Australia, 1829–1897* (Melbourne, 1970), chapter 5; Elizabeth Egglestone, *Fear, favour or affection: Aborigines and the criminal law in Victoria, South Australia and Western Australia* (Canberra, 1976) and Enid Russell, *A history of the law in Western Australia and its development from 1829 to 1979* (Perth, 1980).

44 If a full bench was available the former maximum of three years still applied. The proof of race was on the accused. Protectors were appointed to mitigate the impact of settlement on Aborigines.

regions were being claimed, one justice alone could exercise summary power (if there was not another within 20 miles) and after the granting of responsible government in 1892, the penalty he could authorise had extended to three years, or five years for a second offence.[45]

COLLECTIVE JUSTICE – LAW AND RACE

Under such discriminatory legislation, Aborigines as a group were subjected to extraordinary procedures. This powerful distinction, whereby one's fate at the hands of the law could be determined not simply by one's individual actions so much as by one's membership of a group, was particularly open to abuse in relation to the criminal law. The distinction was certainly not unknown in Britain[46] but was more explicit and more comprehensive in the colonies, where race became deeply embedded in the practical operation of the law.

Susceptible to reduction to physical appearance alone, group membership rendered those who had committed no crime legally liable at least to suspicion, with a very real possibility of prosecution, punishment and worse simply on the basis of perceived identity rather than according to incontrovertible evidence of individual criminal actions adjudicated in a court of law. Conceived and executed in bodily terms in the colonies, law could fortify the already formidable ideological power of race to naturalise discrimination. Indeed, in formulating what amounted to comprehensive regimes of exclusion, law could produce race in the colonies as much as be produced within its parameters.[47]

Paul Hasluck notes that while settler subjects in Western Australia could also 'be tried summarily, and for some offences might also be whipped', indigenous subjects could not elect to go before a jury; they had no right of appeal; and the range of offences for which they could be tried under summary jurisdiction was far greater and their penalties heavier.[48] And race, of course, elaborated the meaning and effects of these extraordinary procedures for Aborigines in ways that were completely unknown for settlers.

It is clear that Grey's endorsement of the summary provisions would be, as Russell had feared, the thin edge of the wedge. But as already observed,

---

45 Hasluck, *Black Australians*, pp. 135–43; Peter Biskup, *Not slaves, not citizens: the Aboriginal problem in Western Australia* (St. Lucia, 1973), pp. 13–25. Biskup observes, pp. 22–23, that the Aboriginal population of the Rottnest Island prison doubled between 1883 and 1884. He notes that although in the 1870s the need for Aboriginal labour together with legislation authorising Aboriginal 'access' to unimproved pastoral leasehold lands eased tensions in some parts of the northwest, this 'precarious adjustment' had broken down by the 1890s.

46 See, for example, the British 1824 vagrancy legislation.

47 For further discussion of the structural basis underlying particular constructions of race in different colonial contexts, see P. Wolfe, 'Land, labor, and difference: elementary structures of race' in *American Historical Review*, 106, pt. 2 (June 2003), 866–905.

48 See Hasluck, *Black Australians*, p. 142.

Grey had not been unaware of the import of his exceptional decision, disclaiming any more general principle throughout the British dominions that native peoples would be subject to a different course of criminal procedure from other British subjects. 'Such a principle would,' he said, 'in many instances contravene the plainest rules of justice …'.[49]

CONCLUSION

In the case of Western Australia, summary procedures were administered by a powerful alliance comprising local magistrates, the police and landowners, whose shared interests provided the framework within which they could perceive and exercise their summary powers.[50] Within the grim politics of the settler-colonial encounter, the possibility to rule by inducing general anxiety and alarm within a designated population and by opening the way for arbitrary prosecution and exemplary punishments could operate in tandem with the rule of law as the nineteenth century wore on.[51] As the next century began and settlers in the individual colonies celebrated their federation, the discrimination to which Aborigines had long been subjected would be further entrenched in the founding documents of the new nation.[52]

It bears reiterating that these demands for extraordinary procedures in the Australian colonies correlated with conflicts over dispossession, suggesting that the installation of the rule of law for the settlers – along with the formation of the nation to come – was contingent upon the capacity to tolerate its abrogation in relation to indigenous peoples. In this sense, the suspension of the rule of law was intimately related to, rather than separate from, its regular operation.

Within this framework, what might otherwise be viewed as an aberration, or quite simply as unlawful or unjust, was actually constitutive of the rule of

---

49 Grey to Fitzgerald, no. 11, 2 June 1848 (TNA: PRO, CO 397/7). In a minute on Irwin to Grey, no. 62, 23 December 1847 (TNA: PRO, CO 18/45), Herman Merivale supported summary procedures for 'the poor creatures' in Western Australia whom he perceived as susceptible to protection rather than equality. Accordingly, 'exceptional laws, marking them, as no doubt they do, as inferiors, are, nevertheless, consistent with the whole policy pursued towards them. They seem a natural part of it.'

50 Hasluck observes that 'in the outback settlements the unavoidable fact is that when [an Aborigine] appears before local justices he appears before people who, as a class, have a very strong interest in his case and who may be the very persons he is alleged to have wronged': *Black Australians*, p. 142.

51 See also J. McGuire, 'Judicial violence and the "civilising process": race and the transition from public to private executions in colonial Australia' in *Australian Historical Studies*, 29, pt. 3 (1998), 187–209.

52 See P. Wolfe, 'Nation and miscegeNation' and J. Chesterman and B. Galligan, *Citizens without rights: Aborigines and Australian citizenship* (Cambridge, 1997).

law, so that in suspending itself, the rule of law maintained itself. Such suspensions created a space in which the 'normal order' could develop – where exclusive sovereignty could be secured, individual property could be defended and the broader liberal political, social and economic order could be fully installed – and bail could be paid. The idea of the rule of law, providing universal equality for those not excluded from its particular domain – that of the nation – could be seen less problematically to prevail.

As Schmitt reminds us, 'There is no rule that is applicable to chaos. Order must be established for juridical order to make sense. A regular situation must be created, and sovereign is he who definitely decides if this situation is actually effective.'[53] Further, as Agamben interprets Schmitt:

> The relation of exception thus simply expresses the originary formal structure of the juridical relation. In this sense, the sovereign decision on the exception is the originary juridico-political structure on the basis of which what is included in the juridical order and what is excluded from it acquire their meaning. In its archetypal form, the state of exception is therefore the principle of every juridical localization, since only the state of exception opens the space in which the determination of a certain juridical order and a particular territory first becomes possible.[54]

Both Schmitt and Agamben assume a European origin impossible to localise in specific temporal or spatial terms, a 'time immemorial'. But in the colonies, in the critical formative stages of establishing state power, we encounter native society as the origin that is to be suppressed – through the constitution of the law that at once presupposes and authorises such suppression. Whether through summary justice legislation, the banning of Aboriginal testimony, exemplary punishments or outright martial law, to name just some of its modes in colonies of settlement, the state of exception helped transfer sovereignty and precipitated indigenous peoples' collective subjection to the racialising and criminalising force of domestic law.

53 Cited in G. Agamben, *Homo sacer*, p. 16.
54 Agamben, *Homo sacer*, p. 19.

Indigenous customary rights and the common law in Aotearoa New Zealand

DAVID V. WILLIAMS

THE UNTIDY PROCESS OF ANNEXATION AND RECEPTION

THE ADVENTURE OF THE common law in New Zealand began with the establishment of a British colonial state in 1840. The process of annexation was untidy and the proper basis for the sovereignty claims that led to the establishment of the state remain doubtful to this day. Initially the territory was annexed as a dependency of New South Wales after a lieutenant governor was sworn in at Sydney on 14 January 1840. In June 1840 the New South Wales legislature enacted an Act to make provision for dealing with land claims and to extend New South Wales law to the dependency.[1] Meanwhile in February the lieutenant governor, Hobson, had commenced negotiations with chiefs of the indigenous Maori tribes of the islands now generally called Aotearoa.[2] A treaty, written in Maori and known as the Treaty of Waitangi, was entered into between the Crown and many of those chiefs. It offered the Queen's protection to Maori and certain guarantees of their rights to land and important treasures. An English translation clearly asserted that the chiefs were ceding their sovereignty to the Crown, but the Treaty itself was not clear on that point. Some Maori remain of the view that the Treaty affirmed the prior power, prestige and authority of Maori and invited the Crown to govern only the European settlers who had already begun to arrive in the territory.[3]

News that those settlers at Port Nicholson (Wellington) were organising their own council independently of the lieutenant governor, led to Hobson rushing out two Proclamations of British Sovereignty over all the islands in May 1840. The proclamation for the North Island purported to be based on

---

1   Act 3 Vict., no. 28 (New South Wales) came into force on 16 June 1840.
2   Aotearoa became the most used Maori language name for New Zealand during the twentieth century: M. King, *Penguin history of New Zealand* (Wellington, 2003), p. 69.
3   See C. Orange, *The treaty of Waitangi* (Wellington, 1987); M. Durie, *Te mana, te kawanatanga: the politics of Maori self-determination* (Auckland, 1998).

the Treaty of Waitangi as a cession of sovereignty owing, he said, to the 'universal' adherence of the chiefs – a wildly inaccurate claim. The justification given for the other proclamation claiming the southern islands was, somewhat oddly, 'discovery'. In terms of European voyagers, the South Island was first partially mapped by a Dutch expedition in 1642 and it was the Dutch who bestowed the European name for the country: New Zealand.[4] The expeditions (and British flag plantings) by the British explorer, Cook, did not begin until 1769. Moreover, there were no British settlers in the South Island to lend credence to any discovery-based claim. Indeed the only significant group of settlers living there in 1840 were French! Hobson's proclamations were taken at face value by the Colonial Office in London, however, and duly gazetted. The imperial Parliament then passed an empowering Act and in November the Colonial Office issued the necessary charters and instructions to erect New Zealand as a separate colony.[5]

The complications arising from New Zealand's brief dependency on New South Wales included a lack of clarity as to the reception date for the deemed arrival of the common law in this new British land. When did the Blackstonian 'birthright of Englishmen' arrive?[6] In 1858 a Supreme Court judgment relating to the imperial Wills Act 1837 decided that that Act was inapplicable in New Zealand because it was a statute that had been passed after the foundation of New South Wales and it had not been expressly incorporated into the laws of that colony. Hence it did not apply in New Zealand either. This decision was arrived at in spite of the fact that the English Acts Act 1854, one of the first Acts of the New Zealand colony's first elected legislature in 1854, had specified that the imperial Wills Amendment Act 1852 did apply in the colony.[7] The General Assembly then rushed through a retrospective declaratory statute. By the English Laws Act 1858, section 1: 'The laws of England as existing on the 14th day of January 1840, shall, so far as applicable to the circumstances of the said Colony of New Zealand, be deemed and taken to have been in force therein on and after that day.' The 1858 Act was re-enacted as the English Laws Act 1908. This was repealed and replaced by the Imperial Laws Application Act 1988 that is now in force.

---

4 The Dutch explorer, Tasman, assumed that he had reached the great Southern land mass known to the Dutch as 'Staten Landt'. Later, Dutch map-makers substituted 'Zeelandia Nova': A. Salmond, *Two worlds: first meetings between Maori and Europeans, 1642–1772* (Auckland, 1991), pp. 24 and 437.

5 D.V. Williams, 'The annexation of New Zealand to New South Wales in 1840: what of the treaty of Waitangi?' in *Australian Journal of Law & Society*, 2 (1985), 41–55.

6 See W.J.V. Windeyer, ' "A birthright and inheritance" ' in *Tasmania University Law Review* (1962), 635.

7 D.V. Williams, 'The foundation of colonial rule in New Zealand' in *New Zealand Universities Law Review*, 13 (1988), 54–67 [The Supreme Court (re-named the High Court in 1980) was the first instance superior court established by the Supreme Court Ordinance

SO FAR AS APPLICABLE TO THE CIRCUMSTANCES
OF THE COLONY

The focus of this paper is on the local circumstances exception, drawn from Blackstonian doctrine, to the general application of English law in British colonies. In particular, a matter of crucial concern in 2003 to courts and the government concerns the significance of the indigenous stream of customary law, known generally as 'tikanga Maori', within the state legal system. To what extent, it has been asked, ought English doctrines of law give way to tikanga Maori conceptions on the ground that a number of common law presumptions and the doctrines of tenure are inapplicable to the circumstances of New Zealand as those circumstances are now understood?

At the outset of colonial rule the lieutenant governor initiated a number of debates between the chiefs of tribes and envoys of the Crown as copies of the Treaty of Waitangi were taken to most coastal regions of the country (including the South Island) for the adherence of local tribes. A crucial element of those debates concerned the future status of customary law systems and of chiefly authority in relation to the new governance authority of the Queen. Numerous oral and written assurances were given to Maori by Crown officials and agents to the effect that: 'The Queen will not interfere with your native laws or customs.'[8] This might have presaged a system of colonial rule similar to that later known as indirect rule, but that was not to be so in New Zealand. This was to be a settlement colony to be peopled as rapidly as possible by British migrants. From the earliest period of Crown colony rule, imperial decision-makers determined that racial amalgamation and assimilation were the policies to be applied to Maori.[9] This meant that, if Maori people were not to be a dying race, then the principle of 'communism' that ran through the whole of their institutions must be eradicated. They would be civilised by an English education, their communal values would be transformed into individualised property values, and their indigenous notions of law and religion would be displaced in favour of western Christian belief systems. As a matter of fact many Maori communities were engaged in vigorous social and economic transformations and an eclectic engagement with western values in a manner consistent with tikanga Maori and chiefly

---

1841. Confusingly, the Supreme Court now is a new second tier appellate body to replace appeals to the Privy Council: Supreme Court Act 2003.]

8   Waitangi Tribunal, *Muriwhenua land report* (Wellington, 1997), pp. 112–14; New Zealand Law Commission, *Maori custom and values in New Zealand law* (Wellington, 2001), pp. 72–74.

9   See A. Ward, *A show of justice: racial 'amalgamation' in nineteenth century New Zealand* (Auckland, 1995); P. Adams, *Fatal necessity: British intervention in New Zealand, 1830–1847* (Auckland, 1977); D.V. Williams, *Crown policy affecting Maori knowledge systems and cultural practices* (Wellington, 2001).

authority.[10] Imperial and colonial policy did not care, however, to wait for an internal transformation of Maori tribal systems. The 1840 promises to respect tikanga Maori were viewed merely as temporary expedients only. Quickly it became evident that New Zealand was to have a mono-legal regime based on English common law. The presence of organised bodies of Scots settlers in southern regions, incidentally, did not entail the application of Scots law there.[11]

The assumption of colonial courts was that all English law – statutes of general application and the common law of England (including the principles and rules of equity) – applied in New Zealand unless a strong case could be put forward for the non-application of a particular provision. Indeed it has been argued by Australian jurists that the emphasis on local circumstances in Blackstonian doctrine was misleading:[12]

> Blackstone's statement that 'colonists carry with them only so much of English law as is applicable to their own situation and the condition of the infant colony' is, like so many of his generalisations, misleading; it would have been nearer the truth if he had said, 'colonists carry with them the mass of English law, both common law and statute, except those parts which are inapplicable to their own situation and the condition of the infant colony'. What became applicable was far greater in content and importance than what had to be rejected.

New Zealand colonial courts certainly preferred to apply English law even when the specifically English context of the law's origins were plain:[13]

> I think, in dealing with this question, we must suppose that we have lying open before us the whole common law and statute law of England in force on the terminal day; and of that great body of law, every provision which was then applicable to the circumstances of the Colony is to be deemed to have been solemnly adopted and legislatively declared to be the law of the Colony by the Legislature of the Colony at a time when it had been fully empowered by the Imperial Parliament to make its own laws. And it seems to me that with respect to the statute law of England the question is not whether the whole of a particular statute, or a chapter of a statute, can be applied in the Colony, but whether the particular enactment, duly interpreted and construed by context and the preamble of the Act, is capable of being applied or not.

---

10 See J. Belich, *Making peoples* (Auckland, 1996).
11 N. Jamieson, 'English law but British justice' in *Otago Law Review*, 4 (1980), 488–502.
12 F.R. Beasley and R.W. Baker, 'The need for co-operation in State and Commonwealth law' in *Australian Law Journal*, 23 (1949), 192.
13 *Highett v. McDonald* (1878) 3 NZ Jur. (NS) (SC) 102, p. 104 (per Johnston J.).

That case concerned section 12 of the Tippling Act – 24 Geo II, ch. 40 – which declared that no action shall be brought for the recovery of a debt for spirituous liquor unless contracted at one time for not less than 20 shillings. This single provision was surrounded by a network of clauses of purely local application in relation to the complex licensing and revenue laws of eighteenth-century England. The New Zealand court nevertheless held that section to be for the purpose of protecting public morals and plainly applicable to every part of Her Majesty's dominions.

The reception of English law in relation to gold mining was discussed in a Court of Appeal decision in 1875 after hearing extensive legal argument. Chapman J. gave a lengthy account of the relevant law and concluded:[14]

> Taking all the cases to be found in the Reports, they are too few in number to establish any exhaustive general rules as to suitableness or applicability of English Statutes to the colonies; and, therefore, 'what shall be admitted and what rejected, must in cases of dispute, be decided, in the first instance by the provincial (i.e. colonial) judicature, subject to the revision and control of the King in Council. (1 Bl. Com. 108.)

Thus empowered by Blackstonian doctrine, the conclusion arrived at by the court was to apply the royal prerogative to gold in New Zealand. In doing so, it followed the leading English case on the matter:[15]

> The auriferous deposits belong to Her Majesty, subject to the gold fields laws of the colony; but Her Majesty could not, therefore, be entitled to foul streams beyond the gold fields to the detriment of grantees of the Crown. In the case of *Mines*, report in *Plowden*, it was held that the King had the right to cut timber on the freehold of a subject so far as was necessary for working a Royal mine under the land. But it would be going beyond the decision in that case to hold that the Sovereign would be entitled to cut timber, if necessary for working the mine, on other closes than that in which the gold was found. A freeholder can maintain an action for polluting, by gold mining, a stream flowing past his freehold, unless the freehold be within the gold field, and the pollution be justified by the regulations made under the Gold Fields Act.

It is not immediately obvious to me why the 1568 *Case of mines* decision arising from the particular historical context of Elizabethan England should be applied in a case concerning a dispute between sheep farmers and gold

14 *Borton* v. *Howe* (1875) 3 CA 5, p. 14.
15 Ibid., p. 18.

miners in southern New Zealand over the fouling of streams by gold mining operations. However, that was the decision of the New Zealand court. Moreover, similar reasoning in two opinions of the Privy Council in following years applied this royal prerogative to a colony in Australia and to British North America.[16]

There are in fact very few New Zealand cases in which it has been held that some rule of common law or an English statute was *not* applicable to the circumstances of the country. Surprisingly perhaps, one of these few cases is *Baldick* v. *Jackson* in which it was decided that a 1324 statute (17 Edw II, ch. 2) deeming whales to be a 'royal fish' as part of the royal prerogative was not in force in this country.[17] Stout C.J. took into account the extensive private commercial whaling in New Zealand since 1829 and his own personal knowledge of Greenland whaling customs (derived from his upbringing on the Shetland Islands).[18] He also pointed out that the Treaty of Waitangi assumed the existence of Maori fishing rights, that the Maori were accustomed to engage in whaling and that a royal prerogative right to whales would thus disturb Maori rights in respect of fisheries.

The Treaty's article 2 protective guarantee over fisheries helped the Chief Justice to his decision refusing to apply the royal fish doctrine to New Zealand. Surely then, by parity of reasoning, the same article's protective guarantee for lands and estates would point to a decision that the royal metals prerogative was inappropriate to the circumstances of the colony. However, just a year after his own *Baldick* v. *Jackson* decision, Stout C.J. made no reference to it (or to the Treaty of Waitangi) when making this comment on the Mining Act 1908: 'There is no doubt that the Mining Act proceeds on the presumption that at common law precious metals belong to the Crown, and the Crown has a right to mine for them: See *Reg* v. *Earl of Northumberland*. This will explain, no doubt, the interference with private property in mining districts.'[19]

In time the increasing body of statutes enacted by the colonial and dominion legislature reduced the number of occasions the courts might be called on to consider whether a pre-1840 English or United Kingdom statute was applicable in New Zealand. As late as 1976, however, the Supreme Court was asked to issue a declaration that the Prime Minister had illegally suspended an Act of Parliament. The Prime Minister, Muldoon, was the

---

16 *Wooley* v. *A-G of Victoria* (1877) 2 App. Cas. 163; *A-G of British Columbia* v. *A-G of Canada* (1889) 14 App. Cas. 295.

17 *Baldick* v. *Jackson* (1910) 30 NZLR 343.

18 D. Hamer, 'Robert Stout, 1844–1930, lawyer, politician, premier, chief justice, university chancellor' in Department of Internal Affairs, *The dictionary of New Zealand biography, volume two, 1870–1900* (Wellington, 1993), p. 484.

19 *Skeet and Dillon* v. *Nicholls* (1911) 30 NZLR 623. See D.V. Williams, 'Gold, the *Case of Mines* (1568) and the Waitangi Tribunal', *Australian Journal of Law and History*, 7 (2003), 157–75.

leader of the party that had just won a general election in which he campaigned vigorously against the 'communist' potential of the previous government's superannuation scheme. By press statement he announced that the super-annuation legislation would be repealed in due course and that compulsory contributions to the scheme should cease immediately. A private litigant persuaded the court that this action was the suspension of an Act by 'regall authority without the consent of Parlyament' contrary to the Bill of Rights 1688. Wild C.J. wrote:[20]

> It is a graphic illustration of the depth of our legal heritage and the strength of our constitutional law that a statute passed by the English Parliament nearly three centuries ago to extirpate the abuses of the Stuart Kings should be available on the other side of the earth to a citizen of this country which was then virtually unknown in Europe and on which no Englishman was to set foot for almost another hundred years. And yet it is not disputed that the Bill of Rights is part of our law.

RADICAL TITLE, ABORIGINAL TITLE AND MAORI CUSTOMARY RIGHTS

Once the colonial state of New Zealand was established, it was plain that New Zealand was to be a settlement colony and that European settlers needed land to be made available to them. Land policy and immigration were therefore crucial to imperial and colonial officials. On the other hand, the cultural and spiritual relationships and interconnections between land and people were central to the precepts of tikanga Maori. The notion of sharing resources with incomers, under arrangements that involved an ongoing commitment to mutually beneficial and reciprocal outcomes, were entirely possible under tikanga Maori. In many parts of the country there had been a number of European sealers, whalers, traders and missionaries who had lived under customary law regimes in the fifty years of contact prior to 1840. The notion of permanent alienation of land, or even of 'ownership' of land as such, was not imaginable however. Hohepa, now the Maori Language Commissioner, wrote about 'whenua' – the Maori word for 'land' – in this way:[21]

> For Maori, whenua has an added meaning, being the human placenta or afterbirth. Through various birth ceremonies the placenta is returned

20 *Fitzgerald v. Muldoon* [1976] 2 NZLR 615, p. 622. See D.V. Williams, 'To remind people of the Bill of Rights 1688' in *Monash University Law Review*, 3 (1977), 243–48.
21 P. Hohepa and D.V. Williams, *The taking into account of te ao Maori in relation to the reform of the law of succession* (Wellington, 1996), p. 10. See T.C. Royal (ed.), *The woven universe: selected writings of Rev Maori Marsden* (Otaki, 2003).

to the land, and that results in each Maori person having personal, spiritual, symbolic and sacred links to the land where their whenua (placenta) is part of the whenua (land). The words 'nooku teenei whenua' (This is my land) is given a much stronger meaning because of the above extensions. Having ancestral and birth connections the above is also translated as 'I belong to this land, so do my ancestors, and when I die I join them so I too will be totally part of this land'.

The paradigms of land tenure written by the Colonial Office in instructions to governors as implemented by the Land Claims Ordinance 1841 were very different. The Ordinance declared that 'all unappropriated lands within the said Colony of New Zealand, subject however to the rightful and necessary occupation and use thereof by the aboriginal inhabitants of the said Colony, are and remain Crown or Domain Lands of Her Majesty'. This was an assertion of the radical title of the Crown to all land. The question then arose as to whether, in order to provide land for settlers, Maori customary rights had first to be extinguished in respect of *all* land, or only in respect of land actually occupied and cultivated at the time (in a fashion that John Locke might understand) by Maori tribes. Earl Grey's 1846 instructions to a new governor, Grey (not a relative), were avowedly based on the opinions of the historian Arnold: '[So] much does the right of property go along with labour, that civilized nations have never scrupled to take possession of countries inhabited only by tribes of savages – countries which have been hunted over but never subdued or cultivated.'

Earl Grey (then Lord Howick) had been the author of a House of Commons Committee report in 1844 arguing for the settlement of waste lands in the colony without undue deference to the 'injudicious proceedings' of the Treaty of Waitangi. Now as Secretary of State he strongly dissented from the notion that aboriginal inhabitants are the proprietors of every part of the soil of any country. For him civilised [i.e. European] men had a right to step in and take possession of vacant territory: '[All] lands not actually occupied in the sense in which alone occupation can give a right of possession ought to have been considered as the property of the Crown.' The governor was expressly empowered to depart from the strict application of these principles but only if it would be impracticable to enforce that policy.[22]

Grey's predecessor, Fitzroy, introduced briefly a policy to waive Crown pre-emption and thus permit settlers to engage in direct purchasing of land from Maori. To clarify the land policy for the future of the colony, Grey initiated a test case in the Supreme Court. In *Queen* v. *Symonds* in 1847 the

---

22 Earl Grey to Grey, 23 December 1846, *British Parliamentary Papers: Colonies New Zealand* (Shannon, 1969), vol. 5, pp. 523–25. See D.V. Williams, *'Te kooti tango whenua': the native land court, 1864–1909* (Wellington, 1999), pp. 108–14.

judges of the Supreme Court asserted the paramount importance of the Crown's pre-emptive monopoly right to purchase lands from Maori. Nevertheless, relying on the Supreme Court judgments of Marshall C.J. and the commentaries of Kent and Story in the United States of America, they took a more liberal view of the scope of aboriginal title than Earl Grey had:[23]

> Whatever may be the opinion of jurists as to the strength or weakness of the Native title, whatsoever may have been the past vague notions of the Natives of this country, whatever may be their present clearer and still growing conception of their own dominion over land, it cannot be too solemnly asserted that it is entitled to be respected, that it cannot be extinguished (at least in times of peace) otherwise than by the free consent of the Native occupiers. But for their protection, and for the sake of humanity, the Government is bound to maintain, and the Courts to assert, the Queen's exclusive right to extinguish it.

This doctrine of Crown pre-emption and aboriginal title was relied on during the Crown colony period, up to 1854, and until 1862 in the early years of responsible government implemented pursuant to the powers granted by the imperial parliament to an elected General Assembly in the New Zealand Constitution Act 1852. Crown pre-emption enabled successive governors to enter into land purchase transactions over very large blocks of land. The deeds signed covered the majority of the land in the country, especially in those areas where the Maori population was low and settler pressures for good pastoral land were great. In the government's view these deeds extinguished Maori customary rights.

An increasing reluctance by Maori tribes to sell land, and the outbreak of war between Crown and Maori forces in several areas of the North Island, led to a change of policy. The Native Lands Act 1862 waived Crown pre-emption and replaced it with a Native Land Court system. This court over the next sixty years investigated the customary title rights to all land blocks not dealt with either in the earlier deeds or under the confiscation proclamations of the New Zealand Settlements Act 1863. Following the court's title investigation, customary title was extinguished and a form of individualised freehold title was then issued to named Maori 'owners'. As was desired and anticipated by the governments responsible for the Native Land Acts, most Maori freehold title land was alienated into the hands of the Crown or settlers within a short period of time after title investigations.[24]

---

23 *New Zealand Privy Council Cases, 1840–1932* (Wellington, 1938), p. 390 (per Chapman J. – the case remained unreported until included in this volume). See D.V. Williams, '*Queen* v. *Symonds* reconsidered', *Victoria University of Wellington Law Review*, 19 (1989), 385–402.
24 Williams, '*Te kooti tango whenua*', pp. 58–62.

CUSTOMARY RIGHTS REJECTED

The *Symonds* approach was affirmed in 1872 in *Re Lundon and Whitaker Claims Act 1871*.[25] Nevertheless, the Supreme Court soon after resiled from its 1847 recognition of aboriginal title rights. In *Wi Parata* v. *Bishop of Wellington* in 1877 the court reinterpreted the reasoning of *Queen* v. *Symonds*. The earlier court's holdings on the radical title of the Crown to all lands were emphasised and the court now took the view that it had no jurisdiction to avoid a Crown grant of land, or in any way to go behind a Crown grant to inquire into the extinguishment or otherwise of any prior customary rights. In the judgment of Prendergast C.J. and Richmond J., delivered by the Chief Justice, the 1841 Ordinance was said to 'express the well-known legal incidents of a settlement planted by a civilised Power in the midst of uncivilised tribes'. The Treaty of Waitangi was dismissed 'as a simple nullity. No body politic existed capable of making a cession of sovereignty, nor could the thing itself exist. So far as the proprietary rights of the natives are concerned, the so-called treaty merely affirms the rights and obligations which, *jure gentium*, vested in and devolved upon the Crown.' Nor did the Native Rights Act 1865 of the colonial Parliament make a difference. That Act speaks, the judges wrote, 'of the "Ancient Custom and Usage of the Maori people," as if some such body of customary law did in reality exist. But a phrase in a statute cannot call what is non-existent into being.' Rather, 'in the case of primitive barbarians, the supreme executive Government must acquit itself, as best it may, of its obligation to respect native proprietary rights, and of necessity must be the sole arbiter of its own justice.'[26]

The *Wi Parata* approach replaced legal obligations to respect indigenous customary rights with an unenforceable and non-justiciable moral obligation on the executive branch of government to deal with those rights as they saw fit. The proclamation of British sovereignty and the concomitant radical title of the Crown entailed the consequence that Crown grants could never be impeached. A number of aspects of the *Wi Parata* judgment did not escape criticism from the Privy Council in later cases. In *Nireaha Tamaki* v. *Baker* and *Wallis* v. *Solicitor-General* the Judicial Committee pointed to the incontrovertible statutory recognition of the existence of customary Maori rights and the capacity of Maori tribes to enter into legal transactions.[27] The colonial judges, however, showed little inclination to respect the admonitions of the final appellate court for the Empire. Nor did they need to, because the

25 *Re Lundon and Whitaker Claims Act 1871* (1872) 2 NZCA. 41, p. 49.
26 *Wi Parata* v. *Bishop of Wellington* (1877) 3 NZ Jur. (NS) (SC) 72, pp. 77–80. See P.G. McHugh, 'Tales of constitutional origin and crown sovereignty in New Zealand', *University of Toronto Law Journal*, 52 (2002), 77–82.
27 *Nireaha Tamaki* v. *Baker* [1901] AC 561; *Wallis* v. *Solicitor-General* [1903] AC 173.

legislature had no compunction about intervening to reverse inconvenient Privy Council decisions and even to bar further litigation by a successful Maori litigant such as Nireaha Tamaki.[28] On one extraordinary occasion the judges in Wellington publicly lambasted the Privy Council, not only for insinuating that the colonial judges were beholden to the executive but also for their Lordships' palpable ignorance, as the colonial bench viewed it, of laws and practices concerning Native land issues. Consistent with the reasoning of *Wi Parata*, Stout C.J.'s protest included the assertion that 'All lands of the Colony belonged to the Crown, and it was for the Crown under Letters Patent to grant to the parties to the Treaty such lands as the Crown had agreed to grant'.[29]

It was the understandings of the chief justices, Prendergast and Stout, rather than of the Privy Council, that were codified into the Native Land Act 1909 which was drafted by the famous jurist, and long serving solicitor-general, Salmond. The non-justiciability of Maori claims that customary title rights had not been properly extinguished was most explicitly dealt with by sections 84 to 87 of the 1909 Act. These sections were re-enacted in 1931 and 1953 consolidations of Salmond's code and remained in force until Te Ture Whenua Maori Act 1993. Salmond's private explanation of these provisions to Ngata, an eminent Maori member of Parliament, was as follows:[30]

> The intention is that when a dispute arises between Natives and the Crown as to the right to customary land, the dispute shall be settled by Parliament and not otherwise. The Native race will have nothing to fear from the decision of that tribunal, and to allow the matter to be fought out in the Law Courts would not, I think, be either in the public interest or in the interests of the Natives themselves.

His memorandum to explain the bill he drafted made it clear that in his view customary title only existed on the basis of the radical rights of the Crown:

> Customary land, since it has never been Crown-granted, belongs to the Crown. It is in a wide sense of the term Crown land, subject, however, to the right of those Natives who by virtue of Maori custom have a claim to it to obtain a Crown grant (or a certificate of title under the Land Transfer Act in lieu of a grant) on the ascertainment of their customary titles by the Native Land Court. This right of the Natives

---

28 Land Titles Protection Act 1902; Maori Land Claims Adjustment and Laws Amendment Act 1904, s. 4.

29 'Protest of bench and bar, 25 April 1903', appendix to *New Zealand Privy Council Cases, 1840–1932*, p. 732.

30 A. Frame, *Salmond: southern jurist* (Wellington, 1995), p. 114 (citing Salmond to Ngata, 22 December 1909, Crown Law Office, Wellington, Case File 84).

to their customary lands was recognised by the Treaty of Waitangi in 1840. In its origin it was merely a moral claim, dependent on the good will of the Crown, and not recognisable or enforceable at law.

Salmond went on to argue that whether or not legislative recognition of Maori custom had created a legal right enforceable against the Crown 'was left an open question by the Privy Council in *Nireaha Tamaki* v. *Baker*'. On the other hand, 'it is settled' by *Wi Parata* that once a Crown grant has been issued then 'the validity of the title so obtained cannot be questioned on the ground that the antecedent Native title to that land had not been lawfully extinguished'.[31] Hence the definition in s. 2 of the 1909 Act is that '"Customary land" means land (vested in the Crown) held by Natives under the customs and usages of the Maori people'.[32] By then, however, the area of land not yet investigated by the Land Court was tiny. Just 490,752 acres remained in 1909, that had been reduced to 190,792 acres in 1911 and it was eliminated as a significant category of dry land shortly afterwards.[33]

The question of Maori customary claims to the land comprised in the beds on inland lakes proved a thorny problem for Crown policy in the years immediately following the Native Land Act 1909. The Court of Appeal affirmed the right of Te Arawa plaintiffs to have the Native Land Court investigate their title to the bed of Lake Rotorua: *Tamihana Korokai* v. *Solicitor-General*. Salmond as solicitor-general engaged in indignant arguments that the judges had failed to understand the nature of the Crown's right to prevent customary title issues being justiciable. The eventual outcome for this and other lakebed issues was to persuade Maori tribes to accept the Crown's assertion of title in return for various forms of compensation, sometimes including a proportion of the fishing licence revenues for fishing in those lakes.[34] For Salmond, 'It could never have been the intention of the Legislature to recognise and give legal effect to any Native claim to the exclusive ownership of the great navigable waters of the Dominion'.[35]

---

31 J. Salmond, 'Memorandum. Notes on the history of native-land legislation'. Now published in full in H. Bassett, R. Steel and D.V. Williams, *The Maori land legislation manual* (Wellington, 1994), app. C, pp. 95–96.

32 A full list of statutory definitions of land in the Native Land Acts 1862 to 1909 is set out in Williams, '*Te kooti tango whenua*', app. 3, pp. 255–59.

33 Ibid., p. 59.

34 *Tamihana Korokai* v. *Solicitor-General* (1912) 32 NZLR 321; Frame, *Salmond*, pp. 115–28.

35 Ibid., p. 127. See also *In re the Bed of the Wanganui River* [1962] NZLR 600 (CA); E.J. Haughey, 'Maori claims to lakes, river beds and the foreshore' in *New Zealand Universities Law Review*, 2 (1966), 29–42.

ABORIGINAL TITLE REVIVES

One might have been assumed that the *Wi Parata* doctrine and its statutory codification had led to the total demise of aboriginal title as a concept relevant to law in New Zealand. The Maori cultural renaissance of the 1970s, however, led to a strong questioning of many of the assumptions of assimilation and integration policies pursued by successive governments over many decades. Furthermore, within governing circles hesitant steps were being taken to move away from the colonial settler picture of New Zealand as a Better Britain in the South Seas and the most loyal of the British Dominions, to New Zealand as an independent nation in the South Pacific.[36] Some scholars speak of the emergence of 'post-colonialism' at this time. This is unhelpful, in my view, as constitutional structures derived from colonial times firmly remained in place – even if from time to time some British imperial and monarchical trappings have been shed. Yet there was indeed in the 1970s a renewed political focus on the Treaty of Waitangi as the foundation of the New Zealand nation. Waitangi Day became the country's national day of commemoration (and also the focus of political protests led by Maori nationalists). There was also an emerging awareness of the position of other indigenous peoples who had become a minority population in their own land. Unlike the peoples of most imperial territories, being de-colonised with the vigorous support of the United Nations at that time, first nation peoples in the Americas, the Pacific Rim, Scandinavia and elsewhere were not being offered the right of self-determination.

In the 1980s legal scholars and practitioners began to seek to craft arguments that would advance the cause of the strong Maori cultural renaissance. Most of that effort was directed towards an enhanced status for the guarantees to Maori contained in the Treaty of Waitangi and enhanced powers for the Waitangi Tribunal created by the Treaty of Waitangi Act 1975. This was consistent with the long history of Maori seeking the ratification of the Treaty as an enforceable legal instrument. These efforts included many court cases, petitions to Parliament, petitions to the British monarch and resolutions of autonomous Maori parliaments and other independent Maori political movements and churches. I was one of the scholars who argued for an enhanced legal status for the Treaty of Waitangi. This was a consensual solemn compact between Crown and Maori, whereas the so-called 'common law' doctrine of aboriginal title was a doctrine of imperial law that accepted the framework of British sovereignty claims. Moreover, that doctrine permitted the Crown to extinguish customary title by overriding Acts of Parliament – including confiscation without compensation and other forms of extinguishment without the explicit consent of the indigenous people.[37]

---

36 See J. Belich, *Paradise reforged* (Auckland, 2001).
37 D.V. Williams, 'Te tiriti o Waitangi – unique relationship between crown and tangata whenua?' in I.H. Kawharu (ed.), *Waitangi* (Auckland, 1989), pp. 84–89.

Maori litigants willing to resort to the courts of the state legal system, not surprisingly, were less concerned with ideological purity and more concerned with favourable outcomes. The decisions of Canadian courts after the landmark judgments in the decision of the Supreme Court of Canada on the Nishga nation: *Calder* v. *Attorney-General of British Columbia* had suggested the possibility of favourable outcomes from reliance on aboriginal title. This possibility was seized upon in the 1980s. Thus, in its first report that contained specific recommendations to Ministers of the Crown, the Waitangi Tribunal wrote in 1983:[38]

> Nonetheless the approach of the New Zealand Courts, and of successive Governments, does not compare favourably with that taken by other Courts and Governments in their consideration of indigenous minorities. In North America for example treaties with the original Indian populations have been recognised by the Courts, and in areas not covered by treaties, common law rights are regarded as vesting in native peoples by virtue of their prior occupation (refer for example, *Calder* v. *Attorney-General of British Columbia* (1973) 34 D.L.R. 145).
>
> The overseas experience must cause us to re-think our perception of the Treaty of Waitangi and of its significance.

That re-thinking was taken a step further in 1986 when the High Court held that, even if customary rights had been extinguished along the adjacent shoreline, customary fishing rights below high-water mark in a coastal area remained unextinguished. The judge, Williamson J., was assisted again by the *Calder* decision and also the academic writings of an expatriate New Zealander, McHugh, in restrictively distinguishing an earlier Court of Appeal decision: *Waipapakura* v. *Hempton*.[39] In the *Waipapakura* case Salmond had argued that tidal waters vested in the Crown by its prerogative free of any customary rights. Stout C.J., for the Court of Appeal, had denied that the explicit saving of 'existing Maori fishing rights' in the Fisheries Act 1908 authorised recognition of customary fishing right claims to harvest whitebait in tidal waters. That was another example of *Wi Parata*-type reasoning that prevailed at that time. Now in 1986, the High Court held that customary rights continued to subsist and continued to have the protection accorded by the aboriginal title doctrines of the common law outlined in the (now remembered) *Symonds* case unless clearly and plainly extinguished by statute or other lawful means. Mere assertion of Crown prerogative rights would not suffice and the onus of proving extinguishment lay on the Crown.[40]

38 Waitangi Tribunal, *Motunui Waitara Report* (Wellington, 1983), para 10.1. [The correct *Calder* citation is: (1973) 34 DLR (3d) 145.]

39 *Waipapakura* v. *Hempton* (1914) 33 NZLR 1065. See Frame, *Salmond*, pp. 104–06.

40 *Te Weehi* v. *Regional Fisheries Officer* [1986] 1 NZLR 680; P.G. McHugh, 'The legal status

After *Te Weehi*, further fisheries litigation in the superior courts, reports of the Waitangi Tribunal and a report of the Law Commission gave detailed attention to the nature and extent of Maori customary fishing rights. It was found that these rights were not merely traditional practices for subsistence living but included commercial opportunities exploited well prior to 1840 by Maori tribes.[41] Subsequent legislation in 1989 and 1992, after negotiations between the Government and Maori negotiators, established a new statutory regime for Maori fisheries, extinguished customary rights to commercial fisheries and established a statute-based regime for non-commercial fisheries.[42] Thus there are now a number of 'taiapure' local fisheries of special significance for customary spiritual or cultural reasons and detailed general regulations to govern the customary take of various fish species in all parts of the country.[43]

ABORIGINAL TITLE REVIVES AGAIN (BUT ONLY BRIEFLY)

Government ministers and legal advisers were taken by surprise with a number of decisions of superior courts in the 1980s. In addition to the cases on customary and commercial fishing rights mentioned above, the Court of Appeal found against the Attorney-General three times within two years. Litigation was launched by Maori to prevent the neo-liberal policies of corporatisation and privatisation undermining the opportunity to make good their claims for the return of Crown land and assets in partial satisfaction of historic grievances. The court thrice found that the Government was in breach of a statutory obligation to not act 'in a manner inconsistent with the principles of the Treaty of Waitangi'.[44] That obligation was originally

of Maori fishing rights in tidal waters' in *Victoria University of Wellington Law Review*, 14 (1984), 247–73; P.G. McHugh, 'Aboriginal title in New Zealand courts' in *Canterbury Law Review*, 2 (1984), 235–65.

41 Waitangi Tribunal, *Muriwhenua Fishing Claims Report* (Wellington, 1988) [app. 5 contains *Ngai Tahu Trust Board* v. *Attorney-General* (unreported), CP 559/87, Wellington, 2 November 1987); Waitangi Tribunal, *Ngai Tahu Sea Fisheries Report* (Wellington, 1992); *Te Runanga o Muriwhenua* v. *Attorney-General* [1990] 2 NZLR 641 (CA) which declared *Waipapakura* to be 'a dubious authority': per Cooke P., p. 654; Law Commission, *The Treaty of Waitangi and Maori Fisheries* (Wellington, 1989).

42 Maori Fisheries Act 1989; Treaty of Waitangi (Fisheries Settlement) Act 1992. Section 9 of the 1992 Act is the extinguishment provision.

43 Fisheries Act 1996, Part IX; Fisheries (Kaimoana Customary Fishing) Regulations 1998/434; Fisheries (East Otago Taiapure) Order 1999/210, (Kawhia Aotea Taiapure) Order 2000/69, (Porongahau Taiapure) Order 1996/349, (Waikare Inlet Taiapure) Order 1997/357, (Whakapuaka (Delaware Bay) Taiapure) Order 2002/20.

44 State-Owned Enterprises Act 1986, s. 9; *NZ Maori Council* v. *Attorney-General* [1987] 1 NZLR 641 (CA) [SOE lands]; *NZ Maori Council* v. *Attorney-General* [1989] 2 NZLR 142 (CA) [Forests]; *Tainui Maori Trust Board* v. *Attorney-General* [1989] 2 NZLR 513 (CA)

thought to be a largely meaningless device to appease Maori. However, the Court of Appeal took seriously the opportunity judicially to create a jurisprudence of principles of the Treaty and this then flowed into the analysis of those principles in Waitangi Tribunal reports.[45]

All this induced successive governments to elaborate a coordinated approach to Treaty issues and then to establish a policy on the settlement of historical Treaty claims. This began with the formulation of principles for Crown action in 1989, a settlement policy in 1994 and a revised settlement policy in 2000.[46] The possibility of Maori claimants relying on customary rights and aboriginal title arguments was specifically addressed by Crown advisers. In respect of historical claims from 1840 to 1992, all customary entitlements are extinguished as part and parcel of the Treaty settlement process that claimants must agree to if they are to receive a Crown apology and the cultural and commercial redress package on offer in direct negotiations. The policy includes a strong denial that Maori may advance anything other than use-rights claims to natural resources. The exploitation and control of natural resources such as water flows, precious minerals, petroleum resources and geothermal resources was firmly stated to be the sole responsibility of the Crown acting in the national interest.[47] Thus a May 2003 Waitangi Tribunal report finding that Maori may have 'a Treaty interest' in relation to petroleum exploitation was summarily dismissed. The Government was not surprised by the finding and it was prepared quickly to reject the Tribunal's recommendations.[48]

The panic that occurred in government circles in June 2003 when the Court of Appeal confirmed the jurisdiction of the Maori Land Court to inquire into customary entitlements to foreshore and seabed lands was quite another matter.[49] The Court of Appeal media release stressed that the court's 'decision is a preliminary one about the ability of the iwi [tribes] to bring their claims. The validity and extent of the customary claims in issue have yet to be decided by the Maori Land Court. The impact of other legislation

---

[Coal]. See also *Huakina Development Trust* v. *Waikato Valley Authority* [1987] 2 NZLR 188 where the High Court held the Treaty of Waitangi relevant to an assessment of 'public interest' even when interpreting a statute containing no reference to the Treaty or to Maori values.

45 New Zealand Law Commission, *Maori custom and values in New Zealand law* (Wellington, 2001), pp. 83–84; Ministry of Maori Development, *A guide to the principles of the treaty of Waitangi* (Wellington, 2001).

46 Department of Justice, *Principles for crown action on the treaty of Waitangi* (Wellington, 1989); Office of Treaty Settlement, *Crown proposals for the settlement of treaty of Waitangi claims, detailed proposals* (Wellington, 1994); Office of Treaty Settlement, *Healing the past, building a future: a guide to treaty of Waitangi claims and direct negotiations with the crown*, 2nd ed. (Wellington, 2002).

47 Office of Treaty Settlements, 1994, pp. 18–22; Office of Treaty Settlements, 2002, p. 28.

48 Waitangi Tribunal, *Petroleum Report* (Wellington, 2003); P. Hodgson, 'Government response to Waitangi Tribunal's Petroleum Report', 21 November 2003, http://www.beehive.govt.nz/PrintDocument.cfm?DocumentID=18433.

49 *Attorney-General* v. *Ngati Apa & others* [2003] 3 NZLR 643 (CA) [*Ngati Apa*].

controlling the management and use of the resources of maritime areas also remains to be considered.'[50] This *Ngati Apa* decision was a modest procedural victory for seven tribes from the north of the South Island. They had resorted to litigation after years of unresolved difficulties over procedures to obtain permission to engage in commercial aquaculture activities in the Marlborough Sounds. Nevertheless, the court ruling created a storm of controversy. The fierce debates on talkback radio, letters to editors, opposition political party rallies and the like about 'public access to beaches' had little or no connection to the narrow findings of the Court of Appeal or to the actual claims of the plaintiffs.

The normal means to resolve ambiguities in the law, following the due process that is supposed to be a fundamental feature of the common law heritage, is to allow a court to hear evidence and to make a ruling based on that evidence. The Government immediately decided that it could not and would not wait. It would introduce legislation to assert Crown ownership over the foreshore/seabed areas.[51] This then provoked a howl of anguish from Maori interests, including the Government's own Maori members of parliament. What followed was a proposal to create a new concept of 'public domain' and to recognise customary rights if and only if those rights stopped well short of ownership rights.[52] It was decided that the Maori Land Court must be deprived of its jurisdiction to hear evidence from the tribes of their claims to customary entitlements in accordance with tikanga Maori, and the High Court must be deprived of its jurisdiction to apply the doctrine of aboriginal title to similar effect. Now no court judgment as to the property rights, if any, that might flow from any proven customary rights will be allowed to proceed. The Government also flatly rejected the recommendations of the Waitangi Tribunal, following an urgent hearing, that called for a 'longer conversation' between the Crown and Maori on these matters.[53] In order to ensure a parliamentary majority for the Foreshore and Seabed Bill when it was introduced in 2004, the 'public domain' concept was dropped and the unambiguous assertion of Crown ownership over the contested lands, with existing customary entitlements extinguished, was re-asserted. In place of existing customary entitlements, the Foreshore and Seabed Act 2004 as eventually enacted provides for a complex regime of court proceedings that purport to permit recognition of the customary rights of Maori in relation to

50 Court of Appeal of New Zealand, 'Media release: seabed case', 19 June 2003.
51 'Seabed owned by the crown says PM', *The New Zealand Herald*, 23 June 2003.
52 Department of the Prime Minister and Cabinet, *The foreshore and seabed of New Zealand: protecting public access and customary rights: Government proposals for consultation* (Wellington, 2003).
53 Waitangi Tribunal, *Report on the crown's foreshore and seabed policy* (Wellington, 2004) [The Waitangi Tribunal is a permanent commission of inquiry established by the Treaty of Waitangi Act 1975 to deal with both historical and contemporary disputes between the Crown and Maori.]

specific foreshore and seabed lands. However, those rights are defined in accordance with the statute's parameters and prescribed preconditions. If Maori litigants might otherwise have been entitled to a property right based on common law aboriginal title, they must now negotiate with the government for such 'redress' as the government thinks fit to offer to them.[54] The trite aphorism that those who do not know their history may be condemned to repeat it seems very apt in the circumstances.

The reason that the Government was so unprepared for the Court of Appeal outcome in the *Ngati Apa* case was that Crown advisers had long assumed the correctness of the 1963 Court of Appeal decision in *In re the Ninety-Mile Beach*. That decision was based on the reasoning of cases such as *Wi Parata*, and *Waipapakura* and the arguments of solicitors-general following in the footsteps of Salmond. *In re the Ninety-Mile Beach* had been the subject of sustained academic critiques.[55] It was inconsistent with the approach in a number of more recent Court of Appeal decisions as well as Privy Council decisions in the past.[56] The protection of the Crown in the privative clauses of Salmond's 1909 Act had been repealed in 1993 and replaced by limitation of actions protections to prevent historic claims being relitigated. This did not protect the Crown in respect of new claims that might arise based on customary rights and aboriginal title doctrines. It was no doubt assumed in 1993 that all customary rights to dry land, the beds of inland waters and fisheries had been extinguished. There was thought to be nothing left for the aboriginal title doctrines to apply to perhaps. Yet Salmond's definition of customary land had been replaced in 1993. The reference to the land being 'vested in the Crown' was removed and the new definition upheld an entirely different conceptual framework: 'Land that is held in accordance with tikanga Maori shall have the status of Maori customary land.'

In *Ngati Apa* the unanimous decision of a five judge bench of the Court of Appeal was that *In re the Ninety-Mile Beach* should be overruled. Tipping J., usually one of the more conservative figures on the Court of Appeal bench, began his judgment:

---

54 The Foreshore and Seabed Act 2004 provides for 'territorial customary rights' (ss. 32–45) and 'customary rights orders' (ss. 46–65).

55 K. Roberts-Wray, *Commonwealth and colonial law* (London, 1966), pp. 626–35; F.M. Brookfield, 'The New Zealand Constitution: the search for legitimacy' in Kawharu (ed.), pp. 10–12; R.P. Boast, '*In Re the Ninety-Mile Beach* revisited', *Victoria University of Wellington Law Review*, 23 (1993), 145–70; P.G. McHugh, *The Maori Magna Carta: New Zealand law and the treaty of Waitangi* (Auckland, 1991), pp. 117–26. See *Ngati Apa*, para. 87 (per Elias C.J.).

56 Recent Court of Appeal decisions include *Te Runanga o Muriwhenua* v. *Attorney-General* [1990] 2 NZLR 641; *Te Runanganui o Te Ika Whenua* v. *Attorney-General* [1994] 2 NZLR 20. Relevant Privy Council cases on appeals from New Zealand include the *Nireaha Tamaki* and *Wallis* cases cited above and *Manu Kapua* v. *Para Haimona* [1913] AC 761. A Nigerian appeal to the Privy Council, *Amodu Tijani* v. *Secretary, Southern Nigeria* [1921] 2 AC 399 was crucial to the reasoning of most of the judges in *Ngati Apa*.

When the common law of England came to New Zealand its arrival did not extinguish Maori customary title. Rather, such title was integrated into what then became the common law of New Zealand. Upon acquisition of sovereignty the Crown did not therefore acquire wholly unfettered title to all the land in New Zealand.... It follows that as Maori customary land is an ingredient of the common law of New Zealand, title to it must be lawfully extinguished before it can be regarded as ceasing to exist.... Undoubtedly Parliament is capable of effecting such extinguishment but, again in view of the importance of the subject matter, Parliament would need to make its intention crystal clear. In other words Parliament's purpose would need to be demonstrated by express words or at least by necessary implication.

Tipping J. went on to stress that 'I have deliberately referred to the common law of New Zealand in this context to distinguish it from the common law of England which of course lacked any ingredient involving Maori customary title or land'.[57] In the event the Court held that the Foreshore and Seabed Endowment Revesting Act 1991 and numerous statutes on the territorial sea and exclusive economic zone and on empowering and vesting land in harbour boards did not conclusively extinguish customary title. Gault P. in particular expressed 'real reservations about the ability of the appellants to establish that which they claim' in terms of an ownership interest under Te Ture Whenua Maori Act 1993.[58] He agreed, however, that the appeal be allowed so as to allow a Maori Land Court hearing to investigate the facts.

The judgment of Elias C.J. and the joint judgment of Keith and Anderson JJ. are of particular interest to the reception of law, and the local circumstances exception to the reception of the entire body of English law, with which this paper commenced. The High Court decision of Ellis J. in favour of the Crown was in error and had to be reversed, according to the Chief Justice, because:[59]

I consider that in starting with English common law, unmodified by New Zealand conditions (including Maori customary proprietary interests), and in assuming that the Crown acquired property in the land of New Zealand when it acquired sovereignty, the judgment in the

---

57 *Ngati Apa*, paras. 183, 185 and 212. There are cases in recent years where New Zealand courts have asserted that the common law as applied in New Zealand may differ from the common law as laid down by the House of Lords on the grounds that the circumstances of New Zealand are different – for example the torts cases *Invercargill City Council* v. *Hamlin* [1996] 1 NZLR 513 (PC); *Lange* v. *Atkinson* [2000] 3 NZLR 385 (CA). However, the stress on the notion of a 'New Zealand common law' is more marked in this case.

58 *Ngati Apa*, para. 106.

59 *Ngati Apa*, para. 13 (case citations omitted).

High Court was in error. The transfer of sovereignty did not affect customary property. They are interests preserved by the common law until extinguished in accordance with law. I agree that the legislation relied on in the High Court does not extinguish any Maori property in the seabed or foreshore. I agree with Keith and Anderson JJ. and Tipping J. that *In Re the Ninety-Mile Beach* was wrong in law and should not be followed. *In Re the Ninety-Mile Beach* followed the discredited authority of *Wi Parata* v. *Bishop of Wellington*, which was rejected by the Privy Council in *Nireaha Tamaki* v. *Baker*. This is not a modern revision, based on developing insights since 1963. The reasoning the Court applied in *In Re the Ninety-Mile Beach* was contrary to other and higher authority and indeed was described at the time as 'revolutionary'.

Further on in her judgment, she said:[60]

The applicable common law principle in the circumstances of New Zealand is that rights of property are respected on assumption of sovereignty. They can be extinguished only by consent or in accordance with statutory authority. They continue to exist until extinguishment in accordance with law is established. Any presumption of the common law inconsistent with the recognition of customary property is displaced by the circumstances of New Zealand (see Roberts-Wray, at 635)....

The approach adopted in the judgment under appeal in starting with the expectations of the settlers based on English common law and in expressing a preference for 'full and absolute dominion' in the Crown pending a Crown grant is also the approach of *Wi Parata*. Similarly, the reliance by Turner J. [in 1963] upon English law presumptions relating to ownership of the foreshore and seabed (an argument in substance re-run by the respondents in the present appeal) is misplaced. The common law as received in New Zealand was modified by recognising Maori customary property interests. If any such custom is shown to give interests in foreshore and seabed, there is no room for a contrary presumption derived from English common law. The common law of New Zealand is different.

With respect, the suggestion that this judgment is 'not a modern revision, based on developing insights since 1963' is hard to justify. A technique of English common law judges through the centuries has been to assert the timelessness of the common law. As McHugh has put it: 'Since the common law's past is designed to solve contemporary problems, presentism necessarily underlies its method.' In relation to the 1980s Court of Appeal decisions on

60 *Ngati Apa*, paras. 85–86.

the principles of the Treaty, McHugh observed: 'The Court of Appeal was using the Treaty of Waitangi less as a means for describing the past than as a means of living in the common law's eternal present. It used the Treaty as a source for timeless "Treaty principles" by which contemporary Crown conduct was to be measured.'[61]

The Chief Justice is certainly wrong from the perspective of an historian to say 'From the beginning of Crown colony government, it was accepted that the entire country was owned by Maori according to their customs and that until sold land continued to belong to them'. On the contrary, as noted above, for the first seven years of the Crown colony it was generally assumed in the Colonial Office and the House of Commons that most of the country was 'waste land' vested in the Crown and that Maori customary and Treaty rights applied only to land actually occupied and cultivated by Maori. Only after the *Symonds* case did the Colonial Office reluctantly accept Grey's advice as Governor that all the land in the country should be treated as subject to Maori customary rights. The strength of the Chief Justice's judgment, for lawyers at least, is not impaired by such an historical inaccuracy. It is, in any case, a legal fiction that the common law applied to the whole country in 1840 when tikanga Maori prevailed as the only law in many areas for decades to come. It is another legal fiction that the New Zealand common law as laid down authoritatively in 2003 is the correct view of the law that had always applied since 1840.

Likewise the judgment of Keith and Anderson JJ. takes a significantly new approach to the reception of English common law without admitting that it is a new approach. They point out that under English law 'without prejudice to public (or common) rights especially of navigation (including anchoring), that the Crown could grant and did grant to subjects the soil below low water mark including areas outside ports and harbours. Those rights could also arise by prescription or usage.' A number of English cases and authorities were cited, and then they say: 'Accordingly, under the law of England which became part of the law of New Zealand in 1840 "so far as applicable to the circumstances of New Zealand", private individuals could have property in sea areas including the seabed. The "circumstances" qualification is well and relevantly demonstrated by the judgment of Stout C.J. in *Baldick* v. *Jackson*.'

That qualification had not been invoked in a number of earlier New Zealand cases discussed in the judgments, nor indeed in the judgment of Ellis J. at first instance. Those decisions had assumed or explicitly stated that Crown prerogative ownership of the foreshore and seabed was entirely appropriate to the circumstances of New Zealand. Salmond as solicitor-general forcibly presented that argument on many occasions. The Court of Appeal, quite rightly in my view, is now distancing itself from those

61 McHugh, 'Tales of constitutional origin', pp. 74, 92.

assumptions. Yet it is odd that the highly exceptional case of *Baldick* v. *Jackson* is treated as if it is a perfectly ordinary application of the local circumstances caveat to Blackstone's views on the application of the birthright of Englishmen in new colonies.

The *Ngati Apa* decision, then, finally and conclusively overrules the *Wi Parata* approach. It no longer has any authority as a precedent in court proceedings. The *Ngati Apa* decision also restores the Court of Appeal's 1980s reputation for being willing to move into unfamiliar legal territory for the benefit of Maori plaintiffs and their putative property rights, even if that approach is contrary to the position strongly advocated for by the Crown as being in the interest of all New Zealanders. Yet at the end of the day, the *Wi Parata* approach lives on not in the courts but in the executive and legislative branches of government. Rather than take time for consideration, the Prime Minister and other ministers immediately after the June 2003 decision lambasted the Court of Appeal for its unexpected judicial activism. They peremptorily dismissed a series of careful recommendations from the Waitangi Tribunal in 2004 suggesting a 'longer conversation' between the Crown and Maori. The Government's line now is remarkably similar to the opinion of Prendergast C.J. in 1877, that 'the supreme executive Government must acquit itself as best it may, of its obligation to respect native proprietary rights, and of necessity must be the sole arbiter of its own justice'.[62] The Cabinet's approach to the 2003 foreshore/seabed consultations with Maori mirrors the views (quoted above) of Salmond writing to Ngata in 1909: '[W]hen a dispute arises between Natives and the Crown as to the right to customary land, the dispute shall be settled by Parliament and not otherwise.'[63] The Foreshore and Seabed Act 2004 imposed the parliamentary 'settlement'.

The adventure of the common law in Aotearoa New Zealand has seen many changes take place since the nineteenth century. In many areas of law new directions have been followed by New Zealand legislators and judges, and a distinctive New Zealand common law has developed. Yet, when it comes to indigenous customary rights as property rights, in some respects the colonialist assumptions accompanying the reception of English law in British colonies in the nineteenth century remain powerful and persuasive for those acting on behalf of the Crown in right of New Zealand to this day.

---

62 *Wi Parata* v. *Bishop of Wellington* (1877) 3 NZ Jur. (NS) (SC) 72, p. 78.
63 M. Cullen, 'Govt aiming for foreshore policy statement by Xmas' 23 October 2003. Media statement (attached to 'Memorandum (No 3) of counsel (TJ Castle) for Ngati Rarua and Ngati Apa', 24 October 2003: Waitangi Tribunal, Wai 1071, doc. 2.142).

Colourful adventures of the law: legal regulation of colour as sign from heraldry to trade mark law

N.M. DAWSON

> When we were children words were coloured
> (Harlot and murder were dark purple)
> And language was a prism ...
> Louis MacNeice

INTRODUCTION: THE 'MYSTERY' OF COLOUR[1]

THE ART HISTORIAN JOHN Gage suggests that colour moves us because history saturates it with associations, connotations and symbolism.[2] At the sensory and perceptual levels, colour has no meaning; colour meaning is created by a combination of culture and language. In the case of purple, for example, its association with opulence and sovereignty is of ancient origin. Originally an expensive dye obtained from molluscs on Mediterranean shores by a process perfected by the Phoenicians around 1500 BC, it became known as Tyrian or royal purple, describing a spectrum of colour rather than a particular shade.[3] In ancient Rome, a senator was identifiable by the broad purple band around the hem of his tunic. Julius Caesar decreed that only members of the imperial household could wear purple robes. In Byzantium, a room in the imperial palace lined with the purple stone porphyria was reserved for the birth of the emperor's children ('born in the purple'). Purple was the colour of the sails of Cleopatra's barge in Shakespeare's vivid

I am grateful to Claire Archbold for her suggestions at an early stage of this project, and to Robert Yorke, archivist, College of Arms, for his assistance with research on heraldic material.

1 G.B. Shaw, *The doctors' dilemma* (1906), act IV: 'I believe in Michael Angelo, Velasquez, and Rembrandt; in the might of design, the mystery of colour, the redemption of all things by Beauty everlasting ...' In the more prosaic language of the scientist, 'the meaning of the term colour is one of the worst muddles in the history of science': J. Gibson, *The senses considered as perceptual systems* (London, 1968), p. 183.

2 J. Jones, 'Rainbow alliance', *The Guardian*, 29 June 2000.

3 S. Garfield, *Mauve: how one man invented a colour that changed the world* (London, 2000), pp. 39–43, H. Zollinger, *Color – a multidisciplinary approach* (Weinheim, New York and

account in *Antony and Cleopatra*. Even today, purple is associated with the coronation and other robes of a monarch. Purple has also enjoyed more transient associations, from symbol of the pop culture of the late 1960s and early 1970s to the colour of economic confidence and the bull market of the beginning of the third millennium.[4] Colour associations may also be created at an individual as well as a universal level, and this may depend at least in part upon the individual's psychological and emotional response to particular colours.[5] 'Hue' is after all an old English word meaning, *inter alia*, beauty: colours and colour shades have aesthetic properties. This was well expressed by the artist Wassily Kandinsky when he said: 'praise be to the palette for the delights it offers ... it is itself a "work", more beautiful indeed than many a work.'[6] John Ruskin also appeared to recognise the aesthetic and psychological impact of colour when he opined that 'the purest and most thoughtful minds are those which love colour the most'.[7] In similar vein, Sir Arthur Bliss wrote a Colour Symphony, the mood of each movement being described by a colour.

Moving back a stage from the cognitive processes of colour association and colour naming, colour perception itself can be affected by neurological function and by external factors such as distance and various chromatic effects. All of these factors contribute to the complexity of colour as a semiotic code. The phenomenon of colour has, for over a century, attracted attention in an increasing range of disciplines, art, chemistry, physics, mineralogy, psychology, anthropology, linguistics, neuroscience, ophthalmology, and others, yet colour as sign is only beginning to attract the attention of legal scholars. That interest is generated by an upsurge in attempts to monopolise the symbolic power of single colour shades and colour combinations not spatially limited, through trade mark registration. This paper explores colour symbolism within other legal frameworks, seeking an understanding of the semiotic function of colour which may be relevant to the resolution of contemporary issues in trade mark law.

Chichester, 1999), pp. 152–53, D. Garnett, *Colour – a social history* (London, 2000), p. 40; V. Finlay, *Colour* (London, 2002), chap. 10, and J. Gage, *Colour and culture: practice and meaning from antiquity to abstraction* (London, 1993), p. 82.

4 'Seeing purple', *The Economist*, 12 May 2001.

5 These factors impede progress towards the creation of global norms of colour measurement which would facilitate trade on the Internet: 'When the world sings the blues', *Times Higher Education Supplement*, 27 October 2000.

6 Quoted in Gage, *Colour and culture*, p. 177.

7 J. Ruskin, *Stones of Venice* (London, 1851–53).

THE LESSONS OF HERALDRY

Colour shades

Heraldry has been defined as the 'systematic hereditary use of an arrangement of charges or devices on a shield'[8] and armorial bearings as 'marks of hereditary honour, given or authorised by some supreme power to gratify the bearer or distinguish families'.[9] This 'shorthand of history'[10] is a discrete symbolic system regulated by separate courts (in England, the High Court of Chivalry,[11] and in Scotland, the Court of the Lord Lyon),[12] with a number of parallels with the use of trade marks.[13] Boutell describes heraldry as 'a symbolical and pictorial language, in which figures, devices and colours are employed instead of letters'.[14] The precise origins of heraldry are obscure, but it appears to have developed more or less simultaneously across Europe in the twelfth century. Doubt has been cast on the traditional view that arms were originally intended to facilitate long-distance recognition of combatants in battle,[15] a more convincing explanation being that they were borne in a non-literate society as a means of personal identification and display. Nevertheless, heraldry was emblematic of chivalry and closely linked, if not with active warfare, then with the tournament where the heralds' function was to recognise armorial bearings and announce the identity of knights in

---

8 T. Woodcock and J.M. Robinson, *Oxford guide to heraldry* (Oxford, 1988, reissued 2001), p. 1.

9 Sir George Mackenzie, *The science of heraldry*, quoted in J.H. Stevenson, *Heraldry in Scotland* (Glasgow, 1914), p. 12.

10 W. Scott-Giles, *Romance of heraldry* (London, 1929), p. 2.

11 See G.D. Squibb, *High Court of Chivalry* (Oxford, 1959); J.H. Baker, *Introduction to English legal history* (4th ed., London, 2002), pp. 122–23, A.R. Wagner, *Heralds and heraldry in the middle ages* (London, 1939), pp. 20–24, L.G. Pine, 'The law of heraldry' in *Solicitors' Journal*, 130 (1986), 387, and P.M. Ashman, 'Heraldry and the law of arms in England' in *Journal of Legal History*, 9 (1988), 50. For heraldry in Ireland, see S. Hood, *Royal roots, republican inheritance – the survival of the office of arms* (Dublin, 2002), E. MacLysaght, *Irish families: their names, arms and origins* (Dublin, 1957), F. Gillespie, 'Heraldry in Ireland' in *Journal of Heraldry Society of Scotland*, 23 (2000), 7, and A. Lyall, 'Irish heraldic jurisdiction' in *Coat of Arms* (n.s.), x (1993), 134, 178, 238 and 266.

12 The Court of the Lord Lyon King of Arms has jurisdiction in questions of heraldry and the right to bear arms, subject to appeal to the Court of Session and the House of Lords: W.M. Gloag and R.C. Henderson, *The law of Scotland* (10th ed., Edinburgh, 1995), para. 2.8; D.M. Walker, *The Scottish legal system* (7th ed., Edinburgh, 1997), p. 282; Stevenson, *Heraldry in Scotland*, and T. Innes, *Scots heraldry* (3rd ed., revised by M.R. Innes, Edinburgh, 1978).

13 See, for example, P. Gwynne-Jones, *The art of heraldry* (London, 1998), p. 25, where the author comments on modern heraldic design 'tapping in particular the geometric formations of the Middle Ages which have so frequently been borrowed from heraldry and turned into many successful modern logos and trade marks'.

14 C. Boutell, *Handbook to English heraldry* (11th ed., London, 1914), p. 3.

15 Woodcock and Robinson, *Oxford guide*, pp. 2–3, and Gwynne-Jones, *Art of heraldry*, pp. 14–15.

the lists.[16] Within a short time, heraldry became a systematised branch of learning, as evidenced by Rolls of Arms compiled by the heralds. Boutell states that 'in the reign of Henry III [1216–72] heraldry in England had confirmed its own claims to be regarded as a science, by being in possession of a system and a classification of its own'.[17] That the practice of heraldry broke free of its connection with the tournament, gradually infiltrating the ranks of civil society, ensured its survival and increased vitality: 'by the end of the fifteenth century, most villages in [England] had their "knight" or gentleman bearing for civilian use a shield of arms.'[18]

When heraldry was in its infancy armorial bearings were self-assumed, but by the fourteenth century, the crown had established a right to regulate the achievement of arms. Grants of arms by English kings were rare and by the fifteenth century delegation of this prerogative function to the heralds had become established practice.[19] The medieval kings also provided the means of establishing title to arms by descent or long user. The High Court of Chivalry, the civil law court which adjudicated on military matters not justiciable at common law, assumed jurisdiction to resolve heraldic disputes.[20] Somewhat later, the crown established a system of heraldic visitations of England (and Ireland) for the purpose of correcting heraldic abuses.[21]

One of the most celebrated cases determined by the Court of Chivalry was *Scrope* v. *Grosvenor*, which lasted for almost five years (1385–90) and involved the testimony of many prominent members of English and Welsh society.[22] The case involved the complaint of Sir Richard Scrope, a soldier of note and at one time the lord chancellor of England,[23] that his arms had been

16 See generally Wagner, *Heralds and heraldry in the middle ages*, and by the same author, *Heralds and ancestors* (London, 1978): 'where the heralds came from is obscure but what bore them up seems certain. It was the sudden vogue of the tournament' (p. 9).

17 Boutell, *Handbook*, p. 4. See also Wagner, *Heralds and heraldry*, pp. 48–55.

18 Gwynne-Jones, *Art of heraldry*, p. 20.

19 The term 'herald' covers three groups of officers of arms in the College of Arms: the Kings of Arms (Garter, Clarenceux, Norroy and Ulster), the heralds strictly so-called (Chester, Lancaster, Richmond, Somerset, Windsor and York), and the *pursuivants* (Bluemantle, Portcullis, Rouge Croix, Rouge Dragon).

20 The history of the Court of Chivalry was extensively researched by G.D. Squibb in a sympathetic account published in 1959: see n. 11 above. Although the court did not sit from 1737 until 1954, by which time it was thought obsolete, it was held in 1954 by Lord Goddard sitting as surrogate for the earl marshal that the court's jurisdiction in relation to heraldic disputes survives: *Manchester Corporation* v. *Manchester Palace of Varieties* [1955] P.133. See C. D'Olivier Farran, 'An ancient court revived' in *Law Quarterly Review*, 71 (1955), 187.

21 Wagner, *Heralds and heraldry*, p. 5: only three visitations in Ireland are recorded.

22 Including John of Gaunt, the future Henry IV and Geoffrey Chaucer for Scrope, and Owen Glendower for Grosvenor. See N.H. Harris, *The controversy between Sir Richard Scrope and Sir Robert Grosvenor in the Court of Chivalry*, 2 vols. (London, 1832), and G. Scrope, 'The Scrope and Grosvenor Roll' in *Coat of Arms* (n.s.), ii (1952), 83.

23 See J. Campbell, *Lives of the lord chancellors*, 10 vols. (4th ed., London, 1856), vol. 1, p. 240 *et seq.*

usurped by Sir Robert Grosvenor. Both had fought in the wars with France. Scrope claimed that he and his ancestors had used the arms in question, *Azure a bend Or*, a diagonal yellow stripe on a blue background, since the Conquest. The case appears at first sight to be one of colour recognition and establishment of exclusive rights to the use of a certain colour arrangement. The court accepted Scrope's evidence of user from time immemorial,[24] and ordered Grosvenor to 'difference' or distinguish his arms by adding a silver border. Regarding this as defeat, Scrope appealed to the king in council. The appeal was determined by Richard II, who considered that the addition of a silver border was an inadequate means of differentiating the arms, given that there were no kinship ties between the parties. Grosvenor subsequently adopted *Azure a garb Or* (a yellow wheat sheaf on a blue background), using the same colours but a different heraldic design. It was not the imitation of colour itself that concerned Scrope, but the imitation of the arrangement on the shield of the heraldic devices. In fact, complaints about usurpation of colour could only be based on arms consisting of a single colour. Instances of the use of 'plain arms' involving one colour only and no other devices, were, however, exceptional.[25] Commonly in heraldry, colour is only part of a complex arrangement of devices on a shield, and no attempt is made by the heralds to ensure that colours used are not too similar to those used by others bearing arms, if the detailed devices or charges are different. A medieval Welsh heraldic writer makes the fairly obvious point that the use of colour alone is inadequate for a symbolic system in which many people actively participate, as there are not enough colours: 'and where colours failed ... they introduced ... the forms of animals, fishes, birds, and other things.'[26]

The purpose of heraldry, personal identification and display, does not require discrimination between different colour shades. 'There are no fixed shades for heraldic colours. If the official description of a coat of arms gives its tinture as *Gules* (red), *Azure* (blue) and *Argent* (white) then, as long as the blue is not too light and the red not too orange, purple or pink, it is up to the artist to decide which particular shades they think are appropriate.'[27] The refusal to become engaged in a process of discrimination among colour shades can doubtless be explained on the basis that heraldic practice was settled before colour science had developed at all. Colours were made from natural dyes, and colour-fastness was not possible. It was also the case that no

24 See Squibb, *Court of Chivalry*, pp. 178–89.

25 G.J. Brault, *Early Blazon* (2nd ed., Woodbridge, Suffolk, 1997), pp. 29–30. Lyall refers to the use of plain red arms by Le Bret of Rathfarnham in Ireland: A. Lyall, *Land law in Ireland* (2nd ed., Dublin, 2000), p. 50. The use of plain arms was also known in Icelandic heraldry: see Gage, *Colour and culture*, p. 83.

26 J. Trevor, *Llyfr Arfau*, a Welsh Book of Arms translated by E.J. Jones, *Medieval heraldry* (Cardiff, 1943), p. 9.

27 http://www.college-of-arms.gov.uk/faq.htm.

consensus existed across cultures as to the meaning of some colour terms, such as scarlet, purple, or the medieval colour term, *perse*, which is now quite obscure.[28] Thus, no reliable means existed to articulate perceived differences in shades of colour. This apparent indifference to colour in heraldry is, however, only superficial. Although the heraldic system has little to say on the subject of discrimination between colour shades, it is instructive on the issue of colour terms.

Colour language

'The identification of one of a range of shades is a conscious and verbalised act, and … is thus dependent upon the available colour-language.'[29] Heraldry has its own specialised colour language within the language of blazon, the terminology used to describe heraldic charges or devices. As blazon evolved over several centuries, a different picture of its colour language emerges according to the era under consideration. A leading heraldic authority, Boutell, states that in English heraldry in its developed state the tinctures comprise two metals (*or, argent*), eight colours (*azure, gules, purpure, sable, vert,* and three more obscure colours – *tenné*, orange or tawny, *sanguine*, blood red, and *murrey*, mulberry or purply red), and eight furs (four patterns based on *ermine*: *ermine, ermines, erminois,* and *pean*, and four patterns based on *vair* (squirrel) – *vair, counter-vair, potent,* and *counter-potent.*)[30] Blazon not only overcame instability in colour shades by association with recognisable physical matter – furs, metals – the colours of which were relatively stable and commonly understood, it was also a means of widening the range of available terms for colour using associational references. It was, however, the colour language of an elite, as Umberto Eco points out:

> … one should remark that a greater variety of colours exists, or existed, in heraldry. But heraldry represents a case of an elaborated code for a cultivated minority able to discriminate more colours and associate more refined names to different hues, as well as memorize aristocratic stocks.[31]

Blazon and in particular the heraldic tinctures attracted considerable interest from semioticians, linguists, philologists and anthropologists in the latter part of the twentieth century. It is considered relevant to a particular colour puzzle: if the human brain is capable of distinguishing millions of colour

28 Gage, *Colour and culture*, pp. 80, 82, and J. Gage, *Colour and meaning: art, science and symbolism* (London, 1999), pp. 52 and 280, and Finlay, *Colour, passim*.
29 Gage, *Colour and meaning*, p. 52.
30 J.P. Brooke-Little (ed.), *Boutell's heraldry* (London, revised edition 1973), p. 27, Woodcock and Robinson, *Oxford guide*, pp. 51–2, Brault, *Early blazon*, p. 60.
31 U. Eco, 'How culture conditions the colours we see', in M. Blonsky (ed.), *On signs* (Oxford, 1985), pp. 157–75, at p. 174.

shades,[32] why is it that colour vocabulary is so limited in any language, usually ranging from eight to eleven colour terms?[33] Much of this discourse takes as its starting point Berlin and Kay's book, *Basic color terms*, first published in 1969, and based on an analysis of 98 languages.[34] The authors found that some languages have as few as two colour terms and most languages have only around eleven basic colour terms. In English, these are white, black, red, green, yellow, blue, brown, orange, pink, purple, and grey. The deficit between the lexicon of colour and perceptible colour shades, has led to the creation of numerous colour indexes to support various branches of science, art and trade, where colours are described by trade names, associational names, actual colour shades, or by classification numbers, such as the Pantone colour code. In the language of blazon, actual colours number only eight of which three are associational, and of the 18 tinctures listed by Boutell, the remaining ten are associational terms. This suggests that because of the imbalance between colour perception and colour language, experience of colour will largely be associational; our experience of green, for example, is expressed by reference to the sea, grass, moss, emeralds, limes, bottles and so on, while our experience of red may be articulated by reference to cherries, rubies, bricks or cardinals.[35]

Thus, even though in the language of blazon which was created specifically to support a symbolic system, there are more colour terms than in ordinary language, the extension of colour vocabulary has been achieved by the use of associational or context-dependent terms. All of this is relevant to modern trade mark law. Widespread hostility to monopolies in trade marks consisting of words was finally overcome in the early twentieth century. In a case involving the Coca-Cola registered trade mark, for example, the United States Supreme Court brushed aside the suggestion that registration conferred an unacceptable language monopoly: 'Plaintiff's rights are limited at the most to two words. All the rest of infinity is open to defendant.'[36] When we consider that several million different colour shades can be

---

32 Eco cites the classification of the Optical Society of America which suggests that between 7.5 and 10 million colour shades can be distinguished: 'How culture conditions', p. 167.

33 The study of colour language developed in the mid-nineteenth century, when William Gladstone, a distinguished classical scholar as well as politician, highlighted the absence of colour terms in Homer's *Iliad*: see Zollinger, *Color*, pp. 123–30, Gage, *Colour and culture*, chap. 5, and N. Mirzoeff, *An introduction to visual culture* (London, 1999), pp. 54–57.

34 B. Berlin and P. Kay, *Basic color terms: their universality and evolution* (2nd ed., Berkeley, 1991). See also M. Sahlins, 'Colors and cultures', in J.L. Dolgin, D.S. Kemnitzer, and D.M. Schneider (eds.), *Symbolic anthropology, a reader in the study of symbols and meanings* (New York, 1977), pp. 165–80, P. Kay and C.K. McDaniel, 'The linguistic significance of the meanings of basic color terms', chap. 17 in A. Byrne and D.R. Hilbert (eds.), *Readings on color, vol. 2: the science of color* (Cambridge, Mass., and London, 1997), pp. 399–441.

35 Gage, *Colour and meaning*, p. 262.

36 *Coca-Cola Corp v. Old Dominion Beverage Corp*, 271 F. 600, 604 (4th Cir.,1921).

perceived by the human brain, the idea of the 'rest of infinity' appears to favour a positive response to the question whether registration of single colours or colour combinations as trade marks should be permitted. The dearth of colour terms, however, tends in the opposite direction. Umberto Eco sees colour as a cultural puzzle 'filtered through a linguistic system', a view shared by the linguist John Lyons, who concludes that while colour as a phenomenon is real, colours are not.[37] It is not only that an impoverished colour vocabulary affects our colour perceptions, but that these are more broadly affected by a range of cultural factors. Eco concludes that it is not possible to base a system of communication on subtle distinctions between colours that are close to one another in the spectrum.[38]

Colour meaning

The third colour point to emerge from a consideration of the heraldic system relates to colour meaning. From time to time, attempts were made to establish a hierarchy of colours, attributing particular qualities or virtues to colours or linking colours to planets and gemstones.[39] For example, in the fourteenth century, an Italian jurist, Bartolus of Sassoferrato, suggested a hierarchy of colours with gold the noblest colour and black the least noble. Although this was not adopted generally even in Italy, the attempt to invest colours with specific meanings was a recurrent theme of European heraldry, especially Italian heraldry, and continued during the Renaissance.[40] It also attracted considerable criticism. Joseph Edmondson, an eighteenth-century heraldic writer observed: 'White, say they, denotes chastity; black constancy; blue loyalty, &c, &c. But as to such ridiculous fancies, the mere mention of them is fully sufficient.'[41] Somewhat earlier, François Rabelais's *Gargantua* had satirised a book entitled *Blason des couleurs* in which Sicily Herald rigidly insisted on particular colour meanings. Rabelais rejected Sicily Herald's choice of meanings, but accepted the general view that colours have *some* meaning. He believed that their meaning could be explained by reference to nature and philosophy rather than by reference to the 'science' of heraldry.[42] The following extract from a Welsh Book of Arms illustrates the complexity of colour meaning and suggests a link with our next line of enquiry, colour restrictions under sumptuary laws:

37 J. Lyons, 'Colour in language', in T. Lamb and J. Bourriau (eds.), *Colour: art and science* (Cambridge, 1995), pp. 194–224, at pp. 197 and 223.
38 Eco, 'How culture conditions', p. 174.
39 M. Keen, *Chivalry* (London and New Haven, 1984), p. 130.
40 Gage, *Colour and culture*, pp. 82–89.
41 J. Edmondson, *Complete body of heraldry*, 2 vols. (London, 1780).
42 Gage, *Colour and culture*, p. 89.

Further concerning the red colour. Red is the third mediary colour, and it lies precisely midway between the extremities white and black as the Philosopher [Aristotle] says .... this colour is forbidden by civil law to be worn without permission, except by a prince; and whoever transgresses may be executed. And why is this colour ordained to a prince ...? Because this colour represents cruelty, and a prince ought to be cruel towards his enemies, and it behoves him to punish disorder ... This colour, too, is borne by the kings of England in their arms ...[43]

Even where heraldic practice was structurally neutral on the specific meaning of colours or tinctures, heraldic literature played a major part in creating and sustaining colour meanings. Furthermore, the heraldic system enabled bearers of arms to create their own personalised colour associations. One way or another, the development of colour meaning prospers in and around heraldry.

SUMPTUARY LAWS

Sumptuary laws are those which regulate consumption and expenditure (*sumptus*), and personal conduct.[44] More specifically, they address three broad areas of personal life: (1) conduct at weddings and other celebrations, and at funerals; (2) the table – consumption of food and drink, and (3) apparel – expenditure on and the style of dress. Known to the ancient Spartans and Greeks, sumptuary laws appeared as a modern phenomenon in a number of European countries (Italy, France and Spain) in the twelfth century, but were not enacted in Germany, Switzerland and England until the fourteenth century. Sumptuary laws in England spanned the period 1327 to 1604,[45] and were first enacted in Scotland in 1429 (or possibly earlier).[46] They were also known further afield, in Japan and the American colonies.[47] They can be explained on economic grounds, limiting consumption in times of shortage

---

43 Trevor, *Llyfr Arfau*, in Jones, *Medieval heraldry*, pp. 17–19.

44 See generally A. Hunt, *Governance of the consuming passions: a history of sumptuary law* (London, 1996), W.A. Hammond, 'Sumptuary laws and their social influence' in *Popular Science Monthly*, 37 (1890), 33.

45 F.E. Baldwin, *Sumptuary legislation and personal regulation in England* (Baltimore, 1926), and W. Hooper, 'The Tudor sumptuary laws' in *English Historical Review*, 30 (1915), 433.

46 F. Shaw, 'Sumptuary legislation in Scotland' in *Juridical Review* (1979), 81, and J. Chisholm, 'The sumptuary laws of Scotland' in *Journal of Jurisprudence*, xxxv (1891), 290.

47 C. Kovesi Killerby, *Sumptuary law in Italy, 1200–1500* (Oxford, 2002), pp. 8–22, and Hunt, *Governance of the consuming passions*, pp. 1, 38–39. Little evidence has been found for the existence of sumptuary laws in Ireland, beyond a number of prohibitions on the wearing of the Irish style of dress and the distinctive popular colour, saffron: J.C. Walker, *An historical essay on the dress of the ancient and modern Irish* (Dublin, 1788), pp. 42 and 49, cited by Hunt, *Governance of the consuming passions*, p. 75.

or economic recession, or promoting consumption of the output of home industry; on moral grounds, curbing excess when luxury and conspicuous consumption were inconsistent with the values of the time, and on social grounds, creating status symbols and reinforcing class divisions in society by differential application of the rules. This was often done by means of regulation of dress, restricting the use of materials and fashions to certain social classes.

Sumptuary legislation regulating dress not infrequently contained colour restrictions. Restrictions on the use of cloth of gold and silver might be seen as an attempt to curb excess, but sumptuary laws often went further, restricting the use of specific colours such as crimson, blue or purple to the higher ranks of society. In France, for example, a law of 1189 provided that no person of common rank was allowed to wear garments of *vair* (squirrel), grey, *zibeline* (sable), or scarlet colour. In Scotland, a statute of 1429/30 placed restrictions on the type and stuff of apparel of various classes. As regards colour, yeomen and commoners were not to wear 'hewyt' (hued) clothing. In 1457/8, a second Act concerning apparel provided that labourers, husbandmen and their wives could wear light blue, green and red on holidays, but on working days they must wear grey or white. This Act also placed certain restrictions on excess in clerical dress.[48]

Several of the Acts of apparel in England contained significant colour restrictions based on social class. For example, an Act of 1463 provided that no person below the rank of lord could wear cloth of gold, sable or purple silk, and a 1533 statute provided that only earls and those of superior degrees could wear cloth mixed with gold or silver or sable, and that only dukes, marquises, earls, barons and knights could wear 'velvet, crimson, scarlet or blue, furs, black genets'.[49] In the regulation of dress, sumptuary laws generally bore more heavily on women than on men, one commentator suggesting the reason that 'a ship is sooner rigged than a woman'.[50] Colour restrictions sometimes served to identify prostitutes, or the marital status of women,[51] but were most commonly used to reinforce social distinctions. A number of instances of more general colour restrictions can be found. Hunt cites a prohibition on the wearing of green or dark blue in Venice after the great plague of 1347–8, 'with the motive of encouraging a general return to

---

48 Shaw, 'Sumptuary legislation', 82–83.

49 1463: 3 Edw. IV, c. 5; 1533: 27 Hen. VIII, c. 13. See Hunt, *Governance of the consuming passions*, chap. 12, Hooper, 'Tudor sumptuary laws', 433, and see generally, Baldwin, *Sumptuary legislation*.

50 Hooper, 'Tudor sumptuary laws', 444. See generally Kovesi Killerby, *Sumptuary laws in Italy*, chap. 6, and Hunt, *Governance of the consuming passions*, chap. 5.

51 Hunt, op. cit., pp. 129–30, referring to a Moravian customary code: married women wore blue, widows white, unmarried women pink, and young girls red; see also Kovesi Killerby, op. cit., p. 9.

happiness',[52] while Gage notes that in 1495 during a storm which caused the Tiber to flood, Pope Alexander VI ordered a procession praying for the storm to abate to dress in white, a colour associated with rejoicing. The pope's master of ceremonies persuaded him that violet, the liturgical equivalent of black, would be more suitable.[53]

Sumptuary legislation may have passed into oblivion, probably by the seventeenth century across Europe, but a number of commentators have observed that sumptuary feeling in society and the associations which sumptuary laws created long survived the abolition of legislative codes.[54] For our purposes, the sumptuary laws illustrate how colour associations and colour meaning can be culturally constructed as part of the public domain and reinforced within a legal regulatory framework.

PRIVATE OWNERSHIP OF COLOUR AS SIGN IN THE MARKETPLACE — THE LAW OF TRADE MARKS

The application of intellectual property law generally

Intellectual property rights in colour and colour shades have been secured under patent law for almost two hundred years. A patent may be granted for a new dye (product) or a new method of dyeing or dye manufacture (process). In the early ninteenth century, a number of patents based on natural dyes were granted. William Perkin's invention in 1856 of mauve (or Tyrian purple as it was first called, with sumptuary ambition), the first aniline dye (based upon coal tar), was the first of many synthetic dyes to be patented, laying the foundation for the synthetic dye industry at a time of rapid expansion of the textile trade.[55] In 1868, a process for the manufacture of a synthetic form of alizarin, a Turkey red dye which had previously been available as a natural dye derived from the madder plant, was patented simultaneously by Perkin in the United Kingdom and by Graebe in Germany, rendering redundant the madder fields of Europe.[56] A more recent example of patent rights to a colour is International Klein Blue (IKB), an ultramarine blue invented by the French artist, Yves Klein (1928–62), and patented in 1957.

---

52 Hunt, *Governance of the consuming passions*, p. 70.
53 Gage, *Colour and culture*, p. 84.
54 Hooper, 'Tudor sumptuary laws', 449.
55 Garfield, *Mauve*; M. Tordoff, *The servant of colour: a history of the Society of Dyers and Colourists: 1884–1984* (Bradford, 1984), pp. 15–44, A.S. Travis, *The rainbow makers: the origin of the synthetic dyestuff industries in W. Europe* (Bethlehem, Pa., and London, 1992), and R.L.M. Allen, *Color chemistry* (London, 1971), pp. 8, 155–56, 183–85.
56 H Levenstein, 'British patent laws – ancient and modern' in *Journal of Society of Dyers and Colourists* (1934), 83, H. Varley, *Colour* (London, 1980), p. 88.

Patents are not generally relevant to our enquiry for two reasons. One is that a colour patent does not necessarily confer a monopoly in a particular shade; others may reproduce the same shade provided that they do not use the patented process.[57] Secondly, in the normal course of events, a colour patent does not lead to a colour shade becoming associated with one trader or individual as the patentee will most likely license the patent to manufacturers of textiles and textile goods. In the unusual case of an association being created between a shade and one person or company, patent law provides no mechanisms for regulating the use of colour as sign; it addresses the technical production of colour, not its semiotic function. Until recently, copyright would also have seemed irrelevant for present purposes. In 2001, however, a paint manufacturer, Farrow & Ball, alleged that ICI had infringed its rights in a range of paint colours used in home decoration ('the National Trust range'), and sued ICI for copyright infringement, passing off and infringement of database right. While the outcome of the case is unknown, the proceedings are evidence of pressure to secure new intellectual property rights in colour and create a context for our consideration of trade marks.[58]

The action for passing off – ownership of goodwill in colour

In the law of passing off, where a trader has established goodwill in a trade mark, trade name, or the get-up (trade dress) of a product or service, relief is available where another trader makes use of a similar mark, name, get-up or other sign so as to deceive consumers.[59] So far as colour is concerned, the law of passing off requires traders wishing to establish rights in the use of a colour to educate the relevant public to associate the colour with their trade. The creation of a new colour meaning is a pre-requisite to success in a passing off action. Where a colour has some other meaning, and all colours do, the trader will only succeed by establishing a 'secondary meaning' that is more powerful in a specific commercial context than other senses in which the colour is understood: it must signal that goods or services emanate from one particular trade source. Colours that are common in the trade are in principle excluded from the protection afforded by a passing off action.[60]

---

57 For patents for various black dyes, see *Vidal v. Levinstein Ltd.* (1912) 29 R.P.C. 245, and Levinstein, 'British patent laws', 87–88.

58 See also *Lambretta Clothing Co. Ltd. v. Teddy Smith (UK) Ltd.* [2003] R.P.C. 41, where an attempt to establish unregistered design right in the colours of a sweatshirt design failed. The definition of 'design' in the Registered Designs Act 1949 has recently been amended to include 'colours' of products but the impact of this change is not yet clear: Registered Designs Regs. 2001, S.I. 2001/3949.

59 C. Wadlow, *Law of passing-off* (2nd ed., London 1995), W.R. Cornish and D. Llewelyn, *Intellectual property* (5th ed., London, 2003), chap. 16.

60 *Schweppes Ltd. v. Gibbens* (1904) 22 R.P.C. 113, *Scott Ltd. v. Nice-Pak Products Ltd.* [1989] F.S.R. 100.

Goodwill in colour has often been protected in passing off actions where colour is used in association with a word mark or device mark or other distinctive sign, so that colour has not been critical to the outcome of the case. An early example is *Knott* v. *Morgan*,[61] where both parties ran omnibus services in London in the 1830s. The plaintiff alleged that the defendant had copied not only colours (of buses and of drivers' uniforms) but also a star and garter device. An injunction was granted by the lord chancellor to prevent deception of the public by these means. Similarly, in 1912 in the USA, the Coca-Cola Company complained that a rival company, Gay-Ola, had copied the colour of Coca-Cola, as well as the colouring of kegs in which the drink was delivered to shops operating soda fountains. Other acts of unfair competition were alleged to have been committed by the defendants. The court enjoined all such modes of deception.[62] Perhaps the most extreme case of colour being protected as one element of get-up or trade dress is the Jif lemon case, where the colour, shape and size of the Jif lemon, a plastic container filled with lemon juice, were protected against imitation, despite their initial genericness.[63] It is, however, equally clear from the case law that the use of the same colour for goods or for get-up of goods or services will not constitute passing off, if the defendant sufficiently distinguishes its products by other means, such as a word trade mark, thus avoiding consumer deception.[64]

Where imitation of colour alone has been the issue, plaintiffs have succeeded in a number of cases involving the use of distinctive colour combinations for drugs.[65] Single colours have been protected only on rare occasions. An unusual example was the Privy Council decision in *White Hudson & Co Ltd* v. *Asian Organisation Ltd*, an appeal from the Singapore Court of Appeal.[66] 'Hacks' cough sweets were sold by the plaintiffs in red cellophane wrappers which became distinctive in use. Non-English speaking consumers in Singapore asked for them by describing them as 'red paper cough sweets'. When the defendants put up their 'Pecto' cough sweets in red wrappers, the plaintiffs successfully sued for passing off. It was not simply that the coloured get-up was more important to consumers than the word trade mark 'Hacks' but that the verbal description of the get-up had become the *de facto* trade mark. The Hacks case is reminiscent of a number of US cases in the 1880s, involving plug tobacco, where coloured get-up was translated by consumers into word trade marks, such as 'the red tin tobacco'.[67] Imitation of get-up was

61 (1836) 2 Keen 213, 48 Eng. Rep. 610.
62 *Coca-Cola Co* v. *Gay-Ola Co*, 200 F. 720 (1912, CCA, 6th Circuit).
63 *Reckitt & Colman* v. *Borden* [1990] R.P.C. 341, H.L.
64 *Cadbury Schweppes Ltd.* v. *Pub Squash Co.* [1981] 1 All E.R. 213, *BP Amoco plc* v. *John Kelly Ltd.* [2002] F.S.R. 87.
65 See Wadlow, *Law of passing off*, para. 6.68.
66 [1964] 1 W.L.R. 1466.
67 E.g. *Lorillard* v. *Wight*, 15 F 383 (Cir Ct., D. Maryland, 1883). See S.A. Diamond, 'The public interest and the trademark system' in *Journal of Patent Office Society*, 62 (1980), 528, 543.

found in such circumstances to constitute unfair competition. In England, the 1937 'pink paraffin' case involved the use of colour *per se* rather than a verbalisation of coloured get-up. The plaintiff established goodwill in the sale of paraffin coloured pink and was able to prevent the sale of pink paraffin by the defendant. There was at that time no business reason for paraffin to be coloured, and the plaintiff was the only trader selling coloured paraffin.[68] Some plaintiffs in other single colour passing off cases have just managed to establish the arguable case needed to obtain an interlocutory injunction.[69]

It is always dangerous to extrapolate a general principle from successful passing off cases, especially where it was clear on the facts that the defendant intended to deceive consumers. Evidence of intention to deceive may well have been the basis of some of the cases referred to above.[70] Where, for example, the plaintiff has the only coloured product on the market and the use of colour is non-functional, the court may well be persuaded that a defendant who uses the same colour intends to deceive. Why the same colour was chosen in such circumstances is 'a question which falls to be asked and answered'.[71] Thus, Whitford J. would later observe that in the pink paraffin case, 'in truth the pinkness of the paraffin was of no great importance'.[72] Similarly, in *Coca-Cola Co* v. *Gay-Ola Co*, the court was not moved by the defendants' argument that the colouring of their beverage derived from the use of caramel, a colouring commonly used in the trade: 'we rest our conclusion here upon the fact that the color was adopted in part as a means of aiding the contemplated fraud.'[73] Just eight years later, the United States Supreme Court would say of Coca-Cola, 'the coloring matter is free to all who can make it *if no extrinsic deceiving element is present*'.[74]

If we turn to the reported unsuccessful passing off cases, we find a marked robustness towards the protection of goodwill in colour alone, and an awareness of the complexity of colour associations. In *Payton & Co* v. *Snelling Lampard & Co*,[75] both parties sold coffee in tins, the plaintiffs' tins being marked 'Royal Coffee' and the defendants' tins marked 'Flag Coffee'. The plaintiffs complained that the defendants' label incorporated the same colours (red, blue and green) as the plaintiffs' label, albeit differently arranged. The House of Lords somewhat peremptorily rejected the plaintiffs'

---

68 *Shell-Mex & BP Ltd. and Aladdin Industries Ltd.* v. *R & W Holmes* (1937) 54 R.P.C. 287. It appears that the plaintiffs later registered the word 'Pink' as a trade mark for paraffin: see *Blue Paraffin Trade Mark* [1977] R.P.C. 473, 481, 485.
69 *Sodastream* v. *Thorn Cascade* [1982] R.P.C. 459, and *SDS Biotech* v. *Power* [1995] F.S.R. 797.
70 E.g. *Sodastream*, *Shell-Mex*, and *Coca Cola*.
71 *Sodastream*, Kerr L.J. at p. 467.
72 *Blue Paraffin Trade Mark* [1977] R.P.C. 473, 486.
73 200 F. 720, 724, Denison J.
74 *Coca-Cola Co* v. *Koke Co*, 254 U.S. 143, 147 (1920), emphasis supplied.
75 [1901] A.C. 308.

case of passing off. The sale of coffee was honestly achieved by the use of the word marks, and everything else was, in Lord Macnaghten's words, 'absolutely irrelevant'. The courts have also been alert to the possibility that by being the first in the market to use a particular colour or colours for certain products, plaintiffs may have placed a new colour meaning in the public domain for the legitimate use of other traders. Thus, the use of pink paper by the *Financial Times* was found to have created an association between business news and pink paper, making it legitimate for the *Evening Standard* to sell a pink business section inside its otherwise white newspaper.[76] Similarly, in *Rizla* v. *Bryant & May*,[77] the plaintiffs had used three colours for different qualities of cigarette papers. The court held that for the defendants to use the same colours in the same way for their products did not amount to passing off; they were using the colours (accurately) to make exactly the same statement as the plaintiffs had made about the quality of their own goods. A contrary finding would have led to an unacceptable monopoly not only of colours but of colour terms, as consumers asked for the plaintiffs' goods by describing them as 'reds', 'greens' and 'blues'.

Greatest hostility has been shown towards plaintiffs who adopt colours that are common to the particular trade and later assert sole title to their use. In the absence of clear evidence of a defendant's intention to deceive, not even a market leader will succeed in this endeavour. In *Imperial Group plc* v. *Philip Morris Ltd*, the use of black and gold for packets of 'Raffles' cigarettes did not amount to passing off, even though there was some evidence of a very high association of black and gold with 'John Player Specials'. Black and gold were commonly used in the trade at the upper end of the market. 'Exclusivity in colour … is not something to be purchased by the expenditure of large sums of money. A trader wanting to establish distinctiveness in get-up must start with a get-up which is distinctive at the time when it is adopted and which remains distinctive in the market.'[78]

Registration of colour as trade marks, 1875–1975

Trade mark registration has been possible in these islands since 1875. The basic requirement for registrability is distinctiveness of the mark or sign, a capacity to distinguish one trader's products from competing products. In addition, entry on the Register requires a degree of definition or precision, as it must be clear to others from an inspection of the Register what exactly the mark is that the applicant seeks to protect. Definitional issues have been problematic in relation to colour but are essentially soluble by reference to

76 *Financial Times* v. *Evening Standard* [1991] F.S.R. 7.
77 [1986] R.P.C. 389.
78 [1984] R.P.C. 293, 310, Whitford J.

international colour standards, such as the Pantone or RAL colour codes.[79]
The requirement of colour distinctiveness is more complex; indeed, it took
three attempts before the registration system reflected the fact that colour
could form at least an element in the distinctiveness of the mark.

Monochrome   The Trade Mark Registration Act 1875 did not refer to colour
and no notice was taken of colour in the Registry, causing Jessel MR to
remark that 'colour is not protected by the Act'.[80] This was probably due to
technical difficulties in the accurate reproduction of colour shades. Special
rules were, however, devised for registration of coloured 'cotton marks'
(made by coloured threads woven into the selvedge of cotton), which were
deposited at several locations and available for inspection.[81] Although the
1875 Act did not allow registration of colours except for cotton marks, this
was not an absolute bar to protection of registered marks actually used in
colour as the experience of the wholesale grocers, Hanson & Son & Barter,
demonstrates. The managing director, Sir Reginald Hanson (1840–1905),
was lord mayor of London in 1886, and an MP for London from 1891 to
1900. His prominence in the City and in wider political circles ensured a high
profile for trade mark litigation in which the firm was involved. The firm sold
French coffee in canisters bearing a red, white and blue label which imitated
another colour sign, the French tricolour. In 1881, it was registered under the
Trade Marks Registration Act 1875 as an 'old mark', that is, one already in use
before the 1875 Act. As the latter Act did not allow registration of colours, the
mark was registered as a colourless parallelogram with three panels or stripes,
the outer two shown on the Register as shaded and the middle one unshaded.
The words 'red, white and blue' were printed below. Despite the monochrome
nature of the registration, Hansons obtained an injunction in 1884, restraining a competitor's use of a similar red, white and blue label for coffee on
grounds of infringement of their registered trade mark.[82]

Colour treated as an accident   The Patents Designs and Trade Marks Act
1883, section 67, permitted trade marks to be registered in a colour. Once
registered, however, the trade mark owner had an exclusive right to use the
mark in that or any other colour. This had the unfortunate consequence that
a trade mark would only be accepted for registration if it was distinctive apart
from colour. When Hansons applied to register the mark described above in

79 *Libertel Groep BV* v. *Benelux-Merkenbureau*, European Court of Justice, 6 May 2003.
80 *Worthington & Co's Trade Mark* (1880) 14 Ch.D. 8, 11.
81 *Re Robinson's Trade Mark* (1880) 29 W.R. 31. See 'Registration of trade-marks in colour' in
    Solicitors' Journal (1881), 254 (part I), and 274 (part II), and B. Sherman and L. Bently, *The
    making of modern intellectual property law: the British experience, 1760–1911* (Cambridge, 1999),
    p. 190.
82 *Re Hanson's Trade Mark* (1887) 37 Ch.D. 112, where this episode is noted at p. 113.

colour under the 1883 Act, for coffee and other goods in the same class, Kay J upheld the decision of the Register of Trade Marks to refuse registration, taking the view that the only distinctive feature of the mark was its colour:

> You may register a mark, which is otherwise distinctive, in colour, and that gives you the right to use it in any colour you like, but you cannot register a mark of which the only distinction is the use of a colour, because practically, under the terms of the Act, that would give you a monopoly of all the colours of the rainbow.[83]

Colour a potential part of distinctiveness   The *Hanson* case was cited in evidence before the 1905 Select Committee on the Trade Mark Bill, whose report led to the Trade Marks Act 1905. Giving evidence to the committee, Fletcher Moulton KC, a leading trade mark lawyer and draftsman of the bill, welcomed a proposed clause allowing registration of marks which depended upon colour for their distinctiveness, a change in the law which would allow 'the very well known mark of Hansons, the great wholesale grocers', to be registered as it was actually used.[84] The clause was enacted in the 1905 Act. Theodore McKenna, solicitor, patent agent and representative of the Trade Mark Owners Mutual Association was, however, more cautious as to the likely impact of the change, saying to the committee that 'it is very difficult ... to give exclusive rights in colour, apart from design and shape'.[85]

Registration of colour alone – the issue crystallises in 1975   The trade mark law concerns of traders like Hansons seem petty today, when the pressing question not yet fully resolved is Theodore McKenna's question, whether registration of colour or colours alone, without shape or design, should be permitted. It was, however, the case that the resolution of Hansons' concerns under the 1905 Act largely laid the colour issue to rest for seventy years. No commercial pressure existed for further change in legislative or judicial policy, here or in other jurisdictions. In the USA, for example, this was actively expressed as the 'mere color' rule: 'over the long history of United States trademark law, few principles were as "black and white" as the prohibition against protection for color alone.'[86]

The initial pressure for change came from the pharmaceutical industry. By the 1970s, the Trade Marks Registry and the courts were faced with the issue of distinctiveness of colour combinations, and later single colours, applied to the entire surface of drugs. The goal was preservation of market

---

83 Ibid., p.116.
84 *Select Committee on the Trade Marks Bill*, q. 108, H.C. 1905, viii, 257.
85 Ibid., q. 1621.
86 J.M. Samuels and L.B. Samuels, 'Color trademarks: shades of confusion' in *Trademark Reporter*, 83 [1993], 554.

share against generic competition, following expiry of patents for the drugs in question, by establishing trade mark rights in the colours that consumers had become used to during the life of the patent. One such case, *Smith Kline & French Laboratories Ltd* v. *Sterling-Winthrop Group*,[87] was heard in the House of Lords in 1975. At the same time, the Court of Appeal was considering an application to register the words 'BLUE PARAFFIN' as a trade mark for paraffin coloured blue.[88] Just before these two legal proceedings were concluded, the Mathys Departmental Committee reported on the state of British trade mark law. Referring to the ongoing colour cases before the courts, the report stated:

> '... We accept that a manufacturer or trader may make an arbitrary choice of a colour or a combination of colours from the limited range of colours available in nature and promote his coloured goods until evidence shows that consumers identify goods of that colour with him. We do not doubt that good promotion can lead to that result, but we do not believe that it should be allowed to lead to a perpetual monopoly by trade mark registration and so place an unacceptable restraint on other traders ... In our view the same reasoning applies as much to combinations of colour as it does to one colour. We believe that in the course of trade distinctions between various combinations of colours cannot be expected to be readily recognisable,[89]

a view which has resonances in Umberto Eco's work, considered earlier. Subsequently, however, in *Smith Kline & French*, the law lords ruled that a colour combination for drugs could be registered as a trade mark: 'the colour combinations have thus been shown to serve the business purpose of a trade mark. *They do precisely what a trade mark is supposed to do.*'[90]

Somewhere between the ontological approach of the Mathys committee, and the teleological approach of the House of Lords in *Smith Kline & French*, is this comment from Buckley LJ in the *Blue Paraffin Trade Mark* case, also decided in 1975, permitting the registration of the words 'BLUE PARAFFIN':

> 'I confess I have felt some anxiety about this aspect of the case .... The registration of the mark will not in itself make it improper for [the opponents] thereafter to sell paraffin coloured blue ... but the existence of the mark may give rise to difficulties of this kind.'[91]

---

87 [1975] 2 All E.R. 578. See also Diamond, 'Public interest and trademark system', 542–43.
88 [1977] R.P.C. 473, decided in 1975.
89 Cmnd. 5601, 1974, para. 55.
90 Op. cit., p. 581, Lord Diplock (emphasis supplied).
91 [1977] R.P.C. 473, 500.

CONCLUSION

The law has moved on since the issue crystallised in 1975 as a choice between a teleological or an ontological approach to trade mark law. In 1995, the United States Supreme Court firmly opted for the former approach, stating in a case involving a colour combination that 'it is the source-distinguishing ability of a mark – not its ontological status as color, shape, fragrance, word or sign – that permits it to serve these basic purposes'.[92] Subsequent US case law and legal comment do not, however, suggest that the matter is fully resolved: registered colour marks may ultimately confer very limited rights. The European Court of Justice, interpreting the harmonised trade mark law of the European Union,[93] has also held colour marks registrable as a matter of principle, but in cautious terms: 'it must be borne in mind that, while colours are capable of conveying certain associations of ideas, and of arousing feelings, they possess little inherent capacity for communicating specific information, especially since they are commonly and widely used, because of their appeal, in order to advertise and market goods or services, without any specific message.'[94] In some European member states, the position has already been reached that minimal differences in colour shading may avoid liability for infringement of registered colour marks,[95] and that injunctive relief will only be granted on the narrowest possible basis.[96]

The burden of this paper has been that history does not support a policy of registration of trade marks consisting of colour alone, not spatially limited. The operation of colour and colour terms in the heraldic system; the treatment of colour in sumptuary law; the sceptical approach to colour goodwill in the law of passing off where goodwill in colour is subordinate to the overarching need for deception; and the satisfactory operation of the registered trade mark system for over a century when registration of colour *per se* was not allowed, in the knowledge that passing off would provide a

---

92 *Qualitex Co. v. Jacobson Products Co.*, 514 U.S. 159, 164 (1995). The court approved the decision in *In re Owens Corning Fiberglas Corp.*, 774 F. 2d 1116 (CA Fed 1985), where a single colour was held registrable.

93 Council Directive 89/104/EEC for the approximation of Trade Mark Laws in the Member States, O.J. L40/1.

94 *Libertel*, n. 79 above. See also the decision of the Federal Court of Australia in *Philmac Pty. Ltd. v. Registrar of Trade Marks* (2002) 56 I.P.R. 452, where colour meaning is carefully considered.

95 See H. Johannes, 'Yellow/black: the monopolised colours of Imperial Austria under the reign of the Habsburgs' in *European Intellectual Property Review*, [2000], 441 (Germany), *Aquatherm GmbH v. Wavin PsA* [2002] *E.I.P.R.* N-33 (Italy). See also C. Schulze, 'Registering colour trade marks in the EU' in *European Intellectual Property Review*, [2003], 55.

96 See, for example, *Re Deutsche Telekom AG*, a decision of the German Federal Supreme Court concerning Deutsche Telekom's 'house colour', magenta (RAL 4010), noted at [2004] *E.I.P.R.* N-61.

remedy for all deceptive uses of colour – all of these considerations point towards a strongly ontological approach to the issue of private ownership of colour shades and colour combinations by means of trade mark registration. This will require recognition of a complex visual and semiotic phenomenon saturated with multiple meanings but unsupported by a commensurate colour vocabulary, a deficit not supplied by Pantone or other colour codes which mean nothing to consumers. The end result may not be an outright refusal, such as that of the Mathys committee, to countenance colour registrations – commercial pressures are probably now too great for a return to that position – rather an extreme caution, such as that articulated by Buckley LJ in the *Blue Paraffin Trade Mark* case, when dealing with requests for private annexation of colour shades.

Charles Hunt's haircut: getting down to the roots of a legal adventure

RICHARD W. IRELAND

THE HAIRCUT OCCUPIES A position of some importance in the history of imprisonment. In practical terms it may be administered to prevent the spread of disease in the conditions of close proximity in which inmates might find themselves. As such it may be seen alongside the compulsory treatment for scabies that was such a regular part of the Victorian penal experience. But the haircut has also a symbolic status, for it removes some of the outward manifestation of the individuality of the prisoner, becoming part of the uni-form which simultaneously marks the similarity of those subject to it, their difference from those imposing it, and the relative power of each group.[1] That such considerations are not merely modern theoretical rationalizations is evident in the observations of the penal pioneer, Sir George Paul, writing as early as 1784, whose words also remind us that different ideas from those mentioned above might also at times inform this apparently trivial practice:

> I consider, [writes Paul], shaving the head as an important regulation first, because it infallibly cleanses the most filthy part of the person, and is the only means of preventing the introduction of vermin to the bedding. Secondly, because it changes the ordinary appearance of the person, and goes far towards preventing prisoners from being recognized upon their return to society, by those strangers who are

---

1 The uniform as a standard part of prisoner and staff equipment in gaols is still establishing itself in the mid-nineteenth century; it was only adopted for all staff in Carmarthen by around 1864, when it is mentioned in the *Twenty-ninth report of the prison inspectors 1864* [3321] xxvi, p. 17. Uniform for prisoners was standard in the gaol before that date. Compare on the question of uniforms J. Thomas, *The English prison officer since 1850* (London, 1972), p. 41 and more generally the observation of Erving Goffman in *Asylums* (New York, 1961), p. 111: 'one of the main accomplishments of total institutions is staging a difference between two constructed categories of persons – a difference in social quality and moral character, a difference in perceptions of self and other.' See the same author's analysis of haircutting at pp. 14 et seq. As to an anthropological argument linking short hair to conformity, see I.M. Lewis, *Social anthropology in perspective* (Cambridge, 1985), pp. 117–18.

daily admitted to a distant view of them when walking in the yards. And thirdly, because so far as the shaving the head is a mortification to the offender, it becomes a punishment directed to the mind, and is (at least so far as I have conceived) an allowable alternative for inflicting corporal punishment intended to be excluded from this [i.e. the prison discipline] system.[2]

The regulation of such a practice then, given its practical and symbolic significance, may be an important, if improbable, area of investigation for those interested in the development of the prison in that most radical period of its change, the nineteenth century.

THE DISPUTE

On 18 August 1846 in Carmarthen gaol in south-west Wales two prisoners, Charles Hunt and Robert Jones, had their hair cut. They were not happy. On the next day the governor of the gaol, with his customary disregard for the proprieties of spelling and grammar, recorded in his journal that

> they had a complaint to make in consequence of their hair being cut yesterday it was requeset to be cut off for cleanliness has it was two long & two thick they are two dissatisfied characters and they wanted to write to the secretary of state which I informed them they could not write a letter until they had been three months in the Gaol according to the secretary of state rules but that they should see a Visiting Justice if they pleased.[3]

They then took their complaint before the mayor, who was a justice of the peace.

Just over a month later the 'Barber of the Gaol' was in action again, apparently working under instruction to leave 'a little side locks and in front of the head'. Hunt, Jones and a third prisoner, James Hargrave, refused to submit to his ministrations 'until they saw the rules to that effect'. The governor,

---

2 Quoted in M.Ignatieff, *A just measure of pain* (Harmondsworth, 1989), pp. 100–01. Note that Paul's second argument is probably of less importance in the following century as prisons become increasingly closed institutions, unlike Paul's own model penitentiary. We will see then that it is the fear that the shaven head will reveal, not conceal, criminal identity which becomes more immediate, *infra* note 7. In an interesting case from Brecon in 1844, a female prisoner, feigning lunacy, was apparently to have her head shaved as treatment for the condition, though it may have been a device to reveal the imposture, see D. Davies, *Law and disorder in Breconshire, 1750–1880* (Brecon, n.d.), pp. 49–51.

3 *Gaoler's journal* (Carmarthen Record Office – hereafter CRO – Acc. 4916), 19 August 1846.

Henry Westlake, instructed his turnkeys to 'see it done', an order apparently directed to the administration of the haircut rather than the revelation of its authority. The prisoners demanded to see the visiting justices, the supervisory authorities of the county gaol, prompting Westlake to seek to keep them apart from each other for fear of combination. Hunt was ordered to the treadwheel yard but refused to go, saying that 'he would go with his own class'. Westlake sent him instead to one of the cells set aside for punishment.[4]

On the next day both the surgeon of the gaol and his assistant attended the institution to inspect the disputed coiffures, 'which they considered it not two close for cleanliness and to keep good health'. David Davies and Thomas Jones MD, both visiting justices, were also called in order to listen to the complaint, but both Hunt and Hargrave were unwilling to show the appropriate level of respect, both proving 'very insolent to their worships'. The justices found the complaint groundless. At this point the important issue of communication to an authority beyond the prison, which had been raised by Hunt a month earlier, was raised again, as both he and Hargrave asked for pen and paper. Hargrave also, significantly, asked for the names of the visiting justices. His letter to the Home Office was apparently intent on naming those he considered culpable in his mistreatment. Westlake refused to allow him to write a letter, ordering him to break stones and placing him in irons when he refused to do so. With the dispute escalating, Jones seems to have had a change of heart and asked the governor if he, Jones, might be kept apart from Hunt and Hargrave, declaring that 'he was very sorry that he ever saw them'.[5]

The following day, 24 September 1846, saw Hargrave complaining about his own segregation from his fellow prisoners and demanding to see a justice again. His wishes were apparently ignored, for on the next day he repeated his demand and refused his soup, insisting that it should be measured. Westlake, embarrassed to find no liquid measure in the gaol, weighed the soup on scales. The turnkey was sent into Carmarthen town to find a justice but, unable to do so, returned without one. Possibly thinking that the increasing difficulty of his position was not recognized in his minimal salary, the turnkey resigned the next day.[6]

On 2 October Hargrave wrote two letters to the Secretary of State at the Home Office. Charles Hunt wrote two days later. Both men had now been incarcerated for more than three months since their conviction. Westlake took the letters to the visiting justices, one of whom volunteered the opinion that they should not be sent. Visiting justices then attended the gaol, asking the other prisoners whether they had any complaints in an attempt, I suspect, to isolate the two who had written. On 6 October two of the justices, both

4 Ibid., 22 September 1846.
5 Ibid., 23 September 1846.
6 Ibid., 24, 25, 26 September 1846.

medical practitioners, signed their own report on the incident and on the following day all the letters were despatched.[7]

Before we turn to the analysis of this chain of events some comments may be in order. Firstly, I must confess that the contents of the letters themselves are a mystery to me. Although it is known from surrounding evidence that the prisoners' complaints touched the matter of insufficient clothing as well as the haircut dispute, no copies of any of the letters, or any replies to them, have been found in either local or central archive repositories.[8] Secondly, it may be observed that, leaving to one side the legality of the haircuts, Westlake's interception of the prisoners' mail, and his refusal to allow them to write before they had served three months of their sentence were themselves arguably actions which were in breach of the Home Office's model rules for local prisons.[9]

7 Ibid., 2, 3, 4, 5, 6, 7 October 1846. In November Hunt again demanded to see the rules when he was ordered to have a haircut. He was sent to the refractory cell. This is at least suggestive of the fact that the earlier complaints had not been upheld by the Home Office, see ibid., 3 November 1846. So too is the action taken by Westlake in another haircut dispute later in the year. John Rees, a borough prisoner, had been sentenced for deserting his wife and family. The clerk to the Borough magistrates sent an order to the gaol instructing that Rees's hair should not be cut 'so that he would not be prevented from getting a situation after is time'. It was cut nonetheless, in the words of the governor, 'according to the rules laid down for the governor's guidance', ibid., 4, 5 December 1846. In his report on the gaol for 1851 (*Sixteenth report of the prison inspectors*, 1851 [1346] xxvii, p. 702), the Inspector J.G. Perry recorded the practice of monthly haircutting with no adverse comment. But note that the later order by justices that 2 vagrants sentenced to 3 days each should not have their hair cut. (*Gaoler's journal*, 7 November 1848) seems to have been followed by the then governor, George Stephens. Hair was cut only every two months in the 1840s in Brecon, see Davies, *Law and disorder*, p. 36.

8 I am greatly indebted to Amanda Bevan of the National Archives for her work on the records at Kew.

9 The 'Graham Rules', the nature and applicability of which are described later in this paper, contain the following:

> 86. He [The Governor] shall allow prisoners committed for examination or for trial, to send and receive letters, unless a visiting or committing magistrate shall have issued an order to the contrary, or unless he shall know a sufficient cause why any such letter should not be sent or received; in which latter case he shall record the fact in his journal. He shall, under the same restrictions, allow convicted prisoners to send and receive *one letter in the course of each quarter of the year.*
>
> 87. He shall inspect every letter to or from a prisoner under charge of [*sic*] conviction of any crime, *except such letters as are addressed to* a visiting justice or *other proper authority*, and in every case where he shall deem it necessary to withhold a letter either to or from a prisoner, he shall record the fact in his journal, and shall without delay lay such letter before a visiting justice for his decision.... [my italics].

See the *Report relative to the system of prison discipline, &c., by the inspectors of prisons* 1843, [457] xxv & xxvi, pp. 20–21. Later Governor Stephens of Carmarthen refuses to allow a convict, W. Smith, to send a letter to his friends as he states he was not entitled to under the gaol regulations. Smith's complaint is investigated by a justice, but the details are elusive (*Gaoler's journal*, 8 September 1849).

THE *DRAMATIS PERSONAE*

At about 11.00 o'clock on the morning of 24 April 1846, a carpenter, Lewis Jones, had noticed two men walking towards a Carmarthenshire farm called Llandawke Upper. One of them had no shoes. This was Charles Hunt, a 31-year-old 'labourer' from Liverpool who had been recently in custody in Derby. At 5 feet 4 ½ inches he was of average height, and favoured flannel waistcoats as he was 'tender-chested'. His companion was James Hargrave, 17 years old and 5 foot 3 ½ inches tall, from Manchester. He was suffering from a hernia, and he too had been in prison previously, at least twice, of which one sentence, for failing to break stones in the union workhouse, had recently been served in Carmarthen under the name of Charles Mackintosh. Both of these men, despite their impoverished condition, were able to 'Read and Write Perfect' according to the (admittedly questionable) judgement of Governor Westlake. About 20 minutes later Lewis Jones saw them coming back in the opposite direction from that they had taken earlier. Charles Hunt was by then sporting a pair of shoes and carrying a bundle on his back.

At some time later Hunt and Hargrave met a third man. This was Robert Jones, a 25-year-old ropemaker from London who was suffering from scabies. Jones had no known previous criminal record and he seems to have had a degree of family support, for his mother sent the sum of £1 15*s*. for him on his eventual discharge from custody. The three men were together when Thomas Morgan, who lived at Llandawke Upper Farm, met them on his way home. He found on each of them items of clothing – corduroy trousers, a shirt, three stockings, a handkerchief, part of a petticoat and a shawl – which belonged either to Morgan himself or to his servant, Ann Lewis.[10]

At trial at Quarter Sessions in July 1848 Hunt and Hargrave pleaded guilty to theft, whilst Jones denied a charge of receiving. All were sentenced to a term of nine calendar months imprisonment with hard labour and were returned to Carmarthen County Gaol, in which they had been held on remand before trial.[11]

---

10 The circumstances of the offence and the details of the offenders are taken from information contained in the witness depositions in the case (C.R.O. Quarter Sessions Box 2), the *Register of felons* (C.R.O. Acc 4916), numbers 126 (Hargrave), 127 (Hunt) and 128 (Jones), and incidental details taken from the *Gaoler's journal*. This latter source also carries references to Hargrave's earlier imprisonment in November 1845. The change of name alerts us to the scepticism with which we should view all but the more 'objective' information contained within official records, see R.W. Ireland 'The felon and the angel copier: criminal identity and the promise of photography in Victorian England and Wales', in L. Knafla (ed.), *Policing and war in Europe* (Westport, 2002), p. 53.

11 Rather curiously neither of the local papers, normally so expansive in their trial reporting, find much to say about the case, despite Jones's 'not guilty' plea, see *The Carmarthen Journal* and *The Welshman*, both 10 July 1846.

The other characters in the drama need not detain us for long. Henry Westlake was a former London policeman, part of the contingent sent to deal with the Rebecca disturbances which had shaken this part of Wales a few years previously. He had taken over the governorship of the gaol in July 1844 at a salary of £150 per annum. A man with a gratifying tendency to record events in almost neurotic detail in his diary he was also burdened with an alleged weakness for drink which was to cost him his job in September 1847.[12] Unfortunately, the name of the other person central to the haircutting drama, the individual responsible for performing the operation itself, is unknown. The practice within centrally-administered convict prisons seems to have developed to entrust chosen prisoners with the task of barber, but Westlake seems to refer to someone brought in to perform the task, and earlier evidence from Carmarthen supports the idea of professional involvement there.[13]

THE CONTEXT: PERSONAL

The haircutting dispute was the most significant clash between Hunt, Hargrave and Jones and the authorities in charge of Carmarthen gaol during their sentences, but it was by no means the only one. Whilst on remand all had apparently behaved satisfactorily. They had not, it is true, been amongst the remand prisoners who had volunteered to assist sentenced men in digging out the well at a time of sickness within the institution,[14] but there seems to be no evidence of any positive misconduct. Once sentenced themselves however, the prisoners, and particularly those two who had previous custodial histories, seem to have courted controversy. On 16 July, less than two weeks after their trials, Hunt and Jones together with another felon, William Jenkins, and three vagrants, George Williams, John Smith and Thomas Harries, lodged a mass complaint about the meat served to them, claiming that it did not satisfy their allowance in that it was not 12 ounces in weight without bone. Westlake tells them that the twelve ounces is inclusive of bone, but on checking he discovers that the regulations are ambiguous: 'it specify in the Local Rules that the prisoners shall have twelve ounces of meat twice a week but it does not mention with or without bone'. Thomas Jones, a doctor and justice of the peace, is found in town and tells the prisoners that the allowance was eight ounces without bone, but his confidence may not have

---

12 *Gaoler's journal*, 29 July 1847 *et seq.*

13 His reference in the *Journal*, 22 September 1846 is to the 'Barber of the Gaol'. A receipt dated 5 April 1841 shows one Isaac Thomas being paid 13 shillings 'for shaving the prisoners', C.R.O. Quarter Sessions Box 2. For prisoners acting as barbers see, e.g., 'One who has endured it', *Five years' penal servitude* (London,1878), pp. 48–49.

14 *Gaoler's journal*, 10 May 1846.

been as great as it appeared, for he told Westlake that the matter would have to be referred to the other visiting justices, who then declare the proper quantity to be twelve ounces with bone.[15]

Thereafter Hunt in particular seems to have been agitated regularly about the quantity and quality of his food allowance. On 7 September, Westlake reports that Hunt

> made a complaint to me that he considered that he should have two pints of soup according to the diet Table of prisoners which he said that he wished to se a Visiting Justice which I went out in Town Immedietly for whom but did not succede but I meet the surgeon of the Gaol & he came Tasted the soup & said it was excellent soup & plenty of it for any working men, and I weighed the soup in the presence of the head Turnkey which it was 2 lbs and ten ounces with out the Mess Tin.

After then refusing to show his sore leg, probably injured on the treadwheel ('the shinscraper' to Victorian prisoners), to the surgeon, Hunt was sent to the refractory cell.[16] On 17 October Hunt complained 'in a most threatening manner' that his bread had not been baked enough, a common worry, for undercooking allowed prisoners to be given what were in fact underweight loaves. On 31 October 1846 Hunt declared himself too weak to work, but was passed fit by the assistant surgeon. Again the prisoner raised the quality of his food as a tactic in the wider dispute, claiming that his bread was sour. Three days later, as the final haircut dispute was simmering, Hunt again complained about his bread.[17]

As their sentences drew to an end the prisoners again took the opportunity to challenge the authority of the governor. On 15 March 1847 Hunt was complaining of the cooking even though he was engaged in it himself! Westlake's record displays his indignation:

> Charles Hunt & James Hargrave and Robert Jones three convicted felons sent their soup back to day & could not give any reason in so doing only Robert Jones said he did not like rice in is soup which their was twenty fours prisoners in Gaol beside them & did not find any fault, but the prisoner Hunt I removed from cooking this morning & I ordered one of the females to cook as I have five in Gaol and sent Hunt to work.

15 Ibid., 16, 17 July 1846.
16 Ibid., 7 September 1846. The Surgeon appears later to have felt 'some compunction' for Hunt and requested his release from the refractory cell. See note of 8 September 1846 pasted on the rear inside cover of the *Journal*.
17 Ibid., 17, 31 October, 3 November 1846. For concern over underweight loaves see P. Priestley, *Victorian prison lives* (London, 1985), p. 159.

Four days later Hunt again sent the soup back, only for it to be eaten and enjoyed by the governor. On the 21st Hunt and on 22nd both Hunt and Hargrave sent back their food. On the release of the three prisoners who had been sentenced together, Westlake was no doubt relieved and recorded that their conduct, particularly that of Hunt and Hargrave, had been 'very bad.[18] At this point the three prisoners disappear from the Carmarthenshire records.

All of which provides us with a kind of grimly entertaining story, a power struggle between a few undistinguished felons and a semi-literate official in a remote county gaol. Without more it would make no particular claim on our attention. I think that there is indeed more though. In the remainder of this paper I hope to show that Charles Hunt's haircut highlights some important tensions in the progress of the 'penal revolution' of the nineteenth century.

THE CONTEXT: INSTITUTIONAL

This is no place to chart in any detail either the process of or the reasons for the changes in the penal system which occurred within the hundred years between the publication of John Howard's *The state of the prisons* in 1777 and the statute which brought all prisons under national control in 1877.[19] Suffice it to say that not only was the nature of punishment considerably changed but so was the site of the governmental authority behind it. Imprisonment became a dominant penal measure within the British Isles and responsibility for its administration moved from local to central government. Such major transitions in the form and administration of punishment were neither unilinear nor uncontested but nonetheless the trends are clearly apparent. Specifically we may note a number of key interconnected developments. Firstly, we can see an assumption of responsibility by central government for penitentiary provision, for example in the construction of the first national penitentiary at Millbank, opened in 1816, and in that of the regime-specific Pentonville in 1842. These new institutions formed an additional and in some way superior tier of penal establishment to that already in existence. As such

18 *Gaoler's journal*, 15, 19, 21, 22 March, 2 April 1847. Earlier (31 October 1846) Westlake had said of Hunt that he was 'one of the mutinous characters I ever haddo with, he made use of very threatening language to me in the cell'.

19 There is much literature on the topic. Sean McConville's work, *A history of English prison administration, 1750–1877* (London, 1981) and *English local prisons, 1860–1900: next only to death* (London, 1995) are essential reading. C. Harding, B. Hines, R. Ireland and P. Rawlings, *Imprisonment in England and Wales: a concise history* (London, 1985) and N. Morris and D. Rothman, *The Oxford history of the prison* (Oxford, 1995) give shorter accounts. The 'theoretical' dimensions of the subject are explored most famously in M. Foucault, *Discipline and punish* (London, 1977), and see also D. Garland, *Punishment and modern society* (Oxford, 1990). My own views on the changes can be found in a forthcoming study '"A want of order and good discipline": rules discretion and the Victorian prison' (Cardiff, 2006).

state provision developed, so did a sense of expertise in penal affairs which led to an increased intervention in prisons traditionally administered solely by local authorities, that is by counties and boroughs. Notable as both cause and effect of this claim to specialist knowledge was the creation of the Prison Inspectorate in 1835. The change in balance of power between local and central responsibility can be seen too in the fiscal changes, notably a significant realignment of funding in 1846.[20] Direct statutory intervention in prison regimes, at first tentative and largely permissive, but developing in confidence and effectiveness as time went on, is evidenced by statutes of 1823, 1835, 1839, 1865 and finally the nationalizing measure of 1877. Detectable in all of these various manifestations of penal change is a principle which is gathering momentum as the century progresses, one memorably captioned by the Webbs as the 'fetish of uniformity'.[21] Expressions of this principle can be found in much of the literature of the period, but it is neatly encapsulated in the words of Sir Walter Crofton, writing in 1871: 'There is want of uniformity in our treatment of prisoners which is fatal to our repression of crime.'[22]

We may pause for a moment to consider in a little more detail a specific manifestation of the process of change: the provision of model prison rules intended for adoption by local gaol authorities. The Gaol Act of 1823 had established 23 such rules, which although neither exacting nor fully comprehensive in nature marked an early declaration of intent.[23] The 1835 statute, 'An Act for effecting greater Uniformity of Practice in the Government of the several Prisons in *England* and *Wales*...', had adopted a rather different approach, insisting that local rules should simply be approved by the secretary of state.[24] It also, of course, was the statute which established the inspectorate, the umbilicus which hereafter connected the central and the local institutional structure. The 1839 Act again returned to model rules but restricted itself to eight only, if the more general provisions on prisoner classification are put to one side.[25] But in 1842, following a report by the prison inspectors, the Home Secretary, Sir James Graham,[26] sent out a list of rules to the chairmen of

20 For which see McConville, *English prison administration*, pp. 258–59.
21 S. and B. Webb, *English prisons under local government* (London, 1922), p. 204.
22 Sir W. Crofton, 'The Irish system of prison discipline', in E.C.Wines (ed.), *Transactions of the National Congress on Penitentiary and Reformatory Discipline* (Albany, 1871), p. 71.
23 4 Geo.IV, ch.64, s.10.
24 5 & 6 Will.IV, ch.38, s.2. Subsequently however, a series of regulations approved by the Select Committee of the Lords, 19 regulations in all, were brought to the attention of county visiting justices in a circular of 12 October 1835. The local magistrates were not however obliged to implement them. Interestingly, the circular in its printed form stated that copies of the Rules of Wakefield Gaol and Coldbath Fields were directed to be sent for the purpose of giving effect to the system of silence in gaols contained within the regulations, but this provision has been scored out in the copy received by the Carmarthenshire justices.
25 2 & 3 Vict., ch.56, s.6.
26 Graham was Home Secretary under Peel from September 1841 to June 1846. He was better

Quarter Sessions. There were no fewer than 195 itemized provisions, most notably those relating to diet but also including regulations concerning such matters as haircutting and letter-writing. In this codification not only was uniformity aimed at but so was its bureaucratic guarantee, accountability. Each prison was expected to keep, on my calculation, a minimum of 21 separate record books.[27]

The triumph of the ideology of centralization seems overwhelming at this point. And if prison history is conceived of as the history of central government intention, as it too often has been, then the process might be thought to be practically complete. But Graham's letter to the local authorities contains words which should caution us against premature judgment. 'I confidently anticipate', wrote the Home Secretary, 'the adoption of the recommendations which I have offered to them [the local benches], for I know that they are actuated by the sincere desire faithfully to discharge their important duties', 'I rely with confidence on the cordial co-operation of the magistracy'.[28] These are the words of a man who knows that he cannot really compel, but only flatter and cajole.

There were a number of reasons for local indifference or even hostility to central control over local gaols around mid-century. Philosophically and politically, some were opposed to a degree of intervention which seemed to run counter to a model of the 'Old Constitution' which saw responsibility for such domestic issues as properly devolved to the justices on the spot.[29] Yet even were this not the case practical and financial circumstances might prove strong disincentives to interfere with a prison regime based on existing local

known in Ireland for trying to bring in a Bill against agrarian crime in the Famine. Interestingly, in the context of this paper, his reputation was tarnished in June 1844 in a scandal involving the interception of mail. See L. Stephen and S. Lee (eds.), *Dictionary of national biography* (London, 1908), vol.VIII, pp. 328–32.

27 See *Report relative to the system of prison discipline & by the inspectors of prisons* (1843) and Appendix. It was not long before the rules were being criticised, see the *Report of the commissioners appointed to inquire into the management of Millbank prison*, 1847, (760) xxx, p. 9.

28 Ibid., pp. 13–14. Graham says that he has 'foreborne' to alter existing (and presumably those contained in statute) rules 'in the first instance'. J.G. Perry told the Carnarvon Committee in 1863 that Graham had had 'no power to impose them on the justices': see the *Report from the select committee of the House of Lords on the present state of discipline in gaols and houses of correction* 1863, (499) ix pp. 5–6, but see also his comments on p. 9. The rule on haircuts, incidentally, reads as follows:

   44. He [the Governor] shall direct that in no case the hair of any female prisoner be cut, except when he thinks it necessary on account of vermin or dirt, or when the medical officer deems it requisite on the ground of health; and the hair of male prisoners shall not be cut except for the purpose of health and cleanliness. He shall see that male prisoners be shaved at least once a-week.

29 'Centralization. No. Never with my consent. Not English.', per Mr Podsnap in Dickens's *Our mutual friend* (1864–65), quoted in K.Hoppen, *The mid-Victorian generation* (Oxford, 1998), p. 104.

buildings and staffing. To take an obvious example, the much discussed 'separate' and 'silent' systems, which relied upon the costly provision respectively of specific architecture or an omnipresent staff vigilance to discipline inmates, were at most mere aspirations for counties whose institutions were largely run on reluctantly provided county rates. Smaller things too though, like diet, had a basis in local customary and fiscal practice stubborn enough to ensure that, despite Sir James Graham's fine words, variation rather than uniformity remained usual.[30] The impotence of central authority may perhaps best be demonstrated by an episode in another Welsh gaol not long after Graham's letter to Quarter Sessions. In July 1843 the noted (I was about to write 'influential', but the events to be discussed suggest both the audience for and the restrictions on that influence) prison inspector Whitworth Russell was sent to investigate allegations of significant impropriety in the administration of Caernarfon gaol.[31] His unequivocal call for the governor's dismissal fell on the deaf ears of a local magistracy content to back their own man, even when he was in the wrong.[32]

In Carmarthen no such scandal occurred. In 1844 the Inspector for the Southern and Western District, J.G. Perry, could report that the Graham rules ('at least in the more important prisons') had had an impact on his circuit and the dietary had been 'generally' adopted with them,[33] but their precise effect in Carmarthen is unknown. Not the least significant point to emerge from Charles Hunt's encounters with Governor Westlake, however, is that in truth the local regulations as to diet were both less clear and arguably more generous than those propounded by the Home Office.[34] Carmarthenshire's compliance with central policy could certainly be limited. Repeated adverse comments on the state of its provision for female prisoners did lead in 1858 to the construction of a new building specifically for them. The Prison Inspector, J.G. Perry, and the head of the Directorate of Convict Prisons, Joshua Jebb, were consulted on the design, but Jebb's plans were rejected by the local bench, who raised both financial fears and criminological objections in the face of what they feared might be a temporary fashion for separation.[35] Perry's subsequent reaction to the building evidenced his

---

30 S. and B. Webb, *English prisons*, p. 133 et seq. Sean McConville notes, in *English local prisons, 1860–1900: next only to death* (London, 1995), at pp. 303–04, that returns to the 1864 Departmental Committee on Prison Dietaries stated that 63 of 140 prisons had adopted the 1843 dietary.

31 *Report on the conduct of the governor of Carnarvon county gaol* 1843 (422) xliii.

32 McConville, *History*, p. 252. He was eventually dismissed in advance of a second inquiry in 1848, see Harding et al., *Imprisonment*, p. 146.

33 *Ninth report of the prison inspectors* 1844 [542] xxix, p. 396.

34 The maximum meat allowance under the Graham dietaries was 16 oz. of cooked boneless meat per week. Note also a dispute concerning a move to cut the Carmarthen dietary, *Gaoler's journal*, 11, 25, 28 April 1846.

35 For the discussion in Quarter Sessions see *The Welshman*, 3 July 1857.

frustration. It was, he remarked, the first new building he had seen in fifteen years which had not been constructed on principles of separate confinement but continued to incorporate the 'exploded' system of association.[36] It was no doubt such experiences which lead to Perry testifying five years later to the Carnarvon Committee on Prison Discipline not only that separation should be enforced, but also that 'certain definite codes of rules for all prisons' should be promulgated.[37] By 1863 there is a sense that the terms of debate have shifted, and are being expressed more directly in terms of the impotence of the centre rather than any justifiable autonomy of the periphery. When the Prison Act 1865 was passed it provided, for the first time, effective sanctions to ensure local compliance with its major tenets.[38]

CHARLES HUNT'S HAIRCUT RE-ASSESSED

In the story of an expansionist centralizing prison administration imposing itself upon recalcitrant or even hostile local officials, as in too much of prison history, it is easy to overlook the role of the prisoner. The tendency to write prison history from the top down, from the ideals of the reformers, the debates of the parliamentary committees and the work of the legislature, the prisoner appears, if at all, as the passive recipient of penal change.[39] Yet prison life viewed from the bottom up, from the details of the lived experience of those inmates and staff who came together daily in the institutions, may give us other insights into the quality and quantity of penal change. It may of course be objected to the contrary that the exploration of particular events, of the kind with which this paper began, has no resonance beyond the individual circumstances of the particular actors concerned. Yet I do believe that the analysis of the dispute over the legitimacy of the haircuts given to Charles Hunt, James Hargrave and Robert Jones may assist our under-standing of the 'penal revolution' at a critical point in its progress.

The first point to make is a simple one, but in a sense it serves to explain why this is indeed such a 'critical point'. The events we have considered are clearly taking place in an era of some uncertainty. The governor cannot properly act entirely at his discretion and his neurotically detailed record of

---

36 *Twenty-fourth report of the prison inspectors*, 1859 [2501 Sess. 1] xi, p. 180.

37 Committee on Prison Discipline (1863) *Report*, p. 6.

38 28 & 29 Vict. 126, ss. 35, 36. Note also the change in the formulation and binding nature of the regulations contained within the Act, s.20 and Schedule 1.

39 Whilst it is true that a developing canon of prisoners' writing in the second half of the century does begin to give more detail of the experiences of those confined in institutions, the authors tend to be people whose offences or social backgrounds make them atypical of the majority of their fellow prisoners. Charles Hunt was no Captain D— S— , Michael Davitt or Oscar Wilde.

events reveals his own desire to be seen to be doing the 'right' thing. If complaints are made by prisoners, even 'difficult' men like Hunt, then the governor's superiors, the visiting justices, must be sought in town to offer their own opinion on the dispute. But the visiting justices are no longer unchallenged in the running of the local gaol, a fact of which Hunt and Hargrave were well aware when they asked for pen and paper to write to the Secretary of State.[40] A further level of authority, removed from the politics, personalities and expedience of the immediate vicinity of the gaol might now be invoked. Whilst it may be true that the rules proposed by the Home Secretary were not in themselves binding it is clear that at the least they could offer a kind of standard against which local practice might be measured. We should not overstate the degree of subservence of the older authority structures at this time though – this is, I have said, an era of uncertainty. We know that a determined governor and a complicit local magistracy could still exercise a degree of autonomy which could be frightening, as we have seen, at Caernarfon, or, even more spectacularly , at the sites of significant mid-century prison scandals, Birmingham and Leicester.[41] Even if such departures from essential standards are clearly regarded as 'wrong', and therefore indicative of this process of external appraisal of local practice, a less brutal departure from central norms is still possible. Over a decade after Robert Jones had picked up the discharge money his mother had sent him and left the hair-cutting dispute behind him, Carmarthenshire's magistracy could still, as has been noted, flout the opinions of important governmental 'experts' by rejecting their opinions and building a non-cellular womens' prison. The overall picture suggests an inexorable drive to central control, but viewed in close-up it reveals an awkward and nervous series of compromises.

The second point to be made is related to the last but is, I think, rather more interesting. If we look at the 'Graham Rules' we see that they are framed in terms of the responsibility of the officers of the prison. The provision concerning haircutting, then, appears in the list of duties to be performed by the governor. But Hunt and Hargrave show themselves to be aware of a 'jural relation' more usually associated with the much later work of the American legal philosopher Wesley Hohfeld![42] They know that one person's duty

40 Note also the possibility of prisoners addressing the Prison Inspector directly on his visit. In Carmarthen, for example, the Inspector, J.G. Perry, took down a long statement from a notorious recidivist character, Mary Ann Awberry, on his visit in 1848, see *Gaoler's journal*, 5 October 1848. In April 1848 there is another major source of controversy in the gaol, when the debtors, annoyed about, inter alia, their freedom to play quoits, petition both the high sheriff and the secretary of state, who seems to have passed the issue on to the inspector. The more laconic Governor Stephens reveals fewer details of the affair than his predecessor would have done (ibid., 7, 14, 15, 29 April, 29 May 1848).

41 For the Birmingham and Leicester scandals see, e.g., S. and B. Webb, *English prisons*, pp. 169 *et seq.*

42 Hohfeld's *Fundamental legal conceptions as applied in legal reasoning* was published in 1919.

implies another person's right. When they demand the 'proper' allowance of food, association with 'their own' class, haircuts to be 'according to the rules' they are clearly invoking rights under rules rather than allowances at discretion. When they write to the Home Office they anticipate the possibility of a vindication of those rights from a source beyond the immediate decision-makers, an external guarantee by a higher authority.[43] It is in this context no surprise, I think, to find that the two epistolaries had previous prison experience elsewhere. It is not merely that they knew how to annoy the local authorities. Their experience had given them at the least a basis of comparison of prison regimes, at most knowledge of their 'rights' and of how to enforce them, or at least how to attempt to do so.[44]

The key word here may be 'attempt', for as we have seen the relationship between the central and the local is still in the process of being resolved. I think, however, that the exploitation of the uncertainty which marked the period did in this case lead to some victories for the prisoners concerned. As the haircut dispute and its associated complaints ran on, the magistrates ordered extra clothing to be supplied to the prisoners.[45] That this is not simply coincidental with the invocation of the authority of the Home Office seems likely, for my reading of the documents suggests to me that the order in question has been nervously backdated by the visiting justices concerned. It was not, I think, the only triumph which the inmates enjoyed. A week after Charles Hunt had complained about the quality of his bread we find Governor Westlake asking the Quarter Sessions for the sum of £2.8s. for a new brick oven.[46]

James Hargrave and Charles Hunt may have suffered the use of irons and the refractory cell for their attitudes towards those who exercised authority

43 The process may, perhaps extravagantly, be compared with the analysis of the birth of the Common Law itself, particularly as formulated by S.F.C. Milsom, when the capacity of tenants to appeal over the heads of their feudal lords conferred uniform legal rights.

44 Of course the extent to which such previous experience had informed the perceptions of the individuals concerned here, or indeed of others, must remain of necessity conjectural. It is however probable that the greater the experience of other prisons and prisoners the greater 'education' they might achieve and transmit. It is also worth mentioning in this context that experiments in displaying prison rules within the institutions may have assisted in the development of this 'rights consciousness'. So the rules and dietary of the Penitentiary at Millbank were specifically directed to be displayed in the prison for the inmates to read (see Rule III, 19 *Rules and regulations of the General Penitentiary Millbank*, 1817 xvi 350) whilst the 1823 Gaol Act in s.12 required the Prison Rules to be displayed (s.36 demanded that bequests to prisoners should also be displayed). There is a surviving certificate from 1841 in C.R.O. Q.S. Box 1 that the Rules under '4 Will.IV [in reality Geo.IV] c.64 s.27' are displayed. I should perhaps also point out that wider 'rights discourses', associated with issues such as Chartism, may well, of course, have informed the consciousness of prisoners. I am indebted to Ann Sherlock for her observations on this point.

45 See the notes dated 1 and 5 October 1846 on the Magistrate's side page of the *Gaoler's journal*, but compare the governor's entry on the 5th.

46 *Gaoler's journal*, 10 November 1846.

over them in the county gaol at Carmarthen. They may indeed have been epitomes of the 'mutinous' prisoner so despised by Governor Henry Westlake. But though the times were uncertain and the concept as yet inchoate these otherwise unknown individuals may have, along with many others in their position still unknown, assisted in the birth of a modern-sounding doctrine. We now call it the recognition of a concept of prisoners' rights.[47]

47 The detailed development of the language of 'rights' in this context, as opposed to their substantive content, is not attempted here. Some observations may however be interesting. In an important early case, *R.v. Justices of North Riding of Yorkshire* ([1823] 2 B & C 286, 107 Eng. Rep. 390) an action was brought to establish the validity of the practice of making full diet for untried prisoners conditional upon treadwheel labour. In dismissing the complaint, significantly in our context brought by a magistrate rather than a prisoner, the language of rights is used only by one of the judges, Best J. (pp. 292–93) and then only in their denial in this matter. In a contemporary commentary, which doubts this decision and discusses also the important 1823 Millbank crisis, in which prisoners were found to have been undernourished, the anonymous author seems careful at one point to distinguish the 'claims' of prisoners from the 'rights' which their country has over them, but his language elsewhere is less precise in marking the distinction. See Anon., 'Prisons and penitentiaries', *Quarterly Review*, 30 (1823), 412, but cf. pp. 407, 411. Commenting upon a strike amongst penal servitude prisoners at Portland in 1858 over entitlement to tickets-of-leave, *The Times* described the action as in defence of 'a species of civil rights', and in 1861 declared, after more disturbances, that 'convicts have their customary rights, according to their conceptions': see A. Brown, 'Legitimacy in the evolution of the prison: the Chatham convict prison outbreak, 1861', in L. Knafla (ed.), *Punishment and reform in Europe* (Westport, 2003), pp. 116, 113. Later on in the century Michael Davitt, from his own experience of incarceration, suggests that the use of the term is widespread. Speaking in the context of the provision of underweight measures of bread and meat, he observes: 'There is not among any other class of men in this country to be found such a constant talk of "rights" of "law" of "justice and of the Home Secretary, as is heard from those who for the time being have forfeited almost all rights, who are avowed enemies of all law, and who know not what justice is when they are defrauding or robbing confiding or unsuspecting victims".' See *Leaves from a prison diary* (London, 1885, repr. Shannon, 1972), p. 139.

The influence of Sir Walter Crofton's 'Irish system' on prison reform in Germany

THOMAS KRAUSE

LINKS BETWEEN IRELAND AND Germany in the field of legal history even if understood in a broad sense do not seem very likely and are thus hard to find at first sight.[1] If one takes a closer look there are a few exceptions such as the 'Irish system' of prison discipline put into effect by the Irish prison reformer Walter Crofton, which had a considerable impact in various countries including Germany.[2]

When Crofton first entered the penological scene in the early 1850s prison reform had been a topic on the agenda for about seventy-five years in many parts of Europe as well as in the United States of America. One of the first and certainly most influential persons that gave attention to it was of course John Howard who started to complain about the 'state of the prisons' not only in England and Wales, as the title of his most famous book might suggest, but also in Scotland, Ireland, and several continental European countries including Germany in the 1770s.[3]

Although he immediately found followers nearly everywhere, the emerging debate about issues of prison reform soon vanished on the continent, when the Napoleonic wars began in the 1790s. This was especially the case in the German territories whose rulers understandably regarded the Napoleonic threat as a more important topic to deal with than penal policy.[4] Only after

---

1 The original version of this paper was presented at the '2003 British and Irish Legal History Conference' in Dublin whose organisers had asked for contributions 'on the penetration of a legal system ... into new lands' and had also especially welcomed papers in the field of 'the legal history of Ireland'. When revising it for publication I have kept footnotes and references to a minimum and have tried to cite works in English where appropriate.

2 Max Gruenhut, *Penal reform: a comparative study* (Oxford, 1948), pp. 87–91. The influence of the 'Irish system' specifically in Germany will be further examined in the main part of this paper.

3 Albert Krebs, 'John Howard's influence on the prison system of Europe with special reference to Germany', in: John C. Freeman (ed.), *Prisons past and future* (London, 1978), pp. 35–51. See also Thomas Krause, *Geschichte des Strafvollzugs: von den Kerkern des Altertums bis zur Gegenwart* (Darmstadt, 1999), pp. 67–68, 124.

4 Krause, op. cit., pp. 68, 125.

1815, when each of them finally regained their respective sovereignty, were they in a position to restart thinking about penal matters, and when doing so had to face the fact that the criminal law of their territories was still based on the 'Carolina', the imperial criminal code put into force by Emperor Charles V in 1532.[5] As one can easily imagine, it was a very bloody code indeed focusing on a variety of capital punishments like beheading, hanging, quartering, breaking on the wheel, burning, etc. as well as corporal punishments including mutilation.[6]

Although the law courts and the prerogative of mercy had developed a somewhat milder practice which also gave room for imprisonment as a penal sanction, it was now felt desirable to formulate a more up-to-date criminal law. This happened in most German territorial states between 1813 (Bavaria) and 1869 (Hamburg) by promulgating new penal codes, all of which considerably restricted capital and corporal punishments (mutilation had already fallen into disuse in the eighteenth century) and introduced various forms of imprisonment as the main penal sanctions instead.[7] This meant that it now became necessary to take a closer look at the existing prisons whose deplorable state had not changed much since the late eighteenth century, as John Howard's immediate German followers had failed to effect prison reforms due to the general political situation just mentioned. The leading figure in this reviving debate soon became the Hamburg district physician Dr Julius (1783–1862) who developed an interest in poor and prison relief and found wide public attention when he delivered a series of lectures about prison discipline at the University of Berlin in 1827.[8] Their publication as a book one year later[9] is generally seen as the starting point for the new discipline of penology or 'prison science' (Gefaengniswissenschaft) in Germany.[10] The most prominent auditor of Julius's lectures was the Prussian crown prince Frederick William who was so impressed by them that he henceforth took a keen interest in prison reform and also gave Julius a post as consultant in penological and prison matters when he acceded to the throne in 1840.

5 Idem, pp. 72, 126. For an account of the 'Carolina' see for example John H. Langbein, *Prosecuting crime in the renaissance : England, Germany, France* (Cambridge, Mass., 1974), pp. 155–209, where a translation of substantial parts of it into English can also be found (at pp. 267–313).

6 Langbein, op. cit., pp. 168–69. See also Richard van Duelmen's well-known book *Theater des Schreckens: Gerichtspraxis und Strafrituale in der frühen Neuzeit* (Munich, 1985), especially pp. 102–20, which was translated into English in 1990 under the title *Theatre of horror : crime and punishment in early modern Germany*.

7 Krause, op. cit., pp. 72, 126.

8 Idem, pp. 68–70, 125; Thomas Nutz, *Strafanstalt als Besserungsmaschine : Reformdiskurs und Gefaengniswissenschaft, 1775–1848*, pp. 239–45. See also Gruenhut, op. cit., p. 59 and Gerlinda Smaus, 'The history of ideas and its significance for the prison system', in: Norbert Finzsch (ed.), *Institutions of confinement: hospitals, asylums, and prisons in western Europe and North America, 1500–1950* (Washington, D.C., 1996), pp. 175–80, 186.

9 Nikolaus Heinrich Julius, *Vorlesungen ueber die Gefaengnisskunde* (Berlin, 1828).

10 Smaus, op. cit., pp. 177–80, 186; Krause, op. cit., pp. 68–70, 125.

When trying to find ways of improving the conditions within the prisons and of reforming their administration, Dr Julius and his followers primarily drew their attention to the British Isles and the United States of America whose institutions of confinement they regarded as models.[11] Especially the two convict systems that had been developed on the other side of the Atlantic, solitary confinement (Philadelphia) and the Auburn or 'silent system' (prisoners worked together during daytime, but were not meant to talk to each other (hence 'silent system') and were kept in separate cells at night time), were widely discussed in Germany during the 1820s, 1830s, and 1840s.[12]

In Ireland the number of capital offences was (similarly to the situation in Germany) considerably reduced in the 1820s and 1830s, which meant that incarceration as a penal sanction became more important there too.[13] This was especially the case when transportation (that had not been at hand in Germany at all due to the lack of colonies) also gradually began to disappear from the arsenal of punishments and was finally given up altogether in 1853.[14] This situation fostered the necessity of developing new, bigger prisons on a national rather than on a local or county scale, the first of which was planned and built at Mountjoy between 1846 and 1850.[15] Shaped to the model of its English predecessor Pentonville, Mountjoy Prison is still in use as a carceral institution today.[16] Only a couple of years after its opening an 'Irish Convict Prisons Board' was newly established in 1854, in order to manage the 'national' convict prisons following an inquiry into their state by a commission that had taken place in 1853.[17] One of its members, Walter Frederick Crofton, was appointed chairman of the 'Convict Prisons Board'.[18]

11 Ibid.

12 Smaus, op. cit., pp. 177–78; Krause, op. cit., pp. 68–70, 125; Nutz, op. cit., pp. 313–33. For a general account of the two American prison systems, see, for example, David J. Rothman, 'Perfecting the prison: United States, 1789–1865', in: Norval Morris and D.J. Rothman (ed.), *The Oxford history of the prison* (Oxford, 1995), pp. 114–24.

13 Patrick Carroll-Burke, *Colonial discipline: the making of the Irish convict system* (Dublin, 2000), pp. 29–31; Sean Aylward, 'The Irish prisons service, past, present and future – a personal perspective', in: Paul O' Mahony (ed.), *Criminal justice in Ireland* (Dublin, 2002), pp. 570–72.

14 Ibid. See also Tim Carey, *Mountjoy: the story of a prison* (Cork, 2000), pp. 35–38.

15 Carey, op. cit., pp. 37–43.

16 See Carey, op. cit. Compare also Ian O' Donnell and Finbarr McAuley (eds.), *Criminal justice history: themes and controversies from pre-independence Ireland* (Dublin, 2003), pp. 15–16 ('Introduction' by the editors).

17 See the works cited infra, note 21.

18 Ibid.

II

Although he soon became *the* Irish prison reformer par excellence, Ireland was not the country of Crofton's birth. Courtrai in West Flanders was where he first saw the light of day on 27 February 1815.[19] He was, however, an Irishman by lineage, coming from a distinguished Anglo-Irish family that had its roots in counties Roscommon and Leitrim. His father, Major Walter Crofton, served with the British army in Flanders at the time of his son's birth, but was killed only months later at the battle of Waterloo. Young Walter Frederick, his elder brother and their widowed mother were then cared for by his father's cousin who lived at Maidstone in England. He saw to the two boys' education which led the younger one to the Royal Military Academy, Woolwich. Walter Frederick Crofton was gazetted 2nd lieutenant, Royal Artillery in 1833 and promoted captain in 1845. Soon afterwards he resigned and made his home in Wiltshire where he served as a county magistrate and (like John Howard) began to take an interest in prison and reformatory affairs. This led to his appointment as a member of a commission to inquire into the state of the Irish prisons in 1853 and as chairman of the newly established 'Irish Convict Prisons Board' one year later. After his retirement from this post in 1862 he was knighted and moved back to England. He continued, however, to spend periods of his life in Ireland, where he inaugurated the industrial school system in 1869 and again served as chairman of the 'Prisons Board' from 1877 until 1878. Sir Walter Frederick Crofton died in Oxford on 25 June 1897 shortly after his 82nd birthday.

III

The origins of the 'Irish system' of prison discipline developed and put into operation by Crofton are to be found in the circumstance already mentioned that transportation as a penal sanction was heavily in decline from the 1840s onwards and stopped altogether in 1853. Its substitution was hard labour and it thus became necessary to organise the execution of hard labour sentences in a way that enabled the convicts to return to society on the completion of their sentences.[20] The prison systems mainly at hand at the time (which also have been mentioned above) were solitary confinement and the 'silent system' or variations of them.

When Crofton came into office in 1854 he did something new and rather different, however, when he introduced a special type of a progressive system

19 The account of Crofton's biography given here is mainly based on Richard S.E. Hinde, 'Sir Walter Crofton and the reform of the Irish convict system, 1854–61' in *Irish Jurist n.s.*, 12 (1977), 115–16.
20 Carroll-Burke, op. cit., pp. 31, 55–60; Carey, op. cit., pp. 35–42; Aylward, op. cit., pp. 571–72.

instead.[21] It was partly based on the 'mark system' having been practised in Van Diemen's Land (the convicts there got marks for their behaviour and thus could slowly progress to a better and more liberal treatment before they finally might be released in advance of the expiration of their sentences for good behaviour on a ticket of leave). This ticket-of-leave system had already been introduced in England as had progressive stages in the treatment of convict prisoners.

What made the convict system developed by Walter Crofton and his colleagues in Ireland distinct though was the third or 'intermediate stage' before release on ticket of leave. It followed the first or 'penal stage' served by both men and women in strict solitary confinement in Mountjoy Prison and the second or 'reformatory stage' where the prisoners worked and lodged in association and were allowed to converse with each other.

The third or 'intermediate stage' as the distinct feature of the 'Irish convict system' makes it different from other prison and progressive stage systems (and it is thus sometimes called 'intermediate system'). It required the establishment of new 'intermediate prisons' which were 'open' prisons where the convicts could prove their reformation and qualification for release on licence. Two such 'open' prisons were founded at Lusk (north of Dublin) for agricultural labours and at Smithfield (in Dublin) for industrial workers.

Although the 'Irish system' operated quite successfully for a number of years, it began to fall into decline shortly after Walter Crofton had resigned his office in 1862 because of poor health. When the last of the 'intermediate prisons' was closed in the mid-1880s, it already had more or less ceased to exist. The reasons for its ultimate failure are complex and varied and shall not be examined here.

IV

When trying to answer the question, in which way Walter Crofton's ideas and efforts influenced prison reform in Germany, one first has to state that this mainly happened in a theoretical way, that is German jurists and penologists received and promoted them in their literary works.

21 The 'Irish convict system' developed and put into effect by Crofton has been dealt with by numerous authors during the last 150 years. The most recent publications to which I mainly refer are the following (in chronological order): Richard S.E. Hinde, 'Sir Walter Crofton ...' (see supra, note 19); Elizabeth Dooley, 'Sir Walter Crofton and the Irish or intermediate system of prison discipline' in *New England Journal on Prison Law*, 7 (1981), 72–96 (reprinted in: O'Donnell and McAuley (ed.), *Criminal justice history* (supra, note 16), pp. 196–213); Patrick Carroll-Burke, *Colonial discipline* (supra, note 13); Tim Carey, *Mountjoy* (supra, note 14), especially pp. 35–130, 250–59; Sean Aylward, 'The Irish prisons service' (supra, note 13), pp. 570–73; O'Donnell and McAuley (eds.), *Criminal justice history* (supra, note 16), pp. 16–17 ('introduction by the editors').

The first person who did this was 'the most famous German jurist of his time' (as he has been called), the law professor Carl Joseph Anton Mittermaier (1787–1867).[22] His writings amount to 31 books, approximately 600 articles and book reviews, and about 12,000 letters of correspondence with colleagues in many European countries and the United States of America in a variety of languages (not only German, but also French, Italian, and English, which was not as common as it is nowadays for a German legal academic). His most important works are a textbook on penal law and several monographs on various aspects of criminal procedure, but he is also regarded as one of the founders of comparative law in Germany and last, but not least, one of the first German penologists. His main penological works are a highly acclaimed book on the death penalty in Europe and three monographs plus a variety of articles about prison discipline, and he was also a regular attendant and sometimes chairman of the international penological congresses taking place from 1846 onwards.

After having visited Pentonville Prison in the 1840s Mittermaier advocated solitary confinement for a number of years, but later took notice of the 'Irish system' in the 1850s and first brought it to the attention of German prison reformers in an article published in 1856.[23] He then continued to propagate and defend it against critics in two monographs about prison discipline published in 1858 and 1860 respectively,[24] and even in his last publication again emphasized the advantages of the 'intermediate prisons' for the rehabilitation of convicts.[25]

22 The most up-to-date sketches of Mittermaier's life and works are the biographical articles by Jan Schroeder, 'Karl Joseph Anton Mittermaier', in: Gerd Kleinheyer and Jan Schroeder (ed.), *Deutsche und europaeische Juristen aus neun Jahrhunderten*, 4th ed. (Heidelberg, 1996), pp. 273–77 (with many further references) and Regina Harzer, 'Mittermaier, Carl Joseph Anton', in: Michael Stolleis (ed.), *Juristen: ein biographisches Lexikon von der Antike bis zum 20. Jahrhundert* (Munich, 2001), pp. 441–42. See also Juergen Friedrich Kammer, 'Das gefaengniswissenschaftliche Werk C.J.A. Mittermaiers' (Dr jur thesis: Freiburg, 1971) and Heinz Mueller-Dietz, 'Der Strafvollzug im Werk Mittermaiers', in: Wilfried Kueper (ed.), *Carl Joseph Anton Mittermaier* (Heidelberg, 1988), pp. 109–37, who especially deal with Mittermaier as a penologist.

23 Mittermaier, 'Die Einzelhaft im Zusammenhange mit dem Strafensysteme, insbesondere mit den Wirkungen der neuern Gesetzgebung der bedingten Begnadigung und mit Besserungsanstalten, nach den neuesten in England gemachten Erfahrungen' in *Archiv des Criminalrechts n. s.* 1856, 578–80.

24 Mittermaier, *Die Gefaengnissverbesserung insbesondere die Bedeutung und Durchfuehrung der Einzelnhaft im Zusammenhange mit dem Besserungsprinzip nach den Erfahrungen der verschiedenen Strafanstalten* (Erlangen, 1858), especially pp. 147–51, and idem, *Der gegenwaertige Zustand der Gefaengnissfrage mit Ruecksicht auf die neuesten Leistungen der Gesetzgebung und Erfahrungen ueber Gefaengniseinrichtung mit besonderer Beziehung auf Einzelnhaft* (Erlangen, 1860), especially pp. 138–45.

25 Mittermaier, 'Der gegenwaertige Stand der Ansichten und Leistungen in Bezug auf Verbesserung der Strafanstalten, insbesondere durch die Einfuehrung der Einzelnhaft' in *Blaetter fuer Gefaengnisskunde*, 2 (1867), 99–105.

If Mittermaier may perhaps be called the 'pioneer' amongst the advocates of the 'Irish system' in Germany, the man that really saw to its breakthrough was another law professor who was more than forty years younger than his senior colleague and lived from 1829 until 1889. His name was Franz von Holtzendorff and he taught at the universities of Berlin and Munich.[26] A specialist in public law (especially public international law) as well as criminal law, he is like Mittermaier also regarded as one of the first penologists in Germany. After Professor Mittermaier had brought the 'Irish system' to the attention of the German public, Holtzendorff soon became interested and felt the desire to find more about it which led him to Ireland where he visited the prisons there and also met Walter Crofton. He soon became a personal friend of Crofton's and thus dedicated the first book he published about *The Irish convict system, more especially the intermediate prisons* to him.[27] During the 1860s he continued to propagate it in monographs and articles in German as well as in English[28] and by lecturing about the topic in the law faculty of the University of Berlin.[29] After his move to the University of Munich in 1873, however, his interest in prison reform and penology in general somewhat declined, and in his later years he no longer was such a vigorous defender of Crofton's ideas as he had used to be.[30]

The third supporter of the 'Irish convict system' that shall be mentioned here is the 'grandseigneur' of 'prison science' in Germany, Dr Julius. He had been a strong follower of the concept of solitary confinement during his time as a consultant to the Prussian king Frederick William IV in penological and prison matters during the 1840s, and it was mainly due to his influence that Prussia's first cellular prison (and the second one in Germany) was opened in 1846 at Moabit (a district of the city of Berlin).[31] After having read Holtzendorff's first book on the 'Irish convict system', however, which he reviewed in his last publication, Julius changed his mind and now propagated that it should henceforth form the basis of prison administration in all German states.[32]

---

26 For an account of Holtzendorff as a penologist see Juergen Bluehdorn, 'Beitraege zur Entwicklung und Pflege der Gefaengniswissenschaft an den deutschen Universitaeten des 19. Jahrhunderts' (Dr jur thesis: Muenster, 1964), pp. 220–32.

27 The German original (*Das irische Gefaengnissystem, insbesondere die Zwischenanstalten vor der Entlassung der Straeflinge*) was published in Leipzig in 1859; the translation into English came out one year later in Dublin.

28 The two monographs are *Reflections and observations on the present condition of the Irish convict system* (Dublin, 1863) and *Kritische Untersuchungen ueber die Grundsaetze und Ergebnisse des irischen Strafvollzuges* (Berlin, 1865).

29 Bluehdorn, op. cit., pp. 129, 220–21.

30 See for example Holtzendorff's article 'Die Richtungen des Strafvollzugs und der gegenwaertige Zustand der sachverstaendigen Meinungen ' in *Der Gerichtssaal*, 39 (1887), 1–35. Compare also Bluehdorn, op. cit., pp. 221–26.

31 See supra, note 12 and the references given there.

32 Julius, 'Review of "Dr Franz von Holtzendorff: *Das irische Gefaengnissystem, insbesondere die*

Whereas Professors Mittermaier and Holtzendorff as well as Dr Julius mainly gave lectures and published scholarly articles about penological matters, the approach of Professor Richard Eduard John was somewhat different. He lived from 1827 until 1889 and taught criminal law at the universities of Koenigsberg (in Eastern Prussia), Kiel and Goettingen.[33] Although he also started to deal with the matter by lecturing about it at Koenigsberg in 1865,[34] he partly left the academic stage a few years later and tried to take an active part in penal law reform. He was inspired to do that, because the 'North German Federation' (consisting of Prussia, the smaller North German territories, and the former free imperial cities) had been founded in 1867 and in connection with that a desire for law harmonisation and common law codes was sensed. Being a criminal lawyer, John undertook to draft a penal code for the North German Federation which was published in 1868 and, inter alia, contained several paragraphs proposing the introduction of a progressive stage system based on the Irish model.[35] His task was not well received though, and neither the official draft code promulgated mainly by the Prussian Ministry of Justice nor the final code that became law in 1871 took notice of his efforts, and thus did not contain any elements of the 'Irish convict system'.[36]

If most German penologists of the nineteenth century were university professors of the criminal law like Mittermaier, Holtzendorff and John, there were others too like Dr Julius, the physician, or men of the church whose duty it was to provide for spiritual welfare and pastoral care within the prisons. A man belonging to this group, the Lutheran pastor and prison chaplain Carl Wilhelm Haenell (1814–1875),[37] was in fact the author of the

Zwischenanstalten vor der Entlassung der Straeflinge (Leipzig: Barth, 1859)'" in *Preussische Gerichts-Zeitung*, 1, no. 51 (1859), 3–4.

33 For John's biography and works see A. Teichmann, 'John, Dr. Richard Eduard', in: *Allgemeine Deutsche Biographie*, vol. 50 (1905/repr. 1971), pp. 688–90.

34 John, *Ueber Strafanstalten: ein populaerer Vortrag* (Berlin, 1865).

35 Idem, *Entwurf eines Strafgesetzbuches fuer den Norddeutschen Bund* (Berlin, 1868), pp. 32–33, 88–95. See also Bernd Koch, 'Das System des Stufenstrafvollzugs in Deutschland unter besonderer Beruecksichtigung seiner Entstehungsgeschichte' (Dr jur thesis: Freiburg, 1972), p. 48, and Herbert Schattke, *Die Geschichte der Progression im Strafvollzug und der damit zusammenhaengenden Vollzugsziele in Deutschland* (Frankfurt, 1979), pp. 101–02.

36 Schattke, op. cit., p. 102. Compare also Werner Schubert, 'Der Ausbau der Rechtseinheit unter dem Norddeutschen Bund : zur Entstehung des Strafgesetzbuchs von 1870 unter besonderer Beruecksichtigung des Strafensystems', in: Arno Buschmann et al. (ed.), *Festschrift fuer Rudolf Gmuer zum 70. Geburtstag* (Bielefeld, 1983), pp. 149, 154–57, 161–65. John himself later revoked his opinion and no longer opted in favour of the 'Irish system' (Koch, op. cit., p. 48, note 2).

37 Biographical information on Haenell, who was also a lecturer in theology at Goettingen University between 1844 and 1847, is hard to find. See Philipp Meyer (ed.), *Die Pastoren der Landeskirchen Hannovers und Schaumburg-Lippes seit der Reformation*, vol. 1 (Goettingen, 1941), pp. 194–95, 329, and Wilhelm Ebel, *Catalogus Professorum Gottingensium, 1734–1962* (Goettingen, 1962), p. 44.

first German textbook on 'prison science' (*Gefaengniskunde*). It was published in Goettingen in 1866 and had the Irish system as its foundation, because it was regarded as the most advanced prison system of its time.[38]

At the time of the publication of Haenell's *Gefaengnisskunde* the topic of prison reform was so widely discussed in Germany that a new journal entirely devoted to it was founded. It was called *Blaetter fuer Gefaengnisskunde* (Journal of Prison Science) and already its third volume from 1868 contained two lengthy articles both called 'Die Uebertragbarkeit des irlaendischen Gefaengniswesens auf deutsche Verhaeltnisse' (Possibilities of adopting the Irish convict system in Germany).[39] The authors were Carl Freiherr (i.e. Baron) von Gross, a judge at the supreme court for the Thuringian states in Jena and chairman of the 'Prison Board of the Duchy of Saxe-Weimar', and Juergen Adolph Elvers, the governor of Leuchtenburg House of Correction in the Duchy of Saxe-Altenburg.[40] Baron Gross had visited English and Irish prisons in 1865 and delivered a public lecture about his experiences at the University of Jena in 1867, which was published in Berlin one year later under the title *Eine Wanderung durch irlaendische Gefaengnisse* (Visits of Irish prisons). What he had seen in Ireland impressed him so much that he proposed the 'Irish system' to be introduced in Germany with one small modification. Hailing from a small territory, he regarded a separate 'intermediate prison' as too expensive and recommended an 'intermediate class' within the existing prisons as the third stage before the prisoners' release on conditional pardon instead.[41] Elvers (who knew Gross personally as he lived in the neighbouring territory) more or less followed Gross's proposals with some minor modifications that need not be explained in detail.[42] His plans, however, were not put into effect, as Leuchtenburg House of Correction where he acted as governor was closed down in 1871 and its prisoners were transferred to the nearest Prussian prison, because the authorities of the tiny state of Saxe-Altenburg regarded it as cheaper to pay for their accommodation abroad instead of providing their own prison system.[43] Baron Gross's efforts did not have any effect either, because the debate about the introduction of the 'Irish system' in Germany came to an abrupt end in 1871, when the new 'Penal Code for the North German

---

38 Gruenhut, op. cit., p. 88.

39 Carl Freiherr von Gross, 'Die Uebertragbarkeit' in *Blaetter fuer Gefaengnisskunde*, 3 (1868), 1–39; Juergen Adolph Elvers, 'Die Uebertragbarkeit', ibid., 89–136.

40 More biographical information about Gross and Elvers than given here could not be traced.

41 Gross, loc. cit. See also Rudolf Plischke, 'Historische Rueckblicke ins 18. und 19. Jahrhundert' in *Monatsschrift fuer Kriminalpsychologie und Strafrechtsreform*, 19 (1928), 424–25, and Schattke, op. cit., pp. 80–84.

42 Plischke, loc. cit., p. 425; Schattke, op. cit., p. 84.

43 W. Jacobi and E. Mueller, 'Die alte Irrenanstalt auf der Leuchtenburg bei Kahla' in *Allgemeine Zeitschrift fuer Psychiatrie and psychisch-gerichtliche Medizin*, 68 (1928), 36–37; Plischke, loc. cit.

Federation' (that became the 'Penal Code for the German Reich' in 1872) was put into force, which did not contain any elements of the Crofton model.[44]

V

All German prison reformers advocating the 'Irish system' that have been mentioned so far were either theorists like Mittermaier, Holtzendorff and the other law professors or prison administrators like Baron Gross and Elvers whose proposals were not put into effect. The fact that Sir Walter Crofton's ideas and efforts were so widely discussed amongst mid-nineteenth century German penologists (as has been shown) does, however, raise the question if the 'Irish system' was actually practised anywhere in Germany.

One of its elements, the ticket-of-leave system (common in England as well), was first introduced in Saxony in 1862 and from there found its way into the 'Penal Code for the North German Federation' in 1871 and one year later into the 'Penal Code of the German Reich'.[45] It was not combined with a progressive stage system as the Irish system was and thus it remained an isolated provision of the law.

There was, however, one rather remote territory in Germany which nevertheless had a reputation for a fairly advanced penal policy (it had for example been one of the first German states to abolish capital punishment in 1849) that did reshape its prison administration according to the model of the 'Irish convict system'. This was the Grandduchy of Oldenburg situated in the far northwest of Germany near the Hansa town of Bremen and not very far from the North Sea. It had its main prison in a small town called Vechta where a man by the name of Friedrich Heinrich Wilhelm Hoyer (1796–1863) acted as governor from 1844 until his death in 1863.[46] Renowned for his humanity, he experimented with nearly all prison systems available on the market during the mid-nineteenth century until he became a dedicated supporter of the 'Irish convict system' and began to introduce it at Vechta around 1860. Like Crofton he also founded an 'intermediate prison' where the convicts had to do agricultural work (mainly cultivating heath and moorland).[47] Although many people regarded Hoyer's efforts with great respect, they were not followed elsewhere in Germany, but were seen very

---

44 Compare Schubert, op. cit., pp. 149, 161–65. See also supra, p. 241 and infra, p. 244.

45 Schubert, op. cit., pp. 164–65; Krause, op. cit., pp. 80, 127.

46 For his biography see Niels Kristian Hoyer, 'Ueber die Familie Hoyer und ihr 200jaehriges Wirken in Oldenburg' in *Oldenburgische Familienkunde*, 28 (1986), 273–74, 279–80.

47 Plischke, loc. cit., pp. 426–27; Gruenhut, op. cit., p. 88; Trude Hauser, 'Geschichte der Strafvollzugsanstalten in Vechta', in: Wilhelm Hanisch (ed.), *Beiträge zur Geschichte der Stadt Vechta*, vol. 3 (Vechta, 1978), pp. 367, 375–77, 393–94; Schattke, op. cit., pp. 88–89; Hoyer, op. cit., pp. 279–80.

much associated with him as a person (again a parallel to Crofton). When Hoyer died rather suddenly and unexpectedly during a holiday in the Rhineland, his 'experiment' (as many called it) was therefore immediately stopped by his successor who reintroduced separate confinement at Vechta Prison instead.[48]

VI

After the termination of the 'Vechta experiment' in 1863 the penological debate about the suitability of the 'Irish system' for German purposes did not stop immediately, but continued for a number of years, before it also came to an end due to the new penal legislation put into force in 1871 and 1872 respectively. The 'Penal Code for the North German Federation' as well as the 'Penal Code for the German Reich' only stated imprisonment and penal servitude as criminal sanctions, but hardly said anything about prison administration and prison systems as such. It was therefore up to the new federal states of the Reich to decide how they wanted to organize their prisons.[49] This situation gave room for a variety of models in the different federal states that did, however, show a general tendency towards separate confinement.[50] In contrast to that, the 'Irish convict system' was still mentioned in penological pamphlets, but was no longer really on the agenda.

As the considerable differences between Germany's federal states with respect to prison administration were soon felt to be unsatisfactory, inter-state-agreements about the principles of prison discipline were put into effect in 1897 and 1923 respectively.[51] The latter ones showed a considerable shift towards a reformative penal policy and officially stated rehabilitation as the main aim of incarceration for the first time in Germany. They also recommended the introduction of a system of progressive stages in the German federal state prisons which had been tested before very successfully in the first juvenile prisons founded from 1912 onwards.[52] These recommendations were followed soon (in Prussia, for example, in 1929) and consequently the first 'open' or 'minimum security' prisons were established where prisoners served the last stage of their sentence before their conditional release. They had a striking similarity to the 'intermediate prisons' propagated and put into use by Walter Crofton in Ireland more than seventy years earlier, which meant that his ideas suddenly became important again.[53]

48 Ibid.
49 Krause, op. cit., pp. 81–82, 128.
50 Ibid.
51 Krause, op. cit., pp. 82–83, 128–29.
52 Idem, pp. 83–84, 128–29; Gruenhut, op. cit., pp. 124–25, 285.
53 Krause, op. cit., pp. 83, 129; Klaus Laubenthal, *Strafvollzug*, 3rd ed. (Berlin, 2003), p. 54.

Although the rehabilitation of offenders was not the main aim and in fact no aim at all of Nazi penal policy,[54] some of the leading penologists and prison reformers of the Weimar Republic raised their voices again after the end of the Second World War and continued to act where they had been forced to stop in 1933. Thus new 'open prisons' were established from the 1950s onwards that still resemble their Irish predecessors established during the 1850s.[55]

Although the 'progressive stage system' as such is no longer practised in Germany today, because it is regarded as being too formalized and not flexible enough, the rehabilitation of prisoners and their preparation for a life without criminal offences after their release is still regarded as the main purpose of imprisonment as a penal sanction.[56] 'Open prisons' do form an important part in this process, and therefore even the most recent German textbooks on prison law and administration still mention the name of Sir Walter Frederick Crofton as their 'spiritus rector'.[57]

For a detailed account, see, for example, Koch, op. cit., pp. 55–75, and Schattke, op. cit., pp. 129–99.

54 Krause, op. cit., pp. 85–87, 130; Laubenthal, op. cit., pp. 56–57. Compare also Koch, op. cit., pp. 76–78, and Schattke, op. cit., pp. 201–210.

55 Krause, op. cit., pp. 92,132.

56 Idem, pp. 93–99, 133–35.

57 See, for example, Laubenthal, op. cit., p. 49.

Law in early Iowa: one adventure

RUSSELL K. OSGOOD

WRITING THE LEGAL HISTORY of an organizing period for a new common law jurisdiction is of course a familiar task. And by now one might question whether the modest permutations of the various American and Canadian jurisdictions that have been studied have been sufficiently distinct to justify the work and space and time consumed in preparing and printing them. At the same time these various stories of adaptation do provide interesting if modest points of comparison, and as I began this project I thought that was the best outcome I might hope for. You and future readers, of course, will be the judges of this ultimately, but I have concluded that Iowa, meaning by that term first the territory of Iowa, roughly from 1838[1] to 1846, and then the early state of the same name, roughly from 1846 to 1860, suggests some modest points of comparison but also a few themes of larger significance.

At first glance, Iowa territory and then the State seems an improbable locale for any truly significant common law innovation or departure for several reasons. First of all, it is relatively small, currently having about 3,000,000 residents and during the periods in question it grew from under 50,000 to around 675,000.[2] Second, for most of the period there was no major central urban agglomeration or legal community, rather a number of modest riverside cities on the eastern border along the Mississippi, at Fort Des Moines near the centre of the state and then on the western border along the Missouri River. Third, Iowa was just being settled which is, of course, a process likely to generate legal claims but it also remained, with Missouri, mainly a place of transiting for people proceeding to further Western settlement and, therefore, not a place likely to witness prolonged or significant court actions or related disputes. For example, the Mormon flight from Nauvoo in Illinois in 1844 following the death of Joseph Smith crossed the middle of Iowa. Earlier, a number of adventurers headed for California and gold passed through in the late 1830s.

There are besides the speed and low density of settlement during the period in question some other factors that now in retrospect, I think, suggest

---

1 I chose this year because it was the year that the territorial Supreme Court for the territory of Iowa was created (and the separate Iowa territory was created) pursuant to a federal statute.

2 R. Acton and P. Acton, *To go free: a treasury of Iowa's legal heritage* (Ames, 1995), p. 59.

why Iowa could have produced some interesting legal developments compared to the 'average' formative period in other common law jurisdictions. Among them and the most significant is Iowa's very homogenous geography. While there are hills of some significance in the corners of Iowa, the state was almost entirely covered by gently rolling tall grass prairie traversed by occasional lazy, muddy rivers, like the Racoon, Turkey, and Skunk, from which extended treed savannas. The effect of the geographic homogeneity on law is not immediately apparent but one begins by noting a vast reservoir of very similar and difficult to work (initially) farmland of very high quality all of it fairly vulnerable to rainfall deficiency.[3] There were and remain few alternative land uses, no forestry and little mining. Another fact contributing possible uniqueness is the lack of a major, logically-sited urban centre. The state's population was originally spread very thinly, although it was and is heavier in the eastern than the western half of the state, reflecting the uniformity of the land type and the dominant use to which it was put. Finally, while Iowa had a number of traversing and peripatetic native tribal groupings it had no dominant, well-organized tribe. Almost all the resident tribes had been pushed or 'treatied' into Iowa shortly before this period and on contact with the advancing Europeans these native peoples, including Sioux, Iowa, Pottawattomies, and Sac and Fox fractured, resisted fiercely occasionally but after the Black Hawk War of 1832[4] presented only intermittent points of resistance rather than a continuing set of major problems. While they fractured, they did, however, constitute a consistent, circulating presence[5] within the state moving from one hunting and low-level farming locale to another. It is worth noting that this happened, no doubt, in large part because they had already been pushed out of their ancestral lands in the woodlands and appurtenant prairies in Illinois, Wisconsin and Michigan[6] and only left Iowa when resettled by further federal treaty action.

3 The mean annual rainfall for Grinnell, Iowa is currently about 36 inches a year compared to 45.5 inches for Rockport, Massachusetts.

4 See generally Wm. T. Hagan, *The Sac and Fox Indians* (1938). The war was occasioned by Black Hawk's efforts to return to Illinois and his defeat produced a formal expulsion of Sac and Fox from Iowa to Oklahoma but a band of them, the Meskwaki, remained in what is now Tama County and have a reservation there.

5 The multiple continuing interactions with Indian peoples is illustrated in a number of legal actions including, for example, *Parker* v. *Lewis*, 2 Iowa 311 (1849). In *Parker* a mill owner (Lewis) was grinding Parker's wheat into flour when a group of Indians appeared and Lewis allegedly sold them some of Parker's flour. Parker was later sued by Lewis in slander on the ground that Parker had said of Lewis to others that: 'He is a thief, he stole my wheat and ground it and sold the flour to the Indians.' Id. at 311. Whether this was a voluntary sale is not clear. As to the continuing presence of bands of native hunters and families during this period see generally, *The history of Poweshiek county, Iowa* (Des Moines, 1880).

6 For an excellent, if succinct, treatment of all the tribes in Iowa, see the appropriate entries in B.M. Pritzker, ed., *A native American encyclopedia: history, culture, and people* (New York, 2000).

DUBUQUE LITIGATION

One hesitates to begin to look at law in early Iowa by reference to perhaps the most significant case, a case that started in the United States district court and ended in the U.S. Supreme Court, *Chouteau* v. *Molony*[7]. It was decided on 23 February 1854 in the Supreme Court following an argument in the December 1850 term. The case was 'a suit for the recovery of land, but not according to the form of the proceedings in ejectment….[but] according to the course of pleading allowed in the courts of Iowa….'[8] It involved a set of interesting land claim issues pitting a claimant whose title was derived from an Indian grant to a pivotal early European figure, Julien Dubuque[9], during the period of Spanish and French sovereignty against a claimant whose title derived from a grant by the United States after the Louisiana Purchase conveyed what was to become Iowa.

Henry Chouteau sought title to a large hunk of eastern Iowa (located between the Little Makoketa River and the mouth of Musquabinenque Creek (later called Tete des Morts)), including all of the now city of Dubuque and its environs, under a land claim traceable to Julien Dubuque. Chouteau and Dubuque's interest originated in an agreement of 22 September 1788 with the Fox Indians for land they then occupied on the western bank of the Mississippi. (They were mainly located in what we now call Illinois.) This territory was then under Spanish and French 'control'. The language of the agreement (in French) turns out perhaps to be determinative. 'Les Renards, c'est à dire, le chef et le brave de cinque villages avec l'approbation du reste de leur gens, expliqué par Mr. Quinantotaye, deputé par eux, en leur presence et en la notre nous soussignés, sçavoir, que les Renards permette à Julien Dubuc, appellé par eux la petit nuit, de travailler à la mine jusqu'à qui lui plaira….'[10] This grant, which appears to be a grant of a mineral right and an easement to mine for lead (and this was done) was confirmed in New Orleans by the Baron de Carondelet, a Spanish[11] official, in New Orleans on 22 October 1796. Before acting, the baron sought advice of a saavy Indian trader of the Dubuque area, one Andrew Todd, who recommended approval of the confirmation of the grant.[12] Carondelet confirmed the grant referencing the

---

7 57 U.S. 203 (1854).   8 57 U.S. 221.

9 Dubuque's grave is set high on a bluff overlooking the Mississippi just south of the centre of the modern-day city of Dubuque.

10 57 U.S. at 222–23.

11 It might seem puzzling that a Spanish official would be the governor of Louisiana a short seven years before the sale of the entire territory by France to the United States. The entire history of the 'title' to the territory is beyond this paper, but it is worth noting that Spain subsequent to 1796 conveyed the territory to France by the secret Treaty of St Ildefonso of 1 Oct. 1800

12 57 U.S. at 222.

language of Dubuque's petition which described his holding more as a fee simple absolute title and this, in turn, was the basis for Chouteau's claim. Dubuque's petition asked Carondolet 'de vouilloir bient lui accorder la paysibles possessions des mines et des terres ...'[13] and Carondolet agreed.

Molony's claim was cleaner. He claimed under a clear written grant from the United States. Pursuant to the Treaty of Paris conveying the Louisiana Purchase all land not subject to established French or Spanish grants was vested in the U.S. federal government. So, if Dubuque's claimed fee simple title was good the United States's grant, by its own terms, conveyed nothing. Conversely, if there was no title in Chouteau, Molony's title was clear because the Indians' rights (if any remained) had been extinguished by a treaty of 1832 made by General Scott and Governor Reynolds.[14]

There were additional complicating factors in the case, including periodic enlargements of the description of the legal interest conveyed to Dubuque's successors in interest, but in the end the Supreme Court held solidly for Molony, the United States' claimant, on the following three grounds. First, the original grant from the Fox to Dubuque, was 'a sale to him of the ... mine, with its allowed mining appendages, with the privilege to search for other mines in the event that ore was not found in that mine; and that the order of Governor Carondelet, upon his petition, was not meant to secure to him the ownership of the lands described in his petition.'[15] Second, the court concluded that to the extent that Governor Carondelet conveyed or intended to convey more than what the original language provided (a mining easement) he exceeded his powers under Spanish law and the enlargement of the grant was void.[16] Specifically, Spanish law provided that the king of Spain had to assent to any extinguishment of an Indian right of occupation and this was never sought or granted from or by the Spanish crown.[17] Finally, the court noted that the mine was very close to the large Fox tribal village of Kettle Chief, which village the Indians continued to occupy long after the grant. The court concluded that this continued occupation corroborated its interpretation of the original grant as conveying, at best, an easement for mining purposes and the mine itself, or any substitute mine, rather than a fee simple title to all of the lands claimed by Chouteau.[18] Thus, Molony's United States title was confirmed.

This litigation was of course handled at the federal level and the Supreme Court's somewhat careful handling of Spanish law is perhaps indicative of the sophistication of the federal courts in dealing with a welter of cross-claims first in the Western Reserve and later in the Louisiana Purchase. But, and we will test this shortly, that the claimant whose claim came from a clear, written *federal* grant should win is also consistent with the results in many of these cases from all of these territories.

13 Id. at 224.
16 Id. at 239.

14 Id. at 224.
17 Id. at 237.

15 57 U.S. at 237.
18 Id. at 241.

HALF-BREED RESERVE LITIGATION

Although we find the term offensive, it is perhaps of some significance that pursuant to a treaty the federal government had acceded to setting aside a parcel for 'half-breeds' within Iowa by the ceding Sac and Fox tribe. The exact definition of a 'half-breed' is elusive but in general both European and native peoples recognized that there was a group of individuals of mixed parentage who were not fully welcomed in either the native or European community. Not surprisingly, the reserve set aside for 'half-breeds' produced a fair amount of litigation and the legal treatment of this statutory and treaty-based reserve provides interesting lessons in what is important in a transient, settling area.

Webster v. *Reid*[19] was tried in the territorial district court in Lee County and then appealed. The district court decision was affirmed by the territorial Supreme Court in Iowa. Reid's title to a significant portion of the 'half-breed' reserve that was created by a Treaty of 4 August 1824 between the United States and the Sac and Fox tribes was located 'between the rivers Des Moines and the Mississippi, and the section of the above line between the Mississippi and the Des Moines ... one hundred and nineteen thousand acres ... [and] is intended for the use of the half-breeds belonging to the Sac and Fox nations; they holding it, however, by the same title and in the same manner that other Indian titles are held.'[20] Reid had acquired title in a series of judicial sales of property. The 1824 treaty was followed by a 30 June 1834 Act of the U.S. Congress which relinquished residual federal title implied in the 'reservation' quoted above. And finally on 16 January 1838 the territorial legislature passed an act for the appointment of three commissioners to review and confirm title to specific parcels within the half-breed reserve which they did and which apparently led to a series of judicial sales and sheriffs' deeds including the one giving Reid his title. In essence, what the 1834 treaty and 1838 act seemed to do was dissolve 'sovereign' or any existing 'reservation' character of the half-breed tract (as there is no separate federal constitutional sovereignty recognized in 'half-breeds') and allowed the free alienation by all owners including half-breeds and those with titles derived from them. Reid's title was premised on a judicial sale, which after notice of the sale, then obliterated all claimants who failed to come forward.[21]

Webster's title, by contrast, and not surprisingly was originally from a Sac and Fox half-breed, one Na-ma-tau-pus. Webster's title was established by hearsay testimony of Na-ma-tau-pus's ownership and then his deed out and through others to Webster in 1838.[22] In essence, the district court blocked the introduction of all the evidence proffered by Webster of his title. In a per curiam opinion by the chief justice, Charles Mason, the Supreme Court upheld the district court judgment. (The case was commenced in the district

19 1 Iowa Reports 615 (Cole's, 1846).   20 Id. at 617.   21 Id. at 629.
22 Id. at 628–29.

court by Reid as an action in the right, not as an ejectment proceeding.) As an initial matter, the Supreme Court held that the federal act of 1834 conveyed to all 'lawful' holders in the half-breed tract a fee simple absolute title: 'Since the taking effect, therefore, of the act of 1834, the half-breed tract has been, to the fullest extent, individual property, and as such was by the organic act of the territory, placed under municipal regulations.'[23]

The court justified its conclusion on the following revealing ground: 'Any other construction would lead to the most serious inconvenience.'[24] The court stated that any other conclusion would render the half-breed tract land 'forever hereafter to be exempt from taxation and from sale under execution' and that such land would never be 'subject to our laws'.[25]

Webster also contended that Reid's entire course of conduct constituted an effort to obtain title by 'fraud' including presumably fraud on the courts by his 'misuse' of the judicial sale/execution process.[26] The court rejected the notion that fraud or irregularity should vitiate Reid's title relying heavily on the presumed formal regularity of such processes. For if this is not presumed then: 'Such a rule would produce the greatest inconvenience, by rendering titles insecure, as well as by discouraging persons from purchasing at such sales.'[27]

The Supreme Court also swept aside any claim by Webster based on his undisputed possession, including possible adverse possession.[28] And finally it reached, by what legal route I am not sure, the issue of the merits of Webster/s proffered testimony of his title from Na-ma-tau-pus. While the opinion to this point can be seen largely as the effort of the legal elite in the territory to stabilize and secure titles by deferring heavily to the presumed correctness of legal proceedings establishing title, including sales at execution, its analysis of the claimed conveyance by Na-ma-tau-pus reveals, perhaps not surprisingly, substantial irritation with half-breeds and even Indian culture, in general. I quote it in full:

> The next point to be considered is the proof of title derived from Na-ma-tau-pus, which was proffered by the defendant [Webster] below, and rejected by the court. It is very questionable whether such proof should have been admitted, even if Na-ma-tau-pus had been fully proved to have been one of the Sac and Fox half-breeds. The title of the lands was in the hands of a purchaser under a sale directed by a court of general jurisdiction. If that judgment were irregular, fraudulent, or founded upon an unconstitutional law, could one of the parties to the judgment obtain a remedy in this collateral matter?
>
> But even if the law should permit such a course, we think there was no sufficient evidence that Na-ma-tau-pus was one of the Sac and Fox

23 Id. at 629.   24 Id.   25 Id. at 630.
26 Id. at 631.   27 Id. at 632.   28 Id. at 633.

half-breeds. The principal witness of this subject was one who did not understand the Indian language. He stated that on one occasion he was in company of several whites and Indians, and that then this individual was said to be a half-breed of the Sac and Fox tribes; at another time the witness took the acknowledgement of the deed from Na-ma-tau-pus, when he herd [*sic*] several persons (a part of whom were under oath) state that they believed him a half-breed of the Sac tribe. His complexion indicated a half-breed. [The] Witness had also heard some persons who had married half-breeds make similar statements as to his pedigree. From the necessity of the case the same strictness of proof is not required in relation to pedigree as for most other purposes, still the same general rules are observed.

The best evidence which the nature of the case admits is required where hearsay evidence in such case is allowed. It is the statements of relatives by blood or marriage who are generally best acquainted with the facts they state.

No evidence of that kind was offered in the present case. But even if the peculiar habits and manners of the Indians be such as to require a further modification of the rule of evidence, at least general reputations in the tribe might have been proved by persons who could understand the language. Bullard [one of the intermediary title holders of Webster] stated that several persons had informed him that such reputation existed. The original hearsay would have been infinitely better evidence than this hearsay of a hearsay.

The principles involved in the instructions asked and refused by the court, have already then [been] substantially discussed. If the conclusions above stated are correct, there was no error in refusing the instructions. Judgment affirmed.[29]

This case says a lot about the principles that animated the law in early Iowa. On display one can see the impatience of the judges with the possibility of unsettled titles. One can also see some distrust, even perhaps contempt,[30] for the informality of Indian ways. Finally, the interpolation of legislation, treaties and decisional law shows the shift away from, or fluidity in applying, a strict common law system as one would expect in a new jurisdiction.

Not surprisingly, *Webster* v. *Reid* was one of a number of cases involving the 'half-breed' track including *Wright* v. *Marsh, Lee & Delavan*, decided in

29 Id. at 634.

30 There are not a lot of other cases directly or indirectly involving native peoples that are reported, perhaps suggesting that Indians were handled extra-judicially. In one territorial case appealed to the territorial Supreme Court, the court held that, in the case of a possible murder charge against one Wau-kon-chaw-neek-kaw, it was not actionable to fail to exclude a grand juror who had heard, and tended to believe a report that a group of Indians had killed the victim. *Wau-kon-chaw-neek-kaw* v. *The United States*, 1 Iowa 437 (Morris, 1844).

1849 and upholding in similar terms the claim of one of several individuals whose title originated in partition proceeding pursuant to the 1832 Act at the expense of an undisputed occupier of land.[31] As in *Webster*, the then state Supreme Court swept aside without any careful requirement of a showing of full statutory compliance an objection to the sufficiency of notice of the then territorial court's partition proceeding based on publication in the *Territorial Gazette* in Iowa City (the then capital).[32] In yet another half-breed tract case and also another action in the right, the state Supreme Court in *Hypfner* v. *Walsh* refused to require an instruction in a partition proceeding as to the legal effect of the situs of land, displaying further impatience with the possible destabilizing effects of legal proceedings dealing with this land.[33]

In none of these half-breed track cases had the court confronted and resolved directly a core issue – why was the half-breed track not deemed to remain a species of 'Indian' property subject to tribal jurisdiction? It is possible that Congress's surrender of its reversionary interest in 1834 could have been viewed as a cession of fee simple title to a group of 'half-breeds.' The answer to this question can be found in a district court decision appended (quite prominently) to the rear of the published report that includes *Wright* v. *Marsh, Lee & Delavan*. In *Telford* v. *Barney* a Judge Olney, also sitting in Lee County, considered a title question arising from land situated in the half-breed track.[34] The *Telford* report is actually a set of papers put together by a 'member of the bar' with obviously a keen eye to posterity.

Telford, like the other Lee cases, involved an original title in a half-breed whose successors', including Barney's, interest(s) were wiped out in what appears to have been an omnibus partition proceeding undertaken in 1841 in Lee County.[35] Telford's title derived, not surprisingly, through Marsh, Lee & Delavan who appear to have been land speculators or consolidators.[36] Barney argued that the Lee County court had no jurisdiction to enter a partition order because the land in the tract was 'Indian' land.

> The argument is that, by the treaty [of 1824 not amended in this regard directly by the treaty of 1834], the half-breeds had the right of possession and governmental jurisdiction, and the act of release added the fee and the right of alienation; that there is no evidence that they had aliened when this partition was made; and that, had they done so, any or all of them, jurisdiction remained though title departed from them, and therefore, without regard to title, the land was Indian land.[37]

The court, if the lawyer's notes are accurate, responded heatedly, bluntly, and to our ears offensively:

31 2 Iowa 94 (1849). This was also an action in the right. Id. at 95.
32 Id. at 98 and 108–09.   33 3 Iowa 509 (1852).   34 2 Iowa 575 (1848).
35 Id. at 576.   36 Id. at 577.   37 Id. at 578.

This tract was within the territory of Iowa, and unless jurisdiction of it actually belonged to some other existing political community, it belonged to Iowa. The right to govern it was not in the Sacs and Foxes. They had parted with that right by the treaty of cession. By that treaty they ceded all their lands in Missouri [meaning Iowa], embraced in specified limits. If it be said this land was not in Missouri, the answer is, the metes and bounds included it, and these must prevail. It was not *reserved* for the use of the half-breeds, but *granted* for their use. The Indians say to the United States, we give you so much land – this for you, that for the half-breeds. They parted with all their rights – possessory title and political jurisdiction. The right to occupy went to the half-breeds. The right to govern went somewhere, either to them or to the United States. It could not go to the half-breeds unless they were, or should become a political community. That they *might*, by assuming that character, have clothed themselves with jurisdiction of their territory is not material, unless they really assumed that character. It is not material what answer the treaty alone would give to the question of jurisdiction, for it does not stand alone. Ten years after, when the Indians had ceded their contiguous lands, and with them had migrated many of the half-breeds, leaving a few females who had married white men, and a few drunken vagrants to annoy the whites, who were beginning to occupy the tract as well as the ceded land, and when no semblance of a half-breed community existed, or could be constructed of remaining materials, Congress, in view of these circumstances, released to them the fee in reversion and the right of pre-emption, severed their joint tenancy, invested them individually, their heirs and assigns, as tenants in common, with the allodial fee simple, and prescribed the rules of alienation and descent, instead of leaving that matter to their own municipal regulations. ... The act treats the half-breeds, not as a people competent to govern, but as natural persons, subject to our national government. They needed laws and congress gave them laws, expecting the land, by operation of these laws, to find its way into the common mass of real estates, thus discountenancing every idea of Indian jurisdiction. When this partition was made there was not, and at no time since the treaty had been, an existing tribe to govern the tract; the materials for constructing such a tribe were hopelessly scattered and lost; congress, in who was the sovereign power, had declared them mere individuals, requiring other law-givers than themselves; the land had lost its distinguishing marks, and Wisconsin and Iowa successively had exercised over it legislation, adjudication, and administration, without question or doubt of right; it was occupied by whites, who had mostly possessed themselves of the titles in common tenancy, and had spotted it over with farms and villages, and had done and suffered such innumerable acts of civil and criminal jurisdiction as if now held void, would bring upon a community of thousands, chaos of rights and ruinous calamities.[38]

The court's brutal logic while unattractive in its racialist aspect is probably correct. The half-breeds were no tribe. There was no argument for reserved tribal sovereignty in the tract except for the Sac and Fox and they surrendered it. The half-breeds never organized and probably could not have organized without some kind of overarching cultural umbrella. Thus, they and their successors lost their lands largely through a partition and a series of judicial sales mediated in the Lee County court.

PRAIRIE FIRE LIABILITY

One of the characteristics of tall grass prairie, whether in Illinois, Minnesota, or Iowa, is that periodic burnings of the prairie are an important element in the maintenance and renewal of the deep-rooted grass ecosystem. It is not clear historically whether the periodic burnings commenced wholly naturally with lightning as their cause or whether they started with the arrival of humans and their campfires. But by the time the European settlers arrived periodic burning was occurring and they adopted it to clear fields and replenish the soil.

Thus, it is not surprising that in 1846 Iowa would pass a law as follows:

> That if any person or persons shall set on fire, or cause to be set on fire, any woods, prairies or other grounds whatever, other than his own, or shall permit the fire set out by him to pass from his own prairie or woods to the injury of any person or persons, every person so offending shall, on conviction thereof, for every such offense be fined in any sum not exceeding $50, and shall be liable to an action to the party injured for all damages which he, she or they may have sustained in consequence of such fire.[39]

In the 1850 case of *De France* v. *Spencer*, Spencer appealed a determination of liability by a district court in a situation in which he admitted setting a prairie fire but argued that no liability should attach because he 'had used proper caution and diligence in preventing [the fire from so spreading]'.[40] Spencer argued that this would be the norm at common law and that one should not read into the statute an intention to abrogate the common law. The court agreed provided that the fire was lit under 'prudential circumstances' and not if the abutting property was very near or there were 'high winds'.[41]

---

38 Id. at 579–80.   39 Iowa Laws of 1846, p. 3, § 1.   40 2 Iowa 462 (1850).   41 Id. at 463.

SUBVENTION OF RAILROADS

It is widely believed that in the early years of statehood Iowa, and in particular its courts, connived in an effort to encourage the building of railroads to
encourage the rapid development of the state. An 1853 case, *Dubuque County
v. Dubuque and Pacific Railroad Co.*,[42] provides considerable support for this
belief. Dubuque County held a referendum and approved providing a
$200,000 credit facility to the Dubuque and Pacific Railroad. A local prose-
cutor challenged this on several grounds. First, he argued that a county could
not subvent a railroad or any private corporation, rather only the State of
Iowa could do so. Second, he argued that this credit facility violated the
overall state constitutional limitation of $100,000 on state debt. Third, he
claimed there were a series of procedural flaws in the vote.

The Supreme Court upheld the county's approval of the credit facility for
the private railroad purpose over a particularly sharp and informed dissent
by a Justice Kinney. The majority held that because the state constitution did
not prohibit a county from doing this, it was permitted to do so.[43] This is, of
course, contrary to more recent American legal notions in which localities,
including counties, are seen wholly as subservient creatures of the state in
which they are situated and not permitted to do anything not explicitly
permitted under what are called 'home rule' statutes. Admittedly such
notions were less developed at the time of the *Dubuque and Pacific Railroad*
case but the result is still surprising. Interestingly, Justice Kinney pointed out
that the state enabling statute which permitted a county judge to certify a
ballot question had been changed in the process of adoption with the italicized
words at the end of the following quotation deleted: 'The county judge may
submit to the people of his county at any regular election ... the question –
whether money may be borrowed to aid the erection of public buildings –
whether the county will construct or aid to construct any road or bridge
which may call for an extraordinary expenditure – *whether the county will
subscribe to any work of internal improvement*.'[44] Kinney notes with some force
that this deletion suggests that counties were not intended to be involved in
making decisions about funding internal improvements for private benefit.

The Supreme Court also held that such subsidization was explicitly permitted by the language of the statute quoted near the end of the preceding
paragraph by holding that a 'railroad' constituted a 'road' within the meaning
of the statute.[45] Justice Kinney argued forcefully that the statutory language
should be construed according to its plain meaning (and therefore narrowly)
because the power to tax is a deprivation of freedom and should always be
narrowly construed.[46] It is certainly linguistically startling that the Supreme

42 4 Iowa 1 (1853).   43 Id. at 2.   44 Id. at 13.
45 Id. at 4.   46 Id. at 10–11.

Court would construe 'road' to include a railroad but then also construe the prairie fire statute not to replace the common law when its fairly clear language appeared to do so.

Finally, Justice Kinney in dissent argued that the act of Dubuque County should be considered to be void because the state constitution at § 2, art. 8 provided that: 'the state shall not directly or indirectly become a shareholder in any corporation.'[47] Justice Kinney concluded that it must also follow that a county could also not hold any such share and that the grant of the credit facility to the railroad constituted the acquisition of a prohibited shareholding. The Supreme Court majority rejected this:

> Under such logic, individuality is blended into mad confusion. A county is magnified into a state, and no distinction recognized. If those state restrictions are applicable to counties, they must be equally applicable to the cities, and citizens of the state. It may, with equal propriety, be said that the citizens of Iowa cannot in the aggregate contract debts exceeding one hundred thousand dollars, and that no citizen can become a stockholder in any corporation. There is quite as much identity and affinity between a citizen and the state, as there is between a county and the state.[48]

It is hard to take this argument seriously, but it constituted the last word and produced a favourable resolution to a controversy for the county and the Dubuque and Pacific Railroad.

SCOPE OF THE HOMESTEAD EXEMPTION

It is fair to assume that the courts of a territory or new state will be presented with a number of questions as to the scope of the rights of debtors and creditors and that in the mid-nineteenth century creditors generally prevailed. Iowa was no exception. In *Charles & Blow* v. *Lamberson*[49] the Supreme Court had to construe the applicability of a series of passed, revised, and repealed homestead laws that protected a debtor's home and usually some limited amount (the limitation being specified in dollars) of appurtenant land. Specifically, the plaintiff (and appellant) in this case had previously sued on a contract debt and recovered. In this action, in the right, involving land in the city of Keokuk the creditor sought to enforce his title procured by an execution sale purchase of the premises based on the prior contract debt judgment. The defendant argued that the premises constituted his homestead.

The facts were complicated by Iowa's recent passage of a 'new' homestead act in 1849 which governed and which required that a claimant had to own

47 Id. at 12.   48 Id. at 3.   49 1 Iowa 435 (Coles, 1855).

and 'occupy' his homestead to perfect a claim of an exemption. In the case of the instant, occupying defendant he owned it and he claimed he had a contractor working on it but he did not, in fact, live there before, alas, Iowa repealed the old Homestead Act (saving protected status only for owner/ occupiers in the text of a replacement code). The Supreme Court held that homestead exemption act language should be construed narrowly: 'And here it is proper to remark, that the property was previously liable to execution, unless exempted by positive enactment. By this we mean that without some special statute making the exemption, all of the property of the debtor becomes subject to levy.'[50] The court then delivered the *coup de grâce* by holding that having a contractor working to prepare a dwelling for occupation did not constitute occupation within the meaning the Homestead Act of 1849.

EARLY MEDICAL MALPRACTICE

In our epoch of vigorous debate about malpractice and possible limits on liability in light of rapidly evolving technology, it is hard to comprehend earlier phases in the development of the notion that health professionals can be liable, but in *Bowman* v. *Woods*[51] the court heard a claim of malpractice against a doctor of 'botanic' medicine. It is not hard to imagine that there were in early Iowa a number of unorthodox medical practitioners traversing the new communities, the isolated farms, and the Western-bound settlers selling, as yet, unproven nostrums; Bowman was one. Woods was pregnant and sought him out to handle her delivery. He did so with disastrous results.

In her action for malpractice, Woods produced a Dr Coffin who was a 'traditional' physician who testified that 'Dr' Bowman had not followed standard and 'traditional' medical practice with respect to the delivery.[52] In his defence 'Dr' Bowman attempted to introduce testimony about what was standard 'botanic' medical practice and the trial court rejected this testimony.[53]

The Supreme Court ruled that this was error.

> As yet there is no particular system of medicine established or favored by the laws of Iowa. And as no system is upheld, none is prohibited. The regular, the botanic, the homeopathic, the hydropathic, and other modes of treating diseases are alike unprohibited; and each receives more or less favor and patronage from the people. Though the regular system has been advancing as a science for centuries, aided by research and experience, by wisdom and skill, still the law regards it with no partiality or distinguishing favor, nor is it recognized as the exclusive standard or test by which the other systems are to be adjudged. The

50 Id. at 441.   51 1 Iowa 441 (Greene, 1848).   52 Id. at 442.   53 Id.

evidence of the experienced practitioner of either system is equally admissible in giving opinions upon questions of medical skill.[54]

The court ordered the testimony admitted.

Bowman is to a modern eye perhaps even advanced in its thinking but surely its tolerant approach to medical treatment reflects the heterogeneity of the populations mixing and travelling through Iowa. And, of course, it reflects the relatively undeveloped state legal and administrative approach to medical practice.

A NOTE PAYABLE IN CORN

Iowa, Ohio, and Illinois turned out to be immensely rich farming areas for corn and later soybeans. Corn is an asset or collateral whether in a silo, in a barn, or in the fields before harvest. Corn is also a method of payment and in a less cash and currency oriented social order an important method of payment. Thus, it is not surprising to find in *Phillips* v. *Cooley*[55] a note payable in and stated as representing 200 bushels of corn. Cooley did not turn over the corn promised or owed on the due date and defended an action of assumpsit on the ground that the obligee had made no demand and also that the note specified no place for delivery. The district court had found for Cooley but the Iowa Supreme Court, relying in part on its precedent in non-corn, non-currency note cases (one involving leather) held that no demand was required and that: 'Independent of the statute, it is a well settled rule, that where no place is appointed for the delivery of specific articles, the debtor must, before the day of payment, ascertain from the creditor, if practicable, where he will receive the goods.'[56]

SLAVERY AND BLACKS[57]

Anyone familiar with the territories west of the Mississippi will know that slavery and the disablement[58] of Blacks, or at least legal uncertainty, as to political citizenship and social equality was familiar in every territory, even those north of the Missouri Compromise line, e.g., 36° 30' north latitude. Thus, it is not surprising to find that one of the first cases reported during the territorial period was a habeas corpus action by one Ralph seeking to halt his return to slavery in Missouri.

54 Id.   55 2 Iowa 456 (1850).   56 Id. at 457.   57 1 Iowa 1 (Morris, 1839).
58 The sad history first of the exclusion of Black children from public schools and then their partial accommodation in separate schools is recounted in *Clark* v. *The Board of Directors*, 24 Iowa 266 (1868), in which the state Supreme Court finally required that all public schools admit Black children on an equal footing with Caucasians.

Ralph had come to be in Iowa territory pursuant to an agreement in 1834 with his master. He and his master had agreed that Ralph would come into Iowa to work in the mines near Dubuque and would use his earnings to pay his master $500 with interest. They further agreed that, in the eventuality that Ralph defaulted on his obligation to make this payment, then Ralph would return to his owner and to slavery.[59] Ralph defaulted on payment and his former owner had him seized and Ralph sought and obtained a writ of habeas corpus from a local district court judge. The case was removed to the Supreme Court of the Territory and the Supreme Court in its opinion noted that it was 'not strictly regular for us to entertain jurisdiction of it at all ...' but the justices concluded that as 'it involves an important question, which may ere long, if unsettled, become an exciting one, and as it is by the mutual assent and request of all the parties' they moved forward to decide the case.[60]

Ralph's arguments were comparatively simple. Either he was freed by an organic statute to that effect of the Wisconsin Territory *or* by the federal statute know as the Missouri Compromise of 1820.[61] The Supreme Court decided the case based on the Missouri Compromise. The slave owner claimed that the Missouri Compromise which established that Iowa was to be a free territory could not, without enabling legislation (none had been passed), mandate non-slavery in Iowa and also that Ralph's slavehood had to be preserved during his work to pay the indebtedness or the Compromise violated the Fugitive Slave Clause of the original U. S. Constitution. The court rejected both of these arguments and held that Ralph had been freed when he came to Iowa permanently to work, citing as authority the great English decision of Lord Mansfield in *Sommersett's Case* (1772). The court held that the language of the Missouri Compromise was 'an entire and final prohibition, not looking to future legislative action to render it effectual'.[62] The court also held that Ralph's failure to pay did not make him a fugitive:

> How the failure to comply with this understanding could render a removal, undertaken with the master's consent, an escape, we are unable to comprehend ... The petitioner is under the same obligation to fulfill this engagement as though, instead of its being the price of his freedom, the debt has been incurred for the purchase of any other species of property. It is a debt which he ought to pay, but for the non-payment of which no man in this territory can be reduced to slavery.[63]

Thus, Ralph was determined to be a free debtor.

59 1 Iowa at 2.   60 Id. at 6.   61 Id. at 2–3.
62 Id. at 8.   63 Id. at 7–8.

ADJUDICATING/GOVERNING

In a feverishly developing, rapidly growing and large (in acreage) area like Iowa it would not be surprising to find confusion in roles between adjudicators and other more clearly administrative public officials. For instance, in the *Dubuque and Pacific Railroad* case, discussed above, the county court crafted and certified the ballot questions pursuant to which the $200,000 credit facility was approved by the voters of Dubuque County.

The territorial Supreme Court entered and then withdrew, in favour of lower or district court jurisdiction, a complex case raising issues of proper roles, *United States, ex rel Davenport v. The Commissioners of Dubuque County*[64]. Previously, the Wisconsin legislature (then having jurisdiction over Iowa) had authorized a popular referendum on the question of whether Rockingham or Davenport should be the capitol of Scott County.[65] (Early American history is dotted with fairly rough fights over which city or town would have territorial or county capitol status.) The Wisconsin statute seemed to give either to the county commissioners *or* the sheriff of Dubuque County the power to judge the results. The election was held, eighteen ballots were challenged and tossed out by the Dubuque Commissioners and this led to the selection of Davenport (Rockingham would otherwise have won.) An 'alternative mandamus' was sought to order this action of the commissioners changed or reconsidered and later a peremptory mandamus.[66]

In an erudite opinion, the territorial Supreme Court reviewed the Wisconsin statute, the various common law administrative writs, and the facts of the case. It concluded that neither the Dubuque commissioners nor the Dubuque sheriff had any power or right to judge the validity of the electors.[67] Further, it noted that there are a number of administrative actions of local officials that are not reviewable at all by mandamus or any of the other extraordinary writs, like a decision to refuse to meet or to make or not make any particular decision when a matter is committed to a public official's or body's discretion.[68] On the other hand, some failures are actionable if there is or would be a 'failure of justice'. The court concluded that mandamus was the only available remedy in the case and was 'necessary'.[69] But it further concluded that it had no jurisdiction as this was a matter for the court of general jurisdiction, the district court, to consider.[70]

On an initial reading there does not seem much that is remarkable in the Scott County capitol case. Perhaps the Supreme Court is more erudite and careful about the precise role of the extraordinary common law writs than one might have expected. Chief Justice Mason labours carefully to appear to be consistent with *Marbury v. Madison's* holding on the scope of mandamus

64 1 Iowa 42 (Morris, 1840).   65 Id. at 44.   66 Id at 45.
67 Id. at 45–46.   68 Id at 47–48.   69 Id. at 51.
70 Id. at 52.

in an appellate proceeding.[71] Two perhaps contradictory themes seem to inform the opinion. The first, unspoken, is that the justices should not generally intervene in politics, even failed politics. Second, and here the careful words of Mason are the best summary:

> The general purpose of this writ is to prevent disorder from a failure of justice or defect of police, rather than to afford a private remedy. In this case the public have an interest in the establishment of the county seat of Scott county, and that interest cannot be adequately secured in any other manner. The entry in the proceedings of the board of commissioners of Dubuque county, was to be the only record of the fact of either town being the seat of justice. Not to have that entry made, therefore, would be a 'failure of justice,' and might occasion a great 'defect of police,' from which disorder might very probably arise. The aid of this writ was, therefore, very properly invoked.[72]

Thus, judicial intervention is countenanced based on the likelihood of violence and unrest, not a wild phantasm in Iowa in 1840 but an ever-present possibility.

OCCUPIERS

No issue is probably more politically explosive than how to treat public domain occupiers in a settling territory or state, like Iowa from 1838 to 1860. A huge flood of people looking for land arrived and a number sought to settle. Some occupiers were already present in 1838, particularly in the half-breed tract, and of course there were native claims that were gradually thinned and in most cases eliminated. Adjudicating between occupiers and titled claimants meant, as noted in the half-breed track cases discussed above, picking between farmers in occupation and 'speculators' who frequently had acquired title by means of a judicial sale or some other legal process, usually one in which the sufficiency of notice to the occupiers was, to be generous, sketchy.

Hill v. *Smith*[73] is a startling opinion that dramatically touches on the esteem with which occupiers were held in early Iowa. Hill apparently sold the improvements on land to which one presumes he had no good title to Smith et al. Smith gave to Hill a note and then refused to pay, saying the underlying contract was illegal. Smith argued that it was illegal because Hill was an occupier or squatter. Specifically, he pointed to a federal statute of 1807 applicable to Iowa due to its status as part of the territory of Wisconsin at that time.[74] This statute prohibited the sale of improvements made on public land domain.

71 Id. at 48–49.   72 Id. at 48.   73 1 Iowa 95 (Morris, 1840).
74 Id. at 99–101.

The territorial Supreme Court held that the underlying contract was not void. First, it found that the federal act of 1807 and the sum of other federal enactments concerning unauthorized settlement of the public domain made such settlement a subject that could give rise to one or more penalties but such settlements were not wholly illegal.[75] ('This seems to correspond with the views of the great English commentator in relation to actions that are merely *mala prohibita*.')[76] Second, it went beyond this to find startlingly, I think, that the federal act of 1807 was of no force and effect in Iowa because it was disused or ignored. 'Fortified by this authority, we pronounce it contrary to the spirit of that Anglo-Saxon liberty which we inherit, to revive, without notice, an obsolete statute, one on relation to which long disuse and a contrary policy had induced a reasonable belief that it was no longer in force. If custom can make laws, it can, when long acquiesced in, recognized and countenanced by the sovereign power, also repeal them.'[77]

In a set of reports filled with cases applying with awkwardness the ancient and even superseded common law forms of actions such as actions in the right, trespass quare clausum fregit, etc. etc., it is worth pondering why the territorial Supreme Court finds this important case involving occupiers' rights to sell their improvements the only case of statutory 'desuetude'. Luckily, the court provided clear answers. First, it unabashedly states that occupiers on the federal public domain were doing good things. They were:

> doing acts which they had every reason to believe would be deemed patriotic and praiseworthy; for leading the way in the introduction of wealth, and civilization, and happiness, into the almost illimitable west; for sacrificing the comforts and endearments of home, and enduring the hardships and privations, and encountering the diseases of a new and untried country; for building up great communities in the wilderness, enlarging our bounds of empire, and vastly augmenting the current of our national revenue.[78]

Second, they hint that such settlements were at least connived in and at best encouraged by the government since 'encouragement to western immigration had become a part of our settled national policy'.[79] Finally, the court states that to apply the act of 1807 would be tantamount to copying an unfortunate example from English history:

> History furnishes us with a parallel example, and one which it may be profitable to contemplate for a moment. Henry the VII, of England, in order to replenish his treasury, had recourse to a measure which (in

75 Id. at 102.   76 Id.   77 Id. at 107.
78 Id. at 106.   79 Id.

order that the plaintiff in error should succeed) must be legitimate here. Availing himself of the services of two judges – the supple instruments of his tyranny – he caused a general system of prosecutions to be instituted upon penal statutes which had never been repealed, but which, by long disuse, had become forgotten and wholly disregarded. Empson & Dudley, when afterwards brought to trial for their share in these transactions, pleaded 'that it belonged not to them who were instruments in the hands of supreme power to determine what laws were recent or obsolete, expedient or hurtful, since they were all alike valid so long as they remained unrepealed by the legislature'. But this plea neither availed them with their judges nor with posterity.[80]

With this flourish the territorial Supreme Court upheld the validity of the note even though it related to the sale of improvements made on occupied land in the public domain in Iowa. The court ended by slyly admitting that its decision would be quite popular politically, but conceded:

It is true, that public opinion would frequently be a very unsafe guide for a judicial decision. The fluctuating feelings of the multitude frequently operated upon by momentary excitement, by prejudice or by caprice, would very improperly be adopted as the standard of truth or sound reason. But where the same opinions are concurred in for centuries, and after passion and prejudice have wholly subsided, such opinions are always founded in truth and justice, and can more safely be followed than those of the most learned and able judges.[81]

The outcome is ultimately not startling but the criticism of Henry VII is interesting and contrasts with the generally favourable citations to Blackstone, Chitty, and Littleton as well as reported English cases in early Iowa cases. In at least one case an antagonism is displayed to a perceived English reverence for 'technicality.' In *Harriman* v. *State*[82] the new state Supreme Court considered a number of objections to the legal propriety of grand jury proceedings. The court swept a number of them aside:

But we have long since dispensed with many of the stringent rules and nice technicalities which the courts of [England] in mercy established, to shield and protect the prisoner against the harsh and sanguinary penalties of their criminal code for light and often trivial offences. Under the extreme severity of laws, which appear to have been enacted [in England] without the slightest regard to human life, and under regulations which did not secure counsel to the prisoner, and seldom a

---

80 Id. at 106–07.   81 Id. at 107.   82 2 Iowa 270 (1849).

prompt, fair, and impartial trial, no wonder that merciful judges, under the promptings of humanity, and being regarded especially as protectors, and counsel for the accused, should seize at trifling and unimportant objections to save the lives of those who may have been arrested for ordinary and often doubtful offences. But in this country, where life and liberty are so tenaciously guarded by our constitutions and laws, where a speedy, public, and impartial trial is uniformly secured to the accused, where, though destitute of friends or means, he is furnished with able counsel at public expense ... the reason for such extreme technicality and unmeaning precision ceases to exist.[83]

There may be a theme here which relates to a number of the cases discussed earlier. In the rough and tumble of life in Iowa the judges seem to have had regular recourse to the threats and exigencies of their situation to resolve doubts in favour of order or orderliness at the expense of technical perfection. This would then also explain resistance to English precedent that exalted precision at the expense of more immediate considerations.

CONCLUSION

Iowa certainly is an illustrative adventure in the adoption of the common law in a new and unique environment. Settlement occurred very quickly; races and peoples mixed and were separated; people traversed, paused, sometimes stayed but more often moved on.

What does the adventure demonstrate? Well, first, I think, to speak generally, these cases show that the line between adjudication, the courts, and being a sheriff, or local official, was not a particularly clear or significant one. In situations of some choice, the courts seem to decide cases not based on abstract and enduring concepts of justice but rather on what might pacify or stabilize a very unstable social situation. Second, the cases show a general adherence to the formats of the common law system as to forms of action but, as is typical in American jurisdictions perhaps, greater liberality in construing or disregarding legislative action in a confusing legal order in which old Wisconsin and federal pre-statehood legislation continued to apply rather awkwardly, to use that term again, to very different situations. Third, the cases show, I think, antagonism to native peoples. It is, of course, clear that they were viewed as inferiors but it is also clear that the two very different cultures, systems of land use, systems of ownership and social organization could not mesh (and both survive) in a desegregated society. These tribes traversed 'their' territories, had no precise sense of even sub-tribal

83 Id. at 279.

ownership, and did not heavily cultivate land. Thus, they were pushed out brutally and, in significant part, this was accomplished in the cut and thrust of litigation in the Iowa territory and early state courts. Fourth, one sees hints that the very heavy agricultural focus of Iowa would eventually affect things like prairie fire liability and consumer and debtor affairs generally in a gentler, more pro-farmer way than in the eastern states. Biology may not be destiny but horticulture in Iowa's case clearly shaped the state's legal destiny. Finally, one sees the classic rugged individualism of the frontier and of mid-nineteenth century America; if you go to a botanic doctor do not try to sue based on the botanic doctor's failure to act like a regular physician.

As a postscript, it might be worth taking this project, when completed, one step further in the sense of pursuing the scope of this adventure, for when Oregon was organized as a state it adopted lock, stock and barrel the laws of Iowa, and it would be interesting to see how the legal mutations of the prairie state, flooded quickly with white settlers pushing out disorganized native peoples, further mutated in the Northwest under very different sociological and geographic conditions.

The firm as an entity before the Companies Acts

JOSHUA GETZLER AND MIKE MACNAIR*

ENTITIES AND CORPORATE FORM

THE CORPORATE FORM OF business organisation is a fundamental feature of modern life and modern law. In pre-modern legal systems there were corporations such as guilds and boroughs that collectively regulated individual and partnership businesses, and which might undertake or have imposed on them service obligations to the state. Such corporations are certainly economic actors, but this is a very different phenomenon from the modern business corporation. The process by which this form came into existence is therefore inevitably a major historical question. It bears on economic theories of the firm and on the law-and-economics analysis of the business corporation; on theories of the relationships of law, economy and society, and most potently of law and the historical development of capitalism in Britain and north-western Europe; and in turn the problem relates to 'development strategies' for the less developed countries and to 'transition strategies' for the post-communist countries.

The standard narrative, which can be found in a summary form in the company law textbooks, is one of a gradual development, first of forms of partnership trading, then of joint stock companies. Joint stock ventures incorporated by royal charter temporarily become common in the later seventeenth and early eighteenth century, but the development is 'set back' by the Bubble Act 1720 and the crash of that year. Incorporation by private statute remains episodically used and becomes commonplace with the growth of railway companies in the early nineteenth century. Then parliament adopts general incorporation by registration in 1844 for regulatory reasons,[1]

---

* The authors are grateful to James Oldham for his contributions to the initial primary researches, and also wish to thank audiences at the British Legal History Conference at Dublin, the American Society of Legal History conference in Washington D.C., and the Tel Aviv Law Faculty Workshop in Legal History.

1 E.g. in order to improve the accountability of the executive officers of enterprises: see A. Bisset, *A practical treatise on the law of partnership* (London, 1847), pp. 194 ff., 217 ff., 248ff.; J. Grant, *A practical treatise on the law of corporations* (London, 1850), pp. 274–309.

and in 1855 accepts limited liability; the 1862 consolidation is the 'first modern Companies Act'.[2]

This narrative involves three underlying assumptions. The first is that it is an inherent feature of law that recognition of a company (or other association) as an entity separate from its human participants is something which lies in the gift of the state. The road not in fact travelled, of the development of forms of corporate personality and limited liability through judicial analysis of contractual and proprietary relations, is treated as blocked by something more than historical contingency. The second is that the explanation of the rise of the corporate form is teleological. The modern corporate business form is assumed to triumph because it is more rational than alternative modes of business organisation, because it maximises utility. The dominant 'nexus of contracts' theory of the corporation in American law-and-economics is a variation on this theme, seeing the corporation as legislatively provided default law.[3] This is still true where, as in Marxisant variants on the story,[4] it is assumed to be more rational for capital rather than for society as a whole. The history then becomes a history of overcoming obstacles to the true view. The third assumption is that economic change determines legal change.

In tracing the rise of the corporation and the corporate economy, artificial legal personality has been deemed essential on many counts, for example through facilitating the bundling of individual investors' assets into a larger corpus of capital bundle; creating an entity with a clear capacity to own, trade, sue and be sued; perpetual succession; management structure with internal and external controls over managers through voting and fiduciary law; and the rise of tradeable shares and limited liability. The rise of large-scale enterprises which require more capital than can be raised by personal networks drives the formation of capital markets, and these in turn drive demand for incorporation.

These historical assumptions combine to suggest that corporate development involving separate legal personality follows a kind of natural law of commercial development, and that free experimentation in economic organization under

2 J.H. Farrar and B. Hannigan, with N.E. Furey and P. Wylie, *Farrar's Company law* (London, 1998), p. 21. The orthodox historiographical positions are set out in B.C. Hunt, *The development of the business corporation in England, 1800–1867* (Cambridge, Massachusetts, 1936) and A.B. Du Bois, *The English business company after the Bubble Act, 1720–1800* (London, 1938), and elegantly summarized in P.L. Davies (ed.), *Gower's Principles of modern company law* (6th ed., London, 1997), pp. 18–48. The new 7th edition of *Gower* (London, 2003) simply omits all historical material, leaving something of a lacuna in the consciousness of legal education and practice.

3 For a recent survey see B.R. Cheffins, 'Corporations', in P. Cane and M. Tushnet (eds.), *The Oxford handbook of legal studies* (Oxford, 2003), pp. 485 ff.

4 See for example P. Ireland, 'Capitalism without the capitalist' (1111) 17 *Journal of Legal History*, 41; M.J. Horwitz, *The transformation of American law, 1870–1960: the crisis of legal orthodoxy* (New York and Oxford, 1992), pp. 65–107.

a benign facilitative state will yield corporate form if all goes well. But recent scholarship has painted a picture of stuttering executive, judicial and above all legislative attempts to create joint stock institutions with workable liability regimes, suggesting a variety of interest-group reasons why free incorporation took time to take off and reconstruct capitalism on a corporate footing.[5]

In this paper we would like to suggest a counter-narrative. Our general thesis is that without the benefit of formalized organizational law the courts (with some help from legislative enactments) were able to construct a veil between investors and traders affording much of the benefit of the limited liability policy of later law. It was the Court of Chancery that led the way here, through fraud-based doctrines for reversing or presuming conveyances in order to protect creditors, and as an outgrowth of this body of doctrine, its regime for partnership insolvency. In other words, the basic concepts of contract, property and debt priorities could result in a workable organizational law – without formal corporate entities created by the state. One hundred years ago Maitland made the surmise that non-corporate associational forms such as trusts and other unincorporated associations under the aegis of Chancery had achieved mighty deeds as vehicles of commerce before the rise of general incorporation.[6] The idea that private law can order commercial associations without State-granted incorporation is also implicit in Max Weber's work on the debt structures of the medieval trading associations of

5 M. Lobban, 'Corporate identity and limited liability in France and England 1825–67' (1996) 25 *Anglo-American Law Review* 397; P. Mahoney, 'Preparing the corporate lawyer: contract or concession? an essay on the history of corporate law' (2000) 34 *Georgia Law Review* 873; H. Hansmann and R. Kraakman, 'The essential role of organizational law' (2000) 110 *Yale Law Journal* 387; R. Harris, *Industrializing English law: entrepreneurship and business organization, 1720–1844* (Cambridge, 2000).

6 F.W. Maitland, 'Introduction' to O. Gierke, *Political theories of the middle ages* (Cambridge, 1900), pp. v–xlv; F.W. Maitland, 'The corporation sole' (1900), 'The Crown as corporation' (1901), 'The unincorporate body' (*c.*1903), 'Moral personality and legal personality' (1903), 'Trust and corporation' (*c.*1904), all in H.A.L. Fisher (ed.), *Collected papers of Frederic William Maitland* (3 vols., Cambridge, 1910), iii, pp. 210, 244, 271, 304, 321, and in H.D. Hazeltine, G. Lapsley and P.H. Winfield (eds.), *Selected essays* (Cambridge, 1936), pp. 73–256; F. Pollock and F.W. Maitland, *The history of English law before the time of Edward I*, 2 vols. (2nd ed., Cambridge, 1898, reprinted), i, 486–97. Maitland's Anglicized version of the 'realist' Gierkean corporate theory has fascinated legal and political scholars, starting with Max Weber himself: *Wirtschaft und Gesellschaft / Economy and society: an outline of interpretive sociology* (Tübingen, 1921–22); G. Roth and C. Wittich (eds.), *Economy and society: an outline of interpretive sociology*, 2 vols. (New York, 1968, Berkeley, 1978), ii, 705–29. For more recent contributions see S.J. Stoljar, 'The corporate ideas of Frederick William Maitland', in L.C. Webb (ed.), *Legal personality and political pluralism* (Melbourne, 1958), pp. 20–44; L.C. Webb, 'Corporate personality and political pluralism', ibid., pp. 45–65; S.J. Stoljar, *Groups and entities: an inquiry into corporate theory* (Canberra, 1973); D. Runciman, *Pluralism and the personality of the state* (Cambridge, 1997), pp. 89–123; A. Macfarlane, *The making of the modern world: visions from the West and East* (Basingstoke, 2002), pp. 83–107.

continental southern Europe.[7] It would follow that the statutory interventions of the 1840s and 1850s fall to be explained on some ground other than the need for workable organisational law.

PRIORITIES IN LAW AND EQUITY

From Elizabethan times, the Court of Chancery in partnership with Parliament had evolved techniques for ordering priorities in debt based on three linked concepts: equitable notions of fraud; reliance by one party on the conduct of another; and assumption and apportionment of risk by agreement. One can fold each of these concepts into the others: it is a fraud to cheat someone of their reliance; parties who order their affairs on an agreed or tacit division of risk should be allowed to rely upon the agreement and not be permitted to resile; and so on. All of this may be summarized as a doctrine of priority based on inter-personal transacting. Economic historians have shown how structures of credit networks operated in early modern England, whereby parties relied on each other for myriad forms of linked inter-personal credit in order to generate spending and investment power, in an era of scarce specie and undeveloped financial markets.[8] The reliance on personal reputation and personal connection to maintain credit helps explain the epidemic of defamation actions in this period, as it could be crucial for persons to maintain general reputation lest their commercial or consumer credit be destroyed: here honour and lucre coalesced.[9] We can describe the shift into

7　M. Weber, *The history of commercial partnerships in the middle ages* (ed. and trans. by L. Kaelber and C. Lemert, Lanham, Maryland, 2003), originally published as *Zur Geschichte der Handelsgesellschaften im Mittelalter: nach südeuropäischen Quellen* (P. Schippers, Amsterdam, 1964); see also M. Weber, *Economy and society*, i, 339–56, ii, 666–731; M. Weber, *General economic history* (ed. and trans. by F.H. Knight, London, 1923), pp. 202–35.

8　C. Muldrew, *The economy of obligation: the culture of credit and social relations in early modern England* (Basingstoke, 1998); L. Neal, 'The finance of business during the industrial revolution', in R. Floud and D.N. McCloskey (eds.), *The economic history of Britain since 1700, Vol. 1, 1700–1860* (Cambridge, 1981), pp. 151 ff; S. Quinn, 'Money, finance and capital markets', in R. Floud and P. Johnson (eds.), *The Cambridge economic history of modern Britain, Vol. 1, Industrialisation, 1700–1860* (Cambridge, 2004), pp. 147 ff; M.J. Daunton, *Progress and poverty: an economic and social history of Britain, 1700–1850* (Oxford, 1995), pp. 236–63.

9　C. Muldrew, *Economy of obligation*, ch. 6, read with R.H. Britnell, *The commercialisation of English society, 1000–1500* (2nd ed., Manchester, 1996), pp. 179 ff.; L. Gowing, *Domestic dangers* (Oxford, 1996), pp. 125–33, R.B. Shoemaker, 'The decline of public insult in London 1660–1800' in *Past and Present*, clxix (2000), 97, and M.C. Finn, *The character of credit: personal debt in English culture, 1740–1914* (Cambridge, 2003). Horwitz and Cooke's calendars of litigation suggest the persistence of inter-personal credit at least to the late eighteenth century: see M. Macnair, 'The Court of Exchequer and equity' (2001) 22 *Journal of Legal History* 75 at pp. 80–81, re-reading the evidence in H. Horwitz and J.

corporate form from 1800 as partly a transition from personal to impersonal credit; certainly the correlations are worth investigating even if we avoid trying to identify a 'great transformation' of legal and economic relations.[10]

The sophisticated *in personam* theories of priority developed by Chancery may be contrasted with the rather mechanistic devices employed by the common law. There was a substantive property approach: *nemo dat* and priority in time of acquisition of an asset or security gave the overall priority. And the procedural techniques were still cruder: first in time to win a judgment and seek execution would prevail. Exceptions could be carved out, as where one could sue as if claiming a debt of the Crown. This was yet another complexity applied to a rather indiscriminate system. By contrast, Equity measured the personal conduct of parties towards each other in acquiring rights. Equity tended to use the common-law first-in-time rule as a long-stop if all else failed, not as a starting point. This priorities law was evolved under the great chancellors in the late seventeenth and early eighteenth centuries. It is part and parcel of an overall *in personam* approach to rights and duties, based on assumption of risk, comparative fault and personal obligation rather than rules for acquisition and defence of property. The old equity is not completely attractive to Lord Eldon C. in the early nineteenth century, and we can see him attempting to introject property notions into equity in many areas, notably in constitution of trusts.[11] But we still see a duality of property-fault concepts in basic areas of private law

Cooke (eds.), *London and Middlesex Exchequer equity pleadings, 1685–6 and 1784–5: a calendar* (London, 2000). The role of reputation in markets is a strong theme in modern microeconomics as well as in recent economic history, with the Champagne fairs attracting attention: see A. Greif, P. Milgrom and B. Weingast, 'The merchant guild as a nexus of contracts' (Hoover Working Papers in Economics, Hoover Institute, Stanford, California, 1990); A. Greif, 'On the social foundations and historical development of institutions that facilitate impersonal exchange: from the community responsibility system to individual legal responsibility in pre-modern Europe', and 'Informal contract enforcement: lessons from medieval trade' (John M. Olin Program in Law and Economics, Working Papers 144 & 145, Stanford Law School, Stanford, California, 1997).

10 Cf. Karl Polanyi, *The great transformation* (New York, 1944). Many examples have been identified by historians of a shift after 1800 into impersonal legal relations, including the decline of paternalistic employment practices, the institution of the New Poor Law, the rise of negligence liability for personal injury, and the move to market justice in contractual exchange: see notably M.J. Horwitz, *The transformation of American law 1780–1860* (Cambridge, Massachusetts, 1977); P.S. Atiyah, *The rise and fall of freedom of contract* (Oxford, 1979); A.W.B. Simpson, *Leading cases in the common law* (Oxford, 1995), pp. 100–34. Criticisms are summarized in J. Getzler, *A history of water rights at common law* (Oxford, 2004), pp. 3–6.

11 *Morice* v. *Bishop of Durham* (1805) 10 Ves. Jun. 522, 535–37, 32 E.R. 947, 952–53; cf. judgment of Sir William Grant M.R. who describes the trust more in terms of fiduciary duty supervised by the court rather than structured property ownership: (1804) 9 Ves. Jun. 399, 32 E.R. 656.

today which are not easily eradicated, as with common law and equitable tracing systems which do not reduce easily into a modernized Romanist unjust enrichment framework. The different treatment of volunteers and purchasers that goes deep in private law also has its source in the comparative equities approach of the Chancery: a person who acquired proprietary rights without giving value was less worthy of protection from risk than one who had given value.

We next need to consider some of the doctrinal machinery of the theory of priority based on inter-personal transacting: presumptive fraud, *bona fide* purchase, reputed ownership, estoppel, and the treatment of trusts as rights sounding through *in personam* claims. It will then become possible to explore how equity's approach impacted on business associations to create multiple funds on which creditors could claim, with order of priorities depending on the nature of their reliance. The effect was a pre-incorporation system that offered many of the effects of separate personality, asset partitioning and limited liability.

CONVEYANCE AS PRESUMPTIVE FRAUD

The Court of Chancery wielded a statutory jurisdiction from the later sixteenth century, grounded in a 1571 statute but possibly older, to reverse presumptively fraudulent conveyances. In brief, conveyances of property made without consideration by a debtor, whether before or after he had contracted a debt, were a presumptive fraud on a creditor with a real claim supported by consideration against the same property. The voluntary conveyance was subject to nullification by the court under a statutory power. The property that had been fraudulently conveyed would then be available to the creditor to satisfy the debt.

The jurisdiction may have been an adaptation of the *actio Pauliana* of the Roman law, echoed in the learned laws of Europe including the canon law. The Roman action was a remedy aiming to prevent debtors favouring their families over creditors. Under this doctrine, an alienation made by a debtor with intention to diminish the estate available to his creditors could be subjected to an action nullifying the transfer, and enforcing *restitutio in integrum*, or restoration of the assets to their previous state. The action could be brought against the donor or donee. It was a fictitious action in that the assumption was that the fraudulent transaction had not occurred.[12] A juris-

---

12 The *actio Pauliana* is set out in Justinian's Digest at D.42.8, with further material at C.9.75 and D.22.1.38.4. See further W. W. Buckland, *A textbook of Roman law from Augustus to Justinian* (3rd ed., revised P.G. Stein, Cambridge, 1963), p. 596; M. Kaser, *Roman private law* (3rd ed. transl. by R. Dannenbring, 1980), art 9, s. 3; J.A.C. Thomas, *Textbook of Roman*

diction of this kind certainly existed in Chancery from 1476.[13] Moreover a statute of 1487, 3 Hen. VII c. 4, explicitly made void all deeds of gift of chattels (not land) to the use of the donor, on the basis that these were commonly made to defraud creditors.[14] At any rate the statute of 1571, 13 Eliz. c. 5, restated the doctrine and gave it statutory force; and the remedy was extended by 27 Eliz. c. 4 in 1585. It is certainly the case that lawyers as eminent as Coke C.J. in the seventeenth century and Lord Mansfield in the eighteenth believed that the Elizabethan legislation merely recognized an existing policy and practice of the courts, and in the Restoration period there was a Chancery jurisdiction going beyond the sixteenth-century statutes.[15] The extent of the inherent curial jurisdiction is unclear: it seems that the common law courts at least could not relieve against a gift made *before* the contracting of a debt.[16] The statute of 1571 must therefore be taken to be the modern juristic foundation of the doctrine; that is, from 1571 legislation occupied the field.[17]

The jurisdiction was probably incapable of being applied to money or fungibles, which as property without earmark irrevocably shift in title upon delivery; hence the legal fiction of nullifying the transfer is blocked, as there cannot be real restitution of the *spes*.[18] The remedy in effect traced the property at law and identified the property as legally remaining in the donor's estate, and hence available to creditors.

The remedy was available only if the person making the conveyance did so either (a) without consideration, in which case there was a presumption of fraud; or (b) with a fraudulent intent to transfer away assets that otherwise would have been available to creditors, in which case the existence of consideration supporting the impeached transaction was irrelevant. For example, if the transferor remained in possession after the conveyance this raised a presumption of fraud under 13 Eliz. c. 5. It was early decided that natural affection for family, which was good consideration to effect a transfer

law (1976), pp. 375–76. Canon law doctrine on the issue, likely to have been available to fifteenth century Chancery officials, can be seen in W. Lyndwood, *Provinciale* (Oxford, 1679), pp. 20, v. sine dolo, 161, v. fraude, 162, v. Rex and 165 v. eo ipso.

13 Y.B.M. 16 Edw IV fo. 9b pl. 9, cited in D.E.C. Yale (ed.), *Lord Nottingham's 'Manual of Chancery Practice' and 'Prolegomena to Chancery and Equity'* (Cambridge, 1965), *Prolegomena*, p. 196 s. 35 & n. 5.

14 The statute is noted by W.J. Jones, *The Elizabethan Court of Chancery* (Oxford, 1967), p. 429.

15 See M. Macnair, *The law of proof in early modern equity* (Berlin, 1999), p. 274, text accompanying n. 66.

16 M. Bacon, *A new abridgement of the law* (London, 1736–69; 6th ed., H. Gwillim, London, 1807), *tit. Fraud*, (C), iii, pp. 307–20.

17 See further W. Roberts, *A treatise on the construction of the statutes 13 Eliz. c. 5 and 27 Eliz. c. 4 relating to voluntary and fraudulent conveyances ... in the courts of law and equity* (1800; U.S. ed., Hartford, Connecticut, 1825), ch. 1 s. 1, 1–29.

18 W. Roberts, *Fraudulent conveyances*, at 420–24; *Scott v. Surman* (1743) Willes 400, 125 E.R. 1235 per Willes L.C.J.

of property without a resulting back under implied trust doctrine, was nonetheless insufficient to protect a transfer from the statutory jurisdiction against fraudulent conveyances, though there were special rules for marriage consideration. 27 Eliz. c. 4 was interpreted to mean that the person making a voluntary conveyance could be presumed to do so fraudulently if he contracted the debt *after* the conveyance as well as beforehand. But for the remedy to apply the creditor must have contracted the debt in good faith (that is without notice of the previous conveyance that might bind him to respect it); and it must have been a real debt in the sense of a direct right to the property or to security or value therein, such as a mortgage loan. The reversal of the conveyance took effect at law as a statutory restitution of legal title; the transfer was rendered 'utterly void, frustrate and of none effect': 13 Eliz. c. 5, s. 2. It did not take effect as a trust to counter against fraud or unconscionable conduct. It was sometimes observed that the statute sounded as a legal remedy and hence the equity court's interpretation of fraud ought not to depart from that of the common law. However, the statutory concept of fraud was quickly assimilated to the presumptive fraud of Chancery. This was a real and not fictitious fraud, whereby fraud was presumed from circumstances, as opposed to fraud at common law which required strong proof of fraudulent intent. Under the statute, as refracted through the equitable doctrine of presumptive fraud, if there was a conveyance either before or after a real debt was contracted, this connoted actionable fraud in the vast bulk of cases.[19]

BONA FIDE PURCHASE

The doctrine of bona fide purchase for value and without notice, which originates in the later fifteenth century, considerably antedates the fraudulent conveyances statutes. The modern rule will be familiar to lawyers: in brief, an equitable interest in property will not bind a bona fide purchaser of a common law interest in the same property for value and without actual notice (knowledge of the equitable interest), constructive notice (carelessness in failing to make appropriate enquiries), or implied notice (actual or constructive notice in his lawyer or agent). The primary form of the doctrine in pre-1875 equity was as a defendant's plea, in bar of both the obligation to answer equitable claims on oath and of substantive equitable relief. However, around 1700 it was significantly wider than the modern doctrine. In the context of the fraudulent conveyances statutes, the doctrine could be a sword as well as a shield, and in the later seventeenth and early eighteenth century it could be

---

19 See generally *Russell* v. *Hammond* (1738) 1 Atk. 13, 14–15, 26 E.R. 9, 10; cf. *Nunn* v. *Wilsmore* (1800) 8 T.R. 521, 101 E.R. 1524 (KB). Roberts, *Fraudulent conveyances*, chs. 2 and 3 gives extensive authorities.

used to bar equitable aid to claims to legal titles, and give the purchaser rights to discovery, etc., against the volunteer holder of a legal title.[20] The effect is that in this period it could be said that creditors are always to be paid before voluntary transferees.[21]

REPUTED OWNERSHIP

In the reputed ownership jurisdiction, the court bars a party from pleading title through purchase for value where there has not yet been a conveyance or delivery and where no publicly observable shift in ownership has occurred. Reputed ownership typically involves transfer of personal property (that is, title to goods and chattels) from Vendor to Purchaser for good consideration, for example where a factor sells goods to a merchant; but the Purchaser then leaves the goods in Vendor's possession so as to create the impression of a reputed ownership in the Purchaser of those goods. Where the Vendor then becomes bankrupt, the creditors of the Vendor may treat the goods bought by the Purchaser as if they are in the Vendor's estate and legally available to the estate's general creditors, and the Purchaser is barred or prevented from asserting ownership despite the purchase for good consideration. The reason is that Purchaser has by his conduct led creditors to rely on the Vendor's false appearance of credit, and by creating such an ostensible ownership Purchaser is barred from asserting title against those who have relied upon the appearances created by the Purchaser. The doctrine is thus close to doctrines of estoppel by representation at law and equity and ostensible agency at law. The court's jurisdiction is not based on fraud by the Purchaser who may well have acted in good faith, but rather fixes on the combination of negligence in allowing the Vendor to have the appearance of title, coupled with fraud by the Vendor in exploiting that false credit. An alternative scenario involves a factor buying goods on behalf of a merchant, where the merchant leaves the goods with the factor and does not take forward delivery; if the factor is bankrupted the creditors can then rely on his reputed ownership of the goods bought with the merchant's value.

20 For the early origins, see the cases cited in D.E.C. Yale (ed.), *Lord Nottingham's 'Manual of Chancery Practice'*, pp. 244 ff., ch. xiv, ss. 1 and 2. Plea of purchase bar to equitable aid of a legal title, examples in id., 204–12, and for more context, D.E.C. Yale, Introduction to Yale (ed.), *Lord Nottingham's chancery cases Volume II* (79 Selden Society, London, 1961), pp. 160 ff. Purchaser's right to ancillary aid of equity against volunteer, H. Ballow (attr.), *A treatise of equity* (Dublin, 1756; 1st pub. London 1737), p. 58; J. Gilbert, *The history and practice of the High Court of Chancery* (Washington DC, 1874; written *c.* 1720–25), p. 279.

21 *Fairbeard* v. *Bowers* (1690) Prec. Ch. 17, 24 E.R. 9; *Jones* v. *Powell* (1712) 1 Eq. Ca. Abr. 84, 21 E.R. 896; *Cray* v. *Rooke* (1735) Cases t. Talbot 153, 25 E.R. 713. These cases concern the priority of voluntary bonds, good at law, after the death of the obligor, but the principles stated are general.

The doctrine was set out by the statute 21 Jac. 1, c. 19 (1623–24), though again the legislation may be seen as a codification of curial practice, also likely to have been borrowed from Civilian doctrine though possibly finding its immediate source in Scots law. The court in the leading 1749 case of *Ryall* v. *Rolle*[22] held that the unequivocal policy of the legislation mandated that reputed ownerships should be enforceable by creditors regardless of purchasers' intentions, and not only against absolute grants and choses in possession made by a bankrupt, but also against grants of fractional interests including securities, equitable mortgages and other choses in action pertaining to goods.

The result is that where a purchaser sets up a reputed ownership through failure to take physical delivery of bought or sold goods, this in juristic effect prevents a full title binding third parties ever passing to the purchaser under a valid executed contract. The purchaser is left with personal rights to the goods only; his property is not thereby made available to creditors of another for he never had a perfected title. The jurisdiction thus protected creditors' reasonable assessment of risk in granting credit to a reputed owner X, in the absence of real or constructive knowledge by the creditors that the property in X's hands had been sold to Y.

GENERAL EQUITABLE ESTOPPEL AS AFFECTING PRIORITIES

A related but more general equitable doctrine, more closely linked to fraud, was what would in modern times be called estoppel by holding out or acquiescence as affecting legal priorities. Thus, for example, in *Hobbs* v. *Norton* in 1683 a purchaser of an annuity under a settlement was relieved against the heir general's legal title under an undisclosed revocation; in *Ibbotson* v. *Rhodes* in 1706 a second mortgagee was relieved against an undisclosed first legal mortgage. In both cases the purchaser had made enquiries of the holder of the legal title against which relief was given; in both this person's silence when questioned lent credit, in *Hobbs* to a vendor, in *Ibbotson* to a mortgagor.[23]

TRUSTS AS *IN PERSONAM*

This general context of priority rules based on personal fault and assumption of risk also significantly affected the trust. Voluntary trusts could be attacked

---

22 *Ryall* v. *Rolle* (1749) 1 Atk. 165, 26 E.R. 107 (Lord Hardwicke C., assisted by Sir William Lee, Lord Chief Justice of the Court of King's Bench, Sir Thomas Parker, Lord Chief Baron of the Court of Exchequer, and Sir Thomas Burnet one of the justices of the Court of Common Pleas).

23 *Hobbs* v. *Norton* (1683) 1 Vern. 136, 23 E.R. 370, North L.K., reversing (1682) 2 Ch. Cas 128, 21 E.R. 1099 (Lord Nottingham C.); *Ibbotson* v. *Rhodes* (1706) 2 Vern. 554, 1 Eq. Ca. Ab. 229 pl 13, Cowper L.K.

under the fraudulent conveyance statutes. The court might refuse relief to volunteer beneficiaries seeking to prevent a conveyance in breach of trusts to preserve contingent remainders.[24] And the liability of third party takers from the trustee was by more than one author explained by reference to the character of the taker as *particeps criminis* or as having personally assumed trustee liability.[25] In the 1736 case of *Morrice* v. *Bank of England*[26] Lord Talbot C. held that beneficiaries who won an equitable decree to recover trust assets from an insolvent estate were to be seen as creditors claiming an *in personam* debt, and, as such, could take priority over creditors who later secured judgment at law. This result did not rest on the basis that equitable property established priority over legal personal claims in the absence of a bona fide taking for value, but rather on the basis of an equal moral right for both equitable and legal creditors to take their rank in order of diligence in obtaining a curial remedy. The implication was that had the legal creditors won judgment first they might have swept the estate. The *in personam* basis of this method of trust claiming is strikingly distinct from modern trust doctrines of tracing and priorities.

With these doctrinal tools the law of ongoing associations, commercial or otherwise, could be subjected to the same general principles of inter-personal reliance. In ascending order of scale, we next consider ownership and liabilities of husband and wife; principles of partnership insolvency; and the equitable treatment of legally incorporated associations.

DISAGGREGATING THE EFFECTS OF COVERTURE

Before the Married Women's Property Acts of 1882 and 1893, a wife's legal personality was merged with and subsumed to her husband's, including her capacity to own separate personal property. Under this doctrine of coverture, the personal goods of the 'feme covert' became the absolute property of her husband (who also had the right to execute conveyances of her land binding for the duration of the marriage), and her ability to contract personal obligations fell under the control and responsibility of her husband. By contrast, the unmarried or widowed 'feme sole' had full legal capacity to own property and to sue or be sued. A husband was liable for his wife's debts during the coverture, and in relation to her debts contracted before marriage he was only liable if the debt was sued upon before the wife died.[27]

---

24 *Tipping* v. *Pigot* (1713) 1 Equity Cases Abridged 385 (E) 2, Gilb. Rep. 34, 25 E.R. 25.

25 M. Macnair, 'The conceptual basis of trusts in the later seventeenth and early eighteenth centuries', in R. Helmholz and R. Zimmermann (eds.), *Itinera Fiduciae: Trust and Treuhand in historical perspective* (Berlin, 1998), pp. 227–29 and sources cited there.

26 (1736) Cases t. Talbot 217, 25 E.R. 745; 3 Swans. (App) 573, 36 E.R. 980; (1737) 2 Brown PC 465, 1 E.R. 1068.

27 *Heard* v. *Stamford* (1735) 3 P. Wms 410, 24 E.R. 1123; Cases t. Talbot 173, 25 E.R. 723 per

There are a number of eighteenth-century cases dealing with wives' property and trading that seem to involve an equitable policy of disaggregation as opposed to the common law policy of aggregation based on the legal identity of husband and wife or supersession of wife's legal personality within her husband's person. For example, it was held in courts of equity that a feme covert being a sole trader according to the custom of London could be bankrupted and her separate effects in trade seized and applied to payment of her debts contracted in such separate trade.[28] Moreover, a feme covert living apart from her husband and acting as a feme sole, he not being liable to her debts, could be made bankrupt.[29] The legal policies of eighteenth-century equity strove to overcome the common law's status and property rules and bring liabilities in line with commercial assumption of risk.

THE JINGLE RULE OF PARTNERSHIP INSOLVENCY

The so-called jingle rule for partnership insolvency provides the strongest evidence of how equity could construct forms of asset partitioning and insert a veil between investors, managers and trading entities. The jingle rule states that the joint creditors of a partnership cannot access individual assets of the partners until the partnership funds are exhausted; and the individual creditors of individual partners cannot access other partners' assets until the personal assets of the partner (including his share of the partnership capital) is exhausted. This system of priority dated from at least the end of the seventeenth century. The Court of Chancery consistently applied the jingle rule to bankrupt partners and partnerships from the time of Lord Nottingham C.[30]

Lord Talbot C. In this case an attempt to make the husband liable after the wife's death for her debt contracted before marriage, i.e. that is to aggregate the liabilities, on the basis of H's acquisition by the marriage and coverture rules of W's personal estate, was emphatically rejected.

28 Bacon, *Abridgement*, tit. Bankrupt, (A), i, pp. 385–7; *Ex parte Carrington* (1739) 1 Atk. 206, 26 E.R. 134; *Lavie v. Philips* (1765) 3 Burr. 1776, 97 E.R. 1094; R.S.D. Roper, *Treatise of the law of property arising from the relation of husband and wife* (London, 1820, 2nd ed. 1826), ch. 18, s. 4. There was some common law basis to this at least in the local courts: *Bowett v. Langham* (1627) Lit. 31, 124 E.R. 121, on the limits of the custom.

29 *Case of Mrs Fitzgerald* (1771) reported *in extenso* in Bacon, *Abridgement*, i, 385–6; *Ex parte Preston*, reported in W. Cooke, *The bankrupt laws* (London, 2nd ed., 1788), pp. 32, 36; and *Corbet v. Poelnitz* (1785) 1 T. R. 5, 99 E.R. 940.

30 Egerton L.K. had discountenanced Chancery handling of merchants' accounts in around 1600, and in 1614 had explicitly prohibited consideration of them, 'for none is to account on oath but to the King only'. By 1636, however, Coventry L.K. had diluted the rule to one allowing existing stated accounts to be pleaded in bar to a claim for a new account, and Lord Nottingham in his *Prolegomena to Chancery* (early 1670s) explicitly rejected both Egerton's rule and his reason for it. By Nottingham's time the Chancery was doing a significant amount of business in partnership and other mercantile accounting. At the same period it

From 1785 onwards, Lord Thurlow C. may have experimented with a *pari passu* regime, and though Lord Eldon C. later expressed some support for the idea, the jingle rule prevailed. It was definitively integrated into modern equity and partnership law in Joseph Story's seminal treatises of 1836 and 1841.[31] The effect of the rule was to segregate partnership capital from the personal fortunes of partners, whether active or passive, not entirely as with full limited liability but to a marked degree.

The jingle rule for payment of partner's debts may be reiterated as follows: business creditors who contract with the partnership firm must first resort to the jointly held partnership property, and private creditors who contract with the partners as individuals must first resort to the separate property, and neither group may pursue a claim against assets in the other category until all first claimants on that estate have been paid in full. The procedural form of the rule is that separate creditors cannot prove a debt through a joint commission of bankruptcy, and creditors of the firm or joint creditors cannot prove a debt through a single commission. Instead, creditors of one type of estate must apply for an account of any surplus in the other type of estate once distribution of that latter estate to its primary creditors is completed.[32]

began to play a larger substantive role in bankruptcy litigation. There is no head 'Bankrupt' in W. Tothill's *Transactions of the high court of Chancery* (London, 1649). The only Chancery bankruptcy case in the English Reports before 1650 – *Meechett* v. *Bradshaw* (1633/4) Nelson 22, 21 E.R. 779 – turns on an independent equity; between 1650 and 1700 around 25% of reported bankruptcy cases are in Chancery reports.

31 J. Story, *Commentaries on equity jurisprudence* (Boston, 1836; 2nd ed., Boston and London, 1839), at pp. 550–58; and *Commentaries on the law of partnership* (Boston, 1841; 2nd ed., 1846), arts. 377–88 – although Story was himself ambivalent about the justice of the jingle rule. Story drew heavily on J. Collyer, *A practical treatise on the law of partnership* (London, 1832), which gives a detailed treatment of insolvency rules pertaining to joint and separate estates at pp. 503–82.

32 For the early development of the rule see *Equity cases abridged* (London, 1732), i, Tit. Bankrupt, C – 'Who may be allowed to come in as creditors', at 54–6, 21 E.R. 869–70; id. ii (c.1750), Tit. Bankrupt, I – 'Concerning joint and separate commissions, and creditors coming in under such commissions'; K – 'What shall be said the bankrupt's estate etc.'; L – 'Of distribution, &c. under a commission of bankruptcy', at 109–19; 22 E.R. 93–101. Other important sources are W. Cooke, *The bankrupt laws* (London, 2nd ed., 1788), which is probably the first modern treatise on bankruptcy, at i, 288–307, and E. Christian, *The origin, progress and present practice of the bankrupt law* (London, 1812–14), ii, 242–75, which give an exhaustive analysis of the origins and nature of the jingle rule. The doctrine forms a subset of the much larger topic of joint and several liability, which has its own distinct features in property law, tort and contract. Seventeenth-century authorities are collected in *Boson* v. *Sandford* (1690) 1 Freeman 499, 89 E.R. 374 (KB). G.L. Williams, in *Joint obligations* (London, 1949), subjects joint and several liability to substantial criticism; for modern developments see A.S. Burrows, 'Should one reform joint and several liability?', in N.J. Mullany and A.M. Linden (eds.), *Torts tomorrow: a tribute to John Fleming* (Sydney, 1998), pp. 101–18.

Edward Christian traced the rule back to the 1682 case of *Craven* v. *Knight*[33] before North L.K., who held that the estate of a 'joint trade' (meaning a partnership) was to be divided into 'moieties' to pay out the joint debts of that trade, and any surplus to be applied to the 'particular debts of each partner'. Any agreement of the partners to apply their partnership assets firstly to separate creditors could not bind the joint creditors. In *Ex parte Crowder*[34] Lord Cowper C. held that creditors could prove their separate debts under a joint commission against a bankrupt partnership, especially where a commission for a small separate estate would be costly and inconvenient; but that the separate creditors would have to contribute to the costs of the joint commission and accept that joint creditors took priority:

> [T]he joint or partnership estate was in the first place to be applied to pay the joint or partnership debts; so in like manner the separate estate should be in the first place to pay all the separate debts: and as separate creditors are not to be let in upon the joint-estate, until all the joint-debts are first paid; so likewise the creditors to the partnership shall not come in for any deficiency of the joint-estate, upon the separate estate, until the separate debts are first paid.

The jingle rule was restated in classic form by Lord King C. as a 'settled ... resolution of convenience' in *Ex parte Cook* in 1728:

> [T]he joint creditors shall be first paid out of the partnership or joint estate, and the separate creditors out of the separate estate of each partner, and if there be a surplus of the joint estate, besides what will pay the joint creditors, the same shall be applied to pay the separate creditors, and if there be on the other hand a surplus of the separate estate, beyond what will satisfy the separate creditors, it shall go to supply any deficiency that may remain as to the joint creditors.[35]

Lord King C. also held that it might be convenient for the commissioners to make accounts of the joint and separate estates at the same time, so that joint creditors could later easily apply to the equity court for any surplus left from the several estates; in all of this the court was concerned to minimize procedural costs and trouble.[36] This procedural device did not disturb the substantive priority rules.

---

33 (1682) 2 Chan. Rep. 226, 21 E.R. 664; 1 Eq. Ca. Abr. 55, 21 E.R. 870.
34 (1715) 2 Vern. 706; 23 E.R. 1064.
35 (1728) 2 P. Wms. 500; 24 E.R. 834.
36 Ibid., at 501. See further *Ex parte Turner* (1742) 1 Atk. 97, 26 E.R. 64; *Ex parte Baudier* (1742) 1 Atk. 98, 26 E.R. 64.

Lord Thurlow C., in decisions dating from 1784, seemingly criticized the jingle rule, and would have allowed joint creditors not only to prove in a separate commission but to rank in *pari passu* against a single partner's separate assets pooled with his proportionate share of the jointly held partnership assets. The logic of this position also would allow a separate creditor to rank in *pari passu* against a single partner's separate assets pooled with his proportionate share of the jointly held partnership assets.[37] There is also, however, one possible decision of Thurlow's inconsistent with the *pari passu* approach, in the 1785 case of *Ex parte Marlin*.[38] The original report only gives the barest facts and a minute of the order of the court, almost certainly Lord Thurlow C. sitting at Lincoln's Inn. At issue was the presence of two partnerships with overlapping memberships and different dates of commencement. The facts were that A contracted individual debts in 1771; then A joined B in a partnership in 1772 ('Firm A-B'); then in 1781 A and B joined with C to form a separate second partnership ('Firm A-B-C'). It appears that Firm A-B continued to exist after the formation of Firm A-B-C; that is, the first partnership (being Firm A-B) was not dissolved and its assets and business were not absorbed upon formation of the second partnership (being Firm A-B-C). Separate commissions of bankruptcy were then issued against A, B and C in 1785. It does not appear in the bare statement of fact whether Firm A-B had any assets remaining or was also regarded as bankrupt. The question was whether the court should order separate accounts of the three partners A, B and C as distinct persons, and also separate accounts of the shares of joint property held by those persons as partners in Firm A-B and Firm A-B-C.

Let us recall some features of account in English legal process. By ordering an account to be taken, a common law court (and later, a court of equity) could require a person handling assets to show all receipts and outlays, a procedural duty; and also to give an account of what is owed to a relevant obligor, either in payment over of actual or expected profits ('surcharge of account') or compensation for lost assets ('falsification of account'), thus enforcing the substantive duties of a fiduciary to a beneficiary, of a debtor to a creditor, and so on. In the specific factual circumstance of *Marlin*, an order of separate accounts would in effect have identified a possible *eight* estates or sets of assets for the satisfaction of different groups of creditors. Those eight distinct estates were A, B and C's separate estates outside the two partner-

---

37 See e.g. *Ex parte Cobham* (1784) 1 Brown's C. C. 577, 28 E.R. 1307; *Ex parte Haydon* (24 June 1785), as reported in Cooke, *Bankrupt laws*, i, 292–93; *Ex parte Hodgson* (1785) 2 Brown's Chancery Cases 5, 29 E.R. 3; *Ex parte Page, In re Remnant* (1786) 2 Brown's C. C. 119, 29 E.R. 69; *Ex parte Flintum, re Oyston* (1786) 2 Brown's C. C. 120, 29 E.R. 69; *Ex parte Copland* (1787) 1 Cox 420, 29 E.R. 1230; and see N. Gow, *Practical treatise on the law of partnership* (London, 1823), pp. 314 (2nd ed., 1825), p. 340, followed in Story's *Law of partnership* (2nd ed., Boston, 1846), ch. xv, art. 377.

38 (1785) 2 Bro. C. C. 15; 29 E.R. 8.

ships; A's and B's respective shares in the joint estate in Firm A-B; and A's, B's and C's respective shares in the joint estate in bankrupt Firm A-B-C.

An alternative course would have been to order joint accounting yielding the following three amalgamated estates: A's personal estate plus his share of Firm A-B plus his share of Firm A-B-C; B's personal estate plus his share of Firm A-B plus his share of Firm A-B-C; and C's personal estate plus his share of Firm A-B-C. Such aggregated accounting would have made both the separate estates and the joint partnership estates of each of A, B and C available equally to their various individual and partnership creditors, and could plausibly be described as a type of consolidation of all the estates into one pool for *pari passu* distribution. The personal creditors of A and B could then have taken from C's personal estate with equal rank to C's personal and partnership creditors, a radical departure from the conventional jingle rule.

In the result, the court in *Marlin* specifically ordered the first scheme of entirely separate accounting. The commission of bankruptcy for Firm A-B-C was first to allow the separate creditors of A, B and C to prove their debts, and after that, 'the surplus, if any, of each respective estate, after full payment and satisfaction of the debts of such estate, be carried over to, and constitute part of, the joint estates' of A, B and C. The payment schedule was therefore as follows: first, A's separate estate was to pay his separate creditors; and the same for B and C's separate estates; next the joint estate of Firm A-B (as one of the 'respective estates' of the debtors) was to pay out extant debts of that estate; and finally any surplus from the above distributions was then and only then to go to creditors of bankrupt Firm A-B-C. The costs regime was that Firm A-B-C was to pay for the application to court, with the other distinct estates being required to bear the costs according to the discretion of the commissioners; hence some costs of the accounting exercise could be shifted to the larger joint estate should surpluses derived from the other estates turn out to benefit the larger firm.

The system set out in *Marlin* of separate account taking and application of separate and joint debts to the respective separate and joint estates was adopted in its entirety by Lord Loughborough C. through a General Order of the Lord Chancellor in 1794. The jingle rule with its overlapping accounting mechanisms thus took effect as a general rule of bankruptcy jurisdiction. The Order[39] allowed separate creditors to prove under a joint commission against two or more bankrupts (such as partners) without an exceptional petition to the Chancery; and also required distinct accounts of the separate and joint estates, with separate and joint creditors having first call on those respective classes of estate and second call on any surplus of the other class of estate.[40] It was not unknown for chancellor's orders to be ignored by

---

39 Reproduced in E. Christian, *Bankrupt law*, ii, 240–41.
40 See further E. Christian, *Bankrupt law*, ii, 240–43 ff.

commissioners and courts and so fall into desuetude.[41] In 1796 Lord Loughborough C. ensured the Order of 1794 would be observed by making a long declaration affirming the jingle rule in the case of *Ex parte Elton*:[42]

> In Lord King's time it was determined, that a joint creditor might be a good petitioning creditor, though the commission is only against one partner; that the joint creditor does no more in taking his execution, passing over his action, than bringing the separate effects to be administered in bankruptcy. … [T]his Court … is to make an equitable distribution among the creditors, to admit all equitable claims upon the effects, and to divide them rateably. It has been long settled, and it is not possible to alter that, that each estate is to pay its own creditors. … But any other joint creditor is in exactly the case of a person having two funds; and this Court will not allow him to attach himself upon one fund to the prejudice of those, who have no other and to neglect the other fund. He has the law open to him: but if he comes to claim a distribution the first consideration is, what is that fund, from which he seeks it. It is the separate estate; which is particularly attached to the separate creditors. Upon the supposition, that there is a joint estate: the answer is 'apply yourself to that: You have a right to come upon it: the separate creditors have not: therefore do not affect the fund attached to them, till you have obtained what you can get from the joint fund.

Lord Loughborough then makes clear the point that a separate creditor can only attach the debtor-partner's share of the partnership assets and no more; the creditor cannot reach the moiety or share of the joint estate of other partners:

> I was led to consider another thing: is it possible to admit a separate creditor to take a dividend upon the joint estate rateably with the joint creditors? *No case has gone to that; and it is impossible; for the separate creditor at law has no right to sue the other partner. He has no right to attach the partnership property. He could only attach the interest, his debtor had in that property.* If it stands as a rule of law, we must consider, what I have always understood to be settled by a vast variety of cases not only in bankruptcy, but upon general Equity, that the joint estate is applicable to partnership debts, the separate estate to the separate debts. (emphasis added)

The core idea here is that under the existing structure of equity doctrine, parties have an expectation that joint and individual debts pertain in the first instance to joint and individual estates, and to displace that expectation

41 Ibid., 239–40.
42 (1796) 3 Ves. Jun. 238, 239–41, 30 E.R. 988, 989–90.

would disrupt parties' allocation of risk in partnership dealings. The veil between joint and individual partner assets is not lifted until one side or the other is exhausted because that is how the parties have contracted their liabilities; the court through its default rules is thus entrenching a form of *quasi*-limited liability that works to protect individual creditors from partnership debts and creditors of the firm from individual debts. In *Ex parte Abell*[43] counsel argued again for the *pari passu* approach and against the jingle rule in *Elton*, especially where there was no extant joint estate available; but Lord Loughborough reaffirmed his commitment to the jingle rule, both on policy grounds and as binding authority.

The rule was affirmed yet again by legislation in 1825.[44] Section 16 of this codifying bankruptcy statute stated that joint creditors of a partnership could petition for a commission against single partners without joining the other partners, but that the lord chancellor should have a power to order a joint commission of a number of debtor partners if expedient. Section 62 affirmed that a joint creditors could prove a partnership debt in a separate commission and vote on assignment of the estate, 'but such Creditor shall not receive any Dividend out of the separate Estate of the Bankrupt or Bankrupts until all the separate Creditors shall have received the full Amount of their respective Debts', unless, that is, the partnership creditor could also properly petition as a separate creditor.[45] The 1825 legislation restated and entrenched the jingle rule after a generation of judicial debate.

Lord Eldon C never quite departed from the jingle rule, but he had serious reservations about its merits,[46] expressed most clearly in *Ex parte Emly*.[47] There he stated:

> [T]he Rule as to joint and separate Estates whatever might have been said against its original Adoption, and much might have been said, is too well settled to be now shaken; it has been settled to that Extent, that when there have been joint creditors to the Amount of many Thousands of Pounds, and Separate creditors to a very trifling Amount, the latter have been allowed to take Twenty Shillings in the Pound, and to sweep away the Estate from the joint Creditors.

43 (1799) 4 Ves. Jun. 837, 31 E.R. 434.

44 6 Geo. 4, c. 16. The impact of the legislation is analysed in Hovenden's notes to *Ex parte Elton* (1827) 1 Ves. Jun. Supplement 369, 34 E.R. 831. The later history is examined in V.M. Lester, *Victorian insolvency: bankruptcy, imprisonment for debt, and company winding-up in nineteenth-century England* (Oxford, 1995).

45 Cf. *Ex parte Clowes*, per Thurlow C (1789), reported in Cooke, *Bankrupt laws*, 2nd ed., p. 264; Bacon, *Abridgement* (7th ed., London, 1832), tit. Bankrupts, iii, 460.

46 See Lord Eldon's lengthy *obiter* regretting the application of *stare decisis* regarding the rule, in *Ex parte Clay* (1802) 6 Vesey 813, 31 E.R. 1322; and *Ex parte Nuttall*, 22 June 1801, reported (1802) 6 Ves. Jun. 813, 815, 31 E.R. 1322, 1323.

47 (1811) 1 Rose's Cases in Bankruptcy 61 at 64; Christian, *Bankrupt law*, ii, 248.

These passages show that Lord Eldon's adoption of Loughborough's rule was not driven by any intellectual conviction that the rule was the best solution for handling partnership insolvencies. Like others,[48] Lord Eldon grasped how arbitrary the jingle rule could be, giving widely variant outcomes in cases where there was a large joint estate, a small joint estate or no joint estate to satisfy significant joint debts.[49]

Despite Lord Eldon's reservations on its merits, the jingle rule prevailed. The result of the Second General Order, the bankruptcy statute of 1825, and the string of decisions following *Elton* in 1796, was to end any experimentation with a general rule for rateable distribution of separate and joint debts from separate and joint partner assets. The *pari passu* approach continued to command vocal adherents outside the courts, notably Edward Christian who attacked the use of Civilian jurisprudence imported from Domat as a source for the English jingle rule;[50] and also Joseph Story who criticized the jingle rule in his influential *Commentaries on the law of partnership*.[51] It is not necessary here to go into the policy arguments adduced for and against the *pari passu* approach in the period after 1800; only to observe that with some reluctance the *pari passu* experiment was put aside. The capacity of one class of creditors to 'sweep an estate' at the expense of another class in dealing with partners was the harsh side of the jingle rule that permitted segregation of the assets of the unincorporated firm.

Lord Eldon attempted with some success to curb the growth of joint stock companies, finding ways to apply the anti-corporate policies of the Bubble Act even after its repeal.[52] For Lord Eldon, corporate form outside direct State grant of privilege and control was an abuse in itself. But he did not remove the entity-producing jingle rule from the law of partnership and he thereby helped English traders to separate investor's benefits and liabilities from those of management and control.

---

48 For example Christian, *Bankrupt law*, ii, 248–49.
49 See also Lord Eldon C.'s discussions in *Ex parte Chandler* (1803) 9 Ves. Jun. 35, 32 E.R. 513; *Gray* v. *Chiswell* (1803) 9 Ves. Jun. 119, 32 E.R. 547; *Ex parte Hall* (1804) 9 Ves. Jun. 349, 32 E.R. 637; *Ex parte Ackerman* (1808) 14 Ves. Jun. 604, 33 E.R. 653; *Dutton* v. *Morrison* (1809–10) 17 Ves. Jun. 193, 207–08, 34 E.R. 75; 2 Ves. Jun. Supplement 471, 34 E.R. 1183; and *Ex parte De Tastet* (1810) 17 Vesey 250, 34 E.R. 95.
50 *Bankrupt law*, ii, 244.
51 1st ed., 1841; 2nd ed., 1846, arts. 377–88.
52 See Harris, *Industrializing English law*, pp. 230–49; S. Banner, *Anglo-American securities regulation: cultural and political roots, 1690–1860* (Cambridge, 1998), pp. 14–87; and more generally, *Gower's Principles of modern company law* (6th ed., London, 1997), pp. 21–46.

CORPORATIONS

Partnerships rather than corporations were the main form of business association in England before 1789.[53] But there was some direct authority on priorities in cases of insolvent corporations.

In *Salmon* v. *Hamborough Company* (1671)[54] the House of Lords allowed mesne process against a company's officers in England as individuals, in order to compel the company to appear where the company had no assets in England and could therefore ignore the conventional distraint order. Further, the company's officers were to be ordered to make calls ('leviations') on the shares to meet company liabilities, with members bound on pain of contempt. This roundabout process of debt enforcement formally preserved the veil between company and members, yet effectively the members could be forced to contribute personally under their contracts with the company to meet the company's liabilities. The remedy thus reflects the general approach we have already seen of dealing with these problems as a set of inter-personal credit and contractual relationships, with fixed property rules serving only as the ultimate default position.

In *Naylor* v. *Brown* (1673),[55] a company assigned a bond debt owed to the company representing £1000 in value to W, to hold on trust for payment of debts to a group of favoured creditors including members of the company who claimed that large corporate debts were owed them, so that upon dissolution of the company these members were found to be 'carving large Shares out of their whole Estate', while outside creditors remained unsatisfied. The outside creditors sued, and Lord Nottingham C.'s solution was not to lower the veil and force the members to meet the company's outside debts[56] but rather to refuse enforcement of the preferential trust and so move the assets in that voided trust to meet outside liabilities. The refusal to consolidate the members' estates or credit with the rights and liabilities of the company is striking in the circumstances, as the reporter observes:

> [T]his Case was more remarkable, because several of the principal Members of the Company had set their Names to the Plaintiffs Bond of £500 under the common Seal [to enhance the appearance of credit], which ... did not legally bind them in their private Capacities.[57]

---

53 Deed of settlement companies were assimilated to partnership law, as is noted below. See further Harris, *Industrializing English law*, pp. 14–36, 110–67, 193–98.

54 1 Cases in Chan. 204, 22 E.R. 763; cited and followed in *Harvey* v. *East India Company* (1700) 2 Vern. 395, 23 E.R. 856.

55 Rep. t. Finch 83, 23 E.R. 44, *sub nom. Naylor & Godfrey* (1674) in *Lord Nottingham's Chancery Cases*, ed. D.E.C. Yale, 2 vols. (73 Selden Society), No. 97 at pp. 55–56.

56 73 Selden Soc., at p. 56.

57 (1673) Rep. t. Finch 83, 84, 23 E.R. 44, 45.

Lord Nottingham's own note of the case explained that 'the members of the Comp[any] ought rather to lose than strangers who trusted to their common seal and were encouraged so to do by seeing some principal members sign, seal and deliver the [bond] instrument under the common seal, though it did not legally bind them'. On review, a member-debtor asked for the company's credits and debts to be consolidated and averaged, so that members could recover pro rata with outside creditors the sums owed them under company loans; Lord Nottingham refused this restructuring because of the taint of fraud surrounding the members' company loans.[58]

Gibson v. *Hudson's Bay Company* (1725)[59] as reported by Strange may also suggest the application of a version of the jingle rule in a corporate case:

> [T]here was a by-law which subjected every member's stock to his debts to the Company, on which the decree was founded.... The plaintiff as assignee of the effects of Sir Stephen Evance a bankrupt, brings his bill against the Company to oblige them to suffer him to transfer stock. The Company insist, that Sir Stephen Evance was their banker, and greatly indebted to them, and that upon the clause in the Bankrupts Act, which directs the commissioners to state the account between mutual dealers, they shall be allowed to hold the stock, and account only for the balance, if any shall appear against them. And of this opinion was the Court, and decreed accordingly.

58 *Brown & Naylor* (1676), 73 Selden Soc., No. 557 at p. 419. There are a number of other cases where the issue is raised, but either left unresolved or dealt with by other means. In *Monteage* v. *Grocers' Company* (1675) 73 Selden Society 240, No. 354 at 240, the court allowed discovery against officers and members of the company, but only to force production of the company's books. In *Curson* v. *African Company* (1682) 1 Vern. 121, 23 E.R. 358; Skinner 84, 90 E.R. 40, an insolvent company had transferred its business to a new company. The old company's creditors sued the new company for payment out of the part-unpaid price which remained in the hands of the new company. Lord Keeper North considered various solutions: to have the new company pay from earmarked trust assets; to allow the new company to be sued directly to avoid circuity of action – though this would require joinder of all parties; or, finally, to hold that the new company was in a position analogous to an executor-trustee *de son tort* with regard to the assets of the old company and hence was liable for its debts. In the end, a solution was reached by consent, so the case had no decision or *ratio*. In *Harvey* v. *East India Company* (1700) 2 Vern. 395, 23 E.R. 856, Prec. Ch. 129, 24 E.R. 62, the court allows sequestration against the company assets where the company itself was found to be in contempt following a decree and distraint against it; arrest of the company was not possible nor was the court prepared to lower the veil and move against the persons of the company membership. Also significant is the equitable jurisdiction to relieve debtors of a company for misnomer of the company in deeds or other documents, which would be fatal to a cause at law: see *Pits* v. *James* (1614) Hobart 121, 80 E.R. 271; *Hinckly* v. *Hinckly* (1674) 73 Selden Society No. 123 at 75; *Tit. 'Mistaking'*, Tothill 131, 21 E.R. 145.

59 1 Strange 645, 93 E.R. 755; 1 Eq. Ca. Abr. 10, 21 E.R. 834; Bacon, *Abridgement* (6th ed., 1807), tit. Bankrupt, (G), i, p. 444.

This may indicate that a stockholder's creditors can only claim against the stockholder's company shares after the company's claims against the stockholder are satisfied, as agreed beforehand between stockholder and company. In effect, the stocks are treated as a contractual liability and asset, and in that sense the corporation resembles a partnership or joint trading consortium, with the superadded advantage of corporate form for the joint trading entity. Likewise, the deed of settlement companies of the eighteenth century, which have often been cited as the precursor of the company form, were in the eye of equity, for the purposes of account, set-offs and liability to outsiders, seen as nothing more than a form of partnership.[60]

CONCLUSION

Corporations law has been praised as the ultimate system for brokering risk and enforcing obligation through law – and damned as the ultimate system for concealing and shifting risk unfairly through legal trickery. The law of priorities based on inter-personal credit that we have been exposing shows how sophisticated the equity courts were in grappling with this puzzle in the era before free incorporation. In doing so, they created a concept of firms as real entities that may have facilitated the later invention of general incorporation. And perhaps most significantly, this historical body of law casts doubt on the assumed importance of artificial legal personality in the operation of commercial enterprises during the span of British industrialization.[61]

---

60 *Meliorucchi* v. *Royal Exchange Assurance Company* (1728) 1 Eq. Ca. Abr. 10, 21 E.R. 834 (Lord King C.). Another possible example is *Dawson* v. *Franklyn* (1713) 4 Bro. PC 626, 2 E.R. 427 (PC).
61 Cf. Harris, *Industrializing English law*, esp. pp. 287–93.

Adventures in training –
the Irish genesis of the 'remarkable and far-sighted' Select Committee on Legal Education, 1846

COLUM KENNY

IN 1971, THE ORMROD committee on legal education in England and Wales described an earlier, 1846, parliamentary report on legal education as 'remarkable and far-sighted'.[1] The 1971 committee stated that 'the history of legal education in England over the past 120 years is largely an account of the struggle to implement the recommendations of the 1846 committee and the effects of that struggle'.[2]

What Mr Justice Roger Ormrod and his colleagues did not say, nor had they any particular reason to comment on the fact in 1971, was that the select committee of 1846 owed its origins and its primary agenda to an Irish adventure in legal training. The twin objectives of this paper are, firstly, to demonstrate why the earlier committee which published such an important and influential report had been appointed and, secondly, to recall the two remarkable Irishmen responsible for its establishment.

Within Ireland, long before 1846, the absence of an institution devoted to professional legal training had become a cause for recurrent complaint. One of the outcomes of the Anglo-Norman invasion of Ireland in 1169 was that the old Gaelic or 'brehon' system of legal education declined until, after some centuries, it perished. It had been an elaborate and sophisticated system, which was older and at least as complex as that system of training which developed at the London inns of court in their heyday.[3]

The common law adventurers who came to Ireland were hostile to Gaelic lawyers and their law schools. However, the adventurers themselves did not establish institutions of their own for legal education. There is an indication

---

1 [Ormrod] *Report of the committee on legal education ...* (Cmnd. 4595, London, 1971), p. 5.
2 ibid., p. 8.
3 D.A. Binchy, 'Lawyers and chroniclers' in Brian O'Cuiv, *Seven centuries of Irish learning, 1000–1700* (Cork, 1971), p. 50; Fergus Kelly, *A guide to early Irish law* (Dublin, 1988), pp. 242–63; Máirín Ní Dhonnchadha, 'An address to a student of law' in Donnchadh Ó Corráin, Liam Breatnach and Kim McCone (eds.), *Sages, saints and storytellers: Celtic studies in honour of Professor James Carney* (Maynooth, 1989), pp. 164–70; Nerys Patterson, 'Brehon law in late medieval Ireland' in *Cambridge Medieval Celtic Studies*, xvii (summer, 1989), 56–57.

that senior practitioners of the common law provided basic training at their houses in Dublin, but young men were expected to travel from Ireland to London to observe the work practices of common lawyers there. The purpose of requiring such journeys to London was at least as much cultural or ideological as it was pedagogic. With one known exception, those who made the sometimes difficult and unpleasant crossing from Ireland to attend the London inns do not appear to have participated in the actual educational exercises of the inns of court. Moreover, periodically, the Irish were the object of overt hostility and prejudice at the London inns.[4]

The fact that the pilgrimage to the metropolis was thought to have an important formative influence on those wishing to practise law in Ireland is clear from what happened in the 1540s, when certain lawyers in Ireland were emboldened to found their own inn of court, namely King's Inns. Upon the foundation of King's Inns, the government in London immediately intervened to oblige the Irish parliament to pass a statutory provision requiring young men to go to London and to reside at an English inn of court as a condition of their being admitted to practise law in Ireland.[5]

In England, Irishmen used the London inns as clubs. They passed their time observing and participating in local life. Generation upon generation enjoyed the social and political ferment of a big city while simultaneously resenting the requirement that a man must live in London before becoming a lawyer in Dublin. One of the unsuccessful demands of the Confederate Irish in the 1640s was that a discrete and competent inn of court be established in Ireland.[6] The statutory provision that Irishmen attend the English inns remained in force from 1542 until 1885, notwithstanding the fact that those inns provided little or no training of any kind from the late seventeenth century onwards. The provision was disliked even by that great Irish supporter of the union between Ireland and Britain, Edward Carson, who was a law student in the 1870s. He described the requirement as 'one of the badges of servitude of the Irish nation'. He resented, especially, the fact that, before being admitted to the Middle Temple inn of court, he like other Irish students was obliged to obtain the signatures of two English barristers as guarantors to vouch for his personal honour, 'lest [as Carson put it] he might steal the silver spoons'.[7]

Earlier, in 1792, when protestant nationalism flourished in Ireland, the benchers of King's Inns had proposed to introduce a very elaborate system of education at their Dublin institution. The old statute that required

---

4   Colum Kenny, *King's Inns and the kingdom of Ireland: the Irish 'inn of court', 1541–1800* (Dublin, 1992), pp. 6–23.
5   Ibid., pp. 28–53.
6   Ibid., pp. 120–24.
7   Edward Marjoribanks, *The life of Lord Carson* (London, 1932), p. 17. Carson later became treasurer of Middle Temple.

residency in London did not preclude such initiatives, although under its chilling influence none appears to have been attempted sooner. Had the system envisaged in 1792 come into existence it might not have been long before the Irish parliament repealed the requirement for residency at an English inn of court. However, the benchers' plan was abandoned in the face of strong objections. Objections arose partly because the proposed system was quite eccentric in its imitation of long discontinued educational practices at the English inns; and partly because practising lawyers suspected that the judges were trying to use the particular proposal to increase their power within the profession. Unlike their counterparts at the English inns of court, lawyers in Ireland remained members of the sole Irish inn after their elevation to the bench. Consequently, for centuries, judges constituted the majority of the benchers at King's Inns.[8]

About this time, there was also an adventure in professional legal training in England which had an Irish aspect. In 1796, the benchers of Lincoln's Inn permitted Michael Nolan to deliver a course of law lectures in their hall. Noonan, a Dubliner practising at the English bar and a future king's counsel, wanted the benchers of Lincoln's Inn to go further and to create an office of law lecturer in emulation of the university professorships in law. He argued that

> Such an institution will not be an absolute innovation, as it will in some degree resemble the ancient one of Reader, which has now fallen into disuse. But as the alteration in the manners of the times and the discipline of the Inns of Court would render the revival of that office inefficacious, I venture most humbly to propose that the office of Law Lecturer should be erected under the following regulations ...[9]

Although Nolan thus avoided an error which had contributed to the demise of the proposal for a course of education at King's Inns just four years earlier, when the benchers of that society had appeared to yearn for archaic institutions, he failed to persuade the benchers of Lincoln's Inn to commit themselves beyond their allowing the lectures by himself. Nevertheless, on the basis of this precedent, two further courses were subsequently permitted to be delivered, one by James Mackintosh (in the law of nature and nations) and the other by Joseph Chitty (in commercial law). Regrettably, the benchers of Lincoln's Inn did not take the opportunity which Nolan had afforded them to provide systematic legal training.[10]

These initiatives at the inns of court in Dublin and London differed from the earlier efforts of William Blackstone at the University of Oxford and

---

8 Kenny, *King's Inns and the kingdom of Ireland*, pp. 247–53.
9 *Lincoln's Inn Black Books*, iv, 66–68; *Lincoln's Inn admission register*, i, 511 (24 September 1784).
10 *Lincoln's Inn Black Books*, iv, 76–77, 120–21.

Francis Stoughton Sullivan at Trinity College Dublin, in that the former were intended to be principally for the benefit of men wishing to become legal practitioners. However, academic initiatives were also limited in scope because the provision of legal courses depended heavily on the enthusiasm of individual lecturers. The universities as institutions showed little sustained interest in the law. This was true even at the University of London, which pioneered certain legal courses in the late 1820s. The courses were closely associated with Andrew Amos, personally. When he moved on to other pursuits, his initiative was not enthusiastically maintained and, as Lord Brougham put it later, the university 'fell off very much'. Although Brougham added kindly that 'the lectures that are given still are very learned and very able lectures', he said of the general state of legal education in England that 'I am sorry to say that it is at as low an ebb as it is possible for education to be in any country'.[11]

However, the experiment at the University of London was one of the sources of inspiration for Tristram Kennedy, when he founded the Dublin Law Institute in 1839. Kennedy was a lawyer and one of two Irishmen later instrumental in the establishment of the 1846 select committee on legal education. He is a key figure in the process of professionalisation in Ireland in the nineteenth century.

Kennedy deserves to be celebrated not simply as an enlightened lawyer but also as both an educationalist and a social reformer. The descendant of one of the leading protestant families of Londonderry, he was later elected to parliament by Catholic voters. Among his other achievements, Tristram Kennedy founded the renowned Carrickmacross lace industry as a means of helping impoverished rural dwellers.[12]

Two of Tristram's brothers were also deeply involved in educational initiatives. In 1828, Evory Kennedy became lecturer in midwifery at the recently opened Richmond Hospital School, Dublin, prior to his employment as master of the Rotunda Hospital in Dublin. He is said to have almost succeeded in being appointed professor of medicine at Edinburgh University. For his part, John Pitt Kennedy became known throughout Ireland for his

---

11 *Sel. comm. leg. ed., 1846* [*Report from the select committee on legal education, together with minutes of evidence ... 1846*, H.C. 1846 (686), x, 1], qq. 3774–77; Holdsworth, *History of English law*, xii, 77–101; H.G. Hanbury, *The Vinerian chair and legal education* (Oxford, 1958), ch. 5; R.B. McDowell and D.A. Webb, *Trinity College Dublin: an academic history* (Cambridge, 1982), pp. 65–66, 100, 138–39, 193. Christopher W. Brooks, 'Apprenticeship and legal training in England, 1700–1850' in Brooks, *Lawyers, litigation and English society since 1450* (London and Rio Grande, 1998), pp. 149–78, suggests that the value of apprenticeship before 1850 is often underestimated in considering the absence of other kinds of legal education at that time.

12 Colum Kenny, *Tristram Kennedy and the revival of Irish legal training, 1835–1885* (Dublin, 1996), pp. 17–61.

views on agricultural instruction and, in 1838, was appointed the inspector-general of the nascent national school system.

Tristram Kennedy himself was called to the bar in 1834, having earlier practised for some years as an attorney and served as the sheriff of Londonderry, He turned his attention to the lack of legal training in Ireland, travelling to Germany and to other European countries to learn about their well-established law schools, as well as communicating with professors in St Petersburg and in the United States about his objective of founding an academy for legal practitioners in Ireland.

Among Tristram's correspondents were two professors at Harvard University who were pioneers of legal education. These men, Joseph Story and Simon Greenleaf, personified a methodology of legal training which Kennedy admired and which was both practical and reflective. Judge Story's attitude to training was recalled in 1952 by the then dean of law at the University of Chicago, Edward H. Levi. Addressing members of the Cook County Bar Association, Levi described Story as being part of a tradition which in a significant sense saw law as a profession of the social sciences and the humanities:

> The institutions and ideas of the common law were to be seen as ordered by a science, but they were to be understood and evaluated in terms of everything known about the nature of man and the nature of society.[13]

One might add that this philosophy was very much that of Tristram Kennedy also, and of his acquaintance Thomas Wyse. Both were practical men of principle.

Kennedy's Dublin Law Institute was founded in 1839 with the support of some prominent lawyers and judges in Ireland. This is not the place to explain why it failed within a couple of years of its foundation. Such explanations have been given by me elsewhere.[14] Suffice it to say that Kennedy and the benchers of King's Inns had a disagreement, and the disfavour of the bench was enough to deter most aspiring and practising lawyers from continuing actively to support Kennedy's venture. His institute closed and he himself, eventually, left the bar for life as a land agent among the poor. Before doing so, he joined forces with Thomas Wyse MP to persuade parliament to investigate legal education in England and Ireland.

The family of Thomas Wyse, who was to help to launch and steer the select committee of 1846, claimed descent from an English knight said to have accompanied Strongbow to Ireland in 1171.[15] The first adventurers of

---

13 Edward H. Levi, *Four talks on legal education* (Chicago, 1952), pp. 42–43.

14 Kenny, *Tristram Kennedy*, pp. 83–131.

15 Thomas Wyse, *Historical sketch of the late Catholic Association of Ireland* (2 vols., London, 1829), i, 43.

the common law arrived with a sword in one hand and a deed of title in the other, and sought to persuade the privileged natives of the jurisprudential superiority of common law principles over Gaelic precedent. Wyse's ancestors became established in Waterford, in the south-east of Ireland, where the family name is still found to this day. Wyse's ancestors also remained true to Roman Catholicism, notwithstanding considerable pressures on people of their origin and class to conform to the Anglican establishment.

Thomas Wyse, himself, was born in 1791 and benefited from the contemporary relaxation of certain penal laws that had hitherto restricted the educational opportunities of his co-religionists. As a young man, Thomas went to London with a band of friends who aspired to be lawyers and was enrolled with them at the inns of court. However, like many before him, he appears not to have intended to use that opportunity to prepare for a career at the bar. He stayed just one year on the books of Lincoln's Inn before proceeding to mainland Europe for an extended period of informal study. In later years he worked closely with Daniel O'Connell in the movement for Catholic Emancipation, but differed from O'Connell in being a federalist rather than a 'repealer' of union when it came to the political relationship between Britain and Ireland. Wyse was a great educational reformer whom Sir Robert Peel complimented as 'the consistent promoter of education in all its gradations'. He has been credited with forcing the government's hand and moulding its legislation on the introduction of primary education, not only in Ireland but also in England. He chaired a parliamentary committee of inquiry on primary education years before he came to chair the select committee on legal education. His many achievements, which include periods in office under Melbourne and Russell and his later appointment as 'envoy extraordinary' to Greece, lie beyond the scope of this paper.[16]

Kennedy greatly admired Wyse's reformist zeal and even honoured him with a special banquet in the hall of the Dublin Law Institute, at Henrietta Street, in January 1841, 'in acknowledgment of the services he [Wyse] had rendered to the cause of education'.[17] It is not surprising that, after that institute was forced to close its doors in 1842, Kennedy turned to Wyse for help in lobbying parliament to reform the entire system of legal education in Ireland. Indeed, Wyse was very active in highlighting various Irish grievances during the conservative administration of Sir Robert Peel, from 1841 to 1845.

On 22 May 1843, at Kennedy's behest, Wyse lay on the table of the house of commons a petition 'for better regulating the legal profession in Ireland'.

16 *DNB*, s.v. Wyse. For a substantial biography see James Auchmuty, *Sir Thomas Wyse, 1791–1862: the life and career of an educator and diplomat* (London, 1939).
17 Tristram Kennedy, *The state and the benchers: being an account of undischarged obligations on the part of both to the law student and the society of King's Inns, with annals and incidents on the origin of, and progress made in, systematic legal education in Ireland during the reign of Queen Victoria* (Dublin, 1878), p. 20.

At the time, the petition was simply 'presented and read and ordered to lie upon the table' but it would later prove to have been the slow-burning fuse that eventually ignited parliament's impatience with the legal profession in both Ireland and England. On that same day, Wyse also gave notice of a motion for 20 June 1843, for a committee 'to inquire into the present state of legal education in Ireland, and the means for its future improvement and extension'. The motion was subsequently adjourned in June and then deferred.[18]

On the morning following the presentation of Wyse's petition, George J. Bell, law professor in the University of Edinburgh, despatched to Kennedy a solicited letter supportive of the Dublin Law Institute. The principal of the institute was slowly gathering ammunition to use against the benchers and in November that same year won from Professor Simon Greenleaf of Harvard University a letter conveying the supportive opinion of the judges of the United States Supreme Court on the general question of reforming legal education. However, the time was not yet ripe to press for further parliamentary action and Wyse held his fire. In 1844, and again in 1845, the motion for the appointment of a committee of the House of Commons was deferred. However, Wyse then undertook to press for an enquiry in 1846.[19]

If Kennedy was primarily focused on legal training, his friend Wyse was not. The latter was more deeply involved in the general university question, having made a major speech to parliament on the subject in July 1844 and easing the way for the bill which would soon establish Queen's Colleges in Belfast, Cork and Galway. Yet, Wyse always bore in mind the need for professional legal education. In August 1844, in the course of a long letter to the Provincial Colleges Committee of Cork, which was largely devoted to the contemporary debate about the nature of university education, Wyse noted incidentally that 'the Provincial Colleges offer great facilities for preparatory or elementary general legal instruction ... but a special institution might with great advantage be established in Dublin'. He praised the Dublin Law Institute and, passing over the awkward reasons for its demise, wrote that,

> it is not here necessary to refer to the circumstances which checked its progress, but a hope may be entertained that it may yet be resumed under still more favourable auspices. I took the first steps to obtain at least a parliamentary inquiry into the practicability of such measure, and yet trust such inquiry will be granted.[20]

18 Ibid., p.21; [Tristram Kennedy], *Legal education in Ireland* (London, 1843), *passim; Hansard, 3*, lxxxv, col. 677 (7 April 1846).

19 *Sel. comm. leg. ed., 1846*, appendix iv, no. 11, pp. 349–50.

20 *Hansard, 3*, lxxvi, cols. 1121f.; Norman Atkinson, *Irish education: a history of educational institutions* (Dublin, 1969), pp. 125–26; Winifrede Wyse, *Notes on education reform in Ireland ... compiled from speeches, letters, etc., contained in the unpublished memoirs of Thomas Wyse* (Waterford, 1901), pp. 93–94.

From the terms of this letter it seems that Wyse and Kennedy had jointly worked out a strategy, whereby the benchers of King's Inns would ultimately have to respond constructively to parliamentary pressure for reform or face the likelihood of the Dublin Law Institute finally receiving statutory recognition. But the progress of the Queen's Colleges Bill and the furious sectarian debate which erupted around it early in 1845 kept Wyse occupied and provided unfavourable circumstances for parliament calmly to consider the matter of legal training.

In the spring of 1846, with winter and the Queen's Colleges Act behind him, Wyse turned his attention once more to legal education. He had never forgotten Kennedy's petition of 1843, each year considering a way of advancing its objectives at an appropriate moment. Finally, on 8 April 1846, parliament considered his motion and ordered that a select committee be appointed to enquire into the state of legal education in Ireland, and into the means for its further improvement and extension. Seven of the committee members nominated on 30 April were Irish, and nine were British. Most were lawyers themselves. Their politics were a balance of conservative and liberal. The bulk of the British members represented constituencies far from the capital, a fact which may have inclined them to view the London inns with some scepticism.[21]

It was scarcely surprising that seven out of sixteen members were Irish as the committee was mandated only to consider the position in relation to legal education in Ireland. The seven were Thomas Wyse himself, who became chairman, Sir William Somerville, a liberal from Drogheda, William Watson, a liberal from Kinsale, Sir Edmund Hayes, a tory from Donegal, Alexander McCarthy, recently elected on the Repeal ticket in Cork city, George Hamilton, a tory for Dublin University and Daniel O'Connell. The endorsement of Daniel O'Connell may have been considered important by the chairman but 'the counsellor' never attended any sessions of the committee. O'Connell, Watson, McCarthy and Hamilton had all been called to the bar in Ireland.[22]

Most of the British committee members were also members of the bar. Thus, Sir Howard Elphinstone was a barrister, magistrate and deputy-lieutenant for the county of Sussex. He had formerly practised as an advocate at Doctors' Commons. He was regarded as a radical reformer and represented the constituency of Lewes. William Christie, representing Weymouth, was a barrister on the western circuit in England. A liberal, he had been private secretary to the earl of Minto when the latter was first lord of the admiralty. William Ewart (who was added to the committee on 24 July) was a barrister and a member of the council of University College, London. Although

21 *Hansard*, *3*, lxxxv, cols. 677–91; *Sel. comm. leg. ed.*, *1846*, preface.
22 *Sel. comm. leg. ed.*, *1846* gives only 'Mr O'Connell' but O'Shaughnessy identifies him as Daniel (Mark O'Shaughnessy, 'On legal education in Ireland' in *JSSISI*, vi (1876), 126).

representing the Scottish constituency of Dumfries, he had sat for a decade for Liverpool and Wigan and was the son of a merchant and broker at Liverpool. He was a radical reformer, approving of triennial parliaments and the ballot amongst other progressive measures. For his part, Andrew Rutherford of Leith was a leading advocate at the Scottish bar. He tended to hold conservative sympathies. Spencer Horatio Walpole, elected for Midhurst earlier in 1846, had been called to the bar in 1831. Richard Godson of Kidderminster was a queen's counsel and author of *A practical treatise on the law of patents for inventions, and of copyright*, of which a number of editions had been published since 1823, and had been appointed counsel for the admiralty in February 1845. Godson was a conservative who voted against the admission of dissenters to the universities. However, he favoured the emancipation of Jews and 'negroes'. Sir Thomas Wilde, of Worcester, afterwards became Lord Chancellor Truro. The other British members were Richard Milnes of Pontefract, who had published an account of his tour in Greece, and Henry Bingham Baring of Marlborough, who was an East India proprietor and tory. The East India Company's college provided its students with some instruction in law.[23]

It was only on 5 May 1846, just ten days before the committee heard its first witness, that the house of commons decided to extend the committee's terms of inquiry to include the state of legal education in England. This was an important and logical development, prompted by the success of Kennedy and Wyse in having such a committee established in the first place:

> Mr Wyse moved that it be an instruction to the Committee on Legal Education (Ireland) to extend their inquiry and consideration to the state, improvements and extension of legal education in England. He understood there was no opposition to the motion, and therefore he would not trouble the house with any observations on the subject. The motion was agreed to.[24]

The committee met eighteen times and examined twenty-seven witnesses. Seven of these travelled over from Ireland (Kennedy, Barry, Lawson, Lyle, Mahony, La Touche and Longfield), while two more were Irish barristers working abroad (Moriarty, Norton), and the testimony of these nine Irishmen (33% of the witnesses) accounts for 115 (38%) of the 302 printed pages of evidence. In the appendix to the report, papers delivered to the committee by

---

23 *Dod's parliamentary companion 1851, passim; Sel. comm. leg. ed., 1846*, pp. 46–56.

24 *The Times*, 6 May 1846. I have found no evidence for a suggestion made to Brooks that an intervention in parliament by Henry Warburton MP was 'evidently' instrumental in having the terms of reference of the committee extended to England, and Warburton himself was not a member of the committee (Brooks, 'Apprenticeship and legal training in England, 1700–1850', p. 173n).

Irish witnesses take up 51 (57%) of the 89 pages devoted to documents which were submitted. The vast bulk of these Irish papers were provided by Tristram Kennedy and related to the Dublin Law Institute.

If, in theory, there were so many weighty members that the committee ran the risk of being unwieldy, in practice only a few of them participated actively in its proceedings. Indeed, four of the members never attended any of the eighteen sessions at which witnesses appeared or the final session at which the report was agreed. These were O'Connell, Wilde, Rutherford and Godson. Moreover, Hayes and McCarthy attended only the very first session, while Baring, Walpole, Watson and Elphinstone were present on just four or five occasions. So who then was most active? The chairman, Thomas Wyse, never missed a session. This was notwithstanding the fact that half-way through the committee's hearings he was appointed secretary to the board of control for India, the liberal Lord John Russell having replaced the conservative Robert Peel as prime minister. Most attentive after Wyse was William Christie, the barrister from the western circuit in England, who missed only one meeting of the committee. George Hamilton of Dublin University, who may have kept the Irish benchers briefed on the committee's activities, was present at sixteen of the nineteen sessions. Richard Milnes, the gentleman from Pontefract, attended twelve. William Somerville's attendance improved markedly following his appointment in July 1846 as undersecretary of state for the colonies. Having missed nine of the first eleven meetings, he managed to make it to seven of the last eight. William Ewart attended three of the five meetings which took place after he joined the committee on 24 July.

As might have been expected, most of the questioning of witnesses was conducted by the chairman himself. It is clear from the report of that questioning that the committee believed all along that the current provision for legal education in England and Ireland was completely inadequate, both in relation to the needs of the public generally and of the profession specifically. The chairman felt strongly that some education in law ought to be part of the general education of any person intent on holding an administrative position in public life. The universities were seen by the committee as the places to provide such basic training and it was thought desirable that substantial law faculties should be established to give a range of new law courses leading together to the award of law degrees or constituting individually portion of the requirement for certain other degrees such as the bachelor in arts. Future barristers and solicitors ought also to attend the university courses, but they would also need special professional training which could be provided at some new institution run by the profession itself. Committee members found themselves contending with the view, which nobody appeared before it to represent but which clearly found expression over drinks in the clubs, that many brilliant and very many adequate lawyers had arisen in the profession without any elaborate scheme of legal education and that there was no need for great and possibly burthensome reforms, 'or, in other words, there is nothing to be hoped for which we do not now possess, from an improved system of legal education'.[25] Questions were regularly aimed at eliciting rebuttals of this viewpoint. The chairman of the committee also angled for witnesses to support examinations, and some did so willingly.[26]

On 25 August 1846 the Wyse committee read and agreed its report and evidence. Next day, Wyse 'brought up' the report in parliament.[27] This, as it happened, was also the month during which blight struck the Irish potato crop for the second year running. Ireland was being overwhelmed by the Great Famine, and Irish public figures may have found little time to reflect on Wyse's considerable achievement.

Wyse's achievement was, indeed, considerable. Within what Ormrod would later describe as 'the amazingly short period of three months',[28] the Wyse committee had completed its work and produced a document which ran to over 450 pages in print. Its fundamental finding was that 'the present state of legal education in England and Ireland ... is extremely unsatisfactory and incomplete'. Its report stood not only as a major record of deficiencies in the system but also as a blueprint for future generations. However, even one hundred years later legal education had still not been organised in the comprehensive way recommended by the committee of 1846 and recognised as desirable by many in public life.

When, in 1971, the Ormrod committee on legal education in England and Wales reported, it acknowledged that the 1846 committee had provided 'a remarkable and far-sighted study of the whole problem of education for the legal profession'. Indeed, 'so relevant to our contemporary problems' did it find the opinions of the earlier committee that it dealt with it at some length and included quotations from it.[29]

The Ormrod report acknowledged that the recommendations of the 1846 committee had been 'directed to the main object of raising the intellectual standard of the profession', and that they had been 'of fundamental importance to legal education in this country', meaning England. It declared that 'the history of legal education in England over the past 120 years is largely an account of the struggle to implement the recommendations of the 1846 committee and the effects of that struggle'.[30] Ormrod, as was noted

25 *Sel. comm. leg. ed., 1846*, p. xxx.
26 See, for example, *Sel. comm. leg. ed., 1846*, qq. 1378–1433 (Andrew Amos) and 3772–3881 (Lords Brougham and Campbell).
27 *The Times*, 26 Aug. 1846.
28 [Ormrod] *Report*, p. 5.
29 Ibid., pp. 5–8
30 Ibid., pp. 7–8.

above, did not advert to the Irish origins of Wyse's committee. More remarkably, A.H. Manchester also ignored that Irish genesis when referring to the committee in his studies of the modern legal history of England and Wales and its sources.[31]

Ormrod summed up the results of the select committee of 1846 in this way:

> It was successful in stimulating the academic study of English law at the universities, which gradually attracted an increasing proportion of intending barristers and, to a lesser extent, of intending solicitors, and so helped to raise the standards of the average barrister and solicitor. It was also successful, in the end, in establishing a system of qualifying examinations for both branches of the profession.[32]

These are glowing words of praise, and some might argue that they tend to obscure other sources of stimulation and reform. There is seldom a single cause of historical development and the committee of 1846 ought to be viewed in its full social and educational context. Nevertheless, its importance was clearly considerable and was still being appreciated long after its members had passed away. As recently as 1998, Brooks has described it as having been 'quite rightly identified as the catalyst which precipitated major changes in the direction of institutional legal education during the second half of the nineteenth century'.[33]

The committee of 1846 never became known as 'the Wyse committee', in the way that the committee of 1971 is still associated personally with the name of its chairman, Roger Ormrod. This was a pity, in my opinion, for the contributions of Thomas Wyse and Tristram Kennedy to the development of legal education in Britain and Ireland deserve to be more widely recognised. Where the impact of the adventurers of the common law on legal training in Ireland had for centuries been baleful, the influence of two Irishmen on the standard of legal training in England after 1846 was clearly beneficial.

---

31 A.H. Manchester, *Modern legal history of England and Wales, 1750–1950* (London, 1980); A.H. Manchester, *Sources of English legal history: law, history and society in England and Wales, 1750–1950* (London, 1984).
32 [Ormrod] *Report*, p. 13.
33 Brooks, 'Apprenticeship and legal training in England, 1700–1850', p. 172.

Politics, law and work in modern Britain: the 1965 Redundancy Payments Act

RICHARD WHITING

THE REDUNDANCY PAYMENTS ACT of 1965 was greeted by Lord Wedderburn as likely to mark a 'decisive move towards a system of labour relations more directly structured by the law' because it introduced 'novel, positive legal rights and duties into the employment relationship'.[1] It gave employees the right to compensation in the form of a lump sum payment if their jobs came to an end. The payment was based on length of service, with the rate of payment increasing for those over 41 years of age. It was meant to compensate for the loss of seniority and other rights built up over time, and destruction of the expectation that a job might continue into the future. It recognised rights built up with one employer over time, not with an occupation, like ship repair, that could be undertaken with a series of employers over any given year. It acknowledged a growing public sense that a job meant much more than could simply be accounted for in the weekly wage; it no longer seemed good enough that when a job came to an end an employer's obligation, having been discharged through the payment for work done, also finished. Instead, if workers had to end their employment, as long as they had worked for two years, they would receive an additional lump sum compensating them for the fact of termination.

The rationale for this Act was straightforward. It was trying to recognise, and therefore reconcile, two dimensions of work. The first was work as a *collective duty* to contribute to society's prosperity; the second was work as an *individual activity* which fulfilled vital needs for social belonging and personal dignity. If work was to be collectively efficient, particular jobs had to come to an end in the interests of the productivity and technical change necessary to sustain growth. Post-war 'full employment' for society as a whole actually implied a good deal of job change for individuals: 'full employment, therefore, cannot mean the right to the same job in the same place for all

---

1 K.W. Wedderburn, 'Trade disputes Act 1965, Redundancy Payments Act 1965', *Modern Law Review*, 29 (1966), 55. I am grateful to the British Academy and the University of Leeds for supporting the research on which this essay is based, and to Kevin Costello for valuable editorial comments and guidance on an earlier draft.

time.'² Accounts of unemployment in the inter-war period not only featured the debilitating effects of joblessness over long periods, but also focused on the wearying and dispiriting search for work.³ It was this latter source of anxiety that post-war economic policy could not alleviate. A vivid example of the insecurity of particular jobs, which caught the public eye, involved the sacking of 6,000 workers by the British Motor Corporation in a move that was announced on Wednesday 27 June 1956 and carried out on Friday the 29th; according to its investigator, 'it came as a rude shock to the nation'.⁴

Shattering though it was, the BMC case was only one dimension of the problem. By the 1960s it seemed likely that a good many employers were hoarding labour for fear of the harm to industrial relations that redundancies brought. It was not that employers were ignoring the sense of insecurity arising from redundancy; rather, they were perhaps giving it too great a respect, as least as far as the efficiency of the economy was concerned. The insecurities surrounding unemployment therefore had to be addressed if economic growth – the emerging imperative for governments in the 1960s – was to be achieved. That entailed responding to the widespread view that an individual developed an interest in a particular job over time which had to be compensated for if disturbed, but also doing so in such a way that productivity growth would not be impeded by labour hoarding. This was the context for the 1965 Redundancy Payments Act introduced by the Labour government. This paper is concerned with the early years of its operation, and the case law it discusses is drawn from reported cases for the period 1966–69.

The Redundancy Payments Act presents two connected problems for analysis. The first concerns its political complexion. Although the Labour government introduced the Act, the Conservatives had shown a strong commitment to legislation which gave employees some protection from abrupt termination of their jobs. They had passed the Contracts of Employment Act in 1963 which required employers to give notice of dismissal linked to the length of employment, and could point to an earlier interest both in 'The Workers Charter' of 1947 and a private members' bill of 1950, supported by, amongst others, Robert Carr, Edward Heath, Iain Macleod and Peter Thorneycroft. This bill, which failed, would not only have obliged employers to set the conditions of their employment, but also the terms on which they would be compensated if dismissed.⁵ These forays

---

2 'Redundancy and severance pay', by Jack Diamond, being a paper submitted to the Labour Party's redundancy study group (People's History Museum Manchester, Labour Party Archive, RD 648/Jan. 1964).

3 See, for example, the experiences cited in William Beveridge, *Full employment in a free society* (London, 1944), pp. 242–43.

4 Hilda Kahn, *Repercussions of redundancy: a local survey* (London, 1964), p. 21.

5 'The Worker's Charter' had been published as an annex to *The Industrial Charter. A*

into legal regulation of severance, and hints towards compensation for dismissal, explain why some Conservatives were disappointed by how tentative the 1963 Act had been, and their government was developing legislation on severance pay when they lost the 1964 election.[6] Labour's interest had been signalled in an unsuccessful private member's bill of Jack Diamond which had intended to provide minimum terms of severance pay for those dismissed for reasons beyond their control.[7] Diamond had also submitted a paper recommending lump sum payments to the Labour Party's redundancy group.[8] It is clear that both Conservative and Labour parties were responding to a national agenda that emphasized the importance of increasing economic growth in Britain. The principles which underlay Labour's 1965 Redundancy Payments Act were accepted by the Conservatives.[9] What lay behind this apparent agreement? The Conservatives had developed a strategy of protection for individual workers as a *quid pro quo* for them accepting greater change at work. They had good reasons to try and articulate and represent individual interests at work. Support for the individual worker fitted in neatly with the post-1945 opposition to socialism and nationalization, and was also relevant to the developing anxieties within the Party about the growing power of trade unions in the 1960s. Labour, perhaps inevitably, did not regard issues of industrial policy as best approached through consideration of the individual worker. The Party's whole ethos was built upon collectivism. It saw a need for manpower planning for the economy as a whole of which redundancy and training policies were components. The adjustments demanded by a dynamic economy would to a degree be eased by the anticipation of changing employment patterns rather than simply compensating for the consequences of decisions by private businessmen. This suggests a question about whether or not some essential differences of complexion lay behind the broad agreement about the Act. What was the relationship of the Act to the competing forces of collectivism and individualism?

The second issue concerns the effectiveness of the law in giving adequate reflection to the varied interests that workers brought to employment. This essay accepts the core assumption of the Act that job loss could be

---

statement of Conservative policy (London, 1947), pp. 28ff. For the private members' bill see *Hansard 5*, vol. 480, cols. 2043–44, 17 Nov. 1950. There is a useful analysis of the development of redundancy policy in Dave Lyddon, 'From unemployment to redundancy pay', in Ad Knotter, Bert Altena, Dirk Damsma (eds.), *Labour, social policy and the welfare state* (Amsterdam, 1997), pp. 105–10.

6 *Hansard 5*, vol. 671, col. 1552, 14 February 1962: speech of William Robson Brown.

7 *Hansard 5*, vol. 658, col. 817, 1 May 1960.

8 'Redundancy and severance pay' (People's History Museum Manchester, Labour Party Archive, RD 648/Jan. 1964).

9 *Hansard 5*, vol. 711, col. 61, 26 April 1965: speech of Joseph Godber.

compensated for by money payment. That view can, of course, be challenged, although it is difficult to see how any political system could guarantee *particular* jobs, as opposed to a commitment to provide work that might entail changes in occupation.[10] What it seeks to assess is the sensitivity with which the Act treated employment and the needs which people brought to their jobs. It considers how far the Act recognised employees' connections to particular jobs, and the various elements that comprised that linkage, whether they be to do with a sense of vocation, the recognition of a particular status, or the importance of a job for meeting family obligations.

The legal dimension has, not surprisingly, to be pursued through a study of process as well as content. The Act allowed for appeals to industrial tribunals, which were intended to provide informal and speedy adjudication within a law designed to give them considerable scope for the exercise of their own discretion. Although the chairmen of the tribunals were to have legal experience, the two other members, one from the employers and the other from labour, were there to provide judgments based on a general experience of working life. Appeals against the judgments of tribunals on points of law were allowed to the ordinary courts; it was there that some legal academics feared a more rigid and unsympathetic approach might be taken by the judiciary.[11]

It is the theme of this essay that the political and social character of the Act can be examined by considering the elements of individualism and collectivism in its operation. Clearly the Act focused on individuals, and applied to many businesses where trade unions had no place. If the Act operated not only in the absence of trade unions but also in disregard of them, then it struck a powerful blow for individualism in industrial relations. This effect would have been diluted the more the trade unions had a place within the Act. The role of the contract of employment in redundancy issues will play a significant part in deciding this issue. This was of fundamental importance in determining the nature of the job as originally established, and therefore the extent to which later changes could be accommodated within it or created a discontinuity in the employment. These issues were at the heart of many disputed redundancy cases. Whether or not an employer had made basic changes in a job, or in offering a new one had made significant departures from the old, usually had to be determined by reference to the contract of employment. However, the law of contract seemed particularly inappropriate for capturing the nature of the employment relationship for two reasons. First, it focused on a precise moment at the start of a relationship which was

10 For a discussion of the values at the heart of the Act, see R.H. Fryer, 'Redundancy, values and public policy', *Industrial Relations Journal*, 3 (1973), 2–19.
11 See, for example, K.W. Wedderburn and P.L. Davies, *Employment grievances and disputes procedures in Britain* (Berkeley, California, 1969), esp. pp. 266–69.

bound to develop organically over time, and which suggested the constant renewal of the contract in the light of continual bargaining between employer and employee.[12] Second, it focused on the individual employee, and with the development of collective bargaining, this seemed an unrealistic way of conceptualising the employment relationship. As one tribunal noted, 'Cammell Laird, like so many other employers, apparently pay little regard to the contractual element in labour relations.'[13] However, the redundancy legislation forced tribunals and courts to consider the terms of contracts of employment, and the extent to which their judgments gave a rounded or narrow interpretation of the employment relationship will be a crucial element in determining the political and social nature of the Act.

It is important at the outset to establish the resilience of the central concept of the Act. It was not a welfare payment rooted in need. A Labour Party political broadcast was therefore thought to be misleading when it included redundancy payments within the 'social wage' as one of the benefits to be claimed by the unemployed.[14] Redundancy payments did have this practical function, but they were principally a form of compensation for disturbance arising from the loss of a job without fault, and not hardship.[15] If a redundant employee subsequently got another job without delay the payment was still fully justified. In terms of the political mood in Britain in the 1960s, there were two pressures acting on this principle. Precisely because redundancy payments were often thought of as part of a welfare system, they were caught up in the anxieties about low income families exploiting the social services to avoid the morally desirable search for work.[16] There was also disquiet about employees who received redundancy payments even though they did not 'need' them because they found work soon afterwards; in the most publicly discussed cases, it happened that workers were quite within the law to be re-engaged by the same employer, as happened in 1966 when two car makers, BMC and Rootes, took back workers who had been dismissed.[17]

The second reason to scrutinize the workings of the Act arose from its cost. Employers contributed to a fund which bore part of the cost of

12 J.R. Commons, *The legal foundations of capitalism* (New York, 1924), p. 286.
13 *Joel and another* v. *Cammell Laird (Ship-repairers) Ltd.* [1969] I.T.R. 206.
14 'Review of working of Redundancy Payments Act 1965', I.S. Dewar to P.J.H. Edwards (both Ministry of Labour), 2 October 1968 (TNA:PRO, Ministry of Labour papers LAB 10/3375).
15 For elaboration of these principles see the views of Dingle Foot, the solicitor-general, in *Hansard, standing committee proceedings (D)*, 1964–5, vol. 2, cols. 75–78, 4 May 1965.
16 'Review of working of Redundancy Payments Act 1965', 'Note of a meeting between Richard Crossman, Secretary of State for Social Services, and Roy Hattersley, Parliamentary Secretary, Department of Employment and Productivity', 1 August 1968 (TNA:PRO, LAB 10/3375).
17 'Review of the working of Redundancy Payments Act 1965', 'The main criticisms of the Act – an evaluation' (TNA:PRO, LAB 10/3365 WG(RP)4.)

redundancy payments, especially in the cases of older workers above the age of 41 who received a higher rate of payment. However, by 1968 the fund was ceasing to be self-financing. At a time when the Labour government was trying to reduce the growth in public expenditure, there were good reasons to make the scheme self-balancing, perhaps by reducing payments to those who secured new employment quickly. This would also have stilled some of the anxieties about the apparent generosity of the scheme in its coverage of those who were far from needy. Nevertheless, the core principle of the Act, that it did not deal with welfare payments to the poor but covered all employees whose jobs had come to an end, and was essentially a form of compensation, remained untouched, and the problem was met by higher contributions from employers.[18]

Besides awarding compensation for disturbance, the Act defined the nature of a job. To do this successfully, the Act had to prioritize 'jobs' over 'work'. The more a job merged into a general activity called 'work' and was organized by an employer who could attach or detach employees at will, the less an employee 'owned' his particular job. The more work was attached to the individual employee, the less discretion the employer exercised. It was in the employee's interest that the Act defined a job as precisely as possible, so that any departure from that definition won compensation, because the individual had been dismissed from 'his' job.

This degree of connection with a particular job was tested in two particular ways under the Act. First, the dismissal had to be for redundancy; it could not arise merely because a worker had been dismissed for misconduct, or because of some inadequacy. It did not apply where there had been re-organisation of work with no diminution in the level of activity. But if a particular function within a business, and the need for a particular employee, had ceased, then there was a redundancy. The definition of redundancy in the Act was very specific both as to function and place. Redundancy arose when 'the requirements of that business for employees to carry out work of a particular kind, or for employees to carry out work of a particular kind in the place where he was so employed, have ceased or diminished or are expected to cease or diminish'.[19] This identified changes taking place within, and not merely between, firms. A company might have been producing car bodies over a particular period, with no sign of diminishing output or requirements in the total number of workers employed. This was a definition of employment as linked with a total quantity of work. But if in the course of its activities, the company had switched from making wooden to plastic bodies, and had therefore got rid of its woodworkers, these

---

18 'Proposals for reducing the cost of the redundancy payments scheme', memorandum by Barbara Castle, 10 June 1968 (TNA:PRO, LAB 10/3370).
19 Redundancy Payments Act 1965, s.1(2) (*b*).

employees would have been made redundant and therefore qualified for a payment. This was a definition of employment as particular jobs.

One of the cases where the specification of particular employment, as opposed to the work of a company, arose was in *Smith* v. *G.K. Purdey Trawlers Ltd.*[20] The applicant was a chief engineer whose expertise lay in steam ships and was unable to operate replacement diesel-engined vessels. The company argued that its work had not changed, it was simply being carried out in different ships and therefore there was no redundancy, merely inadequacy. A company, in its view, had every right to expect that an employee could adapt to new methods and techniques. The tribunal, however, held by a majority opinion that he had been made redundant, because work 'of a particular kind' had ceased. Equally instructive was the judgment of Parker C.J. in *Dutton* v. *C.H.Bailey Ltd*. Here, some boilermakers had refused to sign a new agreement over working practices designed to ensure greater productivity. The tribunal did not see the dismissals as arising from redundancy, but from a breakdown in the bargaining process about a new working arrangement. On appeal Parker C.J. took a different view: without the new agreement the boilermakers would have been redundant because work would have diminished. It was therefore a dismissal for redundancy. The law ran against the grain of Parker C.J.'s thinking: 'I come to this decision with reluctance because it seems to me there should be every inducement for employers to make themselves more competitive, and every reason for employees to do away with their restrictive practices and the like.'[21] But this was the crux of the Act. Precisely because the need for economic growth and improved productivity was so widely accepted as a desirable focus for managerial energies, the consequences of unemployment that was in some cases a by-product had to be compensated for. The Act did not intrude upon managerial decisions to make such changes, but it did demand that the employing class pay a price for them.

These kinds of judgments were not confined to those where a change of process had resulted in, or might in the future cause, reduction in the need for certain kinds of work. In *Ramage* v. *Harper-Mackay Ltd.*[22] the tribunal was careful enough to establish that what had been presented as the case of a salesman failing to meet sales targets had in fact arisen from a strategy to reduce the number of salesmen so that in any year one of them was bound to fail to reach their quota. What disturbs this theme of robust defence of

20 [1966] I.T.R. 508. The case was ultimately determined in the applicant's favour by the technical fact that his written notice had simply informed him that he was being dismissed because his ship was to be sold.
21 [1968] I.T.R. 355. The case is discussed in Cyril Grunfeld, *The law of redundancy* (London, 1971), p. 87.
22 [1966] I.T.R. 503.

particular jobs is the case of *Hindle* v. *Percival Boats Ltd.*[23] In this case, according to Wedderburn, 'Judicial adoption of managerial prerogatives has made nonsense of the Act's protection of the worker's "right analogous to a right of property in his job."'[24] Wedderburn's complaint rested on the way in which, in the Court of Appeal, Sachs L.J., argued that what an employer had said was the reason for dismissal carried more weight than any objective cause that a tribunal or Court of Appeal might discover. As long as the management's motive was genuinely held, there was no need to look further to establish the reason for dismissal. In this case, Hindle was a woodworker with a long employment record with a boatbuilder. The company changed hands, and was increasingly involved in the repair of fibreglass boats. Eventually, Hindle and another man were dismissed because the management claimed their work was too slow to be economical. In other words, the reason for dismissal was inadequacy and not redundancy. Lord Denning M.R. had dissented, claiming that the employer's motive was not a sound guide as to the reason for the dismissal, which to him lay in the changeover from wood to fibreglass. On the face of it, this judgment did seem to rest on an employer's claim, and was at variance with the careful exploration of the facts in *Ramage* v. *Harper-Mackay Ltd.* However, the question of 'motive' as against 'reason' was not ultimately the issue, but rather, how far the impact of the change of materials had worked themselves through sometime before Hindle's dismissal, and the fact that he had worked for some time on fibreglass and possibly wood since the change in the company's direction. It was, on the facts, a genuinely difficult case. Had the dismissals followed the change in materials and the disappearance of work in wood, then the redundancy would have been established.

A specific contract could be helpful in defining the element of capacity and place in a job in the employee's favour. Because in *Charles and others* v. *Spiralynx (1933) Ltd.*,[25] the location of a factory had been specified in a contract, it was judged on appeal that the employers had repudiated it by wanting to move workers only 5 miles away. When a salesman found that he lost an office as a result of a branch closure, but not his job as a salesman, the tribunal's judgment that no redundancy had taken place was overturned on appeal because it was implied in the contract that there would be an office provided. Such a fundamental variation in the contract permitted justifiable rejection by the employee.[26]

The definition attached to a particular employee's work was also tested in a further provision of the Act, whereby an employer could avoid a redun-

23 [1969] 1 W.L.R. 174
24 K.W.Wedderburn, *The worker and the law*, 2nd ed. (Harmondsworth, 1971), p. 133.
25 [1969] I.T.R. 257; see also Mark Freedland, *The contract of employment* (Oxford, 1976), p. 242.
26 *Hall* v. *Farrington Data Processing Ltd.* [1969] I.T.R. 230.

dancy payment if an employee was offered either a similar job to his old one or, if the job differed, it was still a reasonable offer and should have been accepted. It was this provision that established the flexibility in working practices an employer could demand.

The collective interest in efficient labour required that work be interpreted flexibly to take account of changing economic needs. In contrast, from the individual's point of view, if the nature of the employment changed, and it therefore failed to fulfil a sense of occupational identity, or some other function, then it ceased to be the same job. So the question of when an employee might reasonably turn down the offer of alternative employment went to the heart of the tension between societal and individual claims upon work. The balance that was struck between these two claims would clearly be an important test of whether the Act looked to the economic claims of society or the social interests of the individual. Crucially, the Act focused on the judgment made by the employee as to whether the offer of alternative employment was suitable or not. An employer could make what most would consider to be a reasonable offer of a new job, but an employee could still reasonably refuse it, if it did not, from his point of view, meet his requirements. Despite their overall agreement about the purpose of the Act, this was an area where Labour and Conservatives disagreed. The Conservatives wanted a consideration of other interests, including the employer's, in what constituted a reasonable rejection of a job offer.[27] The tribunals received little guidance as to what were the grounds for refusing a reasonable offer of a job. As one tribunal report explained, 'no authority was brought to our attention as to the construction to be placed upon the relevant provisions [of the Act].'[28] What most tribunals decided to do was to apply what one described as a 'subjective test', that is, to see whether, from the particular circumstances of the employee, it was reasonable to refuse the new employment and therefore qualify for a redundancy payment.[29] If tribunals were generous in their interpretation of the employee's interest, but also restrictive in their definition of the job, this was the most favourable stance from the point of view of the employee.

Where a job involved a trade, there was usually a strong case if the new contract involved different kinds of work. A patternmaker who refused an apparent promotion to a clerical job was justified in so doing 'mainly because he had been employed as a craftsman for the whole of his working life and he wanted to continue in a job that he understood and for which he was trained,

---

27 *Hansard, standing committee proceedings (D)*, 1964–5, vol. 2, cols. 115–16, 129–30, 11 May 1965.
28 In *Sheppard v. NCB* [1966] I.T.R. 177; for the question of tribunals' discretion, see Geoffrey Howe's comments in *H C Deb, standing committee proceedings (D)*, vol. 2, 1964–65, col. 135, 11 May 1965.
29 *Rawe v. Power Gas Corporation Ltd.* [1966] I.T.R. 155.

rather than move to a job of which he had no experience and for which he
felt he might not be suitable'.[30] In the case of a french polisher who refused
work as a painter, the tribunal felt that where no specific provision existed in
the contract for such a change, transfer from one job to another did not
permit the employer to move the employee from 'trade to trade'.[31] At another
tribunal, a works manager claimed that they 'could not have men picking and
choosing jobs', but a worker who refused to move from being a bench fitter
to operating a capstan lathe was held to be justified in refusing this new
work.[32] But these judgments did not merely apply to craft workers.
According to one tribunal , 'A man who habitually drives a lorry may well not
wish to be employed on pipe-laying for no matter how short a period, despite
any principle or practice of "interchangeability" which his employer may
seek to put into effect.'[33]

The Tribunals were also aware of the elements of social standing involved in
modifications to a job. A salesman who had failed to increase his sales figures
was offered a position of a warehouseman with occasional spells as a relief
salesman. In the tribunal's view, to have accepted the job in the warehouse
'would have undermined the applicant's relationship with his customers if he
required to meet them as a relief salesman'. Further, he deserved the
compensation of a redundancy payment because the 'loss of position ...
would affect his prospects as a sales representative'.[34]

The way in which alternative employment raised the issue of the occupational status of the employee had been clearly grasped by Clive Jenkins,
general secretary of the Association of Supervisory Staffs, Executives and
Technicians (ASSET). Jenkins had been a virtually lone voice from the trade
unions in arguing for legislation over redundancy, and the two Labour MPs
in the forefront of the campaign, Julius Silverman and John Diamond, were
both sponsored by ASSET. Jenkins was very keen to establish that the offer
of manual work would not count as reasonable alternative employment:

> We are likely to be particularly sensitive to the employers offering manual
> employment as 'suitable' alternative work. Quite clearly, we should resist
> this with great determination and argue that redundancy in our grades is,
> in effect, an end to that particular employment.

He was delighted when an early tribunal ruling confirmed his view.[35]

30 *Souter* v. *Henry Balfour and Company Ltd.* [1966] I.T.R. 383.
31 *Cannon* v. *William King and Sons Ltd.* [1966] I.T.R. 452.
32 *Champion* v. *Hellerman Terminals Ltd.* [1966] I.T.R. 72.
33 *Royle* v. *The Dredging & Construction Company Ltd.* [1966] I.T.R. 233.
34 *Ramage* v. *Harper-Mackay Ltd.* [1966] I.T.R. 503.
35 'Severance pay and tribunal reference', memorandum of Clive Jenkins, 4 Feb. 1966 (University
   of Warwick, Modern Records Centre, ASTMS archive, MSS 79/AS/3/8/107).

The Act also specified place of employment as an important factor in determining the degree of change which an alternative job offer entailed, and here the role of a job in meeting family obligations, or, indeed, the secondary nature of work in relation to other priorities, were clearly established. In a number of cases where the alternative employment required re-location, the age of employees' children, the health of a wife, or the obligation to look after elderly relatives, all played their part in justifying refusal and the award of a payment.[36] In *White, Coker, Sizmur, Osmond and Pisani* v. *Bolding (John) and Sons Ltd.*,[37] disability in one case and a possible break-up of a marriage in another justified refusal to move. While building workers could be expected to move around from site to site, and the provision of lodging allowances indicated an implied expectation of working away from home, there was a view that the mobility expected especially of semi-skilled workers could not be very great, and should be restricted to the locality.[38]

There were, inevitably, cases where tribunals varied in their judgments. While in one case a group was entitled to refuse a switch from a night to a day shift purely on the grounds of their familiarity with the former, in another case where night shift work fitted into the caring of a child, the refusal to move to day work did not justify a redundancy payment.[39] In this latter case, the tribunal referred to the contract of employment details which had not specified night shift work. So far the judgments of tribunals have been portrayed as, for the most part, liberal and sensitive to particular conditions of employment. Indeed, many tribunals went out of their way to stress how far their judgments applied to an individual case and were not meant to bind others. A good many of these cases arose from small scale establishments, often involved white-collar as well as blue collar employees, and without a conspicuous trade union presence. This legal intervention into the nature of work may be contrasted with situations where a trade union presence was strong, especially on the shop floor. Studies of 'custom and practice' showed the development of rules of job regulation which were central to the way work was done and often of far greater importance than formal agreements. These rules operated in the workers' interests; they were 'the product of management error and worker power'.[40]

Both 'custom and practice' and the industrial tribunals embodied, in their different ways, rule setting and rule observance. In the absence of a strong

36 See *Cahuac, Johnson and Crouch* v. *Allen Amery Ltd.* [1966] I.T.R. 313; *Silver* v. *J.E.L. Group of Companies* [1966] I.T.R 238; *Rawe* v. *Power Gas Corporation Ltd.* [1966] I.T.R. 155.
37 [1966] I.T.R. 446.
38 *Moore* v. *R.H.Mc Cullogh Ltd.* [1966] I.T.R. 484.
39 *Morrison and Poole* v. *Cramic Engineering Company Ltd.* [1966] I.T.R. 404; *Jones* v. *W.G. Youngman Ltd.* [1966] I.T.R. 463.
40 William Brown, 'A consideration of "custom and practice"', *British Journal of Industrial Relations*, x (1972), 61.

trade union presence, the law provided an alternative set of rules which did not depend upon fluctuations in bargaining power but which had an external force. In place of the guiding hand of the shop steward and his organisation were the judgments of the tribunals, incorporating both legal knowledge but also the experience of industry. However, despite the fact that tribunals were regarded as embodying a certain amount of 'industrial common sense', they had to negotiate some difficult issues in private law doctrine, such as theories of contractual repudiation and privity of contract.

One of the most closely examined cases involving repudiation of a contract was *Marriott* v. *Oxford Co-operative Society Ltd.*[41] The employee was an electrical maintenance foreman and when his department was run down, the management offered him alternative work as a supervisor. This was a different kind of employment, where he 'would do more manual work with his jacket off'. The reduction in status was accompanied by a reduction in pay. The employee protested, went to look for another job, but carried on working until he found alternative employment . The Divisional Court found that there had been a common law 'consensual variation' in the contract. This was overturned by the High Court, on the grounds that there was definite repudiation of the contract by the employers because of the down-grading in status and pay and without Marriott having any choice in the matter.[42] It was irrelevant that Marriott had carried on working since his contract had been terminated by the operation of law when the employer had unilaterally varied the contract. As was pointed out in commentaries, the decision involved a deviation from the conventional doctrine that a contract was terminated only where the victim immediately 'accepted' the repudiation by resigning from the relationship. Mark Freedland judged it 'a departure which is well justified by the realities of the employment relationship'.[43]

In the course of making his judgment in favour of Marriott, Winn L.J. had pleaded in a more fundamental way for a greater recognition of the special character of the employment relationship:

> in relations between employers and workmen and employers and the workmen's union, there should be, as far as it can possibly be achieved, simplicity; academic discussions as to the operation in certain circum-stances in the law of contract of repudiation and acceptances, and acceptance of offers, novations and counter offers, and so on, should not be allowed to produce waste of time or energy.[44]

41 *Marriott* v. *Oxford Co-operative Society Ltd.* [1969] I.T.R. 125.
42 Winn L.J. in [1970] 1 QB 186.
43 M.Freedland, 'The meaning of dismissal in the Redundancy Payments Act, 1965', *MLR*, 33 (1970), 96.
44 [1970] 1 QB 186.

Simplicity was not always possible, especially where the role of trade unions was concerned. Detailed investigation was required where the fact of a redundancy turned on the incorporation of a collective agreement into the contracts of individual employees. The reason tribunals had to tread carefully lay in the doctrine of privity of contract. A contract was only binding on the immediate parties to that contract. The mere fact that a trade union had made an agreement on behalf of its members with their employer did not make that agreement part of the contracts of employment of individual employees. The collective agreement could not therefore be binding upon them. For that condition to exist, there had to be some specific recognition or acknowledgement of that agreement in the contracts of individuals. Where there was no such acknowledgment that an individual's conditions of employment were bound by collective agreement, tribunals had to exercise some care to establish knowledge and acceptance of such agreements by applicants for redundancy payments. Cases usually arose because an employer wanted to re-organize work in some way (re-grading, or transfer to other functions, for example), believed that a collective agreement gave him the right to do this, and then found individual workers claimed a redundancy payment because their contracts did not include this agreement and therefore their original jobs could be regarded as coming to an end.

In the case of *Joel and another* v. *Cammell Laird (Ship-repair) Ltd.*,[45] two workers refused to move from ship-repair to ship-building work, even though this had been provided for in a collective agreement between the company and their trade union. They claimed that this agreement was not part of their contracts and therefore not binding upon them. Their jobs had therefore come to an end and they deserved to receive a redundancy payment. The tribunal was able to establish that both men knew about the agreement (one of them had been a shop steward), were used to working under trade union rules, and had not 'held themselves aloof' from other benefits provided by the agreement. But the documentary evidence for the importation of the collective agreement into the individuals' contracts was decidedly thin, consisting mainly in the way in which certain documents pointed the employees to the relevant 'package deal' that permitted employers to move workers from ship-repair to ship-building. The tribunal still believed that the applicants had accepted the agreement and therefore could not receive redundancy payments, but the scope of their decision was significantly reduced by its reliance on the practical acceptance by the two individuals rather than the formal incorporation of the collective agreement into their contracts: 'We would emphasise that we have laid great stress upon the personalities and individual situations of the two applicants when in the

---

45 [1969] I.T.R. 206.

employment of the respondents. We by no means intend to imply by our decision that any other employee would be similarly bound.'

The tension between customary arrangements developed at the place of work, and the rules established by law arose most clearly over the number of hours worked, and the pay, to be factored into the calculation of the redundancy payment. Many 'normal' working weeks included regular, if not invariable, amounts of overtime; excluding those from the calculation diminished the sum a worker might have expected to receive based on his own conception of his working week. The law, and the tribunals, only recognised overtime where it was compulsory.[46] Any element in wages that was not strictly earned by the individual, even if it was artificial to regard it so, was excluded. In *Lochead* v. *Ministry of Labour and West Lothian Steel Foundry Company Ltd.*[47] a worker paid by hourly rates also received a bonus calculated on the output of piece workers, which was a fairly common arrangement to reflect the co-operative element in factory work and the need to reward those whose individual jobs could not be assessed on an incentive basis. However, the tribunal ignored this in the calculation of the payment on the grounds that the figure for earnings could only reflect what an individual had done and to accept the bonus in this case would 'open the door to innumerable pleas that some special set of circumstances required some special and novel method of calculating redundancy payment'.

The common law of contract was the basis of all employment relations, and the Act inevitably revealed its significance where, in the day-to-day practice of industrial relations, it had inevitably retreated into a certain obscurity. It is difficult to make an overall judgement as to whether or not employees benefited from this. In certain circumstances the contract helped to define a job more precisely and, therefore, confirmed that a change of conditions ended a job and generated a payment; but in other areas, especially over wages, the definition of earnings in the contract appeared restrictive. In the larger context, the Act certainly embraced an individualist view of employment that ran against rthe collectivist traditions of the labour movement. Did the Act therefore marginalize the trade unions in the process of redundancy? By its very nature it had this effect, since it covered the majority of employees and not merely those who worked where trade unions were active. As an illustration of the consequences of this, only about a quarter of employees in the early years of the Act were represented by trade unions at tribunals.[48] Trade unions had long wanted to keep the law out of industrial relations, and their tradition of collectivism was set aside in the

46 Normal working hours were defined by the Contracts of Employment Act 1963, sched. 2, para.1 (1 and 2). See also Mark Freedland, *The contract of employment*, pp. 17–18.
47 [1966] I.T.R. 547.
48 For figures see Wedderburn and Davies, *Employment grievances*, table 31, p. 252.

focus on the individual. But the issue was perhaps more sharply posed than this. When the legislative process dealing with employment rights started in 1963 with the Conservative government's Contracts of Employment Act, it was frequently remarked that employers and trade unions had made disappointingly little progress in the 1950s through their voluntary efforts on these questions.[49] The usual 'line' of the TUC had been that arrangements for dealing with redundancy could not be established through general rules but were best left to negotiation through collective bargaining.[50] When the Labour MP, Julius Silverman, introduced a private member's bill for a severance pay scheme, the trade union MPs were conspicuously absent.[51] If the process of voluntary bargaining to which the trade unions were committed had failed to generate reforms of practical value to employees, and these reforms by their very nature relied little upon the unions, then this new stage in labour relations had negative implications for collectivism.

It is not difficult to find evidence of views in the labour movement that to even accept the notion of redundancy was to play into the hands of the capitalists. The London district committee of the engineers' union believed 'the lure of redundancy payment erodes the moral fibre of the workers to resist unemployment and the right to work'.[52] But trade union members, and other employees, valued redundancy payments, and trade unions had to come to terms with the legal process. In the early years of the Act, trade union officials did not play a big part in the cases coming in front of tribunals; in 1966 they were involved in 26% of all cases and 20% of those cases selected for published report in 1968.[53] But many were uneasy even with this limited exposure to the system, finding it more formal and intimidating than the national insurance tribunals that they had also experienced. The industrial tribunals dealing with redundancy questions seemed more adversarial than the insurance tribunals, and closer to courts of law. Some were concerned that trade union officials did not have the necessary expertise to cope: 'This is obviously a completely new technique the officer must employ, a technique not obviously acquired without practice and experience. A knowledge of court procedure would be extremely helpful in these cases.'[54] Paul O'Higgins reported that

---

49 See *Hansard 5*,vol. 671, cols. 1536 and 1560, 14 February 1963: speeches of Renton and Carr.

50 Redundancy file, letter of George Woodcock (TUC General Secretary) to G.E. Dearing, National Union of Hosiery Workers, 13 July 1962. (University of Warwick, Modern Records Centre [MRC], TUC archive MSS 292B 107.52/1).

51 Redundancy file, note of 19 Feb. 1964 (MRC, TUC MSS 292B, 107.52/3).

52 Responses to TUC circular letter soliciting views about the Act, 20 March 1969 (MRC, TUC MSS 292B, 107.52/8).

53 Wedderburn, *The worker and the law*, p. 137. See also Wedderburn and Davies, *Employment grievances*, pp. 245–69 for a discussion of the working of the tribunals.

54 'Appointments to Tribunals', D.L. Beard, a district organizer with the Transport and

I remember one very famous trade union leader explaining how he protected the interests of his members when he argued their case for redundancy compensation in front of official tribunals. ' I speak loudly', he said. 'I bang the table and I get my way.' [O'Higgins went on] That man was not always helping his members; because of his ignorance of the rules which decide whether or not a worker gets redundancy compensation he lost many cases for his members which he should have won.[55]

In the early years, some felt that the movement was losing out to the employers because of unequal representation. Noting that the Act was 'absolutely virginal in respect of case law', J. Dunn of the National Union of Mineworkers was concerned that 'the employers are very much alive to this, and you will find that employers or consortiums of employers are engaging counsel and solicitors in order to represent them before tribunals. They recognise that if this is the period when they are establishing case law they can get the level of decisions that are favourable to industry and employers, then that is going to help industry to that extent.'[56]

An early survey showed that employers did rely on legal representation more than employees. In 1966 employers had legal representation in 26% of sample cases compared to 14% of employees' cases, and this had appeared to grow for both the following year.[57] On the other hand, there was greater use by employees of trade unions than by employers of advisors from their trade associations. Moreover, there is evidence which challenges the view that the tribunal system was one in which trade union officials felt out of their depth and where the advantage was slipping away from them. Trade union officials developed a good deal of expertise, and tribunals were aware of the possible disadvantage for applicants being without legal representation and did their best to compensate for it. Moreover, suspicions about the tribunals sometimes turned out to be short-lived: 'Many trade union representatives come before the Tribunal primed with nervous belligerency and when they see the manner in which the proceedings are conducted they go away to a considerable extent reassured.'[58] While the trade unions often had particular grievances about the Act, they nonetheless acknowledged its popularity with their members and the benefits it brought to them.[59] Where unions were

General Workers Union, to G.W. Lothian of the TUC, 26 April 1966 (MRC, TUC MSS 292B 107.52/10).

55 Paul O'Higgins, *Workers' rights* (London, 1976), p. 14.

56 *Report of the 98th Annual Trades Union Congress, 1966* (London, 1966), p. 410.

57 Wedderburn and Davies, *Employment grievances*, pp. 252–53.

58 'Working party on Industrial Tribunals', letter of E.D. Grazebrook (Solicitor's Office) to Lawton (Ministry of Labour), 8 June 1966 (TNA:PRO, LAB 10/3014).

59 See Sir Sydney Ford (National Union of Mineworkers), in *Report of the 99th Annual Trades Union Congress, 1967* (London, 1967), p. 454.

weak, the chance to represent members before a tribunal was some redress against the hostility of an employer, but this legislation did mark a fundamental shift from collectively-asserted customs to individually-defended rights.

A number of points emerge from this analysis. Given the central assumption of the Act – that a money payment was a legitimate form of compensation for the loss of work – the findings of the tribunals both revealed and established sensitive interpretations of the requirements that people brought to their jobs, whether vocational or social. They did so across both white and blue collar occupations, achieving a spread that collective bargaining could not match. Along with the Contracts of Employment Act passed by the Conservatives in 1963 it advanced employees' rights considerably beyond what they had enjoyed under the common law.

A further point should be made of a more general kind. The Act was evidence of creative reform. That is, it had not resulted from unanswerable pressure to do something about redundancy by the mass of employees or their organizations . Studies carried out prior to the Act pointed out that redundancy was of a more pressing and fundamental concern to white collar than to manual workers.[60] Earnings-related unemployment benefit had been higher on the TUC's list of desirable reforms. But the concept of redundancy pay had a powerful logic which fitted in with the broader strategy of economic growth to which both Conservatives and Labour were committed. To demand that people accept a more dynamic economy required a reciprocal gesture of putting some kind of price on their sacrifice; this was the rationale of the Act, effectively articulated and defended in the period examined here.

The Act also needs to be placed within a wider context of views about employment. Its operation had both probed and revealed conventional thinking about the characteristics of jobs and their social functions. This process can be contrasted with two other contemporary perspectives on work. One viewed work as having merely instrumental justification, as it delivered leisure time and the means to enjoy it for the affluent worker. There was no need to search for meaning and fulfilment at work; these would come elsewhere, from associational, recreational, or domestic life. The other was an interest in workers' control, which was driven by the view that political democracy required some supplementation by direct involvement in the responsibilities and rewards of the enterprise. Redundancy pay operated at a different level. Of course, at its heart was a belief that the value of work could be recognised by monetary compensation. But in defining the nature of jobs and the boundaries which limited permissible changes to them as a

60 Dorothy Wedderburn, *Redundancy and the railwaymen* (Cambridge, 1965), p. 160; Alan Fox, *The Milton plan* (London, 1965), p. 28.

route to those redundancy payments, as well as providing independent adjudication of the disputes that arose over these questions, the Act was also setting out notions of fair treatment and recognition of status that were more than just economic, and were at the heart of what people valued in the social aspects of work. The Act acknowledged the potential for employment to have a judicial as well as a purely economic dimension.[61] For the majority of employees there was no mechanism, prior to the Act, for achieving this. Whatever its limitations, the Redundancy Payments Act went some way to recognising the complexities surrounding jobs in a way that other conceptions of work had failed to embody in operational form.[62]

61 For an incisive analysis of the relative capabilities of collective bargaining and the law to influence the distribution of power at work, see Hugh Collins, 'Against abstentionism in labour law', in John Eekelaar and John Bell (eds.), *Oxford essays in jurisprudence: third series* (Oxford, 1987), pp. 79–101.
62 For a valuable discussion of the Irish legislation on redundancy, that also covers some common features with the British experience, see Gavin Barrett, 'The law on "downsizing" – some reflections on the experience of the redundancy payments legislation in Ireland', *Dublin University Law Journal*, 20 (1998), 1–50.

An adventure of the law: the Spanish Champagne case

PETER SPILLER

IN THIS PAPER I examine the English case *J. Bollinger and Others* v. *Costa Brava Wine Co. Ltd.*, popularly known as the 'Spanish Champagne' case.[1] This case provided an 'adventure of the law' in two senses.[2] First, in the intellectual sense, the case marked an advance in the law of passing off which was affirmed and extended in subsequent English cases. Secondly, in the geographical sense, the case reflected the penetration of the common law into new lands, as the precedent it formed was adopted by courts outside of England.

I shall begin by presenting the *Bollinger* case, and in particular the role played by counsel for the plaintiffs, Richard Wilberforce, who later (as a lord of appeal) became known for other significant advances in the law.[3] I shall trace the intellectual adventure of the *Bollinger* precedent in England, and then its geographical adventure in other common law jurisdictions. I shall conclude by drawing together the lessons to be learnt from pursuing the legal adventures of this case.

THE 'SPANISH CHAMPAGNE' CASE: THE START OF THE INTELLECTUAL ADVENTURE

> It has never previously been decided whether a group of persons who produce a product within a geographical area, and thus attach a good-will to the name of the area, can sue a person who produces outside the area and attaches the geographical name to his produce. We say that on general principles there should be a cause of action in such cases.[4]

Bollinger and eleven other companies incorporated under French law took action on behalf of themselves and all other persons who produced wine in the Champagne district of France and who supplied this wine to England and Wales. The plaintiffs argued that their wine had long been known to the trade and public in the United Kingdom as 'champagne' and as such had

1   [1960] Ch. 262.
2   See W.J. Johnston, 'The first adventure of the common law' in *Law Quarterly Review*, 36 (1920), 9.
3   See M. Bos and I. Brownlie (eds.), *Liber amicorum* (Oxford, 1987), p. 235.
4   *Bollinger* v. *Costa Brava Wine Co. Ltd* [1959] RPC 150, 151, per Wilberforce QC.

acquired a high reputation, and that a member of the public or trade would understand 'champagne' to mean their wine. They claimed an injunction restraining the Costa Brava Wine Company, London wine and spirit merchants, from applying the trade descriptions 'champagne' or 'Spanish Champagne' to wine made in Spain or from grapes grown in Spain. The injunction was to restrain the company from passing off such wine as wine produced in the Champagne district.[5]

To appreciate the extent to which this action was an 'adventure of the law', it is necessary to understand the law of passing off as it existed up to that time. The law of passing off in the nineteenth century protected a trader with an exclusive right to a trade mark, name or get-up, and prevented a rival trader using that trade mark to induce potential customers to believe that his goods were those of the original trader.[6] Thus, for example, it was held that a company had an exclusive right to use the name 'Singer' to denote sewing machines of its manufacture; and that no one had a right to use the word for the purpose of passing off his goods as those of the company, or to use the word in any way calculated to deceive or aid in deceiving the public.[7]

By the end of the nineteenth century, there was growing recognition that what was protected by the action for passing off was not simply the proprietary right of the trader in the name, mark or get-up.[8] In 1915, Lord Parker confirmed this trend by saying that the right protected was the 'business or goodwill likely to be injured by the misrepresentation'.[9] Subsequent judges confirmed this approach.[10] In line with this view, a broader form of passing off was recognised. Thus for example, it was held that the goodwill of a football manufacturer's business was injured by someone who sold footballs *correctly* described as being made by the manufacturer. This was because the footballs sold were of an inferior *class* or *quality*, and were represented as the manufacturer's footballs of a superior class or quality.[11]

The Spanish Champagne case heralded an adventure in the law for two reasons. First, the case raised the issue of whether parties who did not have

---

5 The plaintiffs also sought a declaration that the description 'Spanish Champagne' or one including 'champagne' was a false trade description. This aspect of the case will not be examined in this paper.

6 'A man is not to sell his own goods under the pretence that they are the goods of another man' (*Perry* v. *Truefitt* (1842) 6 Beav. 66, 73, 49 Eng. Rep. 749, per Lord Langdale MR).

7 *Singer Manufacturing Co.* v. *Loog* (1882) 8 App. Cas. 15, 38.

8 *Reddaway* v. *Banham* [1896] AC 199, 209.

9 *A.G. Spalding & Bros.* v. *A.W. Gamage Ltd.* (1915) 32 RPC 273, 284. In *Inland Revenue Commissioners* v. *Muller & Co.'s Margarine Ltd.* [1901] AC 217, 223, Lord Macnaghten defined goodwill as the 'benefit and advantage of the good name, reputation and connection of a business' and as the 'attractive force which brings in custom'.

10 *Samuelson* v. *Producers' Distributing Co. Ltd.* [1932] 1 Ch. 201, 210, per Romer LJ, and *Draper* v. *Trist* [1939] 3 All ER 513, 526, per Goddard LJ.

11 *A.G. Spalding & Bros.* v. *A W Gamage Ltd.* (1915) 32 RPC 273, 284, 288.

an exclusive right to use a particular trade name, but who were only some members of a *class* consisting of all those who had a right to use the name, were entitled to protect the goodwill in the name by a passing-off action. While there were only twelve plaintiffs, they formed a small part of a class of traders that was capable of continuing expansion, since they might be joined by any future shipper of wine who could prove the right to the goodwill in England. Secondly, the case was one of novelty and importance because of the nature of the misrepresentation against which the plaintiffs were claiming to be entitled to protection. The alleged misrepresentation was not that the defendants' product was the product of the plaintiffs, or that there was a connecting identity between the two products. The alleged misrepresentation was simply that 'Spanish champagne' was wine of the *kind* that enjoyed the reputation and goodwill which attached to genuine champagne, and in which the plaintiffs had a property right.[12]

The *Bollinger* hearing took place over three days in late October 1959. Leading counsel for the plaintiffs was Richard Wilberforce QC. He had been admitted to the bar in 1932, and (except for his absence during 1939–47 in the War effort) had practised at the bar since then. He took silk in 1954 and by the late 1950s was recognised as a leader of the Chancery bar particularly in areas of commercial law. Leading counsel for the defendants was Sir Milner Holland QC and he was assisted by F.E. Skone James. The presiding judge in the High Court (Chancery Division) was Danckwerts J. He was later described by Wilberforce as a man with great sense and a thoughtful mind, who was open to learned argument.[13]

Wilberforce QC was well aware that his argument would represent an adventure of the law, as there was no precedent to support his case.[14] But so convinced was he of the justice of his cause that, when his junior barrister refused to sign the pleadings, Wilberforce took the unusual step of doing this for himself.[15] However, so confident were the opposing counsel that the action would fail that they successfully applied for the trial of preliminary points of law, so as to avoid the wasting of time in hearing the evidence.[16] Included amongst the points of law to be tried was the question whether the defendants had, as to the alleged passing off of their wine for that of the plaintiffs, 'done any act in respect of which the plaintiffs had a cause of action according to English law'.[17]

12 See *Erven Warnink B.V.* v. *J. Townsend & Sons (Hull) Ltd.* [1979] AC 731, 753.
13 Interview, Lord Wilberforce, House of Lords, 11 June 2002. Harold Danckwerts (1888–1978) was a judge of the High Court 1949–61 and lord justice of appeal 1961–69.
14 *Bollinger* v. *Costa Brava Wine Co. Ltd.* [1959] RPC 150, 151.
15 Interview, Lord Wilberforce, House of Lords, 11 June 2002.
16 *Bollinger* v. *Costa Brava Wine Co. Ltd.* [1959] RPC 289, 290. In a previous hearing, Wilberforce QC had successfully resisted the striking out of the alternative statutory offence claim (*Bollinger* v. *Costa Brava Wine Co. Ltd.* [1959] RPC 150, 153).
17 [1960] Ch. 262, 264.

Wilberforce QC began his presentation by stating the question for determination. This, he said, was whether it was part of English law that, where a number of persons produced goods in a defined geographical area which became known by the name of the area and as such acquired a reputation, those persons had a civil remedy against other persons producing goods outside the area who attached its name to their goods. He admitted that there was no conclusive authority either for or against his contention. He stressed that a true geographical name such as 'Champagne', particularly where it was attached to a natural product such as wine, constituted possibly the most valuable part of the goodwill of the person whose business it was. He observed that the defendants had said that the plaintiffs' action did not comply with the requirements of a passing-off action, as there were not the usual allegations of passing off as and for the goods of the plaintiffs. However, he said that that was 'nihil ad rem [irrelevant] as causes of action are not dispensed on a pigeon-hole basis but are simply an invention of the courts useful in dealing with particular situations'.[18]

Wilberforce QC noted the growing recognition by judges of the principle that the action of passing off protected the goodwill arising from the name in question. He further noted that, if there was only one plaintiff alleging that the description applied to his wine, he would be able to bring a passing-off action. He argued that it was 'illogical and contrary to the general interest to say that a number of persons cannot bring an action but that they can do so if formed into a corporation'.[19] He then pointed to American cases which he had researched in support of his argument.[20] Wilberforce QC was careful to add that he did not contend that there was any general right to restrain competition which was recognised as being in line with public policy. But he said that there came a point, as in this case, at which competition became unlawful because of the elements of misrepresentation and injury to property.[21]

In his reserved judgment delivered less than three weeks later, Danckwerts J accepted and echoed the principle-based argument of Wilberforce QC on the issue of passing off. Danckwerts J adopted the view that the law of passing off protected the goodwill likely to be injured by the misrepresentation in question.[22] He believed that 'the law may be thought to have failed if it can offer no remedy for the deliberate act of one person who causes damage to the property of another'. He declared that there seemed to be 'no reason why such licence should be given to a person, competing in trade, who seeks to attach to his product a name or description with which it has no natural association so

18 Ibid., at 267–68.
19 Ibid., at 268.
20 These cases included *Pillsbury-Washburn Flour Mills Co. Ltd.* v. *Eagle* (1898) 86 Fed. Rep. 608.
21 [1960] Ch. 262, 269.
22 Ibid., at 276.

as to make use of the reputation and goodwill which has been gained by a product genuinely indicated by the name or description'. He added:

> In my view, it ought not to matter that the persons truly entitled to describe their goods by the name and description are a class producing goods in a certain locality, and not merely one individual. The description is part of their goodwill and a right of property. I do not believe that the law of passing off, which arose to prevent unfair trading, is so limited in scope. In my view, the [American] decision in the *Pillsbury-Washburn Flour Mills* case is good sense, ... I think that the law should and does provide a remedy for [this] type of unfair competition ...[23]

The principle so established had a practical effect in the *Bollinger* case itself. Just over a year later, in the trial of the action, counsel for the plaintiffs successfully argued for the grant of an injunction against passing off. Danckwerts J. stated that this was on the basis that a substantial portion of the public were likely to be misled by the description 'Spanish Champagne', and that the use of this description was intended to attract to the Spanish product the goodwill connected with the reputation of champagne and was dishonest trading.[24]

THE 'SPANISH CHAMPAGNE' CASE: THE INTELLECTUAL ADVENTURE IN ENGLAND

> [The *Bollinger* decision] uncovered a piece of common law or equity which had till then escaped notice.... In truth the decision went beyond the well-trodden paths of passing off into the unmapped area of 'unfair trading' or 'unlawful competition'.[25]

In the last four decades of the twentieth century, the *Bollinger* judgment was adopted and applied by English courts. In the *Bollinger* case, the descriptive term in question referred to the geographical provenance of the goods. Furthermore, the class entitled to the goodwill in the term was restricted to those supplying, on the English market, goods entirely produced in the locality indicated by its name (the Champagne district). The incremental extension of the principle beyond the facts of this case meant that the intellectual adventure of the law in this subject-area continued.

---

23 Ibid., at 283–84.
24 *Bollinger* v. *Costa Brava Wine Co. Ltd.* [1961] 1 WLR 277, 291–92. In January 1965, Lord Wilberforce and Sir Geoffrey Lawrence (counsel for the plaintiffs) were feted by the champagne producers' association (*The Times*, 6 Jan. 1965).
25 Per Cross J. in *Vine Products* v. *Mackenzie & Co. Ltd.* [1969] RPC 1, 23.

In the 'Sherry' case, heard in 1967, sherry producers and importers sought a declaration that they were entitled to describe their wines by titles including 'British Sherry' and 'South African Sherry'. This prompted a counterclaim, by the producers and shippers of sherry from the Jerez district in Spain, for an injunction to restrain the plaintiffs from passing off their wines, which were not from the Jerez district, as sherry. In this case it was proved that the grapes were produced and blended in the Spanish province, but that the bottling of the wine was done elsewhere. Cross J. described the case as 'an aftermath of the Spanish Champagne case'. He expressly adopted the principle developed in this case, that there could be passing off without any representation that the goods of the defendant were the goods of the plaintiffs and without evidence that there had been resultant confusion or deception. He granted an injunction restraining the plaintiffs from using the unqualified word 'sherry' in relation to their wines, but (because of the acquiescence of the defendants) did not extend the injunction to the use of the descriptions such as 'British Sherry'.[26]

In the 'Scotch whisky' case, heard in 1970, an action was brought by blenders and exporters in Scotland and England of 'Scotch whisky', most of which was a blend of malt and grain whiskies. The defendant companies were part of an operation which mixed malt whisky with cane spirit and sold this as Scotch whisky. Foster J. held that the defendants had committed the tort of passing off. He noted that, although the plaintiffs were the blenders of 'Scotch whisky', they were also the producers thereof. He held that, as producers, the plaintiffs fell 'within the principle' enunciated in *Bollinger* inasmuch as they were entitled to have upheld the description of their product as 'Scotch whisky'. He held that this description, in all the circumstances, constituted a trade description, since the geographical expression was sufficiently precise and included the origin of the goods.[27]

In 1977, the Court of Appeal recognised the *Bollinger* judgment in the 'Champagne Cider' case. Here the plaintiffs had used the expressions 'Champagne Cider' and 'Champagne Perry' to describe their products, and the French champagne producers counterclaimed, alleging passing off. The majority of the Court of Appeal held that passing off had not been established, in the absence of evidence of actual confusion or deception and of actual damage to the defendants. However, counsel did not suggest that the judgment in *Bollinger* was wrong in any respect, although he attempted to place a gloss on the judgment to the effect that the Champagne Houses were entitled only to a *joint* goodwill in respect of the word 'champagne'. Buckley J. rejected this argument and suggested that Danckwerts J. had accepted that each Champagne House also had a *separate* goodwill entitling it to sue.[28]

26 *Vine Products* v. *Mackenzie & Co. Ltd.* [1969] RPC 1, 6, 23, 26, 29.
27 *John Walker & Sons Ltd.* v. *Henry Ost & Co. Ltd.* [1970] 2 All ER 106, 117.
28 *HP Bulmer Ltd.* v. *J. Bollinger, S.A.* [1978] RPC 79, 98.

In 1979, the House of Lords gave its seal of approval to the *Bollinger* judgment in the 'Advocaat' case.[29] The plaintiffs in this case manufactured and distributed an alcoholic drink known as 'Advocaat', made out of a mixture of eggs and spirits. The defendants manufactured an alcoholic drink out of dried eggs and Cyprus sherry (called an egg flip), which they marketed at a lower price as 'Old English Advocaat'. The House of Lords granted an injunction restraining the defendants from selling or distributing under the name 'Advocaat' any product which was not made out of the plaintiffs' ingredients. Lord Diplock began his judgment by remarking that this was 'an action for passing off, not in its classic form of a trader representing his own goods as the goods of somebody else, but in an extended form first recognised and applied by Danckwerts J. in the *Champagne* case'. He added that the findings of fact in the case disclosed 'a case of unfair, not to say dishonest, trading of a kind for which a rational system of law ought to provide a remedy to other traders whose business or goodwill is injured by it'. Lord Diplock noted that a difference between the 'Advocaat' case and the line of cases which had applied the *Bollinger* principle was that in the latter the name in question had geographical connotations. However, he could see 'no reason in principle or logic' why the goodwill in the name of those entitled to make use of it should be protected in law if the name denoted a product from a particular locality, but should lose that protection if the ingredients of the product were not restricted as to their geography.[30] The concurring judgment of Lord Fraser of Tullybelton was to the same effect. He discerned in Danckwerts J.'s judgment that the key feature was that the class producing goods be clearly defined in some way. He extracted the general principle that 'the plaintiff is entitled to protect his right of property in the goodwill attached to a name which is distinctive of a product or class of products sold by him in the course of his business'.[31]

This principle has remained part of English law to the present day. It came to be applied in England in factual situations far removed from those of *Bollinger* and the other early cases. For example, the principle was affirmed in an action brought by the British Broadcasting Corporation ('B.B.C.') against Talksport Ltd. Here the B.B.C. proved that it was the only British broadcasting service legally entitled to broadcast live radio coverage of the 2000 European Football Championship (Euro 2000). The B.B.C. objected to the representation by Talksport Ltd., a licensed British radio broadcaster, that its Euro 2000 coverage was 'Live'. Harman J. noted that the B.B.C.'s complaint was not that Talksport had represented that its Euro 2000 coverage was in some way connected with or authorised by the B.B.C. Harman J. said

---

29 *Erven Warnink B.V.* v. *J Townsend & Sons (Hull) Ltd.* [1979] AC 731.
30 Ibid., at 739, 740, 745.
31 Ibid., at 753, 755.

that the claim made by the B.B.C. was of 'the wider kind of passing off which first found clear expression' in the *Bollinger* case, namely, passing off where the defendant was representing that his goods or services were of the same distinctive character as those of the claimant. Harman J. found in the B.B.C. case that the element of misrepresentation was sufficiently established, but that the claim failed as the evidence did not show any protectable goodwill.[32]

It must be acknowledged that, on occasions, the principle derived from the *Bollinger* case has been applied in a questionable fashion. The danger of new directions in the law is that they can be used to justify positions at variance with the underlying principles which first stimulated the new direction. The *Bollinger* principle was advanced in the interests of preventing unfair competition, yet some later judgments could be seen to stifle fair competition. In the *Chocosuisse* case, a trade association of Swiss-based chocolate manufacturers obtained relief against Cadbury, a leading manufacturer of chocolate confectionery, in respect of its new chocolate bar named 'Swiss Chalet'. The Court of Appeal found that the trial judge was entitled to hold that Cadbury's designation was taken by a significant section of the public in England to mean chocolate made in Switzerland.[33] In the *Taittinger* case, the plaintiff champagne house succeeded where the defendant's product ('elderflower champagne') was a non-alcoholic fruit cordial. The Court of Appeal acted on evidence that some people in England would confuse the defendant's product with champagne. The court granted relief on the ground that the singularity and exclusiveness of 'champagne' would be eroded, leading to 'insidious but serious' damage to the champagne houses' interest in the name.[34] The courts in cases such as these would have done well to heed Wilberforce QC's qualification in his *Bollinger* argument that he was not proposing any general right to restrain competition which was in line with public policy.[35]

THE 'SPANISH CHAMPAGNE' CASE: THE GEOGRAPHICAL ADVENTURE

> The plaintiffs put forward their claim ... on the basis of what has been described as 'the new-fangled tort' of unfair competition which is said to have sprung up as a result of *Bollinger* v. *Costa Brava Wine Co. Ltd.*[36]

---

32 *British Broadcasting Corporation* v. *Talksport Ltd.*, unreported, High Court (Chancery Division), 19 June 2000.
33 *Chocosuisse Union des Fabricants Suisses de Chocolat* v. *Cadbury Ltd.* [1999] RPC 826.
34 *Taittinger* v. *Allbev* [1993] FSR 641, 668–70, 674, 678. See W.R. Cornish, *Intellectual property: patents, copyright, trade marks and allied rights*, 4th ed. (London, 1999), p. 645.
35 [1960] Ch. 262, 269.
36 *Shaw Bros (Hong Kong) Ltd.* v. *Golden Harvest (H.K.) Ltd.* [1972] RPC 559, 560.

In the last three decades of the twentieth century, the *Bollinger* judgment was recognised and applied in a range of jurisdictions outside of England. Many of the cases in which the judgment was recognised involved facts similar to those of the *Bollinger* case. Thus, within a year of the 'Advocaat' case, a Scottish court was faced with a claim by two Scottish companies which produced blended Scotch whisky in Scotland. The respondents produced and marketed in England an alcoholic drink known as 'Wee M'Glen' which consisted of ginger wine made in England and mixed with Scotch malt whisky. The petitioners alleged that the respondents' manner of presentation to the public created the false impression that the drink was produced in Scotland and was a product of Scotland. Lord Wheatley, in allowing the petitioners' motion, noted that their case was not a classical case of passing off in that it was not said that the respondents were passing off their product as that of the petitioners. He noted that the petitioners' claim was that the effect of the misrepresentation was that it was likely to endanger the reputation and goodwill which attached to Scotch whisky because of its Scottish origin, since it was liable to dilute the distinctiveness of indications of Scottish origin when used in relation to alcoholic beverages. Lord Wheatley referred to the line of cases culminating in the 'Advocaat' case, and said that there was 'ample authority for the proposition that the law of Scotland does not differ from the law of England in this field of law'.[37]

In certain cases, the principle of the *Bollinger* decision was accepted but the passing off action failed because of factors such as unreasonable delay in taking steps to protect the distinctiveness of the name and the consequent goodwill.[38] In Canada, an action was brought in the late 1980s by the Institut National des Appellations d'Origine des Vins et Eaux-de-Vie (I.N.A.O.).[39] The I.N.A.O. was a national organisation that regulated the areas and conditions of production and sale of wines and spirits bearing controlled appellations of origin. The I.N.A.O. and French champagne producers brought an action for an injunction to restrain the use of the word 'champagne'. The defendants were companies which for many years had produced, advertised and sold wines which incorporated the word 'champagne'. In the Ontario High Court of Justice, Dupont J. noted that a contentious issue to be determined was whether the concept of 'shared goodwill' should be approved, so as to allow the sixteen plaintiffs to have a common cause of action. Dupont J. said that there would perhaps have been some merit to the defendants' objection on this point prior to the 1960s, but that the law of passing off had been forced to expand. He said that the judgments from *Bollinger* to the

---

37 *Lang Brothers Ltd.* v. *Goldwell Ltd.*, 1980 SC 237, 245.
38 For the similar Australian history, see *Wineworths Group Ltd.* v. *C.I.V.C.* [1992] 2 NZLR 327, 330–31.
39 *I.N.A.O.* v. *Anres Wines Ltd.* (1990) 71 DLR (4th) 575, 576.

'Advocaat' case made clear that the absence of a connecting identity between the defendants' goods and those of the plaintiffs was not fatal to the claim for passing off. Dupont J. concluded that there seemed to be 'no basis for ignoring the strong precedent set'. He added that '[t]he fact that no Canadian court has considered the question is no reason for this court to shy away from following and applying the English judgments to what it considers an appropriate case'. Nevertheless, on the facts of the case, which showed the length of usage of the word 'champagne' and the absence of deception, the plaintiffs were held not to have established passing off, and so the injunction was refused.[40]

No such difficulty met the plaintiffs in an action brought in the early 1990s by the Comité Interprofessionel du Vin de Champagne (C.I.V.C.) in New Zealand.[41] The C.I.V.C. was a semi-official body created under French law to protect the name 'Champagne' for the wine produced in the district of Champagne in France. The C.I.V.C. and three leading French champagne producers brought proceedings against Wineworths Group Ltd. for passing off, as wine produced in Champagne, a wine not so produced. Wineworths was the New Zealand agent of an Australian company which had marketed in New Zealand a sparkling white wine produced under the name 'Seaview Australian Champagne'. The Court of Appeal affirmed the permanent injunction granted in the High Court against Wineworths. Cooke P. remarked that 'the producers of genuine Champagne had acquired in New Zealand a class goodwill of the kind recognised as entitled to protection in *J. Bollinger* v. *Costa Brava Wine Co. Ltd.*'. He said that there was 'no good reason' why the court should reject the concept of goodwill taken by Danckwerts J. and approved by the House of Lords in the 'Advocaat' case. He added that '[c]ommercial honesty is as important here as anywhere else, and the temptations to depart from it can be no less strong'. Cooke P. held that the facts of the case were not materially distinguishable from those of the Spanish Champagne case, and that '[t]he judgment of Danckwerts J. in that case should be applied here'.[42]

Furthermore, as happened in England, the *Bollinger* judgment was cited in situations entirely unrelated to matters of alcoholic liquor, and attempts were made by counsel to extend the range of the judgment. On occasions Commonwealth courts recognised the development of the law in *Bollinger* and subsequent cases, but were not prepared to grant a remedy to the plaintiffs. In a Canadian case in the early 1980s, action was taken by the authorised dealer of Seiko watches for Canada, who sued a distributing company for passing off. This was on the ground that the latter sold Seiko

40 *I.N.A.O.* v. *Anres Wines Ltd.* (1987) 60 OR (2d) 316, 323, 324, 327.
41 *Wineworths Group Ltd.* v. *C.I.V.C.* [1992] 2 NZLR 327.
42 Ibid., at 330, 333.

watches without the point of sale service and instruction booklet. Estey J. acknowledged that the role played by passing off had 'undoubtedly expanded to take into account the changing commercial realities in the present-day community', and in particular examined the modernising role of the Danckwerts J. judgment. However, Estey J. said that '[a]ny expansion of the common law principles to curtail the freedom to compete in the open market should be cautiously approached', and he held that the extended action in passing off had not been made out in the case at hand.[43]

Nevertheless, Commonwealth courts were prepared to grant remedies in analogous circumstances, to the extent that this was seen to be appropriate.[44] In 1971, the Hong Kong Full Court was faced with a claim by a film distributing firm that its right of property in the film character 'the One Armed Swordsman, Kang Fang' had been infringed in the defendant's film. The 'Spanish Champagne' case played a key role in the hearing and the court's judgment. On the one hand, counsel for the plaintiffs interpreted the judgment of Danckwerts J. to mean that a passing-off remedy lay where a false trade description had been used, even though there was no likelihood of confusion with the goods of the plaintiff by whom the remedy was sought. Huggins J., while expressly agreeing with the *Bollinger* judgment, rejected this argument. He said that that 'would have the effect not of going beyond the well-trodden paths of passing-off but of deserting part of the existing path and blazing a new one'.[45] On the other hand, counsel for the defendants argued that there could be no right of property in a fictional character, and noted that there was no reported English case where such a right of property had been held to exist. Huggins J. remarked that '[w]ith the Champagne Cases fresh in my mind I would find it hard to accept the absence of authority in this field of law as a factor of great weight'. Furthermore, he noted that there were some recent American cases where unlawful competition had been found to arise from the use of a fictional character. He remarked that 'the use made by the English courts (and more particularly by Danckwerts J. in the Champagne Cases) of the American cases is some indication that there is at least a close relationship between the two'. He was therefore content to adopt the words of Danckwerts J. and to say that the decisions in these American cases were 'good sense'.[46] Huggins J. then examined the relevant American case-law, which he approved, and in particular affirmed the power and duty of a court of equity to afford relief in appropriate circumstances.[47]

---

43 *Consumers Distributing Co. Ltd.* v. *Seiko Time Canada Ltd.* (1984) 1 CPR (3d) 1, 2, 13.
44 See also *Scott* v. *Tuff-Kote (Australia) Pty. Ltd.* (1975) 1 NSWLR 537, 541, 543.
45 *Shaw Bros. (Hong Kong) Ltd.* v. *Golden Harvest (H.K.) Ltd.* [1972] RPC 559, 561.
46 [1972] RPC 559, 564.
47 [1972] RPC 559, 566. In the Supreme Court of Hong Kong, judgment was entered for the plaintiffs.

The length of the adventurous path taken by the *Bollinger* judgment was indicated by an Irish case heard in 1994. The first plaintiff in this case, An Post, carried on the business previously carried on by the Minister for Post and Telegraphs as seller and supplier of financial products. The plaintiff and its predecessors in title had been involved for 65 years in the promotion and sale of a financial savings product under the name 'Savings Certificates'. The defendant, Irish Permanent plc, was also involved in the promotion and sale of financial products, and in July 1994 it launched a new product known as 'Savings Certificates' which was very similar (though not identical) to those of the plaintiff. The plaintiff contended that it had acquired a significant, substantial and exclusive reputation in the name and trademark 'Savings Certificates' and consequent goodwill of enormous value. Kinlen J. granted an interlocutory injunction. He remarked that '[t]he action of passing off has evolved so that it is no longer restricted to a trader representing his own goods as the goods of somebody else' and that '[i]ts extended form was first recognised and applied by Danckwerts J. in the champagne case'. Kinlen J. set out the developed form of the action as outlined by Lord Diplock, namely, that it extended to prevent the deceptive use of a descriptive term, in order to protect the goodwill in the descriptive term enjoyed by those entitled to use it. In the light of this, Kinlen J. held that there was 'certainly a substantial issue to be tried'.[48]

CONCLUSION

This paper has traced the legal adventures of a landmark case in the law of passing off. What lessons have been learnt from the intellectual and geographical adventures of this case?

The intellectual adventure of the *Bollinger* case presented the classic process of the incremental extension of the common law. This process was ultimately attributable to the resolve of counsel (in this case Wilberforce QC) to advance a novel claim and to persuade the court of the merits of his cause. The process then advanced through the willingness of judges (such as Danckwerts J. and Lord Diplock) to discern and extend the core principle at work. In time, the legal reasoning of judges from case to case produced a legal principle of increasing refinement and applicability. The overall effect in this situation was the progressive extension of a higher standard of commercial candour than that prescribed by the pre-existing law.[49]

The geographical adventure of the *Bollinger* case reflected the continuing role of the English common law in legal systems beyond its jurisdiction. The

48 *An Post v. Irish Permanent p.l.c.* [1995] 1 IR 140, 151.
49 *Cf. Erven Warnink B.V. v. J. Townsend & Sons (Hull) Ltd.* [1979] AC 731, 743, per Lord Diplock.

advance of the *Bollinger* judgment outside of England was assisted by its confirmation in subsequent cases and by its explicit recognition in the House of Lords. Some of the geographical adventure was of a predictable kind, as in the ready resort to the *Bollinger* judgment in the closely-analogous New Zealand *Wineworths* case. Other aspects of the adventure revealed a greater leap of the imagination, not least in the Irish *An Post* case.

Both the intellectual and geographical adventures of the *Bollinger* case revealed that the advance of the law is not synonymous with success for plaintiffs, as was evident in cases where the court developed the law but found for the defendant on the facts. The intellectual and geographical adventures also revealed the challenge faced by judges in maintaining a sense of balance in the development of the law, and in remaining true to the underlying rationale of a new line of precedent. The rationale of the 'Spanish Champagne' precedent was to be found in the argument of Wilberforce QC and in the judgment in this case. These reflected timeless and universal principles founded in logic and the general interest.

The Irish Legal History Society

Established in 1988 to encourage the study and advance the knowledge of the history of Irish law, especially by the publication of original documents and of works relating to the history of Irish law, including its institutions, doctrines and personalities, and the reprinting or editing of works of sufficient rarity or importance.

PATRONS

The Hon. Mr Justice Keane   Rt. Hon. Sir Robert Carswell
Chief Justice of Ireland   Lord Chief Justice of Northern Ireland

COUNCIL 2003/04

President

His Honour Judge Martin QC

Vice-Presidents

James I. McGuire, esq.   Professor Norma Dawson

Honorary Secretaries

Kevin Costello, esq. BL   Ms Sheena Grattan BL

Honorary Treasurers

John G. Gordon, esq.   Revd R.D. Marshall

Council Members

Ms Rosemary Carson   Dr Colum Kenny
The Hon. Mr Justice Geoghegan   Eanna Mulloy SC
Professor D. Greer QC (hon.)   Professor J.O. Ohlmeyer
His Honour Judge Hart QC   Professor W.N. Osborough
Daire Hogan, esq.   (ex officio)